JOURNAL FOR THE STUDY OF THE PSEUDEPIGRAPHA
SUPPLEMENT SERIES
15

Executive Editor
James H. Charlesworth

Associate Editors
Philip R. Davies
James R. Mueller
James C. VanderKam

JSOT Press
Sheffield

Thunder in Gemini

And Other Essays on the History, Language and Literature of Second Temple Palestine

Michael Owen Wise

Journal for the Study of the Pseudepigrapha
Supplement Series 15

For my parents, Richard and Imogen Wise, and
my parents-in-law, Ed and Esther Chernicky

Published by JSOT Press
JSOT Press is an imprint of
Sheffield Academic Press Ltd
343 Fulwood Road
Sheffield S10 3BP
England

Typeset by Sheffield Academic Press
and
Printed on acid-free paper in Great Britain
by Bookcraft Ltd

British Library Cataloguing in Publication Data

Wise, Michael
    Thunder in Gemini: And Other Essays on
    the History, Language and Literature of
    Second Temple Palestine.— (Journal for
    the Study of the Pseudepigrapha
    Supplement Series, ISSN 0951-8215; No. 15)
    I. Title II. Series
    221.9

ISBN 1-85075-460-8

CONTENTS

PREFACE

This collection of essays finds its common bond in that division of history that we call the Second Temple period, and focuses largely on the latter years of that era. With the new availability of the previously sequestered Dead Sea Scrolls, and with the publication of thirty-year old data from excavations at Masada, there is much new evidence to excite the philologist and historian interested in those years. These essays represent my reflections on a small portion of that new evidence.

It is a great pleasure to acknowledge the help of those colleagues and friends who have given generously of their time and expertise, helping me to avoid numerous blunders and, in general, make this a better book. Professors Dennis Pardee and W. Randall Garr read and commented on most of the chapters. Professor Al Wolters read chapters one and five very carefully, and I have incorporated many of his suggested improvements. Professor Shaye Cohen critiqued chapters two and five; his incisive comments have helped structure those portions. Professor Arthur Droge and Dr. Scott Layton also offered helpful suggestions for chapter two. Professor Norman Golb spent a great deal of time with chapter three, and I have adopted many of his proposed changes. Professor Stephen Kaufman also commented on that portion, and Professor Eugene Ulrich kindly answered certain queries about unpublished biblical manuscripts discussed in the chapter. Professors Gene Gragg and James VanderKam read and discussed chapter six with me. My colleagues Professors Erica Reiner and Robert Biggs advised me regarding cuneiform materials. Also, several of my students—Ms. Deborah Friedrich, Mr. Anthony Tomasino and Mr. Michael Douglas, in particular—read large portions of the manuscript and offered their suggestions. To all of these people I offer my sincere thanks. In addition, I express my appreciation to the administration of the University of Chicago, who awarded me a Junior Faculty Grant in the summer of 1991, so that I could devote myself to this work.

An earlier version of chapter three appeared in *Abr-Nahrain* Supplement 3 (1992), pp. 123-66. Likewise, an earlier version of chapter four appeared in *Revue de Qumran* 15 (1991), pp. 103-32. While the main arguments of these chapters have not changed from their earlier incarnations, it has been possible considerably to augment the data upon which these arguments are based, thanks to the new Scrolls materials. I thank the editors of these journals for permission to include these chapters in the present volume. I also tender thanks to Professor James Charlesworth for recommending my book for this series, and to Professor Philip Davies for accepting that recommendation and for his work in editing the manuscript.

Finally and most of all, I thank my wife, Cathy, for her unfailing love, encouragement and belief in me and my work.

Chicago, 18 September 1992

ABBREVIATIONS

ANRW	*Aufstieg und Niedergang der römischen Welt: Geschichte und Kultur Roma in Spiegel der neueren Forschung*
Ant.	Flavius Josephus, *Jewish Antiquities*
AfO	*Archiv für Orientforschung*
ArOr	*Archiv Orientální*
BA	Biblical Aramaic
BA	*Biblical Archaeologist*
BASOR	*Bulletin of the American School of Oriental Research*
BDB	Brown-Driver-Briggs, *Hebrew and English Lexicon of the Old Testament*
Beyer, *Texte*	K. Beyer, *Die aramäischen Texte vom Toten Meer*
BIES	*Bulletin of the Israel Exploration Society*
BO	*Bibliotheca Orientalis*
Brockelmann	C. Brockelmann, *Lexicon Syriacum*
BZ	*Biblische Zeitschrift*
CAD	*The Assyrian Dictionary of the Oriental Institute of the University of Chicago*
CBQ	*Catholic Biblical Quarterly*
CCAG	*Catalogus Codicum Astrologorum Graecorum*
CP	*Classical Philology*
CPA	Christian Palestinian Aramaic
Dalman	G. Dalman, *Aramäisch-Neuhebräisches Handwörterbuch zu Targum, Talmud und Midrasch*
DISO	C.-F. Jean and J. Hoftijzer, *Dictionnarie des inscriptions sémitiques de l'ouest*
DJD	*Discoveries in the Judaean Desert (of Jordan)*
Drower and Macuch	E.S. Drower and R. Macuch, *A Mandaic Dictionary*
DSS	Dead Sea Scrolls
Eisenman and Robinson	R. Eisenman and J.M. Robinson, *A Fascimile Edition of the Dead Sea Scrolls*
ErIs	*Eretz Israel*
EstBib	*Estudios bíblicos*
GKC	Gesenius-Kautzsch-Cowley, *Hebrew Grammar*
HUCA	*Hebrew Union College Annual*
HTR	*Harvard Theological Review*

IEJ	*Israel Exploration Journal*
IOS	*Israel Oriental Society*
JANESCU	*Journal of the Ancient Near Eastern Society of Columbia University*
JAOS	*Journal of the American Oriental Society*
Jastrow	M. Jastrow, *Hebrew Aramaic English Dictionary*
JBL	*Journal of Biblical Literature*
JJS	*Journal of Jewish Studies*
JNES	*Journal of Near Eastern Studies*
JPOS	*Journal of Palestine Oriental Society*
JQR	*Jewish Quarterly Review*
JRS	*Journal of Roman Studies*
JRelS	*Journal of Religious Studies*
JSJ	*Journal for the Study of Judaism*
JSS	*Journal of Semitic Studies*
JTS	*Journal of Theological Studies*
JSNT	*Journal for the Study of the New Testament*
KB	L. Koehler and W. Baumgartner, *Hebräisches und Aramäisches Lexikon zum Alten Testament*
McCQ	*McCormick Quarterly*
Milik, *Books of Enoch*	J.T. Milik, *The Books of Enoch: Aramaic Fragments of Qumrân Cave 4*
Milik, *Ten Years*	J.T. Milik, *Ten Years of Discovery in the Wilderness of Judaea*
NovT	*Novum Testamentum*
NTS	*New Testament Studies*
OLZ	*Orientalische Literaturzeitung*
Or	*Orientalia*
PAM	Palestine Archaeological Museum (designation used for accession numbers of photographs of Scrolls)
Payne Smith	R. Payne Smith, *Thesaurus Syriacus*
PW	Pauly-Wissowa, *Real-Encyclopädie der klassichen Altertumswissenschaft*
RB	*Revue Biblique*
Reed, *List*	*Dead Sea Inventory Project: List of Documents, Photographs and Museum Plates*
RevScRel	*Revue des sciences religieuses*
REJ	*Revue des études juives*
RevQ	*Revue de Qumran*
RSO	*Revista degli studi orientali*
Schulthess	F. Schulthess, *Lexicon Syropalaestinum*
Schürer	E. Schürer, *The History of the Jewish People in the Age of Jesus Christ*
ScrHier	*Scripta hierosolymitana*

Sokoloff,	M. Sokoloff, *A Dictionary of Jewish Palestinian Aramaic*
Dictionary	
StudOr	*Studia Orientalia*
VC	*Vigiliae christianae*
VT	*Vetus Testamentum*
VTSup	Vetus Testamentum Supplements
War	Flavius Josephus, *The Jewish War*

Abbreviations of the names of biblical books, Qumran texts and rabbinic authors follow the systems used in the *Journal of Biblical Literature,* as listed in the 'Instructions for Contributors', volume 107 (1988) 579-96. References to classical authors are to the standard editions and follow the system of abbreviation used in the *Oxford Classical Dictionary.*

Chapter One

THUNDER IN GEMINI: AN ARAMAIC BRONTOLOGION (4Q318)
FROM QUMRAN

Introduction

'Knowest thou the ordinances of heaven; canst thou set the dominion thereof in the earth?' The author of Job 38.33 doubtless anticipated a negative answer to his question. Ironically, however, the time came when many readers of his book believed that they did, indeed, know those ordinances; when a broad spectrum of Jewish society was intent on seeing that dominion established. The Greco-Roman world that constituted the milieu of late Second Temple Judaism was thoroughly imbued with astrological ideas.[1] In one manifestation or another, astrology reigned. The best minds of the day subscribed to its beliefs. In Rome, the foremost philosophic school, the Stoics, were its strongest advocates.

Astrology's basic notions were not always easy to reconcile with the religious beliefs of the peoples who came under its sway. Nevertheless, reconciled they were. The Greeks, who had earlier lacked star-cults and eschewed worship of the sun, moon and planets, ended by systematizing astrology and supplying the philosophic underpinnings upon which it rests even today. In the case of the Jews, explicit testimony as to how they effected their *rapprochement* is lacking. Despite the negative judgment of biblical passages such as Isa. 47.13-14, it was presumably not too difficult. Counterbalancing biblical support was easy to find. Gen. 1.14-18, for example, states that God created the heavenly luminaries to separate light from darkness, to mark out seasons and years, and to rule over the day and the night. A Second Temple Jew, following the same reasoning as medieval

---

1   For orientation see e.g., F. Cumont, *Astrology and Religion Among the Greeks and Romans* (England, 1912; reedition New York: Dover, 1960).

commentators,[2] might easily find here an endorsement of the power contemporary astrologers ascribed to the celestial bodies. Further, the foundations of astrological divination were entirely logical, provided that one accept the equation—almost universally believed—*Himmelsbild ist Weltenbild.* Happenings on earth mirrored those of heaven, though not necessarily clearly. Indeed, it was that very lack of clarity that provided the *raison d'être* for competing astrological systems.

Abundant evidence shows the importance of astrological ideas in Second Temple Judaism.[3] They had, in fact, penetrated to its very heart. Josephus explains that the seven branches of the menorah in Jerusalem's temple symbolize the seven planets (i.e., the sun, moon and five visible planets, Mercury through Saturn). He adds that the twelve loaves of the bread of the presence embody the signs of the zodiac.[4] In the Jerusalem of his day, just as in Rome, such notions had become the property of the intellectual élite. Among the Jews the interpretation of *omina* was the special province of sacred scribes, who were often attached to the temple.[5] The same peasants that abominated recourse to familiar spirits simultaneously were quick to exploit approved methods of divination.[6] Some Second Temple writers, such as Artapanus and Pseudo-Eupolemus, went so far as to ascribe the discovery of astrology to the patriarch Abraham.[7] The book of 1 Enoch

---

2   E.g., cf. Moses ben Nachman (Ramban) *ad loc.*

3   For useful surveys of the evidence for astrological ideas among the Jews of this period, see J.H. Charlesworth, 'Jewish Interest in Astrology during the Hellenistic and Roman Period', in *ANRW* 20.2, pp. 926-50, and L.J. Ness, 'Astrology and Judaism in Late Antiquity' (Ph.D. diss., Miami University, 1990). It should be noted that Isa. 47 and like passages did have effect. As Charlesworth shows, some Jews of this period certainly opposed astrology.

4   *War* 5.217; cf. 5.214.

5   *War* 6.291. These scribes were then the correspondents of the ancient Mesopotamian *barû*, whose job was also the collecting and interpreting of *omina*.

6   Note the list of 'signs of the times' that foretold the destruction of the temple in Jerusalem in 70 CE., and the provisional government's need to silence overly-loud exponents of such 'morale busters.' See *War* 6.288-315.

7   For Artapanus, see Eusebius, *P.E.* 9.18.1, τοῦτον δὲ φησι πανοικίᾳ ἐλθεῖν εἰς Αἴγυπτον πρὸς τὸν τῶν Αἰγυπτίων βασιλέα φαρεθώθην καὶ τὴν ἀστρολογίαν αὐτὸν διδάξαι. For Pseudeo-Eupolemus, see Eusebius *P.E.* 9.17.1-9 and 9.18.2, and note especially that he says of Abraham ὅν δὴ καὶ τὴν ἀστρολογίαν καὶ Χαλδαϊκὴν εὑρεῖν.

makes the seventh from Adam the discoverer and revealer of the royal science.[8] Daniel, wisest of the wise, bested the Chaldeans at their own arts.

Striking testimony to Jewish use of astrology in this period appears in the texts from Qumran. Among these manuscripts are found at least four astrological works: (1) 4Q186, a physiognomic text written in a cyptic script;[9] (2) An Aramaic text, 4Q561, that may be related to the Hebrew 4Q186;[10] (3) 4QMess ar, which apparently predicts the birth of Noah and includes physiognomic elements;[11] (4) a brontologion (sometimes termed in Greek 'brontoskopion').[12]

As the name indicates, brontologia interpreted thunder in order to forecast the future.[13] They existed well before the rise of

8   See 1 Enoch 41-44 and especially 72-82.

9   J.M. Allegro, 'An Astrological Cryptic Document from Qumran', *JSS* 9 (1964), pp. 291-94 (preliminary publication); *editio princeps* idem, DJD 5, 88-91 and plate XXXI.

10   See Reed, *List,* and J. Starcky, 'Les quatre étapes du messianisme à Qumran', *RB* 70 (1963), p. 503 n. 66.

11   The text is thought to exist in three exemplars, but is only partially published. See J. Starcky, 'Un texte messianique araméen de la grotte 4 de Qumran', *Ecole des langues orientales anciennes de l'Institut Catholique de Paris: Mémorial du cinquantenaire 1914-1964* (Travaux de l'Institut de Paris 10; Paris: Bloud et Gay, 1964), pp. 51-66, and Reed, *List,* under 4Q534-536. 4Q535 and 536 overlap, but their relation to 4Q534 is uncertain. Starcky believed the text was messianic—a possibility that cannot be entirely excluded—but most scholars follow J.A. Fitzmyer, 'The Aramaic 'Elect of God' Text from Qumran Cave IV', *Essays in the Semitic Background of the New Testament* (Missoula: Scholars Press, 1974), pp. 127-60, in identifying the person described in the text as Noah. See also F. García-Martínez, '4Q Mes. Aram. y el libro de Noé', *Salmanticensis* 28 (1981), pp. 195-232.

12   Milik, *Ten Years,* 42; *The Books of Enoch,* 187 (where, in the arbitrary fashion that has come to characterize his more recent work, Milik refers to it as 4QZodiac), and J.C. Greenfield and M. Sokoloff, 'Astrological and Related Omen Texts in Jewish Palestinian Aramaic', *JNES* 48 (1989), p. 202. For clarity I shall refer to this text and those of its genre as 'brontologia' rather than 'brontoskopia', though there is perhaps reason to favor the latter term. For the text see PAM 43.374 in Eisenman and Robinson.

13   For discussions see first the classic study by A. Bouché-Leclercq, *Histoire de la divination dans l'antiquité* (2 vols.; Paris, 1879-82; reprint New York: Arno Press, 1975) 1: 198-204. Also helpful are P. Händel, 'Prodigium', *PW* 23.2 (1959) cols. 2283 and 2296, and K. Berger, 'Hellenistisch-heidnische Prodigen und die Vorzeichen in der jüdisichen und christlichen Apokalyptik', in *ANRW* 2.23.2, pp.

genethlialogical (horoscopic) astrology, and a number came to be included in the vast collection of cuneiform *omina* known as the *Enuma Anu Enlil.*[14] The following example is typical:[15]

> When Rammanu thunders in the great gate of the Moon, there will be a slaying of Elamite troops with the sword: the goods of that land will be gathered into another land. (This is what is when the Moon appears and it thunders.) From Bulutu.

Like all general[16] astrological genres, brontologia are largely descriptive. They concern wars, the weather, crops and domestic animals, disease, the rise and fall of great men—particularly kings— and general disturbances of various sorts. Their interest is in the nation as a whole, rather than in the fate of individuals. Such works were often of lay interest.[17] In the Hellenistic period, they were elaborated far

---

1428-96. Less specifically helpful, but still suggestive, is S.J. Scherrer, 'Signs and Wonders in the Imperial Cult', *JBL* 103 (1984), pp. 599-610.

14 The *Enuma Anu Enlil* is of uncertain date. Though the extant version comes from the Neo-Assyrian period, the existence of commentaries aimed at explaining its by then archaic language argues for a substantially earlier date of composition. The Neo-Assyrian version comprises about 70 tablets, some 7000 omens. The brontologia are part of 'Adad' (tablets 36-50), which contain *omina* drawn from earthquakes, rainbows, clouds and rain as well as thunder and lightning flashes.

15 Quotation from R. Campbell Thompson, *The Reports of the Magicians and Astrologers of Nineveh and Babylon* (2 vols.; London: Luzac, 1900) 2:lxxx (number 256a). Thompson's work is badly out of date. H. Hunger is presently reediting the *Enuma Anu Enlil*. See A.J. Sachs and H. Hunger, *Astronomical Diaries and Related Texts from Babylonia* (2 vols., with a 3rd projected; Wien: Österreichischen Akademie der Wissenschaften, 1988-). Note also E.F. Weidner, 'Die astrologische Serie Enûma Anu Enlil', *AfO* 14 (1941-44), pp. 172-95 and 308-18; *AfO* 17 (1954-56), pp. 71-89 and *AfO* 22 (1968-69), pp. 65-75, and E. Reiner and D. Pingree, *Babylonian Planetary Omens, Part 2: Enuma Anu Enlil* (Malibu: Undena Publications, 1975).

16 General astrology concerns itself with celestial phenomena (eclipses, planetary conjunctions, etc.) and their relationship to nations, ethnic groups and, at times, all mankind. It stands in contradistinction to genethlialogical astrology (noted above), catarchic astrology and interrogatory astrology. Catarchic astrology seeks to determine whether a given moment is propitious for an action begun in it (hence the name < Greek ἀρχή, 'beginning'). Interrogatory astrology provides the answers to questions based on the situation in the heavens at the time when the questions are posed.

17 See S. Eriksson, *Wochentagsgötter, Mond, und Tierkreis: Laienastrologie in*

beyond the Mesopotamian predecessor quoted above.[18] This elaboration was possible thanks to the rise of new mathematical approaches to observation of the heavens. It is especially to Ptolemaic Egypt that we owe this new, more complex class of brontologia and, indeed, astrological lore in general.[19] Thus the best parallels to the Aramaic text I propose to discuss in the following pages date to that period, and are mostly collected in the monumental *Catalogus Codicum Astrologorum Graecorum* (CCAG).[20]

Text and Translation

Fragment I

```
5      [ובלו קשתא בלו|||||||| ובו|||||||| גדיא ב– וב–|
              דולא ב–|| וב[–ֹ–|III ֹוב]–||||[
6      [נוניא ב–|||||  וב–||||||  דכרא ב–|||||||  וב–||||||||
```

der römischen Kaiserzeit (Stockholm: Almquist und Wiksell, 1956).

18 Despite this elaboration, however, it is often possible to recognize Akkadian phrases in Greek dress. The old article, C. Bezold and F. Boll, 'Reflexe astrologischer Keilinschriften bei griechischen Schriftstellern', *Sitzungsberichte der Heidelberger Academie der Wissenschaften* 7 (1911), pp. 3-54, is still useful for Greek-Akkadian equivalents, but the cuneiform evidence must be checked against modern editions of the texts.

19 O. Neugebauer, *The Exact Sciences in Antiquity* (2nd ed., New York: Dover, 1969; reprint of Brown University Press, 1957), p. 56.

20 F. Cumont, F. Boll *et al.*, eds., *Catalogus Codicum Astrologorum Graecorum* (Brussels: In Aedibus Academiae, 1898-1953). I have located thirteen (mostly Greco-Roman) 'more elaborate' brontologia as follows: CCAG 3.50-2; 4.128-31; 7.163-7; 8.3 123-5; 168-9 (attributed to 'David the prophet'); 169-71; 9.2 120-3; 10.58-9 (revealed to Ezra); 60-62; 140-2; 11.1 145-6; 155-7, and *Geoponica* 1.10 (edited by I. de Mueller, *Geoponica sive Cassiani Bassi scholastici de re rustica ecologae,* [n.p, 1895]; the text is reproduced, with brief notes, by J. Bidez and F. Cumont, *Les mages hellenises* [2 vols.; Paris: Société D'Édition Les Belles Lettres, 1973] 2: 182-3). Although all these mss are of Byzantine date, that says nothing of the antiquity of the originals. The situation envisaged is common for classical literary and not-so-literary texts. The Laurential ms of Sophocles, for example, our oldest and best authority for all of his plays, was inscribed in the early eleventh century. The genre 'brontologion' continued to be productive throughout the medieval period; cf. the Modern Greek ms described by P. Marc, 'Eine neue Handschrift des Donner- und Erdbebenbuchs', *Byzantinische Zeitschrift* 14 (1905), pp. 614-5.

תורא ב–||[||]|||||||| ובֿ 3 ובֿ[3]

7   [תאומיא ב3|| וב3|| סרטנא ב3|||| וב3||| אריא
ב3||| וב[3|||||| וב[3|||||||

8   [בתולתא ב3||||||||| וב– 3– וב– | מוזניא] *vacat*

9   [תשרי בו ובו עקרבא בו|| ובו||| קשתא בו||||| וב||||||
ובו||[|||||||] גדיא בו||||||||

Fragment II i

1   ובֿ– ||| וב–[||] סֿרטנא בֿ–||||| וב–|||||| אֿ[ר]יֿא]
בֿ–|||||| [ו]בֿ– ||||||||ii

2   בתֿ[ו]לֿתא בֿ–[|||][||||||| וב 3 ובֿ 3 מֿוזניא בֿ[3|| וב[3||
עקרבא ב3||||

3   ובֿ3||| קש[תא] ב3||[|]|||||| ובֿ3||[|] וב[||||||3||] וב||[|||
גדי]אֿ בֿ[3||3|[|||||

4   ובֿ– 3– דול[א] *vacat* שבֿטֿ בו זֿבֿו[נוני]אֿ בֿ[|||
וב][||||

5   [דכרא ב]|||||| ובֿ[3|||||| ובו][|||||| תורא בו|||[||||
ובו||||||||| תאומיא] בֿ–

6   [וב–|] סרטנא ב–|| [וב]–בֿ–||| וב– |||| אֿריא [ב–|||||
וב–|][||| בתולתא]

7   ב–|||||| וב–בֿ– ||||||| מוזניא ב–||||||||| ב[3 וב3
ע]קֿרבא ב3||

8   [ו]בֿ3||| [קש]תֿא בֿ3|| וב3||| גֿדיא בֿ[3||||| וב[3||||||
וב3||[|]|||

9   דולא בֿ3|||||||| וב– 3– נוניא *vacat*

Fragment II ii

1   אדֿרֿ בו ובו דכרא בֿו|| ובֿו|||| תורא בו||[||| ובו|||||
ובו||||||| תאומיא]

2   בו||||||| בו|||||||||| סֿרטֿ[נא ב– וב–| אֿ[ריא ב–||
וב–|][|| וב–||||

3   בתול[תא] בֿ–|||| ובֿ[–בֿ] מוזניא ב–||[|||||| ב–||||||||
עקרבא]

4   בֿ[–||][||||||||| וב 3 3ֿ|3 קש[תא ב3||| וב3|||] ג[ריא בֿ3||||
וב]3||||

5   דולֿא ב3|||||| וב[3|||||| ובֿ3|[||||||||] נו[ניא] בֿ[|||3|||||||
וב3–|

[מא]על מסבת ירעם [בתורא אם] vacat דכרא 6
[אבן דינת ובמ מלכא בד]רת וחר[למדינתא ע]מל[ו] 7
[לן]בא אלן בזזין ולהוון כפן א.[...]ולערביא להוא 8
[ומן מ]נכריא ומרע דחלה ירעם בתאומיא אם vacat 9

Fragment I

(5) [and on the 7th Sagittarius. On the eighth and the ninth Capricorn. On the tenth and the eleventh Aquarius. On the twelfth and the] thirteenth and the [four]teenth (6) [Pisces. On the fifteenth and the sixteenth Aries. On the seventeenth and the eighteenth Taurus. On the ni]neteenth, the twentieth and the twenty-[first (7) Gemini. On the twenty-second and the twenty-third Cancer. On the twenty-fourth and the twenty-fifth Leo. On the twenty-sixth], the twenty-seventh and the twenty-eighth (8) [Virgo. On the twenty-ninth, thirtieth and thirty-first Libra.] vacat (9) [**Tishri** On the first and second] Scorpio. On the third and fourth Sagittarius. On the fifth, sixth and seve]nth Capricorn. On the eighth . . .

Fragment II Column i

(1) and on the thirteenth and the [fo]urteenth Cancer. On the fi[ft]eenth and the sixteenth L[e]o. On the seventeenth [and] the eighteenth (2) Vi[r]go. On the [ni]nteenth, the twentieth and the twenty-first Libra. On the twenty-[second and the twenty-t]hird Scorpio. On the twenty-fourth (3) and the twenty-fifth Sagitt[arius]. On the twenty-six[th], the twenty-seve[nth] and the twenty-eig[hth Caprico]rn. On the twenty-n[inth] (4) and the thirtieth Aquari[us]. vacat **Shevat** On the first and the second [Pisc]es. On [the third and the] fourth (5) [Aries. On] the fifth, [the sixth and the se]venth Taurus. On the eig[hth and ninth Gemini.] On the tenth (6) [and eleventh] Cancer. On the twelfth, thirteenth and fourteenth Leo. [On the fifteenth and six]teenth [Virgo]. (7) On the seventeenth and eighteenth Libra. On the nineteenth, [twentieth and twenty-first S]corpio. On the twenty-second (8) [and] twenty-third [Sagitta]rius. On the twenty-fourth and twenty-fifth Capricorn. On [the twenty-sixth], twenty-seventh and twenty-e[i]ghth, (9) Aquarius. On the twenty-ninth and thirtieth Pisces. vacat

Fragment II Column ii
(1) **Adar** On the first and the second Aries. On the third and the fourth Taurus. On the fif[th, sixth and seventh Gemini]. (2) On the eighth (and) ninth Canc[er. On the tenth and eleventh L]eo. On the twelfth, thir[teenth and fourteenth] (3) Vi[r]go. On the fifteenth and six[teenth Libra. On the seven]teenth (and) eight[eenth Scorpio]. (4) On the [nin]eteenth, twentieth and twenty-first Sagitt[arius. On the twenty-second] and twenty-thi[rd Cap]ricorn. On the twenty-[fourth and twenty-fifth] (5) Aquarius. On the twenty-sixth, twenty-[seventh and twenty-eigh]th Pis[ces]. On the twenty-ni[nth, thirtieth and thirty-first] (6) Aries. *vacat* [If] it thunders [on a day when the moon is in Taurus], (it signifies) [vain] changes in the wo[rld (?) . . .] (7) [and] toil for the cities, and destru[ction in] the royal [co]urt and in the city of dest[ruction] (?) [. . .] (8) there will be, and among the Arabs [   ] . . . famine. Nations will plunder one ano[ther . . .] (9) *vacat* If it thunders (on a day when the moon is) in Gemini, (it signifies) fear and distress caused by foreigners and by [. . .]

Although the text is lacunose, the restorations for fragment I and II i 1-ii 5 are virtually certain because of the observable pattern in the distribution of the signs of the zodiac over the days of the months. The week is the basic unit of the pattern: two days, two days, then three days. This pattern repeats for the succeeding three weeks of the month, accounting for the first twenty-eight days. Then, if the month is a thirty-day month, such as Shevat, a last zodiacal sign covers the two days, twenty-nine and thirty (thus II i 9). If the month is a thirty-one day month, such as Adar, the last sign covers days twenty-nine, thirty and thirty-one (thus, by spacing, II ii 5). A new month always begins with a new sign, and the signs rotate through the months such that whatever sign begins a month will also end it. In other words, each month requires thirteen signs of the zodiac to cover all its days, and since there are only twelve signs, the sign that began the month comes around again at the end. Accordingly, successive months begin with successive signs of the zodiac, and the following reconstruction of the pattern for the entire year results (see table 1).

By reconstructing the entire year (which must be a 364 day solar year to account for the data that are preserved in the text),[21] it is possible to determine the position of the poorly preserved fragment I. Since גדיא is preserved there in line 9, followed by the ciphers for the number eight, one need merely find that month in which Capricorn covers the days immediately preceding the eighth day. The only month of the year that fits is Tishri. The meager remaining portions of the preceding lines can then be filled out. In this text, then, are preserved portions covering 5/13-6/8 and 10/13-12/31 of the year.[22]

Following the distribution of the zodiac over the days of the year, a new section begins. Here the connection with thunder becomes evident. The first three lines of this section concern an instance where thunder is heard in relation to a sign whose name has been lost. Since, however, the next sign's name of Gemini is preserved, the restoration of Taurus is virtually certain. The rest of the lacunae in the brontological portion of the text are not so easily filled in, however, since here the text no longer patterns mechanically.

If it is correct to suppose that the brontological interpretation of each sign of the zodiac occupied about three lines, as does Taurus, then one can estimate the original length of this scroll. The portions of the text distributing the signs of the zodiac over the days of the year would have covered about one and one-half months per column. Adar occupies only about two-thirds of its column, wherein begin the brontological aspects. These data extrapolate to a twelve column text, provided that the missing beginning did not occupy much space before the distribution of the zodiac began. (Judging from Greek parallels, it is unlikely that a hypothetical prose beginning would have been longer than a line or two). The first nine columns of the text would accomplish the distribution of the signs, and the last three would prosecute the אם ירעם pattern for each of the twelve signs. If these tentative conclusions are correct, then it follows that the preserved portions of this brontologion originally derived from columns V, VIII and IX.

---

21   For a good succinct discussion of this calendar, see S. Talmon, *The World of Qumran from Within* (Leiden: Brill, 1989), pp. 147-85. See also chapters five and six, below.
22   I leave aside the three very small fragments preserving only ciphers, which cannot be located and which, if they could, would not add to our understanding of the text.

Nisan		Iyyar		Sivan		Tammuz		Ab		Tishri		Marchesvan	Kislev		Tebet		Adar	
1	דלא	8	נהלאל	21	חזיז	29	נהלאל	29	נהלאל	11		18		24	אומץ	1	דברא	
2	חזיז	9		16	חזיז	30	חזין	30		12	חזין	19		25		2		
3	מימנא	10	מימנא	17	חזיז	23		Elul		13		20		26	חזיז	3	חזין	
4		11	חזיז	18		18		1		14		21		27		4		
5	סימכא	12	מימנא	19	חזין	25	מימנא	2		15	מימנא	22	מימנא	28		5	מימנא	
6		13		20	חזין	26	סימכא	3	נהלאל	16		23		29	נהלא	6		
7		14	מימנא	21		27		4		17	סימכא	24		30		7		
8	אריא	15	אומץ	28		28		5	סימכא	18		25		Tebet		8	אומצא	
9		16		29	מימנא	9		6		19	אריא	26	סימכא	7		9		
10	בתולתא	17	חזיז	30		10	נהלא	7		20		27		8	אומצא	10	אריא	
11		18	אריא	31		11		8	נהלא	21		28	אריא	9		11		
12	מאזניא	19	אריא	Tammuz		12	חזין	9		22	בתולתא	29		10	סימכא	12	מאזניא	
13		20		1	אריא	13		10	נהלא	23		30	בתולתא	11		13		
14		21		2		14	נהלא	11		24	מאזניא	Kislev		12	אריא	14		
15	עקרבא	22	מאזניא	3	מימנא	15		12	מימנא	25		1	חזין	13		15	עקרבא	
16		23		4		16	חזיז	13		26	עקרבא	2		14	מאזניא	16		
17	קשתא	24	מאזניא	5	נהלא	17	קשתא	14	עקרבא	27		3	מאזניא	15		17	עקרבא	
18		25		6		18		15		28	קשתא	4		16		18		
19	גדיא	26	אומצא	7		19	קשתא	16	קשתא	29		5	עקרבא	17	עקרבא	19	קשתא	
20		27		8	נהלא	20		17		30	גדיא	6		18		20		
21	דליא	28		9		21	גדיא	18	גדיא	Marheshvan		Kislev		19	קשתא	21		
22	כוזא	29	מאזניא	10	דלא	22		19		1	חזיז	6	קשתא	20		22	דליא	
23		30		11		23		20		2		7		21	גדיא	23		
24		Sivan		12	כוזא	24	דלא	21	דלא	3	נהלא	8	גדיא	22		24	דליא	
25		1	מימנא	13		25		22		4		9		23	דליא	25		
26	סימכא	2		14	נהלא	26	סימכא	23		5	סימכא	10	דליא	24		26	אומצא	
27		3	נהלא	15		27		24	סימכא	6		11		25		27		
28		4	אריא	16		28		25		7		12	דליא	26	אומצא	28		
29	דליא	5	חזין	17	קשתא	9		26	אריא	8	נהלא	13		27		29	חזין	
30	חזין	6		18		2		27		9		14		28		30		
7				19	דלא	3	חזיז	28		10	חזיז	15	אומצא	16		29	חזין	31	
				20									16				17	אריא	30	

Table 1. The Mensal Zodiac of 4Q Brontologion

The text raises some important questions of interpretation and significance. What is the relation of the two unequal halves of the work, the 'zodiacal' and the 'brontological'? What does the distribution of the signs of the zodiac over the days of the year signify? Why does the author's zodiac, as it can be reconstructed, begin with the sign Taurus, and not with Aries (note table 1)? Aries was the first sign throughout the Hellenistic world and in later Judaism.[23] What then is the signficance of this shift to Taurus? What does this text imply about intellectual relations between the Jews and their milieu? I shall attempt to answer each of these questions in the following pages. First, however, in order to have the best possible understanding of the text *per se*, it is necessary to discuss the brontological section of the text in more detail, paying brief but particular attention to problems and possible restorations.[24]

Restorations, Problems and Comments

II ii 6 [   ] על מסבת As with the other lines of II ii, approximately a third of this line is missing. The meaning of the word מסבת is the principle problem; to a lesser degree it is problematic whether this form, apparently a feminine noun, is in the absolute or construct state. That, of course, is related to how one understands the preserved על, as the preposition or as the first two letters of a verbal or nominal form. This second problem's possible resolutions are a function of the meaning of מסבת.

מסבת could potentially derive from any of three roots, סאב, נסב or

---

23   For later Jewish lists beginning with Aries (Hebrew טלה) see *Pesiq. R.,* ed. Friedmann, 95, *Pirqe R. El.* 6 and *Sepher Yeṣirah* 5.3. Based on the correspondence between the months of the year and the signs of the zodiac, the four zodiacal circles known from 4th-6th century synagogues apparently also assume a zodiac beginning with Aries. The 7th century inscription from Ein Gedi clearly establishes this calendrical correspondence: Nisan aligns with טלה, etc. For discussion of the synagogues see esp. R. Hachlili, *Ancient Jewish Art and Archaeology in the Land of Israel* (Leiden: Brill, 1988), pp. 301-9. For an interpretation of the Beth Alpha inscription as implying the preeminence of Cancer, see I. Sonne, 'The Zodiac Theme in Ancient Synagogues and in Hebrew Printed Books', *Studies in Bibliography and Booklore* 1 (1953), pp. 3-13.

24   Of all the Greek brontologia, the Taurus portion of CCAG 9.2 120-3 is most like that of the Qumran text's Taurus. The two have in common the elements of the king's court, war, famine and the mention of Arabs.

סבב. The basic meanings of נסב are 'to take, to carry, to lift up.' The only *mem* preformative noun derived from this root thus far known in Aramaic is מיסב, 'taking, lifting up.'[25] This is a masculine noun, of course, while ours is feminine. It would seem, then, that if it derives from נסב, מסבת is a previously unattested word. One might suggest that it is a feminine biform of מיסב, but the basic meanings of the word still yield no obvious sense in our text. Nor do idioms that contain מיסב offer any help. Perhaps the most common such idiom is מיסב אפין, 'showing partiality; hypocrisy.' The idiom is known in Syriac (in the slightly different form ܢܣܒ ܒܐܦ̈ܐ) and CPA as well, but does not seem to have any relevance for the present context. Hypocrisy is not a concern of brontologia, judging from Greek parallels (to be discussed more fully below). And, of course, the second term in the idiom is as vital to its meaning as the first, but is lacking here. Conceivably one might perhaps suggest some relation to a second idiom, מסב ומתן, i.e., 'trade', and thereby to economic matters. These are a central concern of brontologia. The idiom occurs in CPA and Syriac, apparently stemming in each instance, either directly or indirectly, from Jewish influence.[26] But this suggestion suffers from obvious defects and is no more attractive than the others. Perhaps מסבת has some sort of economic connotation, but one cannot prove it from attested derived nouns related to נסב.

Two distinct roots סאב exist in Aramaic, the more common meaning 'to grow old' and the other meaning 'to defile, make ritually unclean.' Clearly the first has little to recommend it in the present context, nor, as a matter of fact, does it give rise to a *mem* preformative noun, masculine or feminine. The latter root occurs in Jewish Palestinian Aramaic and Mandaic,[27] and the derived noun מסאבו, 'uncleanness', could fit here morphologically.[28] Aramaic nouns ending in /u/ are feminine, and in forming the *status constructus* add a *taw* to the form of the *status absolutus*. A graphic form מסבת, lacking the *aleph* and a *mater lectionis* for the final /u/, would not be at all surprising in

---

25 See Jastrow, Brockelmann, Dalman and Sokoloff, *Dictionary,* s.v. Syriac knows an adverb derived from the AtG infinitive, but that hardly seems germane.

26 מסב ומתן is a common phrase in Tannaitic Hebrew, but is apparently of Aramaic origin.

27 See Sokoloff, *Dictionary,* s.v. and Drower and Macuch s.v. SUB I. Cf. Schulthess.

28 Cf. Mandaic *msabta,* 'pollution.'

Qumran Aramaic (or Hebrew). Presumably the vocalization would be מְסָבָה.The problem with this suggestion for the brontologion is that ritual defilement is not a theme one finds in known parallels to our text. If עלמ]א is to be restored—felicitious precisely because of such parallels[29]—then the conceptual problem is still more prominent. A Jew would be unlikely to write or adapt a text predicting the ritual defilement of the gentile world, since by Jewish reckoning it already was defiled.[30]

Alternatively one might propose a restoration more narrowly focused than this type of divination tends to be—but still perhaps possible—in which the root סאב could work. Further, at first glance this restoration resonates with a theme common in the Qumran texts and in Second Temple Judaism generally. Perhaps the text read מסבת על מקד]שא, 'ritual defilement upon the temple.' But I see three problems with this suggestion. First, the use of the preposition על with סאב to express this concept would be discordant; one would instead expect either the preposition ב, or simply the noun in construct with 'temple.' Second, the implication of this restoration would be that usually the temple was ritually pure, but might be defiled from time to time. Prior warning could be had from an omen. The common thrust of the relevant Qumran texts, and works such as Psalms of Solomon, is exactly the opposite. The temple is constantly in a state of defilement, because of improper sacrificial and ritual performance as well as more general attitudes. Third, no mention of temples occurs in the Greek brontologia.[31] Though better than any options suggested by the root נסב, I do not think these connected with סאב are convincing.

Thus we come to the root סבב. It occurs in only a few of the Aramaic dialects, generally those written by Jews who also actively used Hebrew.[32] It does not appear in Syriac or CPA, for example. And

29   The Greek equivalents κόσμος and οἰκουμένη occur with notable frequency in the Greek brontologia. Note e.g., CCAG 4.130.19; 4.131.4; 8.3.124.8; 8.3.168.2 and 8.3 169.1.
30   See G. Alon, 'The Levitical Uncleanness of Gentiles', in *Jews, Judaism and the Classical World*, trans. I. Abrahams (Jerusalem: Magnes Press, 1977), pp. 146-89.
31   Perhaps not much should be made of this absence, however, since references to temples do occur in seismologia, texts whose contents are virtually interchangeable with those of brontologia. Cf. CCAG 7.170.12-26. Further, temples are a frequent topic of Akkadian astrological literature.
32   The root does occur in Mandaic; see Drower and Macuch s.v. SUB II. But in

even where it does occur, it is sometimes suspected of being a borrowing from Hebrew. This is the explanation that Sokoloff offers for the forms מסב and מסובה, which occur in *Echa Rabba*.[33] These are the only examples of the root in the material covered by Sokoloff's lexicon, and since their usage coincides with that of Tannaitic Hebrew, his explanation for them may well be correct. But the root also occurs in the Palestinian Talmud and, although its authors did know Hebrew, the usage there does not perfectly coincide with Hebrew idiom. For example, *Rosh Hashanah* 58a, דהוון אילין מסבין יומא דין, 'For these went around (to announce) today.' The semantics of this use of the *Aphel* of סבב are foreign to those of the corresponding Hebrew *Hiphil*. Still, it must be admitted that many of the uses of the Aramaic in the Palestinian Talmud do correspond to Hebrew idiom; accordingly the independent development of סבב in any of the Aramaic dialects known is at best extremely limited. Further, the form found in the brontologion does not occur, at least with a meaning that would be intelligible in the present context.[34]

Nevertheless I favor the root סבב as an explanation of מסבת, for two reasons. First, there exist in Biblical Hebrew two nouns derived from the root which, while not precisely paralleled in Aramaic, would make sense in the present context. The interplay between Hebrew and Aramaic in the Second Temple Period was so substantial and multifaceted that citing Hebrew evidence here is by no means illegitimate. And second, once that identification is made, a nearly exact parallel appears in a Greek brontologion.

At 1 Kings 12.15 one reads, היתה סבה מעם יהוה 'it was a turn of affairs from the Lord.' The word סבה, derived from סבב, here connotes a change of direction in the temporal affairs of men. The parallel passage in 2 Chronicles 10.15 replaces סבה with נסבה,[35] thus providing evidence of a second (perhaps later) nominal form derived from the root and meaning more or less the same thing, 'turn of affairs,

---

this dialect the root is rare, attested only in the D stem meaning 'to surround s.o.'

33 Sokoloff, *Dictionary,* s.v.v.

34 מסבתא means 'winding staircase.'

35 Note the translation of the problematic MT form נסבה (generally understood as a *Niphil* from סבב, but so difficult both morphologically and semantically that various emendations are proposed) by מסבתא in *Tg. Neb.* Ezek. 41.7. The translator's effort may possibly support the idea that Aramaic speakers could connect the two forms when a different meaning was required as well.

change.' Semantically a meaning akin to this one would fit well in the brontologion, especially when Greek parallels are considered. A brontologion structurally nearly identical to ours reads εἰ ἐν τῷ Κριῷ βροντήσῃ, μεγάλα ἐπικαινίσματα ἔσονται κενά: 'If it thunders, in Aries, there shall be great changes, (made) in vain.'[36] A possible Aramaic equivalent to the essence of this omen would be מסבת על[מא רבן ריקן תהוין; although I do not suggest that precisely this restoration is required, something like it does seem to me the best solution to a difficult problem. Since I owe the reader some solution, this, tentatively, is mine.

II ii 7 עמל למדינתא The term עמל is probably the Aramaic equivalent of the ubiquitous θόρυβος of the Greek brontologia. An interpretation much like that of the Qumran text appears in a Greek brontologion that is similar to the Aramaic exemplar both in specifics and in general approach.[37] It reads Εἰ δὲ ʿΗλίου ὄντος ἐν Κριῷ βροντήσει... θόρυβοί τε κατὰ πόλεις, 'If while the sun is in Aries it thunders...(it means) trouble for (the) cities.'

II ii 7 וחר]ב בד[רת מלכא Because the first two letters of חרב are preserved, and given the context and the Greek parallels, the options for the first word seem to be narrowed to חרב and חרבן. On comparison with ii 9, the lacuna into which the missing letters fit appears to be only four letters and spaces wide. The restoration of five letters and spaces, which would result from וחרן בן בד[רת מלכא, strains this estimate and so must count against the possibility of חרבן. (As will become clear shortly, בד[רת מלכא is virtually certain.) In favor of חרבן is the need for an abstract substantive,[38] presumably an equivalent of Greek ἀπώλεια or perhaps φθορά, common in the parallels.[39] חרבן is a common term for 'destruction; desolation' in Jewish Palestinian Aramaic, CPA, Babylonian Talmudic Aramaic and

---

36 CCAG 8.3.195.6. Note also 8.3.196.21, περὶ τὴν οἰκουμένην καινὸν τίθεσθαι.

37 CCAG 7.163-7; the quotation is from 164.5-7.

38 The Greek brontologia abound in abstract nouns combined with the future indicative of the verb 'to be.'

39 ἀπώλεια is more common in the Greek brontologia, but for φθορά cf. e.g., CCAG 8.3 169.25. The equivalent Akkadian phrases are *laqāt amilūti* and *miqit nīši*. See CAD s.v.v. *laqātu* and *miqittu*.

the targumim.[40] It also appears in Qumran Aramaic at Enoch 76.13.[41] On the other hand, there are arguments in favor of חרב. Certainly it fits the space better. Vocalized חֶרֶב, it could mean 'desolation', although this possibility is not favored by Aramaic usage, wherein חרבן is the overwhelming favorite for expressing this concept. It may be preferable, therefore, to vocalize as חֶרֶב. The common meaning for that word is 'sword', but at least three Aramaic dialects evidence the metaphorical 'war, slaughter, destruction.'[42] Syriac often uses ܚܪܒܐ in this way; the expression ܚܪܒܐ ܕܓܒܐ constantly parallels 'ܓܒܐ ܡܢ ܓܒܐ in both prose and poetry.[43] Mandaic knows *harba* and *hirba* bearing this more abstract meaning.[44] Of greater significance is the usage of 4Q246 (Pseudo-Daniel A). The author of this text, describing messianic times, writes עד יקום עם אל וכלא יניח מן חרב 'until there shall arise the people of God, causing all to cease from warfare.'[45] Taking all the factors into account, I prefer to restore חרב.[46]

בד[ר]ת מלכא is almost a certain restoration in the light of Greek parallels. Theoretically, of course, one might consider other possibilities, such as בבי[ר]ת מלכא, 'in the fortress of the king.' References to the 'court of the king' are so common in the known

---

40   See Sokoloff, *Dictionary,* Schulthess and Jastrow s.v.

41   Milik, *Books of Enoch,* p. 288.

42   A fourth, CPA, may support this meaning with the reading of the Codex Damascus to Ben Sira 46.2.

43   See the examples in Brockelmann.

44   See Drower and Macuch *s.v.*

45   Reading and translation are mine; cf. Eisenman and Robinson, PAM 43.236. The work is not yet fully published. For the most recent discussion, including all the phrases of the text which have appeared in sundry publications, see F. García Martínez, '4Q 246: ¿Tipo del anticristo o libertador escatológico?' in *El misterio de la palabra,* eds. V. Collado and E. Zurro (Madrid: Ediciones Cristiandad, 1983), pp. 229-44.

46   It should not be overlooked that the *resh* is not a certain reading (though to my mind there is little doubt). It is barely possible that the letter is instead a damaged or anomolous *daleth.* If so, a felicitous restoration would be וחד[ו] בד[ר]ת מלכא 'and joy in the royal court.' That reading finds a precise parallel in CCAG 9.2.121.5-6: Ταῦρος.' Ἐὰν βροντήσῃ, σίτου φθορὰν σημαίνει κατὰ τὸν τόπον ἐν τῇ χώρᾳ, χαρὰν ἐν τῇ βασιλικῇ αὐλῇ καὶ εὐωχίαν, 'Taurus: If it thunders, it indicates a destruction of grain in the countryside of that region (sc. where the thunder is heard) and joy with good cheer in the royal court.' The notion of royal joy is common in the brontologia; cf. CCAG 4.128.7-9; 7.164.16-7; 9.2 121.9-10; 10. 61.18; 10.141.25; 11.156.3-4 and *Geop.* 1.10.12-13.

brontologia, however, that it seems pointless to explore such other options.⁴⁷ In any case no other plausible option finds a parallel in the Greek brontologia. Among the Greek astrological corpus do appear parallels for the connection between the royal court and the notion of destruction. An example reads, Εἰ ἐν Τοξότη βροντήσῃ . . . τινας τῆς συγκλήτου τῆς βασιλικῆς αὐλῆς ἀπολέσθαι, 'If it thunders in Sagittarius . . . (it means) some of the council summoned to the royal court will be destroyed.'⁴⁸ Another example:Ὑδροχόος. Ἐὰν βροντήσῃ . . . ἔνεδρον καὶ δόλον περὶ τὴν βασιλικὴν αὐλὴν γενέσθαι, 'Aquarius. If it thunders . . . (it means) ambush and intrigue will surround the royal court.'⁴⁹ A great many other texts predict the destruction of a king or his court, so that notion would not be surprising here.⁵⁰

II ii 7 [   ]אב ובמדינת is difficult to restore with any confidence. It is uncertain whether מדינת is a singular or plural construct, and its meaning is uncertain. Further, the possibilities for [אב are numerous. Although most potential solutions seem very unlikely—an apparent boon—this fortune is offset by the fact that the more probable solutions all have problems. What does seem certain, at least, is that these are the first two letters of a toponym, or of an abstract noun defining a toponym.⁵¹

In earlier Aramaic מדינה refers to provinces or regions, i.e., political subdivisions of various sorts. Later, by extension, it comes to mean 'city.' In fact, this is virtually the only meaning of מדינה in the later Aramaic dialects: Palmyrene, Palestinian Jewish Aramaic, Samaritan,

---

47 E.g., CCAG 7.164.10-11, Σελήνης οὔσης ἐν Ταύρῳ ἐὰν βροντήσῃ . . . δῶρα δὲ ἐν Βασιλικῇ αὐλῇ, 'If it thunders while the moon is in Taurus . . . (it signifies) gifts in the royal court.' Note also CCAG 11.1.157.10-11 and the two further examples that appear above. Cf. Akkadian *bartum ina ekallim ibašši*, 'there will be a rebellion in the palace' (cf. CAD s.v. *bartu*.)
48 CCAG 8.3.197.3-6.
49 CCAG 9.2.123.16-22.
50 Particularly apt parallels to the present context are CCAG 3.52.21; 4.127.22; 7.164.14-15; 9.2.122-6; 9.2 123.9-10; 11.1 156.21-2; 11.1 157.19-21 and *Geop.* 1.10.18-19. The usual equivalent in Akkadian astrological texts is simply *qīt palī* 'end of the government' (CAD s.v. *qītu*).
51 In Aramaic generally, if the noun מדינה fronts a toponym, it is in the construct state, while if the toponym precedes, מדינה is in apposition. Since it is in construct here a toponym (or the equivalent) ought to follow.

and Syriac.[52] Could it mean 'city' here? The possibility has to be considered. Although in published Qumran Aramaic מדינה always bears the earlier connotation,[53] the shift evidently occurred sometime in the period around the turn of the eras. Thus, I will discuss possible restorations based on both possibilities, in this order: (1) מדינה means 'province or district;' (2) מדינה means 'city.'

Only two possibilities for the first category seem at all promising. One is Abilene. The name does not survive in contemporary Semitic records, but presumably would have been written something like אבלין. Located north of Damascus, the region had once been under the control of the Itureans, a warlike Arab tribe who intersected Jewish history particularly at the time of John Hyrcanus I (135/4-104 BCE). He or his son Aristobulus I conquered a portion of the tribe's territories.[54] The region once again came to the fore when, at the death of Tiberias (37 CE), Herod Agrippa I was granted the tetrarchy of Abilene. Simultaneously he received the coveted title of king.[55] When Agrippa died in 44 CE, Abilene apparently fell to the administration of the Syrian legate, until in 53 CE it became a part of the kingdom of Agrippa II.[56] Since presumably this brontologion had some relevance to the immediate circumstances of its composition, and since Abilene did have connections with events in Judaea, it is a reasonable possiblity for the lacuna. Also in favor of ובמדינת אבןלין is the region's official status as a Roman province. Seldom do the Greek brontologia name individual cities,[57] while they devote considerable attention to larger political and ethnic units.[58]

The second possibility, still working with אבןלין or simply אבןל,

---

52   This, of course, is the meaning in which the term was borrowed by Arabic.

53   The materials in Eisenman and Robinson may change this picture, but will take scholars some time to digest. For the situation prior to the facsimile edition's appearance, see Beyer, *Aramäische Texte,* p. 553 s.v.

54   It is uncertain whether it was Hyrcanus or his son, Aristobulus I, who conquered regions under Iturean control. See M. Smallwood, *The Jews Under Roman Rule* (Leiden: Brill, 1981), p. 14.

55   *Ant.* 18.228-37. It is possible that Agrippa did not receive Abilene until Claudius expanded the Jewish king's realm in 41 CE.

56   *Ant.* 20.138. But see note 60 below.

57   They do, however, refer on occasion to 'the city' or 'a city;' e.g., CCAG 9.2.123.31. The point is that they do not give the *names* of cities.

58   E.g., CCAG 7.163-7 mentions as part of its predictions Syria, Judaea, Idumea, Koile-Syria, Egypt, Mesopotamia, Greece and thirty-five additional toponyms.

would take the reading as a reference to Eusebius' πόλις ἐπίσημος. This Abila was located some twelve miles east of Gadara, and, as a member of the Decapolis, controlled a territory of significant but uncertain extent.[59] Alexander Jannaeus conquered the city. Later, Pompey re-established it as a free Greek city. Some scholars believe that it was this Abila, not the one in the Lebanon, which Nero granted to Agrippa II.[60] Apart from that possibility, this city-state evidently played such a small role in the affairs of the Jews in these years that it seems a less likely candidate for restoration than the previous option.[61]

If מדינה means 'city', the most obvious restoration is מדינת אבן]דן, 'the city of destruction.' The description of cities by such metaphors or epithets is particularly well attested in Syriac.[62] The Egyptian city of Hieropolis is called either ܟܘܡܪ̈ܐ ܕ ܟܪܬܐ, 'the city of priests', or ܟܪܬܐ ܕ ܟܘܡܪܘܬܐ, 'city of the priesthood.' In this instance the Syriac is a transparent attempt to render each element of the Greek name by a Semitic equivalent. ܟܪܬܐ ܕ ܐܠܗܐ, 'the city of God', refers to Antioch. ܟܪܬܐ ܕ ܡܠܟܘܬܐ, 'city of the kingdom', is an idiom for the capital city of a region. 'The city of peace', ܟܪܬܐ ܕ ܫܠܡܐ, means Baghdad. And finally, 'the city of holiness', ܟܪܬܐ ܕ ܩܘܕܫܐ, is an appellation for Jerusalem. These abstract nouns encode either an aspect of the given city's character, or the author's attitude toward that city. If the writer of the brontologion used the designation מדינת אבן]דן, it would presumably mean either that the site was a ruin at the time that he wrote, or that in his mind it would or should become a ruin. Further, it is logical to suppose that the city in view would be of such significance that, whether a present or future ruin, it was important to the nation's fortunes. One thinks naturally of Jerusalem, just as in Greek brontologia the city of Rome sometimes makes an appearance.[63]

Were Jerusalem a ruin at the time of the writer, the 'assured results' of the dating of the DSS, or at any rate their *terminus ad quem*, would require substantial revision, along with much scholarship that depends

---

59   For the possible extent of its territory, see M. Avi-Yonah, *The Holy Land* (Grand Rapids: Baker, 1966), p. 175. For its membership in the Decapolis and other data, see Schürer 2, pp. 136-7.
60   See Schürer 2, p. 137 n. 265 for the evidence.
61   A third Abila, located in southern Peraea near Philadelphia and apparently mentioned in *Leviticus Rabba,* is a still more unlikely candidate.
62   See Brockelmann and Payne-Smith s.v. ܟܪܬܐ.
63   E.g. CCAG 8.3. 195.25.

on these conclusions. That the writer did in fact compose his brontologion subsequent to the destruction of Jerusalem is not impossible, but the other option, that he considered the city of David to be doomed, seems more likely. Prophets spewing Jeremiads arose whenever Jerusalem was potentially threatened during the late Second Temple period. The phenomenon was a concomitant of the widespread belief in the city's corruption. The DSS may themselves contain such prophecies.[64] The most obvious example of such a prophet of doom in our period is probably the Jesus ben Ananias who spoke of 'a voice against Jerusalem and the sanctuary, a voice against the bridegroom and the bride' in the years immediately before the outbreak of war with Rome.[65] This prophetic perspective is not sectarian in and of itself. Accordingly, even if מדינת אבן]דן were certainly the correct restoration, one would not thereby be justified in regarding this brontologion as a 'sectarian composition.' What it would be more likely to mean is that the text was composed in the first century CE, when increasingly the conviction grew that, barring radical reforms, God was about to judge his people.

Of the restorations that would fit the lacuna, this one would easily be the most attractive, if only there were certain evidence that מדינה ever meant 'city' at this early date. Abilene and Abila suffer in comparison because, while each played some role in Jewish affairs in the years when the brontologion was probably composed, neither was really significant. Perhaps it is not necessary that they should be. Perhaps, then, I am mistaken in my weighing of the factors involved, but if pressed, I would favor restoring מדינת אבן]דן.

II ii 8 כפן א.[   ]... ולערביא The reference to the Arabs here has several parallels among the Greek brontologia.[66] כפן corresponds to a variety of ubiquitous Greek terms and expressions such as φυτῶν, ἀκαρπία,φθορά, σίτου, πεῖνα and Λιμός.[67] It seems likely that the

---

64   As sometimes understood, 4QTestimonia comes to mind as an example. The possible prophecy of the destruction of Jerusalem comes in the last lines, as the text cites portions of the Psalms of Joshua. For interpretive options, see most recently J. Lübbe, 'A Reinterpretation of 4QTestimonia', *RevQ* 12 (1985-87), pp. 187-98.
65   *War* 6.300-309.
66   E.g., CCAG 7.164.24-7, Σελήνης οὔσης ἐν Διδύμοις εἰ βροντήσῃ,... Ἀράβων δὲ ἀπώλεια, 'If it thunders while the moon is in Gemini . . . (it signifies) destruction of Arabs.' Note also CCAG 9.2 121.7; 9.2.121.12, and *Geop.* 1.10.15.
67   E.g., CCAG 4.128.8 and 10; 4.129.13-14; 7.166.12-13; 8.3.124.11; 8.3

illegible portion referred to a second nation or ethnic group that was to suffer famine along with the Arabs.[68] A particularly close parallel to this line appears in a Greek brontologion cited more than once already; it reads εἰ ἐν Ταύρῳ βροντήσῃ, καθὼς Αἰγύπτιοι γράφουσι...ἐν Αἰγύπτῳ δὲ καὶ Ἀραβίᾳ καὶ ἐν βαρβάροις πεῖναν δηλοῖ, 'If it thunders in Taurus, as the Egyptians write . . . it signifies famine in Egypt and Arabia and among the barbarians.'[69]

II ii 8 באנלן אלן בזזין Probably this phrase does not refer back specifically to the Arabs and the others just mentioned. It seems more likely to be an Aramaic equivalent to certain expressions for warfare one finds in the Greek astrological corpus. אלן באלן equates with the reciprocal element of Greek ἀλληλοσφαγία, which, along with synonymous expressions such as ἀλλήλων σφαγή and θανατώσουσιν ἀλλήλους, appears in nearly all preserved Greek brontologia.[70] The Qumran text's connection of war and famine in a single line also has Greek parallels. One such reads, Ἐὰν ἐν τῷ Ζυγῷ βροντήσῃ, λιμὸς και ἀλλήλων σφαγὴ, 'If it thunders in Libra, (it means) famine and mutual slaughter.'[71]

II ii 8 בזזין The morphology here agrees with the Biblical Aramaic *kethib* of geminate participles augmented by endings.[72] The *qere* of such verbs in Biblical Aramaic presupposes reduction of the murmured vowel to zero, with subsequent contraction of the identical consonants. It is this latter form that occurs most often in the texts from Qumran.[73] Either the brontologion was composed prior to this phonological development; or בזזין is a historical spelling that originated with the text's author; or the scribe responsible for our copy substituted the older form.

195.12; 9.2 121.3 and 5 and 11.1.145.14 and 16. Akkadian terms include *bubūtu* and *dīḫu*; see CAD s.v.v. *bubūtu* and *siḫḫu*.

68   I have no good suggestion for the name of that country. The only groups paired with the Arabs in the Greek brontologia are 'the Egyptians' and 'the barbarians.' In neither case is the Aramaic equivalent (מצריא, נכריא) long enough to account for the ink traces plus the three or four letters missing in the lacuna.

69   CCAG 8.3.195.14-17.

70   E.g., CCAG 3.50.29; 4.130.37; 7.164.25; 8.3 124.5; 9.2.123.16; 10.60.6 and 11.1.156.26. The Akkadian literature expresses reciprocal destruction using phrases such as *alu itti ali*, *bītu itti bīti* and *amilu itti amili*.

71   CCAG 4.129.36. Cf. esp. 8.3.170.1; 9.2.122.22-3; 10.60.10 and 11.1.145.5-6.

72   Dan. 4.4 and 5.8.

73   Note especially 1QapGen 21.28 and 22.4, בזין.

II ii 9 אם The use of this particle rather than the usual Aramaic הן to introduce a conditional sentence signals a loan from Hebrew. אם does not occur elsewhere in Qumran Aramaic, but it does appear in the Aramaic materials from the time of Bar Kochba.[74]

II ii 9 דחלה ומרע מנכריא The Greek brontologia never pair 'fear' with 'sickness/distress' (φόβος and νόσος).[75] The assimilation of the *nun* of מן does not regularly occur in Aramaic, but מנכריא is not particularly surprising. Assimilation can happen in those dialects of Aramaic that were in sustained contact with Hebrew (wherein assimilation of *nun* is common).[76] Probably נכריא is the equivalent of the Greek terms βαρβάροι and λαὸς ξένος. These groups are often the source of difficulties in the Greek brontologia. An especially *à propos* example is the following: Αἰγόκερος."Αν βροντήσῃ . . . εἰς τὴν ἀνατολὴν κουρσεύονται τόποι ἀπὸ ἐθνῶν, 'Capricorn. If it thunders . . . (it signifies that) regions in the east will be cut off by aliens.'[77] The context suggests that the broken word at the end of the line also contained an assimilated *nun,* but I have no evidence in favor of any particular restoration.

---

74 Note especially Mur 20, which may be contemporary with the DSS. This marriage contract probably dates to 64 CE. For the text see DJD 2, 111 lines 6 and 8. For the date see Beyer, *Texte,* p. 309.

75 The semanitic field of νόσος is almost exactly that of מרע. Both refer in the first instance to literal illness, and then by extension to general distress. νόσος is ubiquitous in the Greek texts, in both its literal and figurative senses. Cf. CCAG 4.128.17; 4.131.5 and 13; 7.164.25; 8.3.195.18, etc., and for a clearly literal use note especially 8.3.196.26, νόσους περὶ τοὺς ὀφθαλμούς. Only if one wished to argue that מרע is rather the equivalent of Greek ταραχή—a much less obvious and satisfying suggestion—is it possible to cite a few parallels connecting that word with terms for war: CCAG 7.167.14-17, for example, and *Geop.* 1.10.14.

76 Cf. Jer. 10.11, Dan. 2.45, 4.22 and 4.30, 11QtgJob 31.28 and 35.27, etc. Assimilation is particularly frequent in the Aramaic Bar Kochba correspondence, so it may have been a colloquialism.

77 CCAG 10.141.12-14. Cf. also 3.52.18; 3.52.33-4; 8.3.195.3; 8.3.195.8-9; 8.3.196.9-10; 10.58.4, and esp. 8.3.196.15-21, Εἰ ἐν Ζυγῷ βροντήσῃ . . . τοὺς νεωτέρους καὶ τὰ κοράσια ἀπὸ τῶν βαρβάρων κατέχεσθαι. The coming of foreign peoples plays a significant role in Akkadian astrological lore as well. See CAD s.v.v. *nakru* and *girru.*

The Distribution of the Zodiac

Why does this brontologion distribute the signs of the zodiac over the days of the year, and what is the relationship of that portion of the text to the brontological *omina*? Perhaps the best way to begin a consideration of these matters is to take a look at a Greek text that is a structural twin to the Qumran text. The excerpt comes from a Byzantine manuscript,[78] but, as noted above, it is probable that the original of which this text is a copy dates from Hellenistic times. For the first month of the year, it reads as follows:

Μηνὶ Μαρτίῳ α' Β' Κριός, γ' δ' Ταῦρος, ε' ϛ' ζ' Δίδυμος, η'
θ' ι' Καρκίνος, ια' ιβ' Λέων, ιγ' ιδ' ιε' Παρθένος, ιϛ' ιζ'
Ζυγός, ιη' ιθ' κ' Σκορπίος, κα' κβ' Τοξότης, κγ' κδ' κε'
Αἰγόκερως, κϛ' κζ' Ὑδροχόος, κη' κθ' λ' λα' Ἰχθύς.

In the month of March: the first and the second Aries, the third and the fourth Taurus, the fifth, sixth and seventh Gemini, the eighth, ninth and tenth Cancer, the eleventh and twelfth Leo, the thirteenth, fourteenth and fifteenth Virgo, the sixteenth and seventeenth Libra, the eighteenth, nineteenth and twentieth Scorpio, the twenty-first and twenty-second Sagittarius, the twenty-third, twenty-fourth and twenty-fifth Capricorn, the twenty-sixth and twenty-seventh Aquarius, the twenty-eighth, twenty-ninth, thirtieth and thirty-first Pisces.

Unlike the Aramaic brontologion, whose beginning is unfortunately lost, this Greek text bears a heading that explicitly states the rationale of its zodiacal distribution: Βροντοσκόπιον τῶν δώδεκα Ζῳδίων καθ' ἑκάστην νύκτα -κατὰτὸν τῆς Σελήνης δρόμον, 'Brontoskopion of the twelve signs of the zodiac for each night <according to> the course of the moon.' The Qumran text is therefore a Jewish exemplar of that class of books, widespread in antiquity, known as Σεληνοδρόμια or, in Latin, *Lunaria*. These books employed observation of the moon for their sooth-saying, and were of several

78 Paris. S. GR. 1191 = CCAG 7.193-7.

distinct types.[79]

One type of lunary linked the phases of the moon to the days of the month, thereby determining the fate of people born on a given day. This genethlialogical approach originally based its forecasts on the question of which god oversaw the days and months,[80] but later attached itself specifically to the moon. These texts classified calendar days as 'good' and 'bad', by which designation they entered the official Roman calendar as *dies Aegyptiaci*. Despite the name, they seem originally to derive from Mesopotamia. Good days were at first those of the moon's waxing and bad days those of its waning. Especially significant were the days of transition, when the moon passed from one quarter to the next. Accordingly, the seventh, fourteenth, twenty-first and twenty-eighth days were critical and, generally, unlucky. Such a system proved entirely too logical and easily remembered, however, defeating an important purpose of the *cognoscenti:* to force the uninitiated to consult them—for a slight fee, of course. Consequently, much more complicated systems developed. It would not appear that our text partakes of any element of this type of lunar forecast.

Nor does it borrow from the second type of lunary. These texts focused on the shapes of the moon during the course of the month. A number of different 'phases' were distinquished, usually ten or twelve, but sometimes as many as thirty. Each day of the month bore a name; the first was always called 'the moon's birthday', while others were variously 'rising', 'halved', 'vaulted', and so forth. Like the first, this type of text was genethlialogical, usually based on the day of birth. Later conception forecasts developed, and were popular among medieval Christians.

Finally, a third type of lunary derived its prophecies from the position of the moon as it traveled through the signs of the zodiac. This is a composite type of divination, mixing the originally separate genres of lunary and zodiacal text. Doubtless such lunaries arose from the need for greater complexity that was a function of the constant striving for an 'edge' in the competition among seers. In such lunaries the combination of lunar and zodiacal signs is generally not logical, particularly in the horoscopic versions. The reasoning is rather of the

79   For an interesting discussion see R. Eisler, *The Royal Art of Astrology* (London: Herbert Joseph: 1946), pp. 146-54. In general, Eisler's book must be used with caution, especially where he deals with Mesopotamian materials.
80   Cf. Herodotus, *Histories,* 2.82.

following sort: a man born when the moon is in Taurus is destined to perjure himself or become unhappy because the Cretan queen Pasiphae (who became a moon goddess) fell into an unhappy and adulterous love for a bull.[81] Clearly the Qumran brontologion is an example of the third type of moon-book, but unlike genethlialogical exemplars, it does follow a definite logic. Its assignment of various days of the month is schematic, but is based on the observation and calculation of lunar movement. Some background may be helpful in understanding this aspect of the text.

Early observers of celestial phenomena watched the western horizon at and just after sunset, noting the stars (including what we call planets) that set with and just after the sun. Continuing this observation over a period of years, it became apparent that the sun moved through these constellations, from west to east, and that it took a year to return to where it had begun. The great circle thus described lies at an angle of about 23.5^0 to the equator, and is known as the ecliptic. The zone around the ecliptic to which the sun, moon and planets confined their movements, some 8.5^0 on either side, was the zodiac. In the late Neo-Babylonian period the constellations of the zodiac came to be numbered at precisely twelve, and to bear the names by which we now call them. There were thus twelve divisions, theoretically of unequal size according to the expanse of a given constellation. But in defiance of this inequality, the belt of the ecliptic was arbitrarily divided into twelve equal portions that (as one-twelfth of the circle) each comprised 30^0. Since the sun described this circle once per year, monthly solar movement was likewise 30^0, approximately 1^0 per day.

What about the moon? When one recalls that a full moon comes about with diametric opposition to the sun, and that when the moon is invisible it is in conjunction with the sun, the answer is obvious. In the period of a month, while the sun travels 30^0, the moon, of course, travels not only that distance, but also completes an entire rotation of 360^0. Therefore it covers 390^0 in approximately thirty days, and its daily movement is approximately 13^0.[82] Since each portion of the

81   Eisler, *Royal Art,* p. 154.
82   Actually the movement of both the sun and the moon is variable rather than constant. The daily movement of the moon relative to the sun, for example, varies between about 10° and 14° daily. That fact was known to the ancients, who attained great precision in describing lunar movements. See Neugebauer, *Exact Sciences,* esp. pp. 97-144.

zodiac equals 30^0, the moon requires somewhat more than two days to transverse one sign.

Bearing these facts in mind, one can see how the author of the Aramaic brontologion conceived of his distribution of the signs of the zodiac (it will be helpful to look at table 1). For Nisan, for example, the moon begins in Taurus (for reasons discussed below). Days three and four then fall to Gemini. In reality, of course, the moon would not enter that sign until about a third of day three had passed. This assignment is therefore somewhat schematic and, if the same pattern were to continue, grossly inaccurate. But the pattern changes. Days five, six and seven—three days rather than two—are assigned to Cancer. Again the method is schematic, for the moon would not actually enter Cancer until it had traversed 60^0, requiring approximately 4.6 days. Nearly two-thirds of the fifth day would therefore be inaccurately subsumed under Cancer. Yet the difference would almost exactly even out by the end of the seventh day, since 7 x 13 = 91 and 3 x 30 = 90.[83]

The recurrent pattern of two days, two days and three days is obviously connected to the week. In this it contrasts sharply with the Greek brontologion excerpted above, which makes its assignments on the basis of Greek calendrical practice.[84] The guiding principle behind the Qumran text's divisions, overriding observation and calculation whenever necessary, is the sabbath. The effect of the assignments is to highlight the eternal cycle of the creation week, wherein God rested on the seventh day. It is noteworthy that the zodiacal assignments never shift on a sabbath. Considering that the ancients regarded the moon— along with all the other celestial bodies—as a living being, one may speculate that the author believed that it rested on the sabbath. Like man, its sabbath journeys were severely circumscribed, never enough to move into a new sign of the zodiac.

It is now possible to understand how the two halves of this text relate to one another. When the brontological portion of the scroll says אם בתאומיא ירעם , it does not mean, as Milik had thought, 'If it thunders in the sign of the Twins.' That translation implies the rumble of thunder

---

83 The author was really even more accurate. Since he held to a 364 day solar calendar, he perforce calculated the daily lunar motion at 12.85°. Therefore 7 x 12.85 = 89.95—very close to 90 by the standards of antiquity.

84 Most Greek calendars divided the month into three decades, and counted the days within the decade. See E.J. Bickerman, *Chronology of the Ancient World* (Ithaca: Cornell University Press, 1968) p. 27 and n. 28.

in the portion of the sky assigned to Gemini, i.e., in its portion of the belt of the zodiac. Milik's is a linguistically defensible translation, and ancient brontological parallels are not hard to produce. But it fails to incorporate the zodiacal half of the work. אם בתאומיא ירעם means rather, 'If it thunders (on a day when the moon is schematically) in Gemini.' Such days are scattered throughout the year in schematic concord with lunar movement. Each sign recurs thirteen times and governs a total of thirty days, except for the four signs—Cancer, Libra, Capricorn and Aries—in force on one of the intercalary days. These signs are responsible for thirty-one days of the year.

The complexity of this scheme must have been satisfying to its author. No one was likely to hit upon a proper interpretation of thunder without his tutelage. Adding to the text's gnostic character is another element that almost certainly would not have characterized any competing system of divination. I refer to the fact that the author's zodiac begins with the sign of Taurus. This oddity requires an explanation, and I shall now attempt to give one.

Taurus the First Sign of the Zodiac

Actually there are at least two possible explanations for the text's choice of Taurus as the first sign of the zodiac, one much better than the other to my mind, but either possibly correct.[85] The first involves the *thema mundi* or 'world horoscope.' The second also invokes the *thema mundi*, but combines with it the concepts of precession and apocalyptic chronology.

The *thema mundi* is explicated only in relatively late sources, but as these sources are extremely consistent in their presentation of the idea, it was probably long established[86] (of course, it must have been if it connects with the Qumran brontologion). In the present context our focus is on the question of where the sun stood in the zodiac at the time of the world's birth. Rival doctrines existed. One school held that the

---

85   I see no connection between the prominence of Taurus in the scheme of this text and references to that sign in 4Q186. For the best discussion of ברגל השור in 4Q186, see M. Delcor, 'Recherches sur un horoscope en langue hébraïque provenant de Qumran', in his *Religion d'Israel et proche orient ancien* (Leiden: Brill, 1976), pp. 298-319, esp. 306-7.

86   Thus S.J. Tester, *A History of Western Astrology* (Suffolk: Boydell Press, 1987), p. 119.

sun was then in Aries; this view buttressed the Hellenistic practice of beginning the zodiac with the sign of Aries. After all, the zodiac, as a circle, lacked beginning or end. Some justification was required for the apparently arbitrary beginning assigned by the astrologers.[87] The second school held that the sun was in Leo, not Aries, at the time of creation. This doctrine relied upon the concept of the astrological houses.[88] The house of a planet was considered to be that sign where its power was strongest. Leo was the sun's house, because that is where it stands at the height of summer (c. 20 July-19 August).[89] It would appear that of these two rivals, the Qumran text may have embraced the 'Aries school.'

Advocates of this school differed on the question of precisely where within the thirty degrees of that sign the sun stood at creation. Most commonly it was located at Aries degree 19.[90] Though potentially helpful, merely locating the sun there does not necessarily explain the Qumran text; one must also incorporate a perspective found clearly

---

87   The real reason for beginning the zodiac in Aries was that, in Hellenistic times, the sun rose in Aries at the time of the vernal equinox. But with the discovery of the precession of the zodiac, a better justification was necessary, or astrology's claims to hoary antiquity were in grave danger. I shall return to the problem of precession below.

88   The 'houses' are divisions of the zodiac into four, eight, or, at last, twelve equal portions. The sun, moon and planets moved through these houses during the year, and their locations relative to one another were considered significant for horoscopic astrology.

89   For a very early exemplar see CCAG 9.2.176-9, esp. 177. Cf. Macrobius *Somn.* 1.23-24, *Aiunt enim incipiente die illo qui primus omnium luxit, id est quo in hunc fulgorem caelum et elementa purgata sunt, qui ideo mundi natalis iure vocitatur, Arietem in medio caelo fuisse . . . Cancro gestante tunc Lunam. Post hunc Sol cum Leone oriebatur . . .* Although the exact identity of Macrobius is uncertain, all the options suggested point to a *floruit* around the date 400 CE. See A. Cameron, 'The Date and Identity of Macrobius', *JRS* 56 (1966), pp. 25-38.

90   The oldest certainly dated witness to this view is a calendrical text of c. 15 CE See S.Weinstock, 'A New Greek Calendar and Festivals of the Sun', *JRS* 38 (1940), pp. 37-42, esp. 38-9. Cf. Firmic. 3.1.18, *Retractans itaque genituram mundi, quam diximus a sapentissimis viris prudentissime esse compositam, inveni MC. geniturae in Ariete esse positum. Ob hoc itaque, quia frequenter, immo semper MC. in omnibus genituris possidet principatum et quia hic locus supra primum verticem est et quia ex hoc loco totius geniturae fundamenta colligimus . . .* Firmicus wrote his *Mathesis* in the period 334-337 CE, evidently drawing upon many earlier astrological works.

stated only in certain medieval Christian commentators. These commentators are a valuable source of illumination for the brontologion's underlying presuppositions, since unlike the pagan astrologers, they were concerned to harmonize general astrological notions with biblical teachings. They believed it was necessary to conform the concept of the *thema mundi* with the biblical creation narratives. Bede attempted this feat in his *De temporum ratione* and concluded, *Igitur iuxta zodiaci quidem divisionem xv kalendarum Aprilium die, quando facta est lux, sol Arietis signum ingreditur* ('Therefore according to the division of the zodiac the sun enters the sign of Aries on the *kalends* of the fifteenth of April, when light was created').[91] Thus, since the sun and moon were created on the fourth day, for Bede creation began on 18 March. Then, on the equinox, 21 March, the sun entered Aries.

A combination of the 19 Aries position with an adjusted version of Bede's view may explain the brontologion beginning its zodiac with Tarurus. For if one postulates that the sun was at 19 degrees Aries when, on the fourth day of creation, God created the heavenly lights, it follows that the moon must have been in Taurus. Otherwise it would not have been a 'light.'[92] The moon would have been invisible. The reasoning is as follows. The new moon, the time when the first sliver of the moon becomes visible, cannot occur if less than one day has passed since its conjunction with the sun. In fact between one and three days must pass before the elongation (as this distance between the two bodies is known) suffices to render the moon visible. The average increase of the elongation is 12^0 per day, although it varies between 10^0 and 14^0. The time it takes for the new moon to appear—i.e., the amount of elongation required—depends on the time of year, the observer's latitude, and other variables. Theoretically this measurement could be as little as 10^0. Now, if the sun stood at 19 degrees Aries, the moon might well be imagined as entering Taurus—as being elongated 11^0 from the sun. And, since the Qumran text concerns itself with the movements of the moon through the zodiac, a zodiac beginning with Taurus might be entirely reasonable. Then, at the creation, Year One

---

91   *De temporum ratione* 6.92-4. See *Bedae opera*, pars VI, 2, ed. C.W. Jones (Corpus Christianorum Series Latina CXXIII B; Belgium: Typographi Brepols Editores Pontificii Turnholti, 1977). Bede wrote this work in 725 CE.
92   Pagan astrologers, who had no need to consider the biblical text, usually placed the moon in Cancer at the creation.

Month One Day Four was a new moon. But here this explanation of the brontologion's zodiac encounters a difficulty, *for it presupposes that the beginning of a month was signaled by the appearance of the new moon.*

Almost certainly, the author of this Qumran text would not have agreed that the beginning of any given month must coincide with a new moon. The reason: the calendar that underlies this text and so many other Qumran materials regulated time purely by the sun. The solar year was divided into twelve equal portions—a disconnected remnant of the twelve annual lunations—and, once every three months, an intercalary day was added to bring the total days of the year to 364. As a solar calendar, the day began with the rise of the sun and not, as in the lunisolar calender, with evening. A solar calendar should logically begin with daybreak, of course, and yet it has nevertheless been argued that the calendar of Jubilees began in the evening.[93] The Qumran *mishmarot* texts suffice to put the lie to that approach.

These texts seek to establish the correct rotation of the priestly courses into and out of service in the temple at Jerusalem. They envisage a cycle of six years, the length of time necessary for any one of the twenty-four courses to come around again on the same dates of the year. The system of priestly rotations was tied to the creation narratives by virtue of its connection to the solar calendar, which found its inspiration there.[94] Like the solar calendar itself, then, the rotations were an eternal ordinance, and could serve for dating purposes. One type of *mishmarot* establishes equivalences between its own solar reckoning and a lunar calendar.[95] These texts of equivalents prove that the solar calendar began at dawn. In the first year of the cycle, day one of the solar calendar lacks a lunisolar equivalent. The first day of the lunisolar system is aligned with day two of the solar calendar. The reason for this state of affairs can only be that day one of the solar

93   E.g., J.M. Baumgarten, 'The Beginning of the Day in the Calendar of Jubilees', *JBL* 77 (1958), pp. 355-60. In my view each of the examples Baumgarten draws from Jubilees can be squared with a day beginning at sunrise.
94   A. Jaubert, 'Le calendrier des Jubilés et de la secte de Qumran', *VT* 3 (1953), pp. 250-64. The calendar begins on Wednesday because that was the day when the heavenly luminaries were created and calendrical reckoning became possible. Thus the first three days of creation are not counted, and day four becomes 1/1/1 *Anno Mundi.*
95   See chapter six below.

calendar was half complete when evening came and the lunisolar day began. Rather than reckon with half days, no equivalent appears for solar calendar day one. The day must have begun at sunrise. As the equivalences proceed through the year, the first day of each lunisolar month (i.e., the new moon) recedes further and further from the first day of the month as calculated by the solar calendar. Accordingly, at month six solar day one equates with lunisolar day four; at month nine, day one equates with day six; at month twelve, day one equates with day nine. In the solar calendar that underlies the brontologion, the new moon moved slowly through the days of the month no less than the moon itself passed through the zodiac.

In accordance with the solar calendar it was theoretically possible for nearly a full day to pass between the sun's creation and the moon's. Therefore it is conceivable that the author of the brontologion imagined the two heavenlies to be in conjunction at the moment of their creation.[96] Further, his belief in the solar calendar as the only proper instrument for the reckoning of holy time would presumably mitigate against his construction of a *thema mundi* centered on the moon. In this respect one notes that the Greek brontologion cited above, which is titled as a lunary, begins with Aries at the vernal equinox. Contrary to what one might expect, that brontologion lists the signs of the zodiac according to solar movement even though the text is explicitly concerned with the moon.[97] I suspect that the situation is the same with the Qumran text. If so, we must consider another explanation for a zodiac beginning with Taurus.

Modern astronomers have shown that the earth wobbles slowly on its axis. Their ancient counterparts did not realize that this was the explanation, but they observed that the points where the ecliptic and the celestial equator intersected changed. These 'tropical points'—solstices and equinoxes—were gradually wandering from the zodiacal constellations originally connected with them. The vernal point moved clockwise along the circle of the zodiac. This discovery was made by the Bithynian astronomer Hipparchus (c. 190–after 126 BCE),[98] and set

---

96   Note in this respect that the *mishmarot* are interested in calculating, not the beginning, but the end of lunar months, i.e., the time of conjunction.

97   CCAG 8.3.193. Line 3 begins with the month of March, establishing an equivalence with the Semitic Nisan and the vernal equinox.

98   For what little we know of Hipparchus and his life, see D.R. Dicks, *The Geographical Fragments of Hipparchus* (London: Athlone Press, 1960), pp. 1-18.

out in a work entitled *On the Displacement of the Tropical and Equinoctial Points.*[99] This work, apparently composed in 126 BCE, has not survived;[100] what we know of Hipparchus' argument derives from two writings of Ptolemy (fl. 127-148 CE), the *Almagest* and the *Tetrabiblos.* Hipparchus had access to astronomical observations going back several centuries, and could thereby determine that the chart of the sky had changed somewhat. For example, the star Spica stood in his day at a distance of 6^0 from the autumnal equinoctial point, but in the time of the astronomer Timocharis (fl. c. 300 BCE) it had been 2^0 further distant.[101] The movement of the vernal equinox is known as the precession of the zodiac.

Hipparchus knew that the rate of movement was very slow, requiring some seventy years to wander 1^0. At that rate approximately 2,100 years would pass before the tropical points left one sign of the zodiac to move into the next. Still, the zodiac *was* moving. Astrologers had two choices: they could acknowledge this movement and incorporate it into their horoscopic calculations, or they could explain it away and so preserve all their sidereal doctrines unchanged. Accordingly the discovery of precession resulted in a split in astrological circles, as different groups chose one or the other response to the new facts. Most Hellenistic astrology in the West followed in the steps of Ptolemy, who in his *Tetrabiblos* accomplished an amazing slight of hand. Eisler has described it well:[102]

> In order to give a permanent character to these [ancient stellar] relations which played such an important part in his astrological

In works written by the devotees of astrology—who constantly seek to ascribe to their doctrines the greatest possible age—one often finds the discovery of precession credited to a Babylonian astronomer, Kidinnu, who lived centuries earlier than Hipparchus. Neither cuneiform scholars nor historians of science any longer take this attribution seriously. See D.O. Edzard, ed., *Reallexikon der Assyriologie und Vorderasiatischen Archäologie* (6 vols.; Berlin: Walter de Gruyter, 1976-80) 5, p. 589 and O. Neugebauer, 'The Alleged Babylonian Discovery of the Precession of the Equinoxes', *JAOS* 70 (1950), pp. 1-8.

99   For the title, see Ptol. *Alm.* 2.12.21 and 2.17.12.

100 Hipparchus' sole surviving work, *In Arati et Eudoxi phaenomena commentariorum* (ed. by C. Manitius, [Lipsiae: Teubner, 1894]), is an astronomical commentary, but certainly antedates his discovery of precession.

101 Ptol. *Alm.* 7.2.

102 Eisler, *Royal Art,* 110.

theory, [Ptolemy] hit upon the perfectly arbitrary expedient of separating the 'real' zodiac, represented by the zodiacal constellations constantly and slowly shifting their places relative to the 'tropical points', from a perfectly fictitious zodiac bound to the tropical points, and therefore rotating with reference to the belt of fixed stars through which the sun, the moon and the planets appear to thread their way. This is a perfectly legitimate procedure in so far as it introduces a convenient system of reference invariant with respect to the tropical points—i.e., with reference to the seasons of the solar year, which is still used by modern positional astronomy, and can be seen surrounding every modern celestial globe. But instead of numbering the twelve empty parts . . . of this circle of 12 x 30 degrees with neutral numerical signs . . . Ptolemy preferred to call them by the traditional names of the constellations which appeared to be situated in these twelve sectors at the time when these names were given to the constellations . . . All the alleged influences which the stars themselves, or rather their imaginary configurations in the shape of a ram, bull, lion, crab, goat, fish, etc., were said to exert on the fate of man were now transferred, with an audacious arbitrariness without parallel in the history of pious fraud, to these homomyous (*sic*) but wholly empty sectors of a mere circle of reference . . .

Modern Western astrology still follows the Ptolemaic system, although of course the zodiac has continued to wander, such that on the vernal equinox the sun now rises not in Aries, but in Pisces or even, according to some, in Aquarius (hence 'the age of Aquarius'). But some Hellenistic astrological systems responded to the fact of precession more honestly, and thus kept pace with the best science of their age. In present day India, for example, one finds the descendents of those systems; Eastern astrology, in contrast to that of the West, generally acknowledges the precession of the zodiac. And, I would suggest, the author of the Qumran brontologion took account of this scientific advance in constructing his *thema mundi*.

At the time of the composition of our text, the sun rose at the boundary of Aries and Pisces on 1 Nisan (of the solar calendar). It had risen in Aries since about 2200 BCE. Prior to that time, however, calculation would show that on the vernal equinox the sun had risen in Taurus. Beginning approximately 4400 BCE and lasting until the end of the third millennium, the sun began the year in the sign of the Bull.[103] Therefore, if someone were composing a *thema mundi,* or a variation on that theme, and if he believed that the world had been created in approximately 4000 BCE., he would begin his zodiac with the sign of Taurus. The author of our text apparently held such views.

It has been observed that the chronological data of the Priestly source of the Pentateuch imply that the world will last a total of 4000 years, and that the Exodus took place in the year 2666 AM. (*anno mundi*). The remaining one-third of history would then culminate at about the time of Daniel.[104] Similar speculations, based on systems rather different from that of the Bible, are at the core of apocalyptic eschatology of the sort found in many works composed during the Second Temple period. Such division of history into ages obviously implies a calculated understanding of the age of creation and of where a given author's 'present' is located in the teleological movement of history. For example, the Assumption of Moses measures history by jubilees of fifty years. The entire span of history from creation to judgment is eighty-five jubilees. Thus a fixed period of 4250 years defines the course of history from beginning to end; 1750 of those years intervene between the death of Moses and the end, the writer calculating, as is usual with such works, that his own generation is at or near the climax of events.[105] A different schematization of history appears in the Apocalypse of Weeks now located at 1 Enoch 93.1-10 and 91.12-17. Here the history of the world is divided into ten 'weeks' of uncertain length, each characterized by some great or disastrous event. The three final weeks represent a messianic age, and the author sees the advent of this period in events unfolding around him.[106]

---

103 For various calculations of the precise dates see e.g., A.E. Thierens, *Astrology in Mesopotamian Culture* (Leiden: Brill, 1935), p. 15.

104 See the comments of D.S. Russell, *The Method and Message of Jewish Apocalyptic* (Philadelphia: Westminster, 1964), p. 207.

105 For the chronology compare *As. Mos.* 1.2 and 10.12.

106 The most recent full-scale study is F. Dexinger, *Henoch: Zehnwochenapokalypse und offene Probleme der Apokalyptikforschung* (Leiden: Brill, 1970). For important correctives and supplementation see J. VanderKam, 'Studies in the Apocalypse of Weeks (1 Enoch 93:1-10; 91:11-17)', *CBQ* 46 (1984), pp. 511-23 and S.B. Reid, 'The Structure of the Ten Week Apocalypse and the Book of Dream Visions', *JSJ* 16 (1985), pp. 189-95. Also helpful is J. Licht, 'The Time Reckoning of the Judean Desert Sect and of Other Time Reckoners', *ErIsr* 8 (1967), pp. 66-67 (Heb.).

Several works divide the course of history into a 'world-week' of 7000 years, each 'day' lasting 1000 years on the analogy of the biblical creation narrative.[107] Included here are the Testament of Abraham and 2 Enoch.[108] In this system 6000 years of the present age will be followed by a rest of 1000 years.[109]

Given the work's evident popularity in the circles represented by many of the Qumran texts, the book of Jubilees presents a particularly significant perspective. As the name indicates, the work calculates by jubilee periods. In contrast to the Bible and the Assumption of Moses, however, these periods last forty-nine rather than fifty years each. From creation to the Exodus equates to forty-nine jubilees, i.e., 49 x 49 or 2401 years. According to 50.4 another jubilee passed before Israel entered Canaan; thus the total time from creation to the entry into the Promised Land amounts to 2450 years. But the number 2401 may be the more important figure. Michel Testuz has argued that the forty-nine year periods of Jubilees were not the author's largest denomination. Jubilees of jubilees climaxed his septimal system, so that for him history comprised three eras of 2,401 years each.[110] The book of Jubilees concerns itself largely with the first of these eras, the Age of the Testimony (*l'ère du Témoignage*). The second era, the Age of the Law (*l'ère de la Loi*), begins with the revelation to Moses and is nearly complete, while the third era, the New Age (*l'ère nouvelle*), is about to dawn.

Testuz' suggestion for Jubilees yields an approximate fit with the phenomena of the brontologion. The author of the latter work, basing his approach on the creation narratives, may have fashioned a system that would endure for the ages of Testimony and Law there described. If he believed that history's *dénouement* were imminent, then it would follow that he placed the creation at about 4800 years before his own time. Admittedly this number is somewhat large for the astrological equation, but given the difficulty of deciding precisely when the sun's

---

107 Cf. Ps. 90.4 for a day as lasting a thousand years.

108 *Test. Abr.* 17 and 19 and *2 Enoch* 33.1-2.

109 Note the similar *b. Sanh.* 97b and *b. Abod. Zar.* 9b, which allocate a total of 6000 years including the messianic era. On rabbinic chronology in general see E. Frank, *Talmudic and Rabbical Chronology* (New York: Philipp Feldheim, 1956).

110 M. Testuz, *Les idées religieuses du livre des Jubilés* (Paris: Librairie Minard, 1960), pp. 138-9 and 172-4.

vernal rising entered and left Taurus,[111] the system of Jubilees may nevertheless lie behind the Qumran work.

It is equally possible, of course, that the author relied instead upon another approach that dated the creation some 4000-5000 years before his own time. Whatever approach he embraced, it seems that he wrote under the influence of apocalyptic eschatology. Accordingly, his work represents a remarkably creative *mélange* of Hellenistic science and Jewish beliefs, and proves once again that astrological notions did not rest lightly and superficially at the extremes of Jewish thinking.

Conclusion

We come finally to consider when this work was written and what it may tell us about intellectual relations between the Jews of that time and the broader Greco-Roman world. Apart from the solar calendar, nothing about this text is clearly 'sectarian.' Whether and to what degree the solar calendar was sectarian is debated. Certainly it is true that often—probably usually—during the last two centuries BCE Jewish society was regulated by a lunisolar calendar. But some evidence indicates that within those centuries the solar calendar also ruled from time to time. Since the solar calendar was sometimes enforced by the political establishment, it is not really accurate to describe it as sectarian. This calendar seems to have contended for supremacy at least until the fall of Masada and the end of the first *Bellum Judaicum*.[112] The text's possible affinities with eschatological ideas known to us from Jubilees likewise point to no small sect. I take Jubilees as representative of a substantial portion of Palestinian Jews who resisted the innovations that accompanied a deepening Hellenism.

Based on the many parallels between this text and Greek *brontologia* originating in Ptolemaic Egypt, it seems likely that its basic framework derived from the Egyptian diaspora. Although, as we have seen, many of the phrases it employs have Akkadian antecedents, the elaboration of

111 The shape of the bull was imaginary, after all, and variations were possible. Further, ancient astronometry had to make do with such instruments as the gnomon, the Jacob's staff, the quadrant and the armillary sphere; accuracy never exceeded 2 minutes of arc and was often considerably worse.

112 It will be recalled that among the texts found at Masada was a copy of the *Shirot ᶜOlat Hashabbat,* a work that functions according to the solar calendar. Presumably the *Sicarii* followed this system.

these phrases into a type of Σεληνοδρόμιον well known from Egypt bespeaks a western origin.[113] This conclusion is unsurprising, given the manifold and longstanding relations between Palestinian Jews and their Egyptian brethren.[114] Alexandria was the most important center for every kind of astrological research, and many Jews lived there.[115] Further, that this brontologion exemplifies what Bouché-Leclerq called the 'absorption de la divination météorologique par l'astrologie'[116] accords well with earlier conclusions: the Jews came to astrology comparatively late, when it had already been refined well beyond its Chaldean *Urgestalt*.

As to the text's date I can do no better than suggest a broad time frame into which it might reasonably fit. If it is correct that its author presupposed the concept of precession, then the *terminus a quo* cannot antedate Hipparchus' discovery just prior to 125 BCE. How long would it have taken for Jewish scholars to become aware of the Bithynian's work? We have no way of knowing. It may be safe to assign the earliest possible date for the brontologion's original composition to the first decades of the first century BCE. Presumably the work cannot postdate the First Revolt, giving a *terminus ante quem* of c. 70 CE Whether it is possible to date the work more precisely is doubtful. To my mind there is at best one clue: the word מלכא. If the word is intended to designate a Jewish ruler—not at all certain—then its appearance allows us to eliminate the period 4 BCE-37 CE. Otherwise the text might have been composed virtually anytime in the first

---

113   Thus this brontologion cannot serve as evidence for the theory (reasonable though it is) that cuneiform astrological literature spread to the West only after its translation into Aramaic. For the theory, see A.L. Oppenheim, *Letters from Mesopotamia: Official, Business, and Private Letters on Clay from Two Millenia* (Chicago: University of Chicago Press, 1967), pp. 51-53, and D. Pingree, 'Mesopotamian Astronomy and Astral Omens in Other Civilizations', in H.-J. Nissen and J. Renger (eds.), *Mesopotamien und seine Nachbarn* (Berlin: Dietrich Reimer Verlag, 1982), pp. 613-31.

114   For this period see A. Kasher, *The Jews in Hellenistic and Roman Egypt* (Tübingen: J.C.B. Mohr, 1985).

115   Alexandria is a suggested provenance of the *Treatise of Shem*, a calendologion which apparently dates to the same general period as the brontologion. See J. Charlesworth, 'The Treatise of Shem', in J. Charlesworth, ed., *The Old Testament Pseudepigrapha* (2 vols.; Garden City, N.Y.: Doubleday, 1983-85) 1, pp.472-86.

116   Bouché-Leclerq, *La divination* 1, p. 198.

century BCE—under one of the Hasmoneans or Herod the Great—or later in the first century of the Common Era, when various Herodides held the title of king. The other phrases in the text are so generic that they can support no speculation.

Sometime during this century and a half one or more scholars composed this Aramaic brontologion. They may have worked with a Greek exemplar. They combined the best science of their day with their own understanding of scripture, producing what they surely regarded as the single divinely mandated system of astrological divination. Their approach was based on creation itself. It accounted for the sun, the moon and the stars, giving each their proper place as rulers over human affairs. A theologian might say that they mixed the best of natural revelation with the best of special revelation. Did these men believe that they held a key to a mechanistic universe? Possibly; but the history of astrology is replete with systems that allow for divine intervention and human free will. Perhaps, then, like Dickens' Scrooge they knew only what might be. Either way, they knew more than anyone else.

Chapter Two

THE LIFE AND TIMES OF ANANIAS BAR NEDEBAEUS AND HIS FAMILY

Introduction

Sometimes the historian working with Flavius Josephus feels like a lawyer forced to build his case in court upon the testimony of a felon.[1] While there may be some truth in what the witness says, the problem always is to separate it from self-serving obfuscation and outright lies. This process is rarely simple or certain. What is really needed, of course, is another witness so that the convict's testimony can be double-checked. Unfortunately, such checks on the testimony of Josephus seldom turn up; but in the case of Masada, it appears that now one has.

Among the nearly 700 inscribed ostraca and *tituli picti* that Yigael Yadin discovered during his 1963-65 excavations at Masada was an inscribed sherd from a storage jar that he read 'Kahana Raba Aqavia [*sic*].'[2] He interpreted this *titulus pictus* to mean that the owner of the jar had been a member of one of the families of the high priests. As the name Aqavia (henceforth Aqabiah) is not recorded among the priestly élite at the time of the First Revolt—indeed, the name does not appear in Josephus at all[3]—this discovery elicited virtually no comment from scholars interested in the Masada finds. Apparently there was little more to say about the matter. But now that the Hebrew and Aramaic inscribed materials from Masada have been published, the situation has

---

1   On attitudes toward the works of Josephus, ranging the spectrum from utter credulity to total scepticism, see the convenient sketch by P. Bilde, *Flavius Josephus between Jerusalem and Rome* (Sheffield: JSOT Press, 1988), pp. 123-71.

2   Y. Yadin, The Excavation of Masada—1963/64: Preliminary Report', *IEJ* 15 (1965), pp. 1-120. Yadin mentions the jar on pp. 84 and 111, and provides his interpretation of the inscription on p. 111. See also his less technical *Masada: Herod's Fortress and the Zealots' Last Stand* (New York edition, 1966), p. 189.

3   Cf. A. Schalit, *Namenwörterbuch zu Flavius Josephus* (Leiden: Brill, 1968).

changed.[4]

The final editor, Joseph Naveh, has reread this inscription as
ח]נני[ה כהנא רבא עקביא בריה.[5] Naveh connects the inscription to
Ananias bar Nedebaeus, high priest from 48-59 CE. This man's son,
Eleazar, was responsible for refusing further sacrifice on behalf of the
emperor, and consequently, in Josephus' eyes, it was he more than any
other who precipitated the disastrous war with Rome that broke out in
the summer of 66. Clearly this reading has the potential to cast a
brilliant new light on what Josephus has to say about the background
and course of events at Masada. Before such potential can be explored,
however, one must be satisfied that Naveh's decipherment is solidly
established and that the meaning of the inscription is correctly
understood.

Reading and Interpretation of the Inscription

Judging from the fine photographs that he provides—showing the
inscription from two perspectives—Naveh is correct when he states that
materially the reading is 'almost certain.' Although the inked traces of
the final *heh* of the first name are visible, the two or three[6] preceding
letters of the name seem to have been totally abraded. Given that much
abrasion, it would seem prudent to allow that a *yodh* may once have
preceded the visible *heth* that Naveh takes as the first letter of the name,
and that it, also, has since disappeared. Accordingly the inscription
requires the restoration of a proper name consisting of between four
and six letters. Since only two parts of this puzzle are known, possible
reconstructions might be thought so numerous that no particular
suggestion could bear the slightest weight of historical interpretation.

Yet such is not the case. In addition to material readings, several
other almost equally valuable lines of evidence are available to assist

---

4   *Masada I: The Yigael Yadin Excavations 1963-1965 Final Reports.* Y. Yadin
and J. Naveh, *The Aramaic and Hebrew Ostraca and Jar Inscriptions;* Y.
Meshorer, *The Coins of Masada* (Jerusalem: Israel Exploration Society, 1989).
5   Yadin and Naveh, *Aramaic and Hebrew Ostraca,* 37-8 and plate 30. Naveh
had already supplied the new reading in D. Barag and D. Flusser, 'The Ossuary of
Yehohanah Granddaughter of the High Priest Theophilus', *IEJ* 36 (1986), p. 41, n.
8, but without a photograph.
6   Naveh restores three, but judging from the size of the inscription's lettering
and its spacing perhaps only two are missing.

any attempt at reconstruction: the catalogue of attested Hebrew and Aramaic proper names for the Second Temple period, the linguistic principles behind the formation of such names, and the historical evidence for the names of high priests in the period. Bringing all these guides to bear, the possible reconstructions can be very quickly whittled down. For example, neither attestation nor grammar rules out the name חזקיה. And linguistically the other form of that name, יחזקיה, also cannot be eliminated; a certain tendency existed in the Second Temple period to form proper names with imperfect verbal elements.[7] Yet neither form of the name is that of a known high priest in the period in question.[8] Again, a reading of יחנניה would perhaps work materially, but it is ruled out both morphologically (an imperfect of this geminate verb would almost certainly write only one *nun*)[9] and on the basis of attestation (the imperfect of the verb חנן as an onomastic element is unknown among Hebrew and Aramaic personal names of the First and Second Temple periods).[10] The name חלקיה would work materially and grammatically, but it appears not to be attested at this late date.[11] Given the reading]ח[?]]ה[כהנא רבא and all the criteria that help guide a reconstruction, it would appear that the only names that fit this inscription are Naveh's suggested חנניה and a shortened form of the same name, חנה.[12]

---

7   On the forms of this name see S. Layton, *Archaic Features of Canaanite Personal Names in the Hebrew Bible* (Harvard Semitic Monographs; Atlanta: Scholars Press, 1990), pp. 122-5, and E.Y. Kutscher, *The Language and Linguistic Background of the Isaiah Scroll (I Q Isaᵃ)* (Leiden: Brill, 1974), pp. 104-5. As is well known, יחזקיה ordinarily appears in Chronicles where Kings refers to חזקיה.

8   For the names of the high priests, see E. Schürer, *The History of the Jewish People in the Age of Jesus Christ (175 BC-AD 135)* (3 vols.; Edinburgh: T. & T. Clark, 1973-87). New English Version, rev. and ed. by G. Vermes, F. Millar, M. Black and M. Goodman, vol. 2, pp. 229-32. On the possibility that the name might be that of a heretofore unknown, perhaps sectarian, high priest, see Excursus One below.

9   Morphologically the imperfect of this verb, as attested in the Hebrew Bible, is in all cases but one *yāhōn*. At Amos 5.15, however, one encounters *yehᵉnan*, a *hapax legomenon*. For an attempted explanation of this anomalous form, see GKC § 67cc.

10   Scott Layton (personal communication).

11   R. Hachlili, 'Names and Nicknames among the Jews in the Period of the Second Temple', *ErIsr* 17 (1984), pp. 188-211 (Heb.).

12   For more discussion of this short form of the name see below on Murabbaᶜat 19.

The possible readings of the inscription thus ascertained, Naveh is almost certainly right to identify the man to whom the inscription refers as Ananias bar Nedebaeus.[13] What then does the presence of the vessel at Masada mean? Was Ananias the owner of the jar, and if so, was he ever at Masada? Naveh believes—again, probably correctly—that this jar, along with virtually all of the Hebrew and Aramaic material from Masada, was inscribed between 66 CE and the fall of Masada to the Romans.[14] Such being the case, he concludes[15]

> Most likely Ananias was not alive when this jar was inscribed. *Thus* [emphasis mine] I would hazard the following hypothesis: Ananias the High Priest was not present at Masada; the person who wrote the inscription on the jar was 'Aqavia his son.' The text should be understood not as an indication of ownership, but as a kind of certification that the jar had been qualified by the priest as clean and suited for hallowed produce . . . If the inscription indicated ownership, we would expect to find a waw consecutive [sic] between the name of the father and his son . . . The waw does not appear to have been mistakenly omitted. It seems likely that the qualification of the jar, or its contents, was made by Aqavia; the latter, in order to emphasize his authority, used the name of his father, who had been High Priest in Jerusalem. To this effect Aqavia wrote the name and title of his father first and then his own, although it would have been more correct to write, in the usual way, 'Aqavia the son of Ananias the High Priest.'[16]

13   For other ways of construing the inscription, see Excursus One below.

14   The fall of Masada probably took place in the spring of 74 CE, as opposed to the alternative of one year earlier that Naveh prefers. The evidence on the question is not easily reconciled. For a very succinct discussion, including new evidence from the Greek written materials from Masada (which may have an impact on the question), see *Masada II: The Yigael Yadin Excavations 1963-1965 Final Reports. The Latin and Greek Documents*, eds. H. Cotton and J. Geiger (Jerusalem: Israel Exploration Society, 1989), pp. 21-23 and 62-67.

15   Yadin and Naveh, *Aramaic and Hebrew Ostraca*, , pp.37-38.

16   Naveh apparently does not see that the phrase 'Aqavia the son of Ananias the High Priest' is at least ambiguous and would not, therefore, necessarily be the 'more correct' way in Hebrew or Aramaic to say what he thinks the jar says. If the jar had been inscribed עקביה בר חניה כהנא רבא, it would ordinarily mean that Aqabiah, not Ananias, was the high priest. Such is the usual meaning of the syntagm 'X *ben* / *bar* Y + appositive.' Cf. e.g., Hag. 1.1 and Ezra 3.3 for the

Constrained by his belief that Ananias was dead, Naveh departs from Yadin's original interpretation of this inscription as a notation of ownership. He concludes that because the *waw* is absent between the names of father and son, and 'does not appear to have been mistakenly omitted' (!), the inscription cannot signify ownership. Instead it certifies the jar for use with 'holy things.' In his view, although oddly indirect in its phrasing, the qualification is couched in the name of Aqabiah's father because of that man's greater authority. To capture the nuances of Naveh's interpretation, the jar's inscription might be paraphrased '(In the name of) Ananias the high priest, (purity certified by) Aqabiah his son.'

This analysis has little to recommend it. The absence of a *waw* connecting the names of father and son by no means counts against interpreting the inscription as possessive. The syntax of Aramaic (and Hebrew) inscriptions of ownership allows either conjunction or apposition. The appositional option adopted by the jar's inscriber appears in the Aramaic tomb inscriptions known from the environs of Jerusalem. For example, Isawwiya Ossuary 4 reads שלום יונה, 'Salome, Jonah.'[17] A Mount Scopus ossuary reads יהוחנן בר צביא סרי חיסה, 'Johanan son of Ṣibya, Sarai Ḥsy'.'[18] Other examples might be cited,[19] but perhaps one further inscription will suffice to make the point. The Kallon Family Ossuary 2 is a pellucid illustration of the synonymity of the conjunctive and appositional constructions.[20] Line 1(a) reads מרים יועזר שמעון בני יחזק, 'Miriam, Joezer, Simeon, the

---

biblical evidence, and see S.J.D. Cohen, 'Epigraphic Rabbis', *JQR* 72 (1981), p. 8 and n. 7, for postbiblical evidence. As Cohen shows, even the use of the proleptic suffix in the syntagm בנו של (Aramaic בנה ד/רי) does not suffice in such a phrase to make the second name clearly the high priest.

17   E.L. Sukenik, 'Two Jewish Hypogea', *JPOS* 12 (1932), p. 30, plate 4.

18   L.-H. Vincent, 'Chronique: Hypogée judéo-grec découvert au Scopus', *RB* 9 (1900), pp. 107-8 and plate 2.

19   Siloam Ossuary 1 reads שמעון סבא יהוסף ברה, 'Simeon the Elder, Joseph his son.' See L.A. Mayer, 'A Tomb in the Kedron Valley Containing Ossuaries with Hebrew [*sic*] Graffiti Names', *Bulletin of the British School of Archaeology in Jerusalem* 5 (1924), pp. 56-60. The whole inscription was incised at one time and the bones in the ossuary apparently belonged to a single skeleton. It is possible, therefore, that this ossuary belonged only to the father and was provided by the son.

20   This ossuary has never been fully published. For partial publications see J. Fitzmyer and D. Harrington, *A Manual of Palestinian Aramaic Texts* (Biblica et Orientalia 34; Rome: Biblical Institute Press, 1978), p. 230.

children of Yoḥazaq.' Lines 1-2(b) repeat the same inscription, referring to the same individuals, but insert *waws* between the names of the children: מרים ויהועזר ושמעון בני יחזק. Naveh's missing *waw* is a mere chimera.

His contention that the jar's inscription was intended to certify its use for 'holy things' runs aground on the evidence of all other such jar inscriptions from Masada.[21] These inscriptions in every case explicitly define the jar's fitness for cultic purposes. For example, jar 455 reads simply פסולא, 'disqualified.' Jars 458, 459 and 460 bear slight variations of לקודשא, 'for the holy (things).' Jar 457 is particularly instructive in regard to Naveh's argument, for it reads ישוע טוהר לקדש 'Jesus; pure for holy (things).'[22] For Naveh to be correct would clearly require that, in addition to the names of Aqabiah and Ananias, the word לקדש or its Aramaic equivalent appear on the jar. And jar 457 is further fatal to the suggestion that Aqabiah needed the greater authority of his father in order to certify the jar for cultic use. If a simple priest Jesus could make such a determination, surely the son of a high priest could do the same in his own name.

The editor's departures from Yadin's original suggestion that the jar was inscribed by its owner thus lead to new difficulties at every turn. Naveh's hypothesis was born of his prior understanding that Ananias was dead before the jar could have been inscribed with his name.[23] But once this questionable *a priori* is jettisoned, the true meaning of the jar inscription emerges. This jar from Masada belonged to Ananias bar Nedebaeus and an otherwise unknown son, Aqabiah. The inscription indicates their ownership, and its meaning is simply '(Belonging to) Ananias the high priest (and) Aqabiah his son.' The jar should thus be categorized with the several other large inscribed store jars at Masada that belonged to a father and son. Although their inscriptions are

---

21   Yadin and Naveh, *Aramaic and Hebrew Ostraca*, pp. 32-39 and plates 26-30.
22   טוהר is not a *qutl* noun meaning 'purity' but the adjective meaning 'pure.' The graphic form here can be explained either as a simple error or as an indication of the quiescence of the *heh*. On such quiescence in the late Second Temple period, involving a variety of phonological environments, see e.g., E. Qimron, *The Hebrew of the Dead Sea Scrolls* (Harvard Semitic Series 29; Atlanta: Scholars Press, 1986).
23   Although never explained, Naveh's assumption appears to derive from his reading of *War* 2.408 and 2.433 as duplicate accounts of the same events. His dubious conclusions cast grave doubts on this premise. For further discussion, see Excursus Two below.

incomplete, three such jars can be confidently identified. A fourth may also fit here.[24] Of the certain identifications, jar 504 reads '[PN] and his son;' jar 506, 'Besay and [his] son;' and jar 507, [..]nah and [his] son.' These jars differ from that of Ananias and Aqabiah only by their use of the *waw* rather than the appositional option for expressing possession. All these amphorae are Herodian, serving to store goods on Masada during the century preceding Ananias and Aqabiah. Later, when the fortress fell into Jewish hands, they were conscripted for use by new owners.[25] Accordingly, ceramic typology allows one to discount the possibility that the jar belonging to Ananias and Aqabiah was brought to Masada from Jerusalem by some third party. The conclusion is inescapable: either Ananias or his son (or both) was at Masada in the summer of 66 CE.

Taken together with various facts that Josephus supplies, this conclusion plots a trajectory for reevaluating the rôle that Ananias bar Nedebaeus and his family played in the revolt.[26] And in the light of these clues as to the course of events, it is necessary also to consider the potential significance of Murabbaᶜat 19 (henceforth Mur 19), a writ of divorce composed at Masada in this same period.[27] The following chronological discussion is one way of piecing together the new evidence with the old, long known but—for lack of witnesses other than Josephus—never fully understood.

The Period of the Procurators

The following schema (fig.1) illustrates the interrelationships of those members of Ananias' family who are relevant to the present discussion. I will consider each at his proper place in the narrative. One name, John

24 Yadin and Naveh, *Aramaic and Hebrew Ostraca*, p. 43 and plate 37. Jar 503 can be restored as [PN and] his son', but other restorations are equally cogent.
25 Yadin, *Masada*, p. 96.
26 It would be pointless in the following pages to attempt to catalog each and every disagreement between the position mapped out here and earlier scholarly literature. Earlier writers did not have the advantage of the new evidence. For a full listing of the literature on the Second Revolt, Ananias and Eleazar, and Masada, see the bibliographies by H. Schreckenberg, *Bibliographie zu Flavius Josephus* (Leiden: Brill, 1968); *idem, Bibliographie zu Flavius Josephus: Supplementband mit Gesamtregister* (Leiden: Brill, 1979), and L.H. Feldman, *Josephus and Modern Scholarship (1937-1980)* (New York: Garland Publishing, 1984).
27 DJD 2, pp. 104-109 and plates 30-31.

bar Ananias, is only tentatively connected to that of Ananias because it occurs only once in Josephus' works. The relation of this man to Ananias is inferred on the evidence of the patronym, John's evident high station in society, and his possible involvement with Simon bar Giora, as will be duly explained.

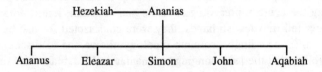

Figure 1. The Family of Ananias bar Nedebaeus

The first mention of Ananias bar Nedebaeus is at the time of his appointment to the high priesthood by Herod, king of Chalcis, in 48 CE.[28] Simultaneously, and perhaps not fortuitously, a new procurator, Cumanus, arrived from Rome. He was the first of five procurators with whom Ananias would have inimical dealings over the next two decades. Some years after Cumanus arrived a controversy arose between the Samaritans and the Jews, stemming from the murder of a Galilean Jew killed in Samaritan territory while making a pilgrimage to Jerusalem. Because Cumanus refused to deal with the situation, the Jews took matters into their own hands. More than one violent confrontation between the Jews and Samaritans followed, eventuating in the involvement of the Syrian governor, Quadratus, and the recall of Cumanus. In the course of investigating the situation Quadratus ordered Ananias and his son, Ananus, the captain of the temple, put in chains and sent to Rome to defend the Jewish actions.[29] Precisely what may have been the involvement of Ananias in this affair is not clear. It is not inconceivable that he was in some measure responsible behind the scenes for the Jewish response to the Samaritans, and that Quadratus acted as he did on the strength of such a suspicion. Perhaps, as Martin Goodman has suggested, Ananias had bribed Cumanus at some point during the scandal.[30] If so, it is likely that Quadratus had knowledge of

---

28   *Ant.* 20.103.
29   *Ant.* 20.131-2, *War* 2.243. E.M. Smallwood, 'High Priests and Politics in Roman Palestine', *JTS* N.S. 13 (1962), p. 24 n. 2, questions whether Ananias himself was sent to Rome on the basis of *War* 2.232-46.
30   M. Goodman, *The Ruling Class of Judaea: The Origins of the Jewish Revolt*

it by reason of his questioning of Cumanus. It is also possible that they had no personal involvement in the dispute, and that Ananias and Ananus were held responsible simply because of their position at the head of the Jewish élite. Such seems to have been the case with Jonathan bar Ananus, the former high priest (36-37 CE) who was also sent to Rome. At any rate Jonathan's inclusion in the Jewish party certainly had a much greater impact on the subsequent careers of both himself and Ananias than any possible involvment in the Samaritan affair. It led, ultimately, to Jonathan's assassination.

While in Rome, Jonathan used his influence with members of the imperial court to secure the appointment of a new procurator, Felix. The motive behind his seeking Felix's appointment becomes clear in the sequel: he knew that Felix would prove malleable.[31] In other words, Jonathan was seeking to increase his own power among the Jews. The royal road to that goal was influence with the Roman procurator.[32] The concomitant of Jonathan's ascendency was, of course, the correspondingly decreased power of others seeking primacy. Ananias, the reigning high priest, therefore stood to lose more by Jonathan's rise than anyone. Thus at the time of Felix's appointment in 52 CE it is possible to discern for the first time the factional maneuvering among the high priestly families that was a significant factor in the outbreak and conduct of the revolt.[33]

A few years after Felix arrived in Judaea, Jonathan was assassinated by the *sicarii* in what Josephus calls that group's first public murder.[34] Josephus claims that this was a murder for hire at the behest of Felix effected through the agency of one Doras, a native of Jerusalem and Jonathan's best friend. But it is doubtful if money really motivated this slaying. As Josephus does not mention Felix's role in the passage of *War* that describes this incident, it is more likely that the charge reflects malicious gossip about the procurator that circulated in the period

---

31   *Ant.* 20.162.

32   On the importance of influence with the procurators on the one hand and the people on the other, see Goodman, *Ruling Class,* pp. 147-50.

33   Goodman, *Ruling Class*, pp. 137-51, on factionalism among the upper classes.

34   Josephus says in *Ant.* 20.163 that it was λησταί who killed the former high priest, but in *War* 2.256 he explicitly calls the murderers σικάριοι.

following the assassination.[35] Josephus probably chose to repeat the
charge in the later *Antiquities* in accordance with the general *Tendenz*
of that work to castigate the procurators. Even if money did change
hands, however, it remains unlikely that the *sicarii* were induced by
this means to kill Jonathan. Rather, they had presumably already
determined to remove him as pro-Roman and saw the money as an
unexpected boon. It would hardly disturb them if the procurator thought
that he had purchased their services; the more mystery surrounded their
surreptitious acts of violence, the better. That would only heighten the
fear that they strove to create in the pro-Roman circles of the upper
class and, one may now suspect, particularly among the high priestly
factions opposed to that of Ananias. For on the basis of the jar
inscription, there can be little doubt that Ananias was intimately
involved with the *sicarii* some years later, at the time of the revolt. It
remains only to ask whether that involvement may have begun already,
and if so what may have motivated the high priest to enter into this dark
alliance.

Central to the question of why Ananias (and, as I hope to show, his
entire immediate family) made common cause with the *sicarii* is the
nature and purpose of that group. This is a problem that has polarized
scholars and which, owing to limitations of space, I cannot consider in
full at this juncture.[36] A few comments regarding the group's

35   Thus Smallwood, 'High Priests', p. 24 and Horsley, 'High Priests and the
Politics of Roman Palestine: A Contextual Analysis of the Evidence in Josephus',
JSJ 17 (1986), pp. 42-43.
36   The nature of the *sicarii* is in part bound up with the question of their
relationship with the Zealots. Although the question had been addressed on rare
occasions earlier, it came to the fore in a polemical exchange between C. Roth and
S. Zeitlin that lasted nearly a decade in the late 1950s and early 1960s. Roth
favored the identification of the groups, while Zeitlin was adamant that they were
distinct. Some of the arguments in this tiresome and frequently *ad hominem* debate
can be found in Roth's, 'Zealots in the War', esp. p. 333 n. 2, and *The Dead Sea
Scrolls: A New Historical Approach* (New York: W.W. Norton, 1965), esp. 85-94,
and S. Zeitlin, 'Josephus and the Zealots: A Rejoinder', *JSS* 5 (1960), p. 388;
'Recent Literature on the Dead Sea Scrolls: The Sicarii and the Zealots', *JQR* 51
(1960-61), pp. 165-69; 'Zealots and Sicarii', *JBL* 81 (1962), pp. 395-8; 'Masada
and the Sicarii', *JQR* 55 (1964), pp. 299-317; 'The Sicarii and Masada', *JQR* 57
(1966-67), pp. 251-70. Although neither man ever really yielded, Roth blinked first
(see *Dead Sea Scrolls*, p. 85 n. 1). In part this debate was fueled and Roth aided by
the publication of M. Hengel's massive study, *Die Zeloten: Untersuchungen zur
jüdischen Freiheitsbewegung in der Zeit von Herodes I. bis 70 n. Chr.* (Leiden:

attractiveness to Ananias will have to suffice. First, most scholars who

Brill, 1961; 2nd enlarged ed. 1976; Eng. tr. by D. Smith, *The Zealots: Investigations into the Jewish Freedom Movement in the Period from Herod I until 70 A.D.*, Edinburgh: T. & T. Clark, 1989). Hengel argued that there existed an organized movement of resistance that was known generally by the term 'Zealot' (Semitic קנא). Originally the *sicarii* were not a distinct group among the ranks of the Zealots in the eyes of the general populace. When Josephus came to describe the group that had followed Menahem bar Judas, however, he did so in the light of the later fragmentation within the Zealot movement, and hence as a way to make an *ad hoc* distinction he called Menahem's followers *sicarii*. (M. Hengel, *Zealots,* pp. 46-51, and cf. pp. 380-404; the latter pages are a reworked and expanded form of his 'Zeloten und Sikarier', in *Josephus-Studien: Untersuchungen zu Josephus dem antiken Judentum und dem Neuen Testament,* ed. O. Betz, K. Haacker and M. Hengel [Göttingen: Vandenhoeck & Ruprecht, 1974], pp. 175-96, and represent his latest word on the question.) Among American and British scholars Hengel does not have much following in this debate. The regnant view is that the *sicarii* must be distinguished from the Zealots on the basis of Josephus' usage of the terms σικάριοι and ζηλωταί. This position was, of course, that defended by Zeitlin, but it owes its popularity much more to the article by M. Smith, 'Zealots and Sicarii'. This article is cited more than any other and includes a very thorough review of the earlier literature. Subsequent writers who have accepted Smith's arguments and distinguish the Zealots from the *sicarii* not just as a matter of Josephus' presentation, but as a matter of historical reality, include S. Applebaum, 'The Zealots: The Case for Revaluation', *JRS* 61 (1971), pp. 164-5; S. Hoenig, 'Qumran Fantasies', *JQR* 63 (1972-73), pp. 249-50; R. Horsley, 'Josephus and the Bandits', *JSJ* 10 (1979), pp. 37-63; idem, 'The Sicarii: Ancient Jewish Terrorists', *JRelS* 52 (1979), pp. 435-58; idem, 'The Zealots: Their Origin, Relationships and Importance in the Jewish Revolt', *NovT* 28 (1986), pp. 159-92; and M. Stern, in 'Zealots', *Encyclopedia Judaica Yearbook 1973,* pp. 135-52 and 'Sicarii and Zealots.' (Yadin never distinguished the groups or indicated an awareness of the question.) Some of Smith's fellow advocates try to go beyond merely distinguishing the *sicarii* from the Zealots, and describe the group sociologically. Stern, for example, in 'Sicarii and Zealots', pp. 300-301, says that (1) the *sicarii* were loyal to the family of Judas of Galilee, whereas the Zealots adhered to no particular family; (2) the leaders of the Zealots were drawn from the Jerusalem priesthood, while the *sicarii* were Galilean in origin; and (3) there were undefined social differences between the groups. Horsley and Hanson, *Bandits, Prophets, and Messiahs: Popular Movements at the Time of Jesus* (Minneapolis: Winston Press, 1985), pp. 190-204, argue that the *sicarii* were a group of Jewish intellectuals. The validity of these attempts at sociological description is open to question. Stern's distinctions appear impossible to maintain in the light of this study, while Horsley and Hanson's conclusion is a *non sequitur* based on Josephus' references to Judas and Menahem as σοφισταί.

have studied what Josephus has to say about the *sicarii* affirm their connection with the so-called 'Fourth Philosophy' whose origin Josephus places at the time of the census under Quirinius.[37] Led by Judas the Galilean, the members of this 'philosophy' rallied to the slogan, 'No ruler but God!' For this reason they resisted the census and violence erupted. If it is right—and I think it is—to see a continuity of ideology between the 'Fourth Philosophy' and the *sicarii,* then here may lie a clue to Ananias' motivation. The real meaning of the slogan 'No ruler but God' is not, as some have concluded, that the group favored a sort of mad dervish-led anarchy and would recognize no earthly leader at all. Certainly the group rejected Roman rule, but its slogan implied the substitution of a theocratic government in which a high priest would serve as the human conduit to the only true king. This had been one Jewish understanding of the required biblical system since the early Hellenistic period at least.[38] Ananias may well have seen himself in the rôle of that high priest.[39] Second, the mention of Doras may help to explain Ananias' involvement with a quasi-terrorist[40]

37   See the comments in Stern, 'Sicarii and Zealots', pp. 263-71.

38   See *Ant.* 12.142 with reference to the phrase κατὰ τοὺς πατρίους νόμους, and the comments on the phrase in V. Tcherikover, *Hellenistic Civilization and the Jews* (New York: Atheneum, 1982), pp. 82-84.

39   Although it often provides a fresh perspective, a basic criticism of Horsley's body of work is that he consistently undervalues the power of religious ideas as motivators, not only for peasants but also for the upper classes. For example, on p. 52 of 'High Priests' he says as follows: '. . . the high priests and other notables, in their sober realism less affected by apocalyptic visions . . .' He goes further on p. 62 of 'Josephus and the Bandits', saying '. . . Jewish apocalypticism had permeated the society as a whole with the exception of the upper classes, the High Priests and Sadducees.' This is a simplistic analysis, a result of Horsley's overemphasis on class distinctions at the expense of other ways of viewing ancient societies. And now, most recently, he seems to deny the presence, and thus the importance, of apocalypticism generally; see R. Horsley, *Sociology and the Jesus Movement* (New York: Crossroad, 1989), pp. 96-99. For apocalyptic as reflecting various groups in the Judaism of the period, including at least some of the upper classes, see e.g., C. Rowland, *The Open Heaven* (New York: Crossroad, 1982), pp. 212-3.

40   Horsley, 'Terrorists', seeking to lend some rigor to the designation 'terrorist', tries to find parallels for the actions of the *sicarii* in those of modern terrorist organizations. He sees the *sicarii* as an impotent group of rebels whose only choice was between different types of violence. Nonviolent means of effecting their purposes were 'denied them by the regime' (p. 444). I am not sure that his

group. Doras' connection with the crime, even if it is merely hearsay and calumny, is instructive as to the group's constituency. As Doras was unquestionably a member of the élite of Jewish society, it shows that some Jews suspected (and, as discussed below, Josephus may have known for certain) that the leadership of the *sicarii* came from the circles of the highest levels of society. This is a suspicion that the finds from Masada tend to corroborate, quite apart from Ananias' involvement with the group. A letter found there written on an ostracon, unfortunately badly broken, begs its recipients at Masada to repay a loan of 500 *denarii*. This was no trifling sum in an era when a laborer earned only one *denarius* per diem.[41] A tag reads קתרא בת, probably to be understood as 'the daughter of Qatros.'[42] This was a name associated with one of the four high priestly families, the family of Boethus. Another tag reads שלום הגלי[לית], 'Salome the Galilean.' Perhaps the gentilic means only to distinguish the name's bearer from the mass of Judaeans at Masada, but it may equally well be understood

understanding of the group is entirely accurate, given their alliance with the most powerful figure in the 'regime;' nor is it clear to me that the *sicarii* were 'terrorists' in the modern sense. Of the five characteristics that Horsley lists on p. 439 as defining 'terrorists', two (sabotage against the occupying military; indiscriminate public violence) are not in evidence in Josephus' descriptions of the *sicarii*. Of the other three, at least one (kidnapping) seems not to have been a general activity, but was planned by Ananias and limited to his 'targets.' The remaining two characteristics (selective symbolic assassination; more general violence against the wealthy and powerful) may be applicable, but can equally well be understood in a different light. The assassinations may be understood not as the powerless sending a message to the powerful, but as factional violence within the ranks of the powerful themselves. The attacks on the wealthy have an eschatological aspect to them that Horsley neglects; they need not be thought of as 'terrorist' actions *per se*. Thus I am dubious about the use of the term 'terrorist' in its modern sociological sense when describing the *sicarii*. My use of 'quasi-terrorist' reflects that hesitancy, and I use the term 'terrorist' in the following discussion in its ordinary rather than technical sense.

41 Yadin and Naveh, *Aramaic and Hebrew Ostraca*, 554 (pp. 49-50 and plate 45).

42 Yadin and Naveh, *Aramaic and Hebrew Ostraca*, 405 (p. 22 and plate 22). Naveh points out the inscribed weight found in the excavations at Jerusalem and dating from the destruction in 70 CE, which reads קתרוס דבר, 'belonging to the son of Qatros.' With due caution he also notes that קתרא may be unconnected with the family of Qatros, and may instead mean 'rock.'

as a marker of upper class heritage.[43] The inscribed materials in Greek from Masada may also point to upper class presence there, if it is true that the upper classes tended to be more Hellenized and that use of the Greek language in preference to Hebrew or Aramaic would reflect this phenomenon.[44] Thus Ananias' involvement with the *sicarii* may not have been particularly anomalous for his class; many upper class people may have either believed in the group's ideology or found it convenient for political reasons to associate themselves with it. This point leads to the third consideration: Ananias joined with the *sicarii* in order to gain leverage in the factional strife among the high priestly families.[45]

At *Ant.* 20.179 Josephus begins an explicit description of the factional strife that probably best explains Ananias' involvement with Jonathan's assassins. Although it is narrated at the point that Agrippa conferred the high priesthood upon Ishmael bar Phiabi in 59 CE—and thus, apparently, when Ananias lost that position[46]—it is likely that the situation here described had been festering for some time. A crucial sentence in the portion has suffered in textual transmission, but Louis Feldman is certainly correct in his choice of reading.[47] It reads

---

43   Yadin and Naveh, *Aramaic and Hebrew Ostraca*, 404 (p. 22, plate 22). Hachlili, 'Names and Nicknames', p. 199 notes that such gentilics often served to identify Judaeans of upper class origins.

44   See the comments on the Masada jars inscribed in Greek belonging to Salome and Zenon in Cotton and Geiger, *Latin and Greek Documents,* pp. 10 and 184-92. Zenon and Salome each owned many jars (numbered for publication 867-90), which may indicate that they were relatively wealthy.

45   For entirely different reasons M. Goodman, 'A Bad Joke in Josephus', *JJS* 36 (1985), p. 198 n. 9, comes to similar conclusions about the role of the *sicarii* in the factional struggles. He thinks they were likely protagonists in these affairs because, if they were simply bandits or anti-Roman fanatics, it is strange that the procurator Albinus could be persuaded to release them. And, if they were no more than simple revolutionaries, presumably they would have been executed forthwith rather than being held for some time in confinement.

46   On the problem of the dates of Ananias' high priesthood, see D.R. Schwartz, 'Ishmael ben Phiabi and the Chronology of Provincia Judaea', *Tarbiz* 52 (1983), pp. 177-200 (Heb.).

47   H. St. John Thackeray, R. Marcus, A. Wikgren and L.H. Feldman, *Josephus* (Loeb Classical Library, 9 vols.; Cambridge: Harvard University Press, 1926-65). Feldman's choice of the reading in A is preferable to Niese's selection of the reading of M, W, the Latin and Eusebius on the grounds that the readings in the other manuscripts are explicable only if one begins with that of A. It seems clear

ἐξάπτεται δὲ καὶ τοῖς ἀρχιερεῦσι ἔχθρα τις εἰς ἀλλήλους καὶ στάσις καὶ πρὸς τοὺς ἱερεῖς καὶ τοὺς πρώτους τοῦ πλήθους τῶν Ἱεροσολυμιτῶν.... Feldman translates, 'There now was enkindled mutual enmity and class warfare between the high priests, on the one hand, and the priests and the leaders of the populace of Jerusalem, on the other.' Are we really to believe that the high priests, having put aside their natural rivalries, were now in league against the ordinary priests and wealthy citizens? The situation envisaged by Feldman's rendering contradicts everything one would expect socio-politically and what Josephus says or implies elsewhere. In particular, it is hard to imagine the high priests *qua* high priests warring against the wealthy citizens. Further, his is not the most natural construction of the Greek.[48] Feldman's dichotomy between the high priests and the other groups apparently derives from an unusual interpretation of ἀλλήλους. It seems that he applies the reciprocal pronoun to both 'high priests' and 'other groups.' His translation of στάσις as 'class warfare' then follows from this understanding of ἀλλήλους. But in fact ἀλλήλους should refer only to the high priests. I therefore propose the translation 'Now a sort of enmity and factionalism inflamed the high priests against one another, and against the ordinary priests and leaders of the Jerusalem laity.'

Accordingly, this portion of *Antiquities* correlates with *War* 2.274-276, which is set just after the arrival of Albinus—broadly at about the same time as the disturbed passage. Here Josephus describes wealthy men gathering groups and terrorizing those in favor of peace with Rome. Groups of thugs again surround different high priests in *Ant.* 20.213-214. From a conspectus of these passages what was happening is clear. Factions were forming by which various high priestly families, prominently those of Jonathan and Ananias, were vying for power. These families, attaching to themselves as many of the aristocrats and

that the phrase ἔχθρα τις εἰς ἀλλήλους καὶ was lost from Niese's manuscripts by parablepsis. The phrase then turns up but slightly altered in a different position in the sentence in the (now incomprehensible) text of the Epitome. It should also be considered that A is the best manuscript of its family; in fact Niese generally favors it. See B. Niese, *Flavii Josephi Opera* (7 vols; Berlin: Weidmannos, 1885-95), *ad loc.*

48   S. Cohen, *Josephus in Galilee and Rome* (Leiden: Brill, 1979), p. 156 n. 182 also takes issue with Feldman's translation. He comments that Feldman has translated as if the Greek contained a μὲν . . . δὲ clause.

lower echelon priests as possible, attacked one another in various ways. Thus, when Josephus makes the pathetic charge that the high priests sent slaves to the threshing floors to rob the ordinary priests of their tithes, such that 'the poorer priests starved to death,'[49] one should understand that the high-priestly factions were strong-arming the adherents of another faction, not oppressing the lower classes per se. In this social context Ananias' alliance with the *sicarii* is more easily explicable. Indeed, the suspicion is not out of place that it was on his orders that Jonathan was assassinated. Just as he had lost the most by Jonathan's increased influence, so he stood to gain the most with him out of the way. The ideology of the *sicarii* could justify his ruthlessness. Ananias' involvement with them was, of course, a secret whose disclosure would mean his death—but then no one knew any of the members of the *sicarii* except the other members.[50]

Perhaps these factional disputes were at least one factor behind the behavior of the *sicarii* as Josephus describes it near the end of Felix's procuratorship and at the beginning of that of Festus. They were burning and looting the villages of those who refused to adopt their anti-Roman stance.[51] Some of these villages were presumably the property of wealthy Jerusalemites who opposed Ananias' faction.

Josephus juxtaposes his description of these activities of the *sicarii* with a note that Festus sent an army against an 'imposter' (γόητος) who had promised his followers salvation (σωτηρία) and 'rest from evils' (παῦλαν κακῶν—undoubtedly to be understood in terms of the Deuteronomic concept).[52] Although Josephus does not here explicitly specify the connection between this would-be messiah and the *sicarii,* it is suggestive that he more than once repeats this sort of juxtaposition.[53] Evidently the reader is to infer a connection. At one point Josephus develops this connection between groups espousing the *sicarii* philosophy and messianic expectation more clearly. Jonathan the

---

49   *Ant.* 20.181.

50   Perhaps these connections with the *sicarii* could shed some new light on the narratives in Acts involving Paul and Ananias, set roughly in this period. As 'zealots for the Law', the *sicarii* would have been most upset with Paul's activities, and it seems likely that they or similar groups lie behind the term 'Jews' as used by the author of Acts in these passages.

51   *Ant.* 20.172, 185-87.

52   *Ant.* 20.188. Cf. Deut. 12.9 and the lexica *s.v.* מנוחה.

53   E.g., *War* 2.264-65.

Weaver in Cyprus attracted radical elements who had fallen victim to the 'madness of the *sicarii*' (ἡ τῶν σικαρίων ἀπόνοια) that had been exported from Palestine, and, following the protocol for such figures, led them into the desert to encounter their God after the manner of Israel's wilderness wanderings.[54] Such episodes are paradigmatic of the major weakness of the alliance between Ananias and the *sicarii* in Jerusalem, and foreshadow what was to happen with Menahem. The *sicarii* were powerfully motivated by eschatological beliefs and were thus particularly susceptible to messianic claimants.[55] From time to time such divisive figures did indeed arise; indeed, it is not impossible that Ananias portrayed himself as such in order to cement the devotion of certain of his followers.[56] By virtue of their varying eschatological expectations the *sicarii* were volatile and prone to factionalism.

By the time that Albinus arrived as procurator in 62 CE, the *sicarii* had become so numerous, and their actions so bold, that even this indifferent and incompetent man was compelled to act against them. Josephus reports that the procurator bent his efforts to their destruction.[57] Curiously, he connects to this statement the declaration that Ananias was now continually advancing in reputation and esteem with the people of Jerusalem by giving them money. The particle δε that connects these sentences admits of more than one understanding. Feldman translates it 'now'—apparently understanding it as a weak copulative. But I suspect that it may be intended in a more adversative sense. Josephus is hinting that the futility of Albinus' efforts at destroying the *sicarii* was rooted in the opposition of the man now becoming the most powerful leader of the Jews, Ananias. Indeed, in the parallel passage in *War,* Josephus flatly declares that wealthy adherents of the revolutionary cause used bribes to blunt the force of Albinus' intentions.[58]

---

54   *War* 7.437-50.

55   Cf. Matt. 24.5 'Many will come . . . saying "I am the Messiah", and will mislead many.' That mentality that characterized the *sicarii* was undoubtedly widespread among the Jews even before the time of the revolt with Rome.

56   Cf. the expectations in certain Qumran texts of a priestly messiah alongside a Davidide. For a stimulating if overly synthetic discussion, see S. Talmon, 'Waiting for the Messiah: The Spiritual Universe of the Qumran Covenanters', in *Judaisms and Their Messiahs at the Turn of the Christian Era,* ed. J. Neusner, W.S. Green and E. Frerichs (New York: Cambridge University Press, 1987), pp. 111-37.

57   *Ant.* 20.204.

58   *War* 2.274-76. Josephus neither mentions names nor uses the term *sicarii,* but

Ananias' other method of preventing Albinus from decimating his secret army was a brilliant piece of indirection. He had the *sicarii* kidnap the secretary of his son, Eleazar. They then ransomed him by 'sending' to Ananias, saying that if he persuaded Albinus to release ten of their own now in prison, they would release the secretary.[59] Ananias did what they had 'asked,' and the plan worked perfectly. By this device Ananias was simultaneously able to deflect certain suspicions that had apparently arisen that he was himself involved with the *sicarii*, and to prevent Albinus from prosecuting his program against the group. Indeed, the gambit worked so well that Ananias and his collaborators repeated it again and again, using, of course, members of Ananias' own household as the kidnap 'victims.' Josephus reports that the numbers of the *sicarii* subsequently rose to their previous levels and that they once again began to 'work evil' against the whole land.

Here there can be no question that, as Mary Smallwood had argued even before the evidence of the jar inscription, Ananias was playing a 'double game.'[60] Drawing on the vast stores of his enormous wealth, he gained power with both the procurator and the 'people' ($\delta\tilde{\eta}\mu o\varsigma$)[61] by the judicious use of bribes and other sorts of enticements. Simultaneously he employed the *sicarii* to eliminate anyone who resisted too strongly the movement toward his ultimate goal: revolt from Rome. By such means he built up a powerful faction among the

it seems clear that the passages are parallel.

59 *Ant.* 20.208-210.

60 Smallwood, 'High Priests', p. 28; *Roman Rule*, pp. 281-82. Her argument was accepted by G. Baumbach, *Jesus vom Nazareth im Lichte der jüdischen Gruppenbildung* (Berlin: Evangelische Verlag, 1971), pp. 49-61, and G. Theissen, *Sociology of Early Palestinian Christianity* (Philadelphia: Fortress, 1978), p. 70. It was emphatically rejected by Horsley, and in fact served as the impetus for his reexamination of her whole approach in his article 'High Priests' (see esp. pp. 23 and 46). The jar inscription clearly vindicates her against such critics. But Smallwood believed that Ananias' policy changed later and that by 66 CE he was a part of the peace party ('High Priests', pp. 29-30). It is now clear that such was not the case and that Ananias continued his double game right up to the time of his death.

61 The exact meaning of such Greek political terminology in the context of Jerusalem is problematic, as that city was not a *polis*. I understand the term here to mean those portions of the 'people' whose alliance Ananias would seek, i.e., the wealthy and well-connected. For a discussion of the terminological problems see Horsley, 'Zealots', pp. 186-7, and V. Tcherikover, 'Was Jerusalem a Polis?' *IEJ* 14 (1964), pp. 63-74.

élite of Jerusalem who, while presumably largely ignorant of his activities with the *sicarii,* were personally indebted to him. These could be relied upon to support him when the dénouement came, provided that reasonable alternatives had been eliminated. (The elimination of such alternatives was a primary motivation for the subversive half of the double game.) Those on the dole from Ananias included the current high priest, Jesus bar Damnaeus. The kidnap episodes also show that Eleazar his son was fully aware of the game; in fact now and later he played a very big part in his father's plans. Despite appearances, the two were by no means estranged at any time before Ananias was murdered.[62] Eleazar's part was simply played out on the other side of the double game from his father's.

When Jesus bar Damnaeus was removed as high priest and replaced first by Jesus bar Gamaliel and then by Matthias bar Theophilus, Ananias kept his position as the power behind the throne (ὑπερεῖχεν) through bribery.[63] The situation under Matthias is particularly instructive. This man was the high priest when the war broke out. The position of high priest was, of course, formally the most powerful in Judaea apart from the procurator. The holder of that office ordinarily further consolidated his power by appointing one of his sons (or perhaps another close relative) to the second most powerful position, that of captain of the temple. The captain of the temple had oversight of the cultus and the whole body of officiating priests. Commanding troops, he served as the chief of police over the temple area. Following the usual pattern Ananias had appointed his son Ananus captain of the temple for at least part of his own decade as high priest.[64] But now when Matthias held the office of high priest it was not one of his own sons or relatives who filled the second spot—even though Matthias had

---

62   In addition to the evidence of the inscription by which this fact now becomes apparent, Josephus gives hints to the same effect in that (1) Ananias had redeemed his son's secretary; and (2) Ananias had refused to turn over his son to the Roman authorities when Florus demanded that those responsible for publicly demeaning him be brought forth. For Eleazar bar Ananias as one of those involved see Goodman, 'Bad Joke', pp. 195-99.

63   *Ant.* 20.213, 223.

64   From subsequent events it appears that Ananus was now dead. He had apparently been the eldest son, some ten to fifteen years older than Eleazar judging from the periods in which they served as captain. On Eleazar as a young man of perhaps thirty when the revolt broke out, see Goodman, *Ruling Class,* p. 211.

four sons.[65] Instead it was Eleazar bar Ananias who served. This is a tell tale index of the enormous power that Ananias had come to wield as a result of his strategies. When Florus arrived as the new procurator in 64 CE, Ananias was the most powerful man in Judaea. What is more, he was a secret revolutionary, and his plans were building rapidly to a crescendo.

The Period from Summer 66 to Spring 67 CE

Early in the summer of 66 CE, Ananias decided that the propitious moment to launch his revolt had arrived. He had control of the most powerful coalition among the high priestly families, one that included many of the priests and wealthy laity in Jerusalem. His control over the *sicarii* gave him a strong link with the general populace who were generally well disposed to the idea of revolt from Rome. Their disposition in this direction had been helped along considerably by Florus' excesses; the time had come when influence with the procurator was no longer of any importance, since revolt would obviously sever that connection. Ananias' son, Eleazar, was in position as the captain of the temple. By this appointment the conspiracy gained control over the central revolutionary symbol, the temple—and, not incidentally, a certain number of troops. What was needed was a secure launch pad for the first stage of the action.

Masada was the perfect choice. Virtually impregnable, it could harbor the revolutionaries while the brushfire was fanned out of control. And it had two additional points in its favor. It was known to contain Herod's armory, with enough weapons and armor to equip 10,000 men.[66] Since the Jews were at a tremendous disadvantage against the Romans in regards to military equipment, this was no small consideration. Second, in the event that plans went awry, Masada could serve the sanctuary purpose for which Herod had originally designed it. To start the revolt Ananias needed to take Masada.

Josephus does not describe the precise mechanism by which the Jews were able to gain the summit and take control from the Roman garrison there.[67] Long before the publication of the jar inscription, Shaye Cohen

---

65 *War* 6.114.
66 *War* 7.299.
67 *War* 2.408. See the discussion below regarding the relationship of this passage to 2.433.

had speculated that the seizure may have been achieved with the aid of a group of leading priests who could have approached the Romans unsuspected, since the upper classes largely collaborated with the Romans in their exercise of power.[68] Now that the inscription proves the involvement of just such priests, this suggestion receives new impetus, although one can imagine other ways in which the capture may have happened.[69] Among the group taking control of Masada, Aqabiah bar Ananias undoubtedly figured prominently, perhaps indeed as commander. It is not impossible that Ananias himself was involved in the ploy, but he was in Jerusalem not long after, so that seems less likely. That he was still alive when Masada fell into Jewish hands is now virtually certain. If he was not among the group that took the fortress, the inscription indicates that he was expected to come at some point in the not-too-distant future. One may surmise that Aqabiah was among the Jewish garrison that now took up residence at Masada and that preparations for a protracted stay now began. A very small part of those preparations was inscribing the jar whose use he expected to share with his father.

Success at Masada was the signal for the second step—cessation of sacrifices accepted from or on behalf of gentiles.[70] The way in which Josephus phrases this decision is important: μηδενὸς ἀλλοτρίου δῶρον ἢ θυσίαν προσδέχεσθαι. Although a clear consequence would be cessation of sacrifice for the emperor and thus war, from the Jewish point of view that was not the act's central significance. A powerful current in the stream of eschatological thinking among the Jews of the late Second Temple period was the purification of the land from gentiles (ἀλλότριοι).[71] The purifying process would begin in the

68 Cohen, *Josephus in Galilee*, p. 193.
69 One wonders, for example, if the ruse may have involved the Jews who supplied the Roman camp. Perhaps the *sicarii* or others in the employ of Ananias managed to infiltrate their number and surprise the Romans when their guard, long used to the routine of the suppliers, was momentarily inattentive. This scenario is suggested by a bread stamp. The stamp, bearing the name 'Josephus', was impressed into the plaster of one of the inside walls at Masada. The implication is that at least one Jew who had once supplied the Romans with bread joined the rebels at the very beginning, when they were first preparing Masada for their own use. For the stamp see Cotton and Geiger, *Latin and Greek Documents,* 211 and plate 44.
70 *War* 2.409.
71 Note in this connection *Pss. Sol.* 17.22 and 45, which depict the messiah

temple, of course, then encompass Jerusalem and ideally spread in every direction throughout Judaea. All Jews would recognize the pregnant meaning of Eleazar's refusal to allow sacrifices by gentiles. Given the power of eschatological appeals, this move was a masterstroke guaranteed to win wider support for Ananias' nascent revolt. It would also provoke the hostilities for which Ananias had so carefully laid a foundation.

Greatly alarmed, members of the high priestly coalitions opposed to Ananias urged that sacrifices be resumed.[72] Certain others who protested the cessation actually belonged to Ananias' faction but were as yet unaware of the double game. He planned to bring them to heel at the proper time, which was not yet. In any case Eleazar had a stranglehold on the necessary mechanisms and could assure that sacrifice would not be resumed. He controlled the temple hierarchy and had the support of the strongest of the revolutionary group (νεωτερίζοντες). This group was very numerous and included many of the priests. I would suggest that there was considerable overlap, if not complete identity, between these 'revolutionaries' and a portion of the upper class leadership of the *sicarii*.[73] In other words, the forces of the *sicarii* were now distributed so as to achieve their goals, some at Masada, some in the temple, and still others elsewhere in Judaea.

In the course of the machinations aimed at restarting the sacrifices, the ruling élite decided to plead for help from Agrippa II and Florus, the latter having now withdrawn to Caesarea.[74] Agrippa did in fact help, sending troops to try to force the issue. The fact that the delegation to Florus included Ananias' son, Simon, has misled scholars into thinking that Ananias opposed his son Eleazar. With the inscription, however, it is possible to recognize that the delegation was simply another facet of Ananias' brilliant scheme. He did not really

cleansing Jerusalem from polluting gentiles in the eschaton. The same antipathy to gentiles is evident in the pattern of omissions from Deuteronomy where it is quoted in the Temple Scroll. See my 'The Eschatological Vision of the Temple Scroll', *JNES* 49 (1990), pp. 155-72. Perhaps the actions of the *sicarii* in raiding En Gedi are connected to this concept; Josephus specifically says (*War* 7.255) that they regarded the (collaborationist?) Jews living there as 'aliens' (ἀλλόφυλοι).

72   *War* 2.410.

73   The finds at Masada prove without question that the so-called *sicarii* there ensconced included a great many priests and that tithing laws on their behalf were strictly observed.

74   *War* 2.418.

oppose Eleazar, nor did Simon. But Ananias was not yet ready to tip his hand and reveal to the aristocracy his true rôle in recent events. If he did, he presumably stood to lose a good part of his support in their ranks. The revelation had to wait until they had no retreat—a time that did indeed come, but unfortunately for Ananias only after he was dead. Thus Ananias pretended to support efforts at forcing the resumption of the sacrifices. He even appeared to be in the forefront of such efforts, and thus continued to strengthen his support among the élite. As to the delegation itself, he had nothing to fear; it had no chance for success and he knew it. Even if Florus did send troops—a vanishingly small probability—there was no reason to believe they would have any more success than those who, with Florus leading, had recently failed to win to the temple and set things aright. It was much more likely that Florus would refuse to send help, as he had lately been accused by the Jews of intolerable provocations.[75] Florus' best hope of vindication from those charges was simply to do nothing and, letting events take their course, prove the rebelliousness of the Jews and so justify his earlier drastic actions.[76] Accordingly Ananias had nothing to lose and everything to gain by playing along with the anti-revolutionaries for a bit longer.

Thereafter fighting broke out between forces in favor of Eleazar's action and those opposed. Eleazar and his men seized control of the lower city, using the temple as their home base. But they were unable to advance to take the upper city. Fighting continued for seven days with neither side able to establish a decisive advantage over the other.[77] It was clear that if Eleazar were to take control of Jerusalem he was going to have to add something to the equation. He needed reinforcements. In light of the jar inscription, I would argue that *War* 2.425 describes their arrival. The portion recounts the irruption into the temple precincts of a group of *sicarii* on the eighth day of the fighting, which corresponded to the festival of wood offering. H. St.J. Thackeray translates,

> The Jews in the Temple excluded their opponents from this ceremony, but along with some feebler folk numbers of the *sicarii*—so they called the brigands who carried a dagger in their bosom—forced their way in; these they enlisted in their service . .

75   *War* 2.333.
76   Thus Cohen, *Josephus in Galilee*, p. 190.
77   *War* 2.424.

This translation gives to Josephus' account a certain slant that is absent from the Greek. Thackeray renders συνεισρυέντας as 'forcing their way in,' but it really just means 'flowing in with, coming in together with.'[78] He translates προσλαβόντες as 'enlisted,' when it might just as well mean 'received, took to themselves.' Indeed, a well attested meaning is 'take to oneself as helper or partner.'[79] The cumulative effect of Thackeray's renderings is to give the impression that the *sicarii* enjoyed no prior relationship with those in the temple, and that their entry was resisted. Later, some sort of *modus vivendi* having been negotiated, the *sicarii* fought side by side with their former opponents. They fought against those in the temple one day, alongside them the next. Not very plausible; something like the following is probably closer to the actual events.

The two warring sides agreed that, in spite of their differences, the wood carrying had to take place as ordained in the Law. Neither side would allow anyone to take part in it, however, who might possibly be an able-bodied partisan of the other side. For this reason it was agreed to allow only feeble and elderly people to enter the temple courtyard with the wood. That was the compromise. But Eleazar took advantage of this concession made by the anti-revolutionaries (who had perhaps been persuaded by Ananias, still usefully on that side of the game) to bring in the reinforcements he needed. Presumably it would not have been difficult to get instructions to the *sicarii* outside the temple, perhaps at Masada, perhaps in Jerusalem. Various underground tunnels and viaducts led out of the temple precincts and the city.[80] Those *sicarii* then arrived during the wood carrying ceremony, perhaps disguised (as on other occasions) so as to appear elderly or crippled.[81] Joining the

78 Cohen, *Josephus in Galilee,* p. 194, n. 28 agrees that Thackeray has overinterpreted συνεισρυέντας.
79 H.G. Liddell and R. Scott, *A Greek English Lexicon* (9th ed., Oxford: Clarendon Press, 1940; with a supplement, 1968), *s.v.* προσλαμβάνω.
80 For this system, cf. *War* 2.446-48 and 5.102, and see the comments of J. Price, *Jerusalem Under Siege* (Leiden: Brill, 1992), pp. 98-100 and 286-90.
81 Cf. *War* 4.560-63, where Josephus describes members of the Zealots from Galilee as wearing women's clothes and makeup while carrying a dagger hidden in their garments. The passage casts some doubt on the distinctiveness of the *sicarii* as the only 'dagger-men.' In the present context, it suggests that some assassins got close to their victims by disguising themselves as women (Josephus accuses them of transvestism, which strictly speaking is a possible way of construing their actions; as it was opprobrious, it was the interpretation of events that pleased him).

group that was entering the temple, they made their way to their compatriots.

It is not only that the Greek allows this understanding, and that the jar inscription mandates a connection between Ananias' family and the *sicarii*. What really confirms this point is the aftermath. For it was only after these *sicarii* had made their way in to join Eleazar's forces in the temple that he was able to take control of the upper city from Agrippa's troops.[82] With this action the anti-revolutionaries were swept aside, and what remained was essentially a mopping-up operation.[83] The course had been set. That the sacrifices would not resume, and that the Jews would indeed revolt, was now certain.

The movement for revolt had entered a new stage. The question was no longer whether there would be one, but who would lead it. And it was now that treachery was hatched within the ranks of the *sicarii,* as Menahem bar Judas made his bid to lead.

Menahem was among those *sicarii* stationed within Jerusalem; whether he had been with Eleazar's forces from the beginning, or whether he had been among those entering at the time of the festival of wood is impossible to say. Up until now he had been willing to play a subservient rôle to Eleazar and Ananias (whose true colors he certainly knew). Seeing that the revolt had been guaranteed by Ananias' brilliant manipulations, he evidently felt that the former high priest was no longer essential for success. He returned to Masada, probably on orders from Eleazar or, secretly, Ananias, in order to break into Herod's armory there and provide the swelling ranks of Jewish revolutionaries

It is likely that such disguises were used by the various revolutionary groups whenever it was essential to keep their identities secret.

82   *War* 2.426.

83   The destruction of Ananias' house along with those of Agrippa and Berenice (*War* 2.426) can be attributed to the fact that most of the revolutionaries were necessarily ignorant that Ananias was the real choreographer of the events thus far. The destruction of the public archives (427-28), often seen as a bid for support from the lower classes, was perhaps not so cynically conceived, even if it did have that result. It was a consequence of the belief in the arrival of the eschaton, a 'jubilee' in which all debt would be cancelled and there would be no poor. That such ideas were a part of the current eschatological milieu is clear from the Qumran text 11Q Melchizedek, for example. This eschatological midrash juxtaposes the concepts of the eschaton and a general restoration of property by combining Isa 61.1 with Lev 25:13. See most recently E. Puech, 'Notes sur le manuscrit de 11QMelkisédeq', *RevQ* 12 (1985-87), pp. 483-513.

with much-needed weapons.[84] Arriving there, the unsuspecting *sicarii* previously stationed at Masada as a garrison—including Aqabiah— welcomed him and his news of the successes in Jerusalem. Arming himself and those whom he had brought with him, all hand-picked supporters of his scheme (τοὺς γνωρίμους), he returned to Jerusalem fully armed and claiming to be the messiah.[85] Presumably those left behind at Masada remained uninformed of his intentions.

When he returned to the city, Menahem was able to take control of the revolt from Eleazar and his supporters, who lacked his weaponry and could not hope to withstand a face to face confrontation. Menahem now assumed direction of the seige of Herod's palace. Hiding there were the notables and chief priests who had led the anti-revolutionaries, among them Ananias and his brother Hezekiah.[86] Ananias and Hezekiah were in the palace in keeping with their pre-dénouement rôle as leaders of the aristocracy against the revolt. It was these two men that Menahem really wanted. Caught unprepared by Menahem's treachery, it was too late to pull back the curtain and make known their true sentiments about the revolt. Once in the murderous grasp of Menahem's intimates, any protestations that they might make in its favor were hardly going to be regarded as sincere. They were helpless.

Caught short by Menahem's actions, Ananias had waited just a little too long to bring the two wings of his forces together. True, it could not have been done much earlier. Only now, when the revolutionaries had all but taken full control of the city and the Jews had no alternative but to carry through with the revolt, could Ananias have made that move without losing large numbers of his supporters among the élite. Earlier they would not simply have deserted his side, but would have gone over *en masse* to his opponents' factions, quite likely to that of Ananus bar Ananus. Thus he waited; presumably he would have made his true position clear very shortly—but Menahem acted first.

Menahem had to kill Ananias in order to make good his own claim to leadership of the *sicarii* and the revolt in general. Finding Ananias and his brother hiding in a sewer or canal near the palace, Menahem's

---

84   *War* 2.433.
85   Josephus describes it as οἷα δὴ Βασιλεὺς. On the messianic significance of this phrase and of Josephus' general characterization of Simon, see e.g., Horsley and Hanson, *Bandits*, pp. 119-27.
86   *War* 2.429.

followers dispatched them.[87] In their eyes the men were merely two leaders of the opposing forces, but Menahem, upon whose orders they acted, knew better. Proof of his intentions is found in the fact that none of the other nobles and leaders who had been beseiged along with Ananias and his brother was put to death.[88] Menahem had selectively targeted the Rasputin of Jerusalem. Josephus chose his words well when he said that Menahem reacted to Ananias' death with joy, knowing that he no longer had any *rival* (ἀντίπαλος).[89] Menahem had betrayed his erstwhile ally.

Eleazar and his supporters, unable to defeat Menahem in straight combat, determined to overthrow his coup by strategy. They plotted to attack him while he was in the temple, where although he had his bodyguards (ζηλωτὰς ἐνόπλους) few of his supporters could enter. Eleazar's faction rushed upon the man, aided by certain others (δῆμος) who had once been part of Ananias' faction and now wanted revenge on his murderer. Menahem's followers were routed and he himself, fleeing, was later hunted down and killed along with his lieutenants.[90] Josephus reports that a relative of Menahem's, Eleazar bar Jair, managed to escape to Masada along with 'a few' (ὀλίγοι) others who had supported the coup. Josephus would have the reader believe that this man went on to become the leader or 'tyrant' of the forces there, but there is reason to question this assertion. Those fleeing to Masada would have had to deal with the garrison left behind, which some evidence[91] suggests was not privy to Menahem's plan. They would not necessarily be willing to receive—much less submit to—the straggling remnant of his failed bid. Further, while the term 'few' is imprecise, it is hardly likely to encompass the 960 inhabitants of Masada present when it fell. The group that fled Jerusalem cannot simply and uncritically be equated with those who died at Masada some eight years later. It is obvious that much must have happened, some of which Josephus hints at, but most of which he chooses not to describe or of which he was ignorant. His imprecision concerning the leadership of

---

87 *War* 2.441.

88 This conclusion arises from the absence of any mention of such deaths, which Josephus, ever eager to portray the rebels as unfavorably as possible, would surely not have neglected to mention.

89 *War* 2.442-43.

90 *War* 2.445-48.

91 See below on the coins associated with Aqabiah.

the *sicarii* in general[92] does not inspire confidence in his narrative here; further, as I shall discuss below, he had particular reasons for obscuring the facts about Eleazar bar Jair.

The question for Ananias' faction was how to proceed now that their leader was dead. Josephus provides few details of this period of the war, but it seems that all remaining revolutionaries united temporarily behind his son, Eleazar. This was clearly a fragile union, and it only lasted a few months. The high-priestly factions had never ceased vying for power, and Eleazar was not the force his father had been. But under his leadership the insurgents captured the fortress of Cypros near Jericho and, persuading the Romans to leave, garrisoned Machaerus as well.[93] It was also apparently with Eleazar in charge that the Jews were able to rout Cestius Gallus at Beth Horon, and even capture many of the Romans' arms and supplies.[94] Apart from this unpredictable victory

---

92   Cf. *War* 7.297 with 2.408, 433. At 7.297 Josephus credits Eleazar bar Jair with leadership of the *sicarii* when they first took Masada. At 2.408 he does not mention who was the leader, while in 2.433 it is Menahem. In my view the episode of 7.297 is the same one referred to in 2.408, while 2.433, as discussed below, was a separate incident. Josephus' claim that Eleazar was at the lead in the summer of 66 I regard as a falsehood, arising perhaps from ignorance but also possibly from historiographic need (see below). The real leaders in 66 were members of the Jerusalem élite, in particular the family of Ananias. Horsley, 'Terrorists', pp. 453-4, sees 7.297 as yet a third incident. In his reconstruction, when Eleazar bar Jair fled Jerusalem, he took Masada from a rebel garrison that had taken it at 2.408. The line of interpretation established here, however, based on both the inscription and on Josephus' hints connecting Ananias and the *sicarii,* is more comprehensively explanatory as well as more plausible. Having taken the fortress by a strategem themselves, is it likely that a revolutionary garrison would fall victim to a similar ploy just a short time later? The basis for Horsley's distinction between the two passages may be Thackeray's translation. In 2.408 Thackeray renders λάθρα 'by a strategem;' at 7.297 he translates δόλῳ 'through treachery.' These are precisely the terms Horsley uses in his own discussion of the portions. According to his note *ad loc.,* Thackeray himself equated 7.297 with 2.408. Presumably his use of different English words to describe the method by which Masada fell was no more than stylistic. The Greek terms λάθρα and δόλος are very largely synonymous, both referring variously to treachery, stealth, or strategem. See Liddell and Scott, *Greek Lexicon, s.v.v.* Thus the text does not imply by its alternation between the terms that the incidents described are distinct, and other criteria must make that decision.

93   *War* 2.484-6.

94   *War* 2.521.

over the Roman forces, the strategy that Eleazar followed for the first steps of the revolt was probably that already plotted before his father's death. The seizure of the major fortresses as quickly as possible ties in with the capture of Masada. But after Beth Horon Eleazar's coalition broke down and another of the factions, that led by Ananus bar Ananus, seized control of the rebellion.

The key passage regarding both the organization of the revolt up to this time and the breakdown of Ananias' faction after his death is *War* 2.562-66.[95] Josephus recounts that after the victory over Cestius Gallus a realignment occurred. In Thackeray's translation,

> The Jews who had pursued Cestius, on their return to Jerusalem,
> partly by force, partly by persuasion, brought over to their side
> such pro-Romans as still remained; and, assembling in the
> Temple, appointed additional generals to conduct the war.

Josephus goes on to say that Eleazar bar Simon (later leader of the Zealots) was specifically denied command at this point, and he provides the names of the commanders according to the regions to which they were assigned. Eleazar bar Ananias[96] received the command of Idumea, along with an otherwise unknown Jesus bar Sapphas. His brother (?) John bar Ananias took charge of the provinces of Gophna and Acrabetta. Josephus himself, of course, received the two Galilees. Supreme command of the Jewish war effort devolved upon Ananus bar Ananus and Joseph bar Gorion.

The Jewish historian here claims that 'additional' ($\pi\lambda\epsilon$íονας) generals were now appointed. Who, then, had been the generals until this time? Josephus' silence on this point is intentional. He wants to obscure the fact that the ruling classes had been responsible for the revolt all along; he wants it to appear as though they were goaded into revolt by an upswell of popular sentiment catalyzed by 'bandits' and 'imposters' and, when no other option remained, took over so as to

---

95 Cohen, *Josephus in Galilee,* p. 197, is dubious of the historicity of the details in this passage, especially since most of the generals here appointed are never mentioned again, even when Josephus narrates the Roman conquests of their districts. Given the extremely sketchy descriptions Josephus provides for those battles, however, it seems to me that Cohen is unduly pessimistic and that not much should be made of the absence of these names later.

96 Reading 'Ανανίου at 566 instead of Νέου, an emendation agreed upon by virtually all students of the passage.

minimize the damage and guide a rapproachment with Rome.[97] Despite
his omissions, however, a critical reading of Josephus suffices to put
the lie to this claim. And if it were needed, the jar inscription
connecting Ananias with the *sicarii* decisively proves the *Tendenz* in
the Jewish historian's portrait. One must conclude that a revolutionary
government had existed prior to the point when Josephus chooses to
mention one, and that when he does, he is really describing another,
albeit bloodless, coup. Prior to the victory over Gallus the supreme
commander had been Eleazar bar Ananias. His brother John was likely
another leader, as was, perhaps, Aqabiah. The other leaders now
shunted aside included apparently Niger the Peraean, who had been in
charge of Idumea (ἄρχοντι τότε, 566), Eleazar bar Simon, who had
played a major rôle in the defeat of the Romans at Beth Horon, and
Simon bar Giora, who had been in command of Acrabetta.[98] When
Josephus says that *additional* generals were now appointed, he is
obscuring the fact that *new* generals were now appointed. Nothing
makes this fact more apparent than the new rôle assumed by Eleazar
bar Ananias. After all, he had taken over Jerusalem by force and fought
off Menahem's challenge. He had established himself as supreme
leader against the opposition of many of the élite. It is hard to believe
that he would now voluntarily accept a subservient position as a general
in Idumea. The only reasonable conclusion is that his power was no
longer supreme and that he was forced to step aside. Unlike Simon bar
Giora and Eleazar bar Simon, however, he retained enough influence to
guarantee himself at least some position of authority, and to choose
where he would serve as general (as I will argue below).

The full effect of Ananias' death was only now coming to be
realized. The high priest had forged his faction through a powerful
combination of persuasion, force and money, the cumulative effect of
which his son could not equal. Eleazar, still a young man, was unable
to hold his father's faction together. Nevertheless, his wealth and
remaining supporters did give him some voice in the changeover. Over
the months between Ananias' death and the reorganization described in
2.562-66, people loyal either to Ananias' person or to his purse began

---

97   Cohen, *Josephus in Galilee*, pp. 184-7; T. Rajak, *Josephus: The Historian
and His Society* (Philadelphia: Fortress, 1984), pp. 108 and 128-32 and Goodman,
Ruling Class, pp. 167-75.
98   For Simon bar Giora as commander in Acrabetta see *War* 4.504 and
Goodman, *Ruling Class*, p.163.

to drift away. This drift was, of course, by no means unassisted; many of these leaders ended up aligned with Ananus bar Ananus. Those switching camps included Gorion bar Nicomedes and his son, Joseph bar Gorion. The latter was rewarded for his shift by receiving co-command of the new government alongside Ananus.[99] Also included were Ananias bar Zadok, a leading Pharisee (although low born), Judas bar Jonathan, and Josephus himself.[100] It is not unlikely that Josephus

99   In *War* 2.448-51, Gorion bar Nicomedes, Ananias bar Zadok and Judas bar Jonathan constituted the negotiating team Eleazar sent to the Romans to bargain for their exit from the city. Presumably he sent men chosen from his most trusted and highest ranking co-conspirators and, I would suggest less confidently, fellow *sicarii*. Along with most scholars, I assume that Gorion bar Nicomedes was the father of the leading general on the basis of the uncommon name. Joseph later died in the internecine strife among the Jews, *War* 4.358. That Ananias bar Zadok and Judas bar Jonathan later belonged to Ananus' faction is apparent in the fact that they were chosen as part of the delegation to recall Josephus from command in Galilee. Cf. *War* 2.451 and 628 and *Vita* 197, 290, 316 and 332 (Judas is consistently called 'Jonathan' in *Vita*, on which see Thackeray's notes *ad loc*).

100   In *Vita* 20-21 Josephus describes an episode about which he is conveniently silent in *War*. He admits that at the time that Menahem was in control of the revolt, he was himself hiding in the inner temple—although he does not say who else was there. In fact he was with Eleazar's forces, for they were the ones who had control of that area. His excuse for hiding in there is that he had been warning against war with Rome so loudly that he thought his life in danger from the revolutionaries under Menahem. This is a patent lie, of course. If he had really been warning so vociferously against war with Rome, he (1) would not have taken refuge with Eleazar, who was the leader of a pro-war faction, and with whom he was not likely to be safe as a true pro-Roman (why not hide elsewhere, or flee the city, as did so many true pro-Romans?); and (2) would presumably never have been given a command in the later war effort. I would suggest that the reason Josephus even brings the matter up in the *Vita* is that it was common knowledge that he had been there among Eleazar's partisans, and that it was now necessary somehow to explain his presence in the temple. Presumably the charge of consortion with Eleazar had been an element of the case brought against Josephus after the war as a one-time adherent of the *sicarii*. Josephus was forced to admit this accusation in *War* 7.448-50. He was brought up on these charges before Vespasian at the instigation of Jonathan the Weaver, who was trying to save his own life by cooperation with the Roman authorities. Evidently there was enough substance to the charges that Vespasian thought them worth investigating, a fact that Josephus has to admit; that the charges might well have been proven emerges from the fact that after Vespasian had investigated, he did not simply dismiss them. Josephus is again forced to admit that it was only after Titus interceded that the case against him was dismissed. The fact of the charges, including his presence in the temple with Eleazar, was evidently

was enticed to change loyalties both by his observation that Eleazar could not hold power and by a promise of command tendered by Ananus.

The Period to the Fall of Masada

The true significance of *War* 2.562-66 is then the victory of the faction headed by Ananus over the remnants of that once led by Ananias. They would continue in power for about a year, until their leaders were killed and anarchy erupted in the city. Josephus never mentions Eleazar again. What happened to him? The question has seldom been addressed,[101] but I would suggest that he made his way to Masada. In favor of this suggestion is a constellation of circumstantial or uncertain evidence that can admittedly produce no definitive conclusion but that, taken as a whole, is very provocative. This evidence is (1) the 'coincidence' that Eleazar was appointed a general in Idumea, which just happens to be where Masada was located—a fortress with which his family had certainly had previous connections; (2) the behavior of Simon bar Giora, a one-time general under Eleazar, after the rise to preeminence of Ananus' group; (3) coins associated with the jar inscription that suggest that Aqabiah, at least, was still at Masada a year after Eleazar's fall from power, and perhaps longer; and (4) Mur 19. I shall consider these points in turn.

It seems unbelievable that the assignment of Eleazar to command the very portion of Palestine, Idumea, in which was located the fortress that his family had planned to use as a refuge should be coincidental. His fellow commander in Idumea was Jesus bar Sapphas, and it is sometimes suggested that this man was appointed along with Eleazar to keep an eye on him. Perhaps; but it should be borne in mind that

so well known that Josephus could not simply say nothing. His preposterous excuse proves that the charges of involvement with the *sicarii* contained some element of truth. It is this fact that perhaps explains his knowledge of their actions, for after all they were perforce a secret organization. How else, for instance, would Josephus have known to connect the assassins of Jerusalem with those burning villages in other parts of Judaea, since there were other groups who might have been responsible?

101 Roth, *The Dead Sea Scrolls*, p. 20, suggests that Eleazar was put to death after the Roman conquest of Galilee, along with other leaders of the revolutionary government.

Idumea consisted at that time of two toparchies, one centered at Beth Gubrin and the other at En Gedi.[102] It seems plausible that two generals were assigned to Idumea, one for each toparchy, simply because of the region's importance to the war effort. Eleazar would then have sought control over the toparchy of En Gedi. In any case, the fact that both Eleazar and his brother John were given appointments instead of simply being stripped of all power prompts the suspicion that he had retained sufficient influence to manipulate his assignment. It appears highly plausible that he chose Idumea precisely because of Masada. He may well have intended to use it as a base of operations in a future bid for a return to supreme power. Josephus later says that Simon bar Giora sought domination in Acrabetta and Idumea because they could serve as an excellent base from which to launch an all-out assault on Jerusalem.[103] The strategic value of Idumea would likewise not have escaped Eleazar, and, it will be noted, John bar Ananias just happened to be assigned to Acrabetta. Unfortunately, lack of sufficient manpower and the apparent refusal of the Idumeans to accept the Jerusalem appointments ultimately stymied this plan, if such it was.[104]

After Ananus had taken power, Simon bar Giora raised an army of 'brigands' (λῃσταί) in Acrabetta and began conducting raids. Eventually this harassment grew so severe that Ananus sent an army to

---

102 *War* 3.54-55; cf. M. Avi-Yonah, *The Holy Land from the Persian to the Arab Conquests (536 B.C. to A.D. 640): A Historical Geography* (rev. ed.; Grand Rapids: Eerdmans, 1966), pp. 95-96.

103 *War* 4.513.

104 Since Josephus says almost nothing about the war in Idumea, the suggestion that the Idumeans refused to accept the appointments is based on inference and analogy. Josephus implies in *War* 4.359-62 that it was the Idumeans who colluded with the Zealots in putting Niger the Peraean to death. As he had been assigned to serve under Eleazar and Jesus in Idumea (*War* 2.566), Niger's mere presence in Jerusalem argues that things had not gone too well earlier. Perhaps the attack on En Gedi by the *sicarii* from Masada (*War* 4.398-405) was in part an effort to enforce the assignments. It may be also that the Idumeans refused the appointments of Jesus and Eleazar because they doubted that such generals, lacking military experience as they did, could be effective against the Roman attack expected in the spring or summer of 68 (cf. the comments of Goodman, *Ruling Class,* p. 189). Josephus' experiences in Galilee, as recounted in both *War* and *Vita,* furnish an analogical explanation for the Idumeans' refusal to accept commanders in whose appointment they had no say. Josephus was able only with great difficulty to overcome similar resistance on the part of certain groups in Galilee. Those assigned to Idumea were evidently not so successful.

deal with the problem and Simon had to flee. He fled directly to Masada, where he remained until Ananus' death—a period of about a year, from late 66/early 67 until the winter of 67/68. While there, he went out on raids against the Idumeans with the men of Masada.[105] The possible connections of these activities with Ananias' sons is intriguing.

First, it must be emphasized that Simon bar Giora had been a general allied with Eleazar when the latter was still in supreme command. They must have had a personal relationship and mutual confidence for that to occur. Having worked together in the early stages of the revolt, these men would have had a deep bond. Then, as noted, it was John bar Ananias who was in command in Acrabetta, which is where Simon chose to raid. That Simon had personal connections there already is probable, but John's complicity in his activities is to be suspected, especially if, as Goodman has suggested, Simon's brigandage were directed solely at supporters of Ananus.[106] And why did Simon flee to Masada? Of course, it was beyond Ananus' reach, but surely there were many other places where he could have escaped the commander's attention—especially since he fled with a tiny and impotent band.[107] Why did he feel confident of a good reception at Masada?

Josephus says that when Simon first arrived there, he was met with a certain suspicion and had to camp below the main fortress. Later he was allowed into the complex. The fear was probably that Simon would try to usurp the leadership of the group—a not ill-founded suspicion, since Simon was a messianic pretender. Such appeals were precisely what had divided the *sicarii* more than once in the past, most recently with Menahem. But gradually Simon managed to allay these fears, and he lived at Masada for about a year. This lengthy stay implies an essential harmony, such as one might expect if two old comrades-in-arms had once again joined forces. It is easy to reconcile the length of Simon's stay at Masada with the idea that Eleazar bar Ananias was in command there. On the other hand, Simon had been opposed to Eleazar bar Jair at the time of Menahem's coup. That fact does not mean, of course, that in the light of changed circumstances the two could never have joined in pursuit of a common goal. But one must wonder why bar

105 *War* 2.652-54, 4.504-08.
106 Goodman, *Ruling Class*, p. 205.
107 According to *War* 4.505, when Simon arrived at Masada his troupe consisted largely of women.

Jair would have jeopardized his leadership by taking Simon in, whereas Eleazar bar Ananias would have done so on the basis of an old friendship. At any rate, later Simon did make precisely the sort of bid for supremacy at Masada that had prompted the suspicions in the first place. Simon urged them to accompany him in his planned attack on Jerusalem. Josephus says that they refused because they 'had grown used to their fortress, and feared to journey far from their den, so to speak.'[108] But how could the historian have known the true motive for their refusal to accompany Simon? In fact he supplied this motive for historiographic reasons. It was crucial for his argument that it appear that the same group that left Jerusalem for Masada in late 66 CE remained in the fortress until its final destruction eight years later. Therefore the historian here depicted them as hibernating animals.[109] But the real question was likely the acceptance or rejection of Simon's messianic claims, pressed with renewed vigor now that Ananus was dead and the leadership of the revolt once more uncertain. Presumably there were those among the group at Masada who did accompany Simon when he left.[110] But perhaps the majority remained with whomever was now leader at Masada—Eleazar bar Ananias, if my apprehensions are correct.

A third reason to suspect that Eleazar bar Ananias went to Masada not too long after losing the power in Jerusalem is archaeological. Yadin's original report on the excavations twice gave details on the finds of the locus (1237) in which the jar inscribed with Ananias' name was discovered. He said,[111]

> The elongated casemate (locus 1237), having a length of 27 m, should be mentioned in particular. In the time of the Revolt this casemate was partitioned by thin walls into at least four dwelling units. In each unit we found ovens and other installations, and in one of them there were also several amphoras, with interesting

108 *War* 4.507-8.
109 The term φωλεός, 'den', is used in literature particularly of the caves where bears hibernate and whence, of course, they virtually never exit during their winter's sleep. See Liddell and Scott, *Greek Lexicon*, s. v.
110 Stern, 'Sicarii and Zealots', pp. 277 and 285, proposes that among Simon's forces at Jerusalem were substantial numbers of *sicarii*. He does not mention any such following Simon from Masada, but rather sees them as drawn from various other bands throughout Judaea.
111 Yadin, 'Excavations', pp. 84 and 111, respectively.

inscriptions [including Ananias' jar] . . .

The inscription [that with Naveh's correction refers to Ananias] .
. . is specially noteworthy. The owner of this vessel belonged to
the family of the High Priests; in his room, which was in the
fortress wall, were found together with typical objects of the
period of the Revolt, many coins . . .

The catalog of Masada coins has now been published, listing a total of
39 bronze coins assigned to locus 1237.[112] The coins date from the time
of John Hyrcanus I (II?) to the time of the First Revolt. The most
significant in the present context are the eleven *prutot* dating to the
second year of the revolt, i.e., Nisan 67-Adar 68 CE.[113] It is of course
impossible to prove that these coins certainly belonged to the occupant
of the room in which they were found and were not, for example,
dropped by some visitor. Nor is it possible to prove beyond doubt that
the jar found with them, inscribed with the names of Ananias and
Aqabiah, was not appropriated by someone else after Ananias' death.
But if someone else had taken this jar one would expect that he would
have scratched out the names of its former owners and replaced them
with his own. Other jars from Masada—including one from the very
same locus, 1237—bear analogous modifications to their original
inscriptions.[114] The most natural interpretation of the evidence is that
the coins belonged to the jar's owner and that the owner was none other
than Aqabiah. If so, then Aqabiah was alive at Masada until the latter

112   The coins of Masada are published in Yadin and Naveh, *Aramaic and Hebrew
Ostraca,* 69-132, with plates 61-81. According to the consecutive numbering
system that Meshorer employs, the coins found in locus 1237 are numbers 103,
144, 595-6, 610-23, 688-89, 1278-80, 1756-60, 2022-23, 2172-3, 2802-03, 4413-15
and 4618-19.
113   Five of the coins are of the type that Meshorer has designated Year Two Type
11, two of the type he calls Year Two Type 11a, two of Type 12, and two so badly
preserved that no specific identification was possible. See Yadin and Naveh,
Aramaic and Hebrew Ostraca, 101-113, and Y. Meshorer, *Ancient Jewish Coins,
vol. 2: Herod the Great through Bar Cochba* (New York: Amphora, 1982) pp. 109
and 260.
114   Jar 458 originally bore a Hebrew inscription, קודש 'holy (things)', in formal
script. Its owner added in cursive an *alef* at the end and a *lamed* at the beginning,
thus supplying the preposition 'for' and converting the language of the inscription
to Aramaic, לקודשא.

part of 67 at the earliest. He may well have been there considerably longer, and these were simply the coins—low denomination 'pocket change'—that he happened to have in his possession when the fortress fell. If he was at Masada at any point in or after the second year, however, then he was there after Ananus took over in Jerusalem. This fact simultaneously raises serious questions about Josephus' assertion that Eleazar bar Jair was the leader at Masada, and argues that Eleazar bar Ananias was at Masada.

When Eleazar bar Jair fled Jerusalem with 'a few' other survivors of Menahem's group, Josephus reports that he went to Masada and there became leader. Perhaps this really is what happened. But as noted above, it requires events to have followed a certain course that is, to say the least, improbable. It is much more likely that when Eleazar bar Jair returned to the fortress, accompanied by a small and beaten band, he would have met with an indifferent reception, or worse. For knowledge of Menahem's plan at the time he left Masada would certainly have precipitated a battle between Ananias' supporters and Menahem's. Nothing supports the assumption that Menahem's forces had won such a battle, or that it even occurred. The coins suggest otherwise. And in the interval between Ananias' death and the overthrow of Menahem, news of the events had surely traveled to the fortress where some of those most concerned were housed. Perhaps the inhabitants were divided by Menahem's actions, and bar Jair had some friends awaiting. But Aqabiah was also still there, and, if so, then yet other partisans of Ananias' family would have been (else Aqabiah could not have survived). If Eleazar entered at all, then, it was only after the sort of negotiations between factions that Josephus describes so frequently in his account of events in Galilee. And if bar Jair was there at all, it is unlikely that he became the leader, since Aqabiah at least was also there. Later Eleazar his brother may have been as well, and apparently others of the ruling élite.[115] These would never have countenanced the rule of the low born bar Jair, any more than they had countenanced that of his relative Menahem. Indeed, the only explicit reason that Josephus gives for Menahem's murder by the upper class supporters of Eleazar bar Ananias was their distaste at his attempt to rise above his birth. They could not abide a lower class ruler.[116]

---

115 See the reference to a debt of 500 *denarii* above.
116 *War* 2.443. The élite could not bear the rule of one 'lower than themselves' (ἑαυτῶν ταπεινότερον).

The coins found in his cell, locus 1237, therefore strongly suggest
that Aqabiah was at Masada until late 67 at the earliest. He would then
have been there well past the time—indeed, a full year past the time—
when Ananus outmaneuvered his brother Eleazar and took control in
Jerusalem. Eleazar having arranged to take command in Idumea and
having no reason to remain in Jerusalem, it is only natural that he
would have joined his brother at Masada. There he could take up the
tattered remnants of his father's plan for revolt and try to fashion them
into some new garment. There he could rule while plotting a return to
power in Jerusalem. And in view of the evidence of Mur 19, Eleazar
may well have remained at Masada until the final debacle.

Mur 19 is a גט (document of divorce). The portions crucial for the
present discussion are the first line, which bears the date, and the
signature of one of the witnesses. The first line reads in Aramaic
באחד למרחשון שנת שת במצדא, 'on the first of Marheshvan, year six
at Masada.' The original editor of Mur 19, J.T. Milik, thought that this
date referred to year six of Provincia Arabia, i.e. 111 CE.[117] But there
are grave difficulties with this solution to the line. First is the date
formula itself. Among the materials of the Babatha archive are a fair
number of contracts that were indubitably executed in Provincia
Arabia, and these always include in their date formulae an explicit
reference to the dating system being followed. Where preserved, the
Greek contracts contain a version of the phrase κατὰ δὲ τὸν τῆς νέας
ἐπαρχείας 'Αραβίας ἀριθμὸν, 'according to the numbering of the
new Province of Arabia,' or at least a reference to the consuls of the
given year.[118] According to prepublication information, the Aramaic
and Nabatean documents contain an equivalent phrase such as ועל מנין
הפרכיה דא or some similar reference to the dating system.[119] Without
question the Judaean custom of the time, both prior to the First Revolt
and following, was to specify the dating system under which a contract
or legal document was executed.[120] Thus the line from Mur 19 almost

---

117   DJD 2, pp. 104 and 106.
118   See N. Lewis, ed., *The Documents from the Bar Kokhba Period in the Cave of
Letters: Greek Papyri* (Jerusalem: Israel Exploration Society, 1989), numbers 5, 11,
12, 14, 15, 16, 17 etc.
119   See e.g. Y. Yadin, 'Expedition D—The Cave of the Letters', *IEJ* 12 (1962),
pp. 238-46.
120   Thus Mur 18, dated to the second year of Nero, and the thirteen published
Hebrew and Aramaic documents from the time of Bar Kochba in which are fully or

certainly is not dating by the system of Provincia Arabia. And yet the line almost certainly constitutes a full dating formula.[121] Why then does it not refer to a ruler or an era?

The analogy Yadin found for the dating formula of Mur 19 was the coins of the First Revolt. Unlike the great mass of Hasmonean, Herodian, Bar Kochba and other Second Temple Jewish coins, these do not refer to a dating system or ruler's name. The observable correspondence between numismatic inscriptions and legal documents in periods of Jewish history on either side of the First Revolt argues that legal documents of the First Revolt would likewise have lacked such references. Perhaps the coins reflect the lack of an agreed upon Jewish leader, or the slogan of the Fourth Philosophy: 'No ruler but God.' Yadin was impressed with this analogy. He was equally impressed with the fact that his excavations at Masada had turned up absolutely no evidence of Jewish habitation at Masada at the time of Bar Kochba or in the several decades preceding. Thus he thought no Jews could have lived at Masada in 111. These two lines of evidence led him to propose that Mur 19 was written at Masada at the time of the

nearly fully preserved the portions bearing dates. The Bar Kochba documents range from April/May 132 to Sept/Oct 135 and date according to the era of 'the redemption of Israel', (i.e., Bar Kochba's seizure of Jerusalem), or to the year of Bar Kochba's rule. They can be arranged chronologically thus: Ḥev 42, Mur 22, the I.O.U. of unknown provenance, Mur 23, Mur 24, Mur 29, Kefar Baru, Mur 25, Ḥev 44, Ḥev 45-46, Ḥev 47, 'Kephar Bebayu' (now known to come from Kefar Baru), and Mur 30. For the documents see DJD 2; Yadin, 'Cave of Letters', pp. 248-57; J.T. Milik, 'Deux documents inédits du Désert de Juda', *Bib* 38 (1957), pp. 264-68; M. Broshi and E. Qimron, 'A House Sale Deed from Kefar Baru from the Time of Bar Kochba', *IEJ* 36 (1986), pp. 201-214, and idem, 'I.O.U. Note from the Time of the Bar Kochba Revolt', *ErIsr* 20 (1989), pp. 256-61 (Heb.). According to m. Gitt. 8.5, a bill of divorcement with an irregular dating is invalid.

121   On the extreme rarity of legal documents that give the year without reference to the counting system or ruler, see E. Koffmahn, *Die Doppelurkunden aus der Wuste Juda* (Leiden: Brill, 1968), pp. 42-45. Recently A. Yardeni has published an Aramaic ostracon from an unknown find spot that she places roughly in the period of this discussion. It dates to 'year thirteen' but apparently makes no reference to a dating system (although a word is illegible at the crucial point in the text, so one cannot be certain that no reference is made). Even if the ostracon made no such reference, however, its relevance for this discussion is tangential at best. It is not a legal text, but some form of private note for bookkeeping purposes. See A. Yardeni, 'New Jewish Aramaic Ostraca from Israel', *Tarbiz* 58 (1988), pp. 119-23 (Heb.).

First Revolt.[122] Yadin was almost certainly right, and his view has won acceptance.[123]

If Yadin was indeed correct, Mur 19 dates to October of the sixth year of the revolt, i.e., October 71 CE. Presumably the inhabitants of Masada had continued to date their legal documents by the system adopted when the revolt began, even though by 71 Jerusalem had fallen and the temple was in ruins. The woman whose divorce decree this was must have left Masada after receiving it, and probably made her way up the coast of the Dead Sea to the entrance of the Wadi Murabba'at, whither other refugees of the revolt had also fled.[124] A less likely possibility is that she made her way home and that, at the time of the Second Revolt some sixty years later, her document was among the family papers she or her descendants snatched up before fleeing to Murabba'at.[125] And thus it came to be among the materials discovered at Murabba'at in this century. In any event, the document was executed at Masada and its signatories were resident there. The last signature on Mur 19 is therefore very intriguing: שהד אלעזר בר חננה 'Eleazar bar Ḥananâ, witness.' The patronymic, חננה, is a short form or hypocoristic of the name חנניה. Such forms of Yahwistic names are known beginning in the Iron Age and continuing to this period.[126] Accordingly,

---

122 Yadin, 'Excavations', p. 119 n. 112.

123 Koffmahn, *Doppelurkunden,* pp. 42-5; R. Hestrin, et al. *Inscriptions Reveal* (Jerusalem: Israel Museum, 1972), p. 189 (Heb.), and Beyer, *Texte,* p. 307. Naveh is uncertain, suggesting that the document may derive from Jews associated with the Roman garrison at Masada that existed from 73 (*sic*) to at least 111 (*Aramaic and Hebrew Ostraca,* 11). I do not share his confidence that Jews would have been permitted to live at Masada alongside the garrison. Naveh makes his suggestion on the basis of evidence for Nabatean presence at Masada, which he cannot explain during the period of the revolt. I have a different view; see note 136 below.

124 Note that according to *War* 7.275, the *sicarii* of Masada had established their control over the region (χώρα) surrounding the fortress, which the Romans had to win back before they could begin the seige. Thus at Murabbacat she may well have been within territory still controlled by the rebels. A coin of the year 42/43, three dated to 58/59, and one to 69/70, together with pottery that parallels that of Qumran II, indicate that refugees occupied the Caves of the region during the First Revolt. See the discussion by R. de Vaux in 'Archéologie', DJD 2, pp. 29-47.

125 It is less likely that the woman returned home because the Romans had employed a 'scorched earth' policy in conquering the villages of Judaea. Thus there may well have been nothing left to which to return. Cf. *War* 4.488-89.

126 For Iron Age examples, see G. Barkay, 'Excavations on the Slope of the Hinnom Valley, Jerusalem', *Qadmoniot* 17 (1984), p. 106 (Heb.), for פלטה <

the man who witnessed this writ of divorce was named Eleazar bar Ananias. Was he possibly the son of Ananias bar Nedebaeus?

The likelihood of this identification is a function of two variables: the frequency of the names he bore among the population of Jewish males generally, and the number of men at Masada at this time. According to the most thorough study of male Jewish names of the period of the Second Temple, nine percent of men were called Eleazar and six percent Ananias.[127] The number of men bearing both names would then be approximately one in two hundred (0.54%). And, since the names could occur in either order, the number of men named Eleazar bar Ananias would be something like one in four hundred (0.27%). Granted, even Hachlili's thorough study may be inaccurate to a certain extent, since the surviving materials from which the data were drawn may not be a fully representative cross section of contemporary society. And my calculation does not begin to approach a statistician's rigor; nevertheless, it may serve as an approximation. One may cautiously state that only one in several hundred men was likely to bear the name Eleazar bar Ananias. Now, according to Josephus, the total number of defenders on Masada when it fell to the Romans was 960. Josephus is not always very accurate with his numbers, of course, but this figure harmonizes reasonably well with the remains found during the modern excavations. Of this total of 960, how many were men? Although

---

פלטיה; P. Bordreuil, *Catalogue des sceaux ouest-sémitique inscrits* (Paris: Bibliothèque Nationale, 1986), p. 52, for another example of the same name; and N. Avigad, *Hebrew Bullae from the Time of Jeremiah: Remnants of a Burnt Archive* (Jerusalem: Israel Exploration Society, 1986), p. 41, for מיכיה > מיכה. For the Persian period, see Y. Aharoni *et al.*, *Excavations at Ramat Rahel: Seasons 1961 and 1962* (Rome: Centro di Studi Semitici, 1964), p. 46, for the very name found on Mur 19: חנניה > חננה. Note also the name מחסיה > מחסה, comparing Cowley, *Papyri*, 8:1 and 8:36. Greco-Roman period examples are Masada jar 499, incised with the name מתתיה > מתתה (Yadin and Navch, *Aramaic and Hebrew Ostraca*, 42 and plate 36); DJD 2, 74:15, where one finds the spelling מתתא; and another example of this latter spelling, on an ossuary from Dominus Flevit (P.B. Bagatti and J.T. Milik, *Gli scavi del 'Dominus Flevit' parte I: La necropoli del periodo romano* [Jerusalem: Tipografia dei P.P. Francescani, 1958], p. 92). Along with additional examples of this pattern for shortened Yahwistic names, the key to their interpretation and vocalization is found in the Hebrew Bible. Judg 17 gives the long and short forms of such a name borne by a single individual: cf. vv. 1, 4 and v. 5ff.

127   Hachlili, 'Names and Nicknames', esp. p. 189.

excavations. Of this total of 960, how many were men? Although Josephus makes it clear that entire families died there, since Masada was a fortress one might expect the population to be skewed toward adult males. Materials found at the site, however, particularly coins of the fifth year, suggest that a number of refugees came there during the war and after the fall of Jerusalem.[128] Such refugees could be of either sex and any age. And Josephus specifically states that new recruits came to Masada all along, presumably with families in some cases.[129] The normal ratios may hold, then, and of the 960 or so total inhabitants one may expect there were three or four women and children for every man. On this basis there may have been as few as 200 to 300 men at Masada.[130] If so, then only one or two at most would be expected to bear the name Eleazar bar Ananias.

This method of arriving at a number is obviously very approximate. Still, considering the other evidence that points to a connection between Eleazar, his family and Masada—even after Ananus' rise—it is entirely conceivable that the man who witnessed Mur 19 was Eleazar bar Ananias bar Nedebaeus.[131] Coming to Masada in late 66, he apparently remained there until at least late 71. Of course, even if Mur 19 was not signed by the high priest's son at Masada in 71, the other considerations argue he may still have been there at some time. And if he were there, it is hard to believe that Eleazar bar Jair was in charge. Why then does Josephus say he was, and why is he silent about Eleazar bar Ananias, if indeed he was the real leader?

---

128 Note the appearance on a list of names of 'the Gadarians' (הגדראין; Yadin and Naveh, *Aramaic and Hebrew Ostraca*, 420:2, 24 and plate 24.) The gentilic could refer to several different towns in Palestine, notably the capital of Peraea or the city southeast of the Sea of Galilee.

129 *War* 4.405, προσδιαφθειρομένων αὐτοῖς καθ' ἡμέραν ἑκασταχόθεν οὐκ ὀλίγων.

130 I.A. Richmond, 'The Roman Siege-Works of Masada, Israel', *JRS* 52 (1962), p. 144, estimates 500 fighting men. That total would not materially affect the estimate of the number of men named Eleazar bar Ananias.

131 A number of the inscribed materials found at Masada refer to an Eleazar, while others mention a 'son of Ananias.' Unfortunately none of these inscriptions contains both the name of the son and the patronym. One can only say, therefore, that the inscriptional materials in no way discourage the theory of Eleazar's presence at Masada. See Yadin and Naveh, *Aramaic and Hebrew Ostraca*, 381, 390, 392, 406, 470, 476, 510, 511, 697.

Conclusion

A number of explanations are possible for Josephus' silence about Eleazar at Masada. He may have been ignorant of Eleazar's presence there, particularly if the son of Ananias died or for some other reason was not at Masada when it fell. If such was the case, then Josephus may have been right in saying that Eleazar bar Jair was the leader when Masada was taken. But historiographic and literary tendencies could equally well explain Josephus' treatment.

Here one must bear in mind this writer's well known bias in favor of the upper classes to which he himself belonged. It was the Jewish historian's intention to absolve the members of the élite from all blame for the revolt against Rome, and to lay it at the feet of his ubiquitous ληϲταί. Unquestionably this feature of Josephus' presentation of the events goes a long way in explaining why he would not want to admit that Eleazar bar Ananias was at Masada at the end, and indeed, why he would not want to admit that Ananias himself was ever there. Josephus needed lower-class leadership, the refuse of first century Judaean society, at Masada. Eleazar bar Jair would do nicely. But this explanation does not really go to the heart of the matter. Josephus needed Eleazar bar Jair to be the general of Masada, whatever the facts. And he wanted to portray the inhabitants of the doomed fortress as essentially the same 'few' who had accompanied bar Jair in his flight from Jerusalem. As alluded to above, it does not take much reflection to see that this last point in particular is very unlikely to be true.

The coins of Masada clearly demonstrate that people came and went during the years of the revolt, probably to and from Jerusalem where the coins were minted. Also among the finds at Masada are some thirty dockets giving directions for supplying their holders with bread. Two of these strongly suggest substantial movement to and from Masada. One refers to 'the porters' (סבליא).[132] The term סבל in Aramaic sometimes has a special connotation: 'bearing corn or grain.'[133] This meaning is likely to apply here. These 'porters' were responsible for bringing supplies of grain to Masada from places outside.[134] The second

---

132 Yadin and Naveh, *Aramaic and Hebrew Ostraca*, 560:1 (p. 53; plate 46).
133 Brockelmann and R. Payne Smith, *s.v.* ܣܒܠ.
134 In light of the Aramaic Bar Kochba letters, which show that grain deported at En Gedi and was then distributed by two of Simeon bar Kosiba's lieutenants (one of whom bore the hitherto unexplained name 'Masabbala' = 'grain merchant' [?]),

docket refers to bread being supplied to 'the camp.'[135] Such a term makes little sense within the confines of the fortress itself. It must mean that there were soldiers from Masada on assignment somewhere outside the walls, presumably harassing the Romans or Idumeans. Evidently they were supplied from Masada. Several inscribed jars indicate that Jews from Nabatea had come to Masada, either directly or via Jerusalem.[136] Mur 19 is still another indication of coming and going; and even Josephus himself gives hints of movement here and there.[137] With substantial movement into and out of Masada, it is likely that there would be some turnover in the population over an eight year period. But in spite of its intrinsic improbability and hints to the contrary from a variety of evidence, Josephus has bewitched many historians into believing his story: the *sicarii* fled to Masada, sealed themselves off from the outside and passively sat out the war, finally dying without even a single sally against the enemy.[138]

This is not likely to be what really happened, nor is it likely that

one might suggest that the grain came from that site. Note also Greek papyrus 740 from Masada, the 'Letter of Abaskantos to Judas.' The letter is of uncertain date, but may derive from the years of the revolt. It apparently refers to 'lettuce' (μαρούλια), which almost certainly would have been brought from the nearby oasis of En Gedi. See Cotton and Geiger, *Latin and Greek Documents,* pp. 85-88 and plate 8.

135 Yadin and Naveh, *Aramaic and Hebrew Ostraca,* 566:2 (p. 54; plate 46).

136 Jar 468 bears an Arabic (= Nabatean?) proper name, and jars 514 and 515 are inscribed with Nabatean cursive script. See Yadin and Naveh, *Aramaic and Hebrew Ostraca,* 40 and 44, and plates 32 and 39, respectively. It is not unlikely that, at the outset of the revolt, it was necessary for Jews living in Nabatea to flee to Judaea. For this possiblity the case of Babatha at the time of the Second Revolt furnishes a perfect analogy. It may also be worth mentioning in this connection that among the Dead Sea Scrolls is at least one in the Nabatean script. See chapter three below, note 21.

137 E.g., his occasional mention of raids on Idumean villages, and his note in *War* 4.405 that new recruits came often.

138 Thus e.g., Applebaum, 'The Zealots', p. 165; Zeitlin, 'Sicarii and Masada', pp. 253-54; and even Smith, 'Zealots and Sicarii', p. 19. Horsley and Hanson, *Bandits,* p. 214 are at least well aware of the problem, saying 'The subsequent history of the Sicarii [after their flight to Masada] would appear to invoke either a major inconsistency or a dramatic fluctuation in behavior'. In 'Terrorists', pp. 454-5, Horsley offers several possible explanations for this behavior, but admits that 'none of them is completely satisfactory.' Still, he is never led to question the veracity of Josephus' story.

those at Masada when it fell were the same group that had first taken refuge there in 66 CE. Josephus obviously had little information about what went on at Masada between the outbreak of the war and its final stand in 74 CE. His *sicarii* at Masada are to a certain extent an artificial construct. They are an element in the historian's effort to come to terms with the tragic consequences of the revolt against Rome. The Jews, God's chosen people, were again the losers; again their temple lay in ruins. Once again, to paraphrase an ancient prophet, the wicked had swallowed up those more righteous than they. For Josephus—as for earlier biblical writers and most of his contemporaries—the explanation was to be found in the notion that the people had sinned. But Josephus went further and pointed specifically to the cause of the people's sin: the 'Fourth Philosophy.' Its most prominent advocates he sealed off at Masada for a final retribution.

As David Ladouceur has shown, the principle of divine retribution permeates the seventh book of *War*. By means of the two speeches that he places in Eleazar bar Jair's mouth at the end, Josephus portrays the suicides by Masada's defenders as acts of penance and retribution. Ladouceur notes, 'In Josephus, as the Sicarii have over and over again murdered their own countrymen, so in their final moments they are forced to murder those closest to them, their own families, and at last themselves.'[139] But for Josephus' portrayal to be most effective, he needed an essential equivalence between the defenders of Masada in 74 CE and the Jerusalem assassins of the early 50's. His account therefore works to that end, obscuring any difficulties with such a depiction in terms of historical realities. The concept of retribution structures the entire Masada account, and helps explain both the presence of Eleazar bar Jair and the absence of Eleazar bar Ananias.

Perhaps the key passage in terms of bar Jair and Masada is *War* 7.324-25. Josephus makes bar Jair say πρῶτοί τε γὰρ πάντων ἀπέστημεν καὶ πολεμοῦμεν αὐτοῖς τελευταῖοι, 'For as we were first of all to rise in revolt, so we are the last to wage war with them.' The explanatory power that Josephus sought to invest in this phrase is manifest in the emphatic placement of πρῶτοι and τελευταῖοι. He does not mean to refer only to the proximate beginning of the revolt in 66 CE. He has in mind what he considers the real beginning, when the

---

139 D. Ladouceur, 'Josephus and Masada', in *Josephus, Judaism and Christianity,* ed. L.H. Feldman and G. Hata (Detroit: Wayne State University Press, 1987), pp. 95-113. The quotation appears on p. 104.

'Fourth Philosophy' arose and the seeds of revolution first were planted. That, of course, was at the time of Quirinius in 6 CE, and the leader had been Judas the Galilean, a forebear of Eleazar bar Jair.[140] For the retribution that Josephus required to be accomplished, then, it was necessary that bar Jair or some other known descendant of Judas be the leader of Masada's rebels. Only then could the end correspond to the beginning and the circle of God's retributive justice be closed; the sins of the father would be visited upon the son.

In the nature of things I cannot prove that Eleazar bar Ananias was at Masada at the end or that Eleazar bar Jair was not the leader when the fortress fell.[141] On the other hand Josephus' account is certainly tendentious and therefore open to question. The evidence for Eleazar bar Ananias' involvement with Masada earlier in the revolt, though

---

140   *War* 7.253; cf. 2.118.

141   Yadin regarded the discovery of the famous 'lots' as stunning proof of the veracity of Josephus' account—'the most dramatic find of the entire dig' (Yadin, *Masada,* 197). One of these 'lots', now published as 437 (Yadin and Naveh, *Aramaic and Hebrew Ostraca,* 28 and plate 25), is inscribed, as Yadin thought, בניאיר. Yadin took this to mean 'ben Jair', whom, following Josephus, he considered to be Masada's leader. This interpretation is open to question. The words can as easily be read 'Sons of Light' (בני אור). Naveh admits as much, but argues that since the other 'lots' all refer to a single individual, consistency requires that this one also refer to one man—thus 'ben Jair.' In his words, this interpretation is 'unequivocally preferable' (p. 29). I must, nevertheless, equivocate. First, the function(s) of these 'lots' is not really known; Yadin's interpretation raises a number of difficulties. Therefore it is uncertain whether a single consistent interpretation should be sought. If it is decided that consistency is indeed important, the fact is that the other 'lots' are all inscribed with nicknames rather than actual names, with the possible exception of 431 (perhaps unfinished), 435 (not really understood) and 433 (which may in fact be a nickname). Ben Jair is not a nickname. Jair was a birth name among the Jews of this period. Thus if consistency be sought there is more than one way to get it: either the inscriptions all refer to single individuals, or they are all nicknames. 'Sons of Light' would be a fine nickname for two brothers, say, in an eschatologically oriented military troop. I am reminded of the similar nickname borne by brothers in another eschatological group, the disciples of Jesus of Nazareth. According to Mark 3.17, Jesus nicknamed John and Jacob the sons of Zebedee 'Sons of Thunder' (Βοανηργές, ὅ ἐστιν υἱοὶ βροντῆς = Hebrew בני רגש?). Of course, even granting Naveh's problematic assertion, the mere presence of a 'ben Jair' at Masada does not automatically equate with the Eleazar who bore that patronym. Even if it did, it would prove no more than his presence. With the inscription on Ananias' jar, his leadership would still be at issue.

largely inferential, deserves careful consideration. More definite is the connection of the family of the high priest Ananias bar Nedebaeus to the fortress and the *sicarii* at the beginning of the revolt and earlier. This connection does not depend solely on the new evidence of the inscription חנ[נ]י[ה כהנא רבא עקביא בריה. Perhaps unwittingly, Josephus had already furnished sufficient clues to raise suspicions, as Mary Smallwood's work, for example, demonstrates. What the inscription provides is a needed hermeneutical key to Josephus. Its testimony is that vital—heretofore missing—second witness to the events and their meaning as Josephus presents them. The new testimony makes it is possible to extract a consistent line from Josephus while uncovering at least some of his inaccuracies and intentional distortions.

In this connection the more abstract significance of the inscription is that it once again brings us face to face with the essential problem of Josephus' trustworthiness. Nowhere is this problem more sharply in focus than in the case of Masada. Scholars have long realized that the speeches the historian places in Eleazar bar Jair's mouth are his own invention. And recently questions have been raised about whether the suicides he describes really took place, at least in the way Josephus says they did.[142] Now there is reason to wonder who was the general at the end. A sceptic might justifiably conclude that Josephus describes suicides that never happened motivated by speeches that were never given by a man who was never there.[143]

---

142 S.J.D. Cohen, 'Masada: Literary Tradition, Archaeological Remains, and the Credibility of Josephus', in *Essays in Honour of Yigael Yadin,* ed. G. Vermes and J. Neusner (= *JJS* 33 [1982]; Totowa, New Jersey, 1983), pp. 385-405.

143 Cf. the words of Smallwood, *Roman Rule,* p. 338, 'Is the truth of the matter that ... Josephus' story is a myth serving the patriotic purpose of covering up the ignominy of the final Jewish surrender and at the same time the apologetic purpose of absolving the Romans of the barbarity of a final massacre of women and children?'

Excursus One: The Identity of 'Ananias the High Priest'

Apart from the option adopted above, three other possible ways of construing the inscription come to mind, none of which Naveh seriously discusses. These alternatives are: (1) the inscription refers to three individuals— Ananias the priest, Rabba, and the latter's son, Aqabiah; (2) the owner of this vessel was merely a member of one of the high priestly families;[144] (3) the reference is to a high priest Ananias, but he is not the son of Nedebaeus; instead he is an otherwise unknown sectarian high priest whom the occupants at Masada established in that role. In my view, none of these alternatives is sufficiently likely as to merit serious consideration. My reasoning is as follows.

Reading the inscription as a reference to three men is perhaps the best of the three alternatives listed. Still, two considerations tell strongly against it. First is the fact that the name רבא (and its variants) never appears in any Second Temple text or source. Evidently Aramaic in origin, it is attested as early as the texts from Elephantine, and is known in other Aramaic dialects as well.[145] In the not inconsiderable sources surviving from ancient Palestine, however, the first definite record of the name is in the Mishnah. The second problem arises upon comparision with the other jars from Masada. Of those bearing inscriptions, none belonged to more than two individuals—and few even to two.

When the inscribed sherd was first unearthed, Yadin believed that it referred merely to a member of one of the high priestly families. The term ἀρχιερεῦς at this period, as known from the New Testament and Josephus, can refer to either (1) the functioning or former holder of the office; or (2) the male members of the families of those men.[146] It

---

144 Naveh does acknowledge the possibility of Yadin's suggestion in a footnote on p. 37, but he gives it no real consideration.

145 See e.g., W. Kornfeld, *Onomastica Aramaica aus Ägypten* (Wien: Walter Kornf, 1978), p. 71, and J. Stark, *Personal Names in Palmyrene Inscriptions* (Oxford: Clarendon Press, 1971) 49. For Jewish Palestine, however, apart from two uncertain readings in materials from Murabba^cat (J.T. Milik, DJD 2, 24 E 2; 38 4 3), it is unattested before the third century CE. See Hachlili, 'Names and Nicknames', p. 190.

146 See Schürer 2, pp. 233-35. The theory of J. Jeremias, *Jerusalem in the Time of*

appears that as few as four families provided all the high priests in the period from Herod to the destruction of the Second Temple. The term may generally be said to refer to the members of those families,[147] whether actual occupants of the high priesthood or not. Thus Yadin's suggestion was entirely plausible on his former reading, 'Kahana Raba Aqavia' (although the word order is problematic). But with Naveh's improved decipherment this interpretation is very difficult to defend. If both men were merely members of the high priestly families, obviously Aqabiah would have just as much claim to the title 'high priest' as would his father. After all, both were equally blue-blooded. If this were the intention of the inscription, one would have expected to read on the jar חנניה עקביא כהניא רברביא, or perhaps חנניה עקביא בני כהנא רבא. But since the actual wording of the inscription distinguishes between the status of the two men, it apparently requires that the first name refer to a man regarded as a (onetime) functioning high priest.

As for the third option, that the reference is to a sectarian high priest of some sort, it is true that Josephus reports that the Zealots appointed a high priest of their own during the course of the revolt, selecting one Phannias bar Samuel by lot.[148] And in the same vein, some have suggested that the Teacher of Righteousness of the Qumran texts was a sectarian high priest.[149] Yet on closer examination neither of these apparent parallels encourages the possibility of a sectarian high priest at Masada.

The Zealots had taken control of the temple at Jerusalem before they made their new appointment. Prior to that time so far as we know they

---

Jesus (Philadelphia: Fortress, 1969), pp. 175-81 is compatible with Schürer's approach to the question.

147 Jeremias notes that these four families—those of Phiabi, Boethus, Ananus and Camith—produced at least 22 of the 25 high priests in the Herodian-Roman period (Jeremias, *Jerusalem*, 194; see also Schürer 2:234). The filiation of the other three, including Ananias bar Nedebaeus, is unknown, but it is likely that these men also belonged to one of the four families. On the basis of this likelihood, the principle of 'family solidarity' that was observably at work among the élite families at the time of the revolt (see Goodman, *Ruling Class,* p. 210 with an impressive number of examples) and the discovery at Masada of a tag reading בת קתרא, one might very tentatively assign Ananias to the family of Boethus (with which קתרא = Cantheras was associated). For the tag, see note 42 above.

148 *War* 4.155, *Ant.* 20.227.

149 E.g., H. Stegemann, *Die Entstehung der Qumrangemeinde* (Bonn: Privately printed, 1971), pp. 102 and 210-220, with notes 328-29.

had no 'sectarian' high priest. It was precisely the possession of the temple that catalyzed their action. Custom dictated that the high priest should officiate there on Sabbaths, at the feast of the new moon, and at the three pilgrim festivals. And of course, only the high priest could enter the Holy of Holies on the Day of Atonement. Without a high priest to officiate at the temple on that occasion, it is unclear how it could take place at all. If they had not selected their own high priest, the Zealots would have had to countenance the activity in the temple of the *quondam* 'nonsectarian' high priest. That man belonged to an opposing faction. Once they had taken control of the Jerusalem temple, therefore, they found it expedient to appoint a 'sectarian' high priest. But there was no temple at Masada. Consequently, unlike the Zealots, its residents had no need of a new high priest. Nothing indicates that they rejected the temple at Jerusalem, and they were apparently content to worship in a synagogue when they could not go there.

The suggestion that the Qumran Teacher of Righteousness was a high priest rests on a misunderstanding of the syntagm 'proper name + הכהן.'[150] Thus the probability that the Ananias referred to in this jar inscription was a sectarian high priest set up at Masada is exiguous. The case for connecting this *titulus pictus* with Ananias bar Nedebaeus can never be airtight, of course; but it is as solid as one is likely to find when attempting to reconcile realia with ancient historical narrative.

---

150 See my article 'The Teacher of Righteousness and the High Priest of the Intersacerdotium: Two Approaches', *RevQ* 14 (1989-90), pp. 587-613.

Excursus Two: The Relation of War 2.408 and 2.433

As noted above, Naveh's conclusion that Ananias bar Nedebaeus had died before the *sicarii* took Masada apparently depends on his reading of *War* 2.408 and 2.433 as duplicate accounts of the same events. This understanding was certainly defensible before the inscription under discussion here entered the picture. Indeed, it has been the view of many scholars who have pondered the relation of the two passages, and it may fairly be called the consensus position.[151] On this construction 2.433 recounts the one and only capture of Masada by the Jews, led by the man, Menahem, who was soon to murder Ananias. This reconciliation of the passages provides neither time nor rationale for Ananias to visit Masada. Yet, as a number of scholars had pointed out even before the inscription's publication, the equation of the two passages is by no means straightforward.[152]

One should note that Josephus calls the protagonists of 2.408 'some of those most fervently agitating for war' (τινὲς τῶν μάλιστα κινούντων τὸν πόλεμον). As there were a variety of rebels (στασιασταί) in Jerusalem and Judaea at this time, there is no particular reason to assume that this phrase refers to the *sicarii*. In 2.433, on the other hand, Josephus is manifestly concerned at least in part with that group, as he names one of its leaders, Menahem bar Judas. Further, the two passages describe different courses of action. In 2.408, the insurgents gain possession of the fortress by a trick (λάθρα), and killing the Roman garrison, install one of their own. In 2.433 there is no mention of any sort of dealing with the Romans nor of taking the fortress. It seems to be assumed that Masada is already under the control of the Jews. Menahem simply breaks into Herod's armory in

151 See, for example, P.W. Barnett, 'Under Tiberius All was Quiet', *NTS* 21 (1974), pp. 566; S.G.F. Brandon, 'The Zealots: The Jewish Resistance Against Rome, A.D. 6–73', *History Today* 15 (1965), p. 640; Goodman, *Ruling Class of Judea*, p. 169 n. 19 (Josephus' account is 'confused'); H.P. Kingdon, 'Who Were the Zealots and Their Leaders in A.D. 66?' *NTS* 17 (1970), p. 68; C. Roth, 'The Zealots in the War of 66-73', *JSS* 4 (1954), p. 340 (implicitly); Smallwood, *Jews Under Roman Rule*, p. 292 n. 119; Smith, 'Zealots and Sicarii', p. 18 n. 94, and Stern, 'Sicarii and Zealots', p. 274 (implicitly).

152 Scholars who take issue with the consensus include R.A. Horsley, 'Sicarii', 453, and Horsley and Hanson, *Bandits*, p. 212. Cohen, *Josephus in Galilee and Rome*, p. 193, does not come to a firm conclusion, but leans toward distinguishing the two accounts.

order to provide weapons for Jerusalemites and other 'brigands' (ληϲταί). 2.408 and 2.433 apparently refer to different groups and recount different events. If these two passages are understood as separate incidents, with some weeks between them—an entirely natural reading—then the constraints behind Naveh's labored interpretion of the jar inscription fall away.

Indeed, the decisive factor in the interpretation of the two passages and their interrelationship is the new jar inscription—once it is correctly understood, of course. A straightforward reading of the inscription as possessive requires that they refer to separate incidents. Accordingly, my differences with Naveh boil down to procedures: I would argue that the interpretive circle must begin with the jar, only afterwards coming round to Josephus. One must not allow the Jewish historian's tendentious narratives to mute the simple but elegant testimony of a sherd that, unlike him, was in a sense an eyewitness to the events at Masada.

Chapter Three

ACCIDENTS AND ACCIDENCE: A SCRIBAL VIEW OF LINGUISTIC DATING OF THE ARAMAIC SCROLLS FROM QUMRAN

Introduction

Habent sua fata libelli. As Terence remarked, books in Greco-Roman antiquity had their own fates—fates that were notoriously capricious. Any number of accidents could befall a book once it left the author's hand and was released to the public. Yet modern students of the language of such books have generally ignored the problems thus posed. Pursuing the study of accidence, they underestimate the potentially insidious effects of ancient caprice on their results. The fact is that accidents affect accidence.

Since all the Dead Sea Scrolls (DSS) lack colophons, linguistic analysis arose alongside paleographic typology as a method of dating the Aramaic texts.[1] The method's application began in earnest in 1958. In that year E. Y. Kutscher published a linguistic analysis of the Genesis Apocryphon (1QapGen) in which, *inter alia,* he attempted to establish the date of its composition on the basis of eight linguistic criteria.[2] Comparing the Qumran text principally to *Reichsaramäisch* and Biblical Aramaic (BA) on the one hand and to Palmyrene and Nabatean on the other, he concluded that it derived from the '1st century BCE[–1st century CE].'[3] His was not the first nor the only

---

1   The problems involved with paleographic dating are well described by R. Eisenman, *Maccabees, Zadokites, Christians and Qumran: A New Hypothesis of Qumran Origins* (Leiden: Brill, 1983), pp. 28-31 and 78-89, and S.A. Kaufman, 'The Pitfalls of Typology: On the Early History of the Alphabet', *HUCA* 57 (1986), pp. 1-14.

2   E.Y. Kutscher, 'The Language of the 'Genesis Apocryphon:' A Preliminary Study', *ScrHier* 4 (1958; [2]1965), pp. 1-35. Kutscher had already sketched his views in 'Dating the Language of the Genesis Apocryphon', *JBL* 76 (1957), pp. 288-92.

3   Kutscher, 'Preliminary Study', p. 22. Because of the way in which Kutscher

linguistic analysis of this scroll, but Kutscher's study soon ousted all rivals.[4] Although often cited in its own right, the influence of the study was greatly extended by the work of Joseph Fitzmyer, who adopted Kutscher's method and results in his commentary on 1QapGen.[5] Kutscher's work has become a benchmark to which constant reference is made, both in technical discussions and in many handbooks on Qumran and Second Temple Jewish literature.[6] Other students of the

phrased his conclusion, one generally finds his dating cited *either* as first century BCE *or* as first century CE; seldom have subsequent scholars paid attention to his extremely tentative wording. Despite that tentative wording, and the fact that he had reached his conclusions about the date of 1QapGen when virtually none of the Qumran and Bar Kochba Aramaic material had yet been published, Kutscher evidently maintained his view of the problem until his death. See his 'The Genesis Apocryphon of Qumran Cave I', *Or* 39 (1970), pp. 178-83, and 'Aramaic' in *Current Trends in Linguistics* 6 (The Hague: Mouton, 1970), pp. 402-3.

4   Other early studies of the language of the text include S. Zeitlin, 'Dating the Genesis Apocryphon', *JBL* 77 (1958), pp. 75-76 (the text is medieval); H.H. Rowley, 'Notes on the Aramaic of the Genesis Apocryphon', in *Hebrew and Semitic Studies Presented to Godfrey Rolles Driver,* eds. D. Winton Thomas and W.D. McHardy (Oxford: Clarendon Press, 1963), pp. 116-29 (the text dates from the second century BCE); and G.L. Archer, 'The Aramaic of the 'Genesis Apocryphon' Compared with the Aramaic of Daniel', in *New Perspectives on the Old Testament,* ed. J. Barton Payne (Waco, Texas: Word, 1970), pp. 160-9 (Kutscher's date is right).

5   J. Fitzmyer, *The Genesis Apocryphon of Qumran Cave 1: A Commentary* (Rome: Biblical Institute Press, 1971), pp. 16-19.

6   A few examples chosen from among different kinds of discussions will give some idea of the extent of the study's influence: J. Barr, 'Hebrew, Aramaic and Greek in the Hellenistic Age', in *The Cambridge History of Judaism Volume Two: The Hellenistic Age,* eds. W.D. Davies and L. Finkelstein (Cambridge: University Press, 1989), pp. 92-3; D.J. Harrington, 'Palestinian Adaptations of Biblical Narratives and Prophecies I: The Bible Rewritten (Narratives)', in *Early Judaism and its Modern Interpreters,* eds. R.A. Kraft and G.W.E. Nickelsburg (Philadelphia: Fortress Press, 1986), p. 244; M.A. Knibb, *The Qumran Community* (Cambridge: University Press, 1987), p. 183; H. Lignée, 'L'Apocryphe de la Genèse', in *Les Textes de Qumran,* eds. J. Carmignac, P. Guilbert, É. Cothenet and H. Lignée (Paris: Éditions Letouzey et Ané, 1961-63), 2, pp. 215; L. Moraldi, *I manuscritti di Qumran* (Turin: Unione Tipografico, 1971), p. 607; T. Muraoka, 'The Aramaic of the Genesis Apocryphon', *RevQ* 8 (1972-75), pp. 7-51 *passim;* G.W.E. Nickelsburg, *Jewish Literature Between the Bible and the Mishnah* (Philadelphia: Fortress Press, 1981), pp. 265 and 272; and idem, 'The Bible Rewritten and Expanded', in *Jewish Writings of the Second Temple Period,* ed. M. Stone (Philadelphia: Fortress Press, 1984), p. 106.

Aramaic Qumran texts have ratified his method by applying it to the
dating of the Aramaic New Jerusalem (5Q15),[7] 4QAmram,[8] the Prayer
of Nabonidus (4QPrNab),[9] the 4Q Enoch texts,[10] and the Targum to Job
(11QtgJob).[11]

Among Kutscher's followers the most meticulous exponent of dating
by analyzing linguistic features has been Michael Sokoloff. His edition
of 11QtgJob serves as a parade example of the method's strengths and
weaknesses.[12] While Kutscher had relied on only eight linguistic
criteria in his analysis, Sokoloff expanded the repertoire to thirty-two.
Mainly comparing BA, 11QtgJob and 1QapGen, he grouped his results
into five categories viewed from the perspective of the targum. He thus
arrived at the following schema:

1. Linguistic phenomena like BA   16
2. Between BA and 1QapGen   6
3. Like 1QapGen   3
4. Later than 1QapGen   3

---

7   J.T. Milik, DJD 3, p. 184.
8   P. Kobelski, *Melchizedek and Melchireša^c* (CBQMS 10; Washington, D.C.:
Catholic Biblical Associates of America, 1981), p. 26.
9   J.T. Milik, '"Prière de Nabonide" et autres écrits d'un cycle de Daniel,
fragments de Qumrân 4' *RB* 63 (1956), p. 407.
10   M. Sokoloff, 'Notes on the Aramaic Fragments of Enoch from Qumran Cave
4', *Maarav* 1 (1979), 202-3, referring to 4QEn^a.
11   Thus in the *editio princeps*, J.P.M. van der Ploeg and A.S. van der Woude, *Le
Targum de Job de la Grotte XI de Qumrân* (Leiden: Brill, 1971), pp. 3-4, and since
in M. Delcor, 'Le targum de Job et l'araméen du temps de Jésus', *RevScRel* 47
(1973), pp. 239-40; J.A. Fitzmyer, 'The First Century Targum of Job from Qumran
Cave 11', in *A Wandering Aramean: Collected Aramaic Essays* (Missoula:
Scholars Press, 1979), pp. 164-5; S.A. Kaufman, 'The Job Targum from Qumran',
JAOS 93 (1973), 325-6; T. Muraoka, 'The Aramaic of the Old Targum of Job from
Qumran Cave XI', *JJS* 25 (1974), pp. 441-42, and idem, 'On the Language of the
Targum to the Book of Job from Qumran', *Proceedings of the Sixth World
Congress on Jewish Studies* 1 (1977), pp. 159-65 (Heb.). Delcor and Fitzmyer
agree with the date suggested in the *editio princeps*, i.e., the latter portion of the
second century BCE. Kaufman suggests the first century BCE, while Muraoka
proposes 250-150 BCE. Based on a small portion of the targum published prior to
the *editio princeps*, S. Segert came to conclusions about the date similar to
Sokoloff's (see below); see 'Sprachliche Bermerkungen zu einigen aramäischen
Texten von Qumran', *ArOr* 33 (1965), pp. 201-2.
12   M. Sokoloff, *The Targum to Job from Qumran Cave XI (Ramat Gan: Bar-
Ilan University*, 1974), pp. 9-25.

5. Inconclusive or traits common to all three   4

Sokoloff concluded,[13]

> . . . most of the linguistic traits of [11QtgJob] analyzed in this
> chapter are either common with BA or are intermediate between
> BA and [1QapGen]. In a few traits [11QtgJob] agrees with
> [1QapGen] while in several it is linguistically later than
> [1QapGen]. The date of composition of [11QtgJob] is thus placed
> sometime between [Daniel] and [1QapGen], and—if a date may
> be hazarded—probably sometime in the late second century BCE.

Reviewers of Sokoloff's volume were enthusiastic about his linguistic
rigor,[14] and as a whole the book is strong in this regard, particularly in
its exploitation of comparative Aramaic evidence.

But fundamental problems undermine this attempt at linguistic
dating of the targum. These problems include Sokoloff's treatment of
the 'lynchpins', BA and 1QapGen;[15] his decisions about how to

---

13   Sokoloff, *The Targum to Job*, 25.
14   G. Vadja, in his review in REJ 14 (1975), p. 169, refers to Sokoloff's 'grande
précision à l'investigation linguistique;' see similar indications of approval in the
sampling represented by P.S. Alexander, *JTS* 27 (1976), pp. 166-8; P. Grelot, *RevQ*
9 (1977), pp. 267-71; L. Frizzell, *CBQ* 37 (1975), p. 427; B. Jongeling, *JSJ* 6
(1975), pp. 117-20; T. Muraoka, *BO* 35 (1978), pp. 318-22; D. Pardee, *JNES* 36
(1977), pp. 216-7; G. Pfeifer, *OLZ* 73 (1978), pp. 562-3; N. Sarna, *IEJ* 26 (1976),
pp. 151-3, L. Schiffman, *JBL* 95 (1976), pp. 158-60; J.A. Soggin, *RSO* 50 (1976),
pp. 404-6, and P. Wernberg-Møller, *JSS* 24 (1979), pp. 119-20.
15   With regard to BA, Sokoloff is insufficiently attentive to the fact that BA is
itself not a uniform entity. The language of Daniel is not exactly that of Ezra; the
consonantal texts reflect a language somewhat different from that of the vocalized
traditions. Furthermore, no less than the DSS, our evidence for BA is also scribal,
so that the language of the period in which the books of Daniel and Ezra were
composed is not exactly what has come down to us. The collection of forms found
in the Masoretic Text (MT) is to an unknown extent 'arbitrary.' This problem is
particularly acute with regard to Sokoloff's orthographic analysis, and appears in
clear relief when one compares the published Qumran portions of the Aramaic of
Daniel with the MT. These fragments cover almost exactly half of the verses of
Daniel 2–7, in whole or in part (105 verses are represented, with only eight
overlapping between any two MSS). They are published in D. Barthélemy, DJD 1,
pp. 150-2; E. Ulrich, 'Daniel Manuscripts from Qumran. Part 1: A Preliminary
Edition of 4QDan[a]', *BASOR* 268 (1987), pp. 17-38; and *idem*, 'Daniel Manuscripts
from Qumran. Part 2: Preliminary Editions of 4QDan[b] and 4QDan[c]', *BASOR* 274

categorize his data;[16] the fact that fully half of his categories revolve

(1989), pp. 3-26. A collation of 1Q71, 1Q72, 4QDan[a] and 4QDan[b] in terms of Sokoloff's categories results in the following:

Categories involving alternation between *aleph* and *heh* (see note 17 below): 1ab.1 4QDan[a] 6 differences from MT 4QDan[b] 2 differences from MT // 1ab.2 4QDanb 1 difference (etc.) // 1ab.4 4QDan[b] 1 // 2 1Q71 2 1Q72 2 4QDan[a] 3 4QDan[b] 3 // 6 1Q72 1 4QDan[a] 4 4QDan[b] 2. Other categories: 3 1Q72 1 // 4 1Q72 2 // 5 1Q72 5 // 8 4QDan[a] 2 4QDan[b] 1 // 9 4QDan[a] 2 4QDan[b] 3 (relevant, but not equivalent, changes) // 13 4QDan[a] 1 // 14 4QDan[a] 3.

The variations from the MT total 47, or about one for every two verses of the biblical text. Here it is important to emphasize that many of the verses found in the Qumran Daniel mss are very fragmentary; presumably, if they were fully attested, the number of variants would increase significantly. And it is fair to presume that if more than four mss containing portions of Aramaic Daniel had turned up in the Caves, the number of variants would have multiplied still further. As for Sokoloff's treatment of 1QapGen, he builds his case for dating 11QtgJob in part upon an unquestioned acceptance of Kutscher's dating for the apocryphon (which date he understands as first century BCE). With the date of 1QapGen thus settled, after his analysis of the targum he simply backdates from that lynchpin. Yet in his own analysis of 11QtgJob, he explicitly or implicitly rejects all but three of Kutscher's eight criteria for linguistic dating. One would think that Sokoloff would then find it necessary to reconsider the date of 1QapGen, but he does not.

16   The difficulties here include, *inter alia*, the following:

(1) The *question of which categories to use*. Sokoloff never justifies his selection. Obviously the choice of categories is crucial because it has the potential to prejudice the final conclusions. For example, Sokoloff does not include Kutscher's criterion of the absence or presence of ית. The particle occurs in 11QtgJob but not in 1QapGen. In Sokoloff's terms, therefore, it would be a category in which the targum was 'later than 1QapGen.' Also, he does not include word-order as a category. Its inclusion might have changed the complexion of his study somewhat (see Muraoka, 'Aramaic', 441-2, and cf. R. Buth, 'Aramaic Word Order from the Perspectives of Functional Grammar and Discourse Analysis [Ph.D. Dissertation, UCLA, 1987], pp. 430-56 and 466-72).

(2) The *categorization of data typologically earlier than BA*. Sokoloff operates on the assumption that BA is the *terminus a quo* for his linguistic analysis, but strictly speaking both Qumran texts occasionally manifest earlier forms than one finds in BA. For example, Sokoloff's category 10, regarding the 3f.pl. forms: the consonantal text of BA does not distinguish these from 3m.pl., but both Qumran texts do. In the same vein, Sokoloff treats phenomena of 11QtgJob which are 'like BA' as the equivalent of 'earlier than 1QapGen' (note here even the physical arrangement of his data on p. 25). In fact, of course, 'like BA' could also mean 'later than 1QapGen' (e.g., the way the two handle etymological /ś/, Sokoloff's category 5), or 'inconclusive' (Sokoloff's category 9, for example, amounts to one

in which all three texts really represent the same treatment of the linguistic situation, although Sokoloff ends up categorizing the targum as 'like BA', making it appear earlier than 1QapGen).

(3) *The categorization of data in cases where 1QapGen and 11QtgJob differ both from BA and from each other.* This material should be considered 'inconclusive', but Sokoloff regularly categorizes it elsewhere—always with the effect of making the targum appear older. For example, with regard to the elision of *aleph* in I-*aleph* verbs, BA always retains the letter except in certain forms of אמר. 11QtgJob sometimes retains, sometimes elides the *aleph,* but more often retains it (the ratio is 10:3). Concerning 1QapGen Sokoloff says on p. 16 'Though the evidence in GAp and *in other QA texts* is sparse, it seems to show a greater tendency to elision than in Tg1' (emphasis mine). When Sokoloff brings in other texts here arbitrarily—he does not do so for all of his categories, only a select few—he obscures the actual relationships between BA, 11QtgJob and 1QapGen. In fact the evidence of the apocryphon is precisely the opposite of his statement: the scroll always retains the *aleph,* for a ratio of 7:0 (תאמר 2:13, 20:26; אול imperative (!) 5:10, 20:23, 27; 21:13; תאכלון 11:17). If any distinction were to be made between the Qumran texts, one would think that 1QapGen should antedate 11QtgJob—but Sokoloff concludes that here 11QtgJob is 'between' BA and the apocryphon.

(4) *The category Sokoloff characterizes as being 'between BA and 1QapGen'.* As in point 3 above, Sokoloff often considers the phenomena of 11QtgJob as 'between' when it could better be said that both Qumran texts are simply unlike BA. The development implied by the word 'between' is not always apparent. Sokoloff's category 1ab.3 exemplifies my point. This category treats the alternating use of *heh* and *aleph* to represent the final syllable of the infinitive of the derived verbal conjugations. BA mostly uses *heh,* 11QtgJob uses the two equally (4:4), and 1QapGen always uses *aleph.* Sokoloff concludes therefrom that the targum is midway between the two other texts, and so it is, of course, with respect to scribal usage. But is that really the same as being 'between' chronologically? For the dialects covered by G. Dalman, *Grammatik des Jüdisch-Palästinischen Aramäisch* (reprint Darmstadt: Wissenschaftliche Buchgesellschaft, 1981), for example, the attestation on this point is mixed (pp. 281-2; Dalman is not attempting to give a complete listing). The same can be said for the language of Targum Neofiti (D. Golomb, *A Grammar of Targum Neofiti* [Chico: Scholars Press, 1985), 130, 133, 135, and 176-85). Thus on this point 11QtgJob is more like a dialect of (Sokoloff's) later 'Middle Western Aramaic' than it is like either of the other texts with which Sokoloff compares it. No chronological development is evident.

(5) *The superficial grouping of evidence in a way that obscures complex interrelationships.* Space precludes a full discussion, but this problem particularly plagues Sokoloff's categories 2, 9, 12 and 14. Category 14, the pronominal possessive suffixes, is a clear example. Here the targum is the same as the consonantal text of BA except for 3f.pl. (but note: this *is* a difference). 1QapGen varies from BA, but Sokoloff concedes that the difference is largely orthographic.

around what is really a single phenomenon, the alternation of *heh* and
aleph;[17] and his implicit premise that linguistic factors are best assessed

His case therefore essentially rests on the apocryphon's forms אזוי for the expected
אחוהי (one occurrence) and מדיתון for the expected מדינתהון (also one occurrence).
The second form is actually a scribal error, however; there are problems not only
with this word but with several around it (see S.A. Kaufman, 'The History of
Aramaic Vowel Reduction', in *Arameans, Aramaic and the Aramaic Literary
Tradition,* ed. M. Sokoloff [Ramat Gan: Bar-Ilan University, 1983], pp. 51-2). One
is left with a situation in which each Qumran text differs from BA once. How
should such situations be adjudicated? Sokoloff's conclusion: 11QtgJob here is
'like BA', and therefore older than 1QapGen. This is an understandable conclusion,
perhaps, but it is by no means mandated. Sokoloff's method does not provide for a
more nuanced appraisal of such cases.

17   Sokoloff never addresses the fact that these two letters were virtually silent
and thus homophones. As *Vokalträger*, the alternation of these letters can be
regarded neither as a problem of morphology nor of phonology, although Sokoloff
treats it as both in different connections. In fact the alternation is a problem only of
orthography or, more properly, 'graphology' (implicit in the term 'orthography' is
the dubious assumption that there was a single standard followed by all groups and
individuals who produced texts). The scribes and authors of the Qumran texts could
not hear the difference between an *aleph* and a *heh*, and, since ancient composition
and copying were both done as much by ear as by eye (see the discussion below),
'errors' or variations could easily enter a text—or not. Taking the case of the use of
the *Haphel* vis à vis the *Aphel*, for example (whatever the meaning of their
alternation in earlier texts such as Cowley's collection versus the Hermopolis
papyri—see E.Y. Kutscher, *A History of Aramaic Part I* [Jerusalem: Hebrew
University, 1973] pp. 87-8 [Heb.]), a selection of noteworthy forms underscores my
point for the period of the Qumran texts. (I draw examples from both Aramaic and
Hebrew texts, since this phenomenon applies to both; in Judaea these languages
had entered into an *adstratum* relationship during the Persian era). In 5/6HevEp 1
line 3 (see the photograph in Y. Yadin, *Bar Kokhba* [London: Weidenfeld and
Nicholson, 1971], p. 122) one reads the following phrase ית חנטיא די החת חנון, 'the
corn which Hanun brought down'—a *Haphel*, in a text fully sixty years younger
than 1QapGen could possibly be (note: Beyer, *Texte,* 351 misreads this phrase; J.
Fitzmyer and D. Harrington, *A Manual of Palestinian Aramaic Texts* [Rome:
Biblical Institute Press, 1978], p. 158 does not include it). Similarly, an ostracon
which A. Yardeni recently published in 'New Jewish Aramaic Ostraca from Israel',
Tarbiz 58 (1988), pp. 123-7 (Heb.), contains the *Haphel* הסקת twice (lines 4 and 8)
alongside an equal number of *Aphels*. Yardeni dates the ostracon to the first century
CE. In the year 128 CE the *hypographeus* to Papyrus Yadin (= PapYad) 18, Judah b.
Eleazar Khthousion, wrote הקתת 'I hereby give (my daughter in marriage)'—see N.
Lewis, Y. Yadin and J. Greenfield, (eds.), *The Documents from the Bar Kokhba
Period in the Cave of Letters* (Jerusalem: Israel Exploration Society, 1989), pp.

by counting rather than weighing.[18] In fact, operating on his

142-3 and plates 18-19. Here again a *Haphel* turns up in a text much later than 1QapGen. In Hebrew texts, one encounters אשכיל for השכיל at 4Q381 15 8 (see E. Schuller, *Non-Canonical Psalms from Qumran: A Pseudepigraphic Collection* [Atlanta: Scholars Press, 1986]). And—one last example—in a Hebrew contract from the time of Bar Kochba one reads הלו אחכרתי לך, '... this I rent to you for payment in kind' (photograph Yadin, *Bar Kokhba*, p. 179). With *Haphels* attested in Aramaic texts firmly dated later than the latest possible date for 1QapGen, and with *Aphels* appearing in coeval Hebrew texts, the point should require no further elaboration. How then is the fact that only *Aphels* occur in the apocryphon to be explained, since it is not a chronological indicator? Scribal leveling, a constant feature of scribal textual transmission, is a likely possible answer; so is the possibility that this usage, along with other features peculiar to 1QapGen, was the habit of a particular scribal school. For further discussion of the alternation of *heh* and *aleph*, see E.Y. Kutscher, *The Language and Linguistic Background of the Isaiah Scroll* (IQIsaᵃ) (Leiden: Brill, 1974), pp. 505-10, and E. Qimron, *The Hebrew of the Dead Sea Scrolls* (Atlanta: Scholars Press, 1986), §§ 100.51, 100.7, and especially 200.11.

18   Sokoloff simply counts up his forms (sometimes they do double duty, as in categories 16 and 18) and decides that 'most' of them support his conclusion as to dating. But should two instances of אן rather than הן in 1QapGen, for example, really count only as much as the apparently substantial loss of distinction between status absolutus and *status emphaticus* in 11QtgJob? Incidentally, the question of the loss of this distinction is complicated. On the one hand Muraoka, 'Aramaic', 432, adduces a number of examples in addition to those suggested by Sokoloff, and concludes that the breakdown in the distinction of usage reflects an Eastern provenance for the targum. Kaufman's contrasting observation on this phenomenon should also be borne in mind ('Job Targum', 324): the use of the *status* may be distinct, and simply reflect an understanding different from that of the MT on whether a given Hebrew phrase in Job is definite or indefinite. Regardless of how the instances in the targum are resolved (Kaufman's position, by its very nature, can be neither proved nor disproved), some evidence does suggest a breakdown had occurred in (certain speech communities of [?]) Judaean Aramaic by the time of the First Revolt. One reads in a fragmentary letter found at Masada the phrase כול אנשא, where the intended meaning can only be 'every man' (cf. 11QtgJob 26:3 בר אנש versus 28:2 בני אנשא). And in Murabbaᶜat 19, lines 6 and 18, one finds the contrast אנתא and אנת, '(as a) wife', where the referrent and meaning are the same in both instances. The witness of the latter text is particularly valuable, for its many peculiarities are best explained as the attempt of someone other than a professional scribe at composing a legal document. It is *ipso facto* better evidence for linguistic change than is a scribal copy of a literary text. For the fragmentary letter see J. Aviram, G. Foerster and E. Netzer (eds.), *Masada I: The Yigael Yadin Excavations, 1963-65. Final Reports. The Aramaic and Hebrew Ostraca and Jar Inscriptions,*

assumptions, one could turn Sokoloff's conclusions on their head, and argue that 1QapGen is older than 11QtgJob.[19]

But I do not want to operate on Sokoloff's assumptions. Instead I want to consider more carefully the question of the fate of books, and its implications for linguistic dating as a method. In what follows the focus will be on two aspects of first-century Palestine that were inextricably bound up with the production and subsequent fate of the Aramaic DSS: (1) the linguistic milieu in which scribes and scholars pursued their goals, and (2) the nature of the book culture in the Greco-Roman world. As Sokoloff's attempt so clearly exemplifies, linguistic dating of the texts is at best fraught with difficulties. But is it even possible? I will argue that it is not.

The Use of Aramaic in Palestine

The linguistic milieu informing the composition and copying of the Aramaic DSS was remarkably rich.[20] The Jews of Palestine used

Yigael Yadin and Joseph Naveh. The Coins of Masada, Yaacov Meshorer (Jerusalem: Israel Exploration Society, 1989), #556 and plate 45. For Murabbaᶜat 19 see J.T. Milik, DJD 2, 104-9 and plates 30-31. On its dating to the time of the First Revolt, see Y. Yadin, 'The Excavation of Masada—1963/64: Preliminary Report', IEJ 15 (1965), p. 119 n. 112, and E. Koffmann, *Die Doppelurkunden aus der Wuste Juda* (Leiden: Brill, 1968), pp. 42-5; R. Hestrin, *et al.*, *Inscriptions Reveal* (Jerusalem: Israel Museum, 1972), p. 189 (Heb.), and Beyer, *Texte*, p. 307.
19 On the basis of the problems discussed in notes 15-17 above, I would rearrange Sokoloff's data as follows: Similar to BA—1ab.2; 5; 16; 17; 18; 20—total 6; Between BA and 1QapGen—1ab.9; 2; 6—total 3; Similar to 1QapGen—1ab.6; 1ab.10; 10—total 3; Later than 1QapGen—1ab.8; 7; 15; 19; 21—total 5; Inconclusive—1ab.1; 1ab.3; 1ab.4; 1ab.5; 1ab.7; 1ab.11; 3; 4; 8; 9; 11; 12; 13; 14—total 15. Seen in this light, Sokoloff's conclusion that most of the phenomena of 11QtgJob point to a time of composition near BA does not hold up. And one can approach the matter in yet another way: arrange the data from the perspective of 1QapGen, *mutatis mutandis*, rather than from that of 11QtgJob. In such a scheme I would group the following data of Sokoloff's study in a category entitled 'Similar to or earlier than BA:' 1ab.1; 1ab.4; 1ab.5; 1ab.7; 1ab.8; 1ab.11; 5; 7; 9; 10; 11; 15. One thus reaches a total of fifteen categories in which 1QapGen resembles BA, as opposed to a mere six for 11QtgJob.
20 This statement obviously assumes a Palestinian provenance for these texts. The assumption seems warranted in view of where they were discovered, and in view of the lack of any categorical indications to the contrary. But if it is true, as discussed below, that the Aramaic DSS were composed in a form of Aramaic

Hebrew, Greek, Latin and, at least for writing, Nabatean in addition to Aramaic; alongside Hebrew, Aramaic was the most widely employed.[21] The question is, how did this situation come to pass? How did Aramaic come to play such a significant role among the Jews, not merely as a written language, but also as a spoken one? Space precludes more than a brief sketch, but essentially there are two competing models that seek to answer this question. The differences between the two models are to some extent merely a matter of emphasis, but the implications to which the different emphases give rise result in contrary evaluations of linguistic dating; they therefore loom large in the discussion at hand.

The first model is that of the spreading *lingua franca*. This model undergirds Fitzmyer's approach to linguistic dating in particular. *Linguae francae* arise because of linguistic diversity, and the need for communication among groups who do not speak each other's vernaculars.[22] During the Assyrian hegemony a form of Aramaic served this function (at least in the West), and for the period of the Neo-Babylonian and Persian empires this practice continued.[23] Subsequent

which was used throughout the Near East for literary works, their original composition, at any rate, certainly could have been elsewhere. The scripts in which they have been transmitted argue that their tradents were Palestinian.

21   See the discussion by J.A. Fitzmyer, 'The Languages of Palestine in the First Century A.D.', in *A Wandering Aramaean: Collected Aramaic Essays* (Missoula: Scholars Press, 1979), pp. 29-56. To his discussion of Latin and Greek add now particularly the materials in J. Aviram, G. Foerster and E. Netzer (eds.), *Masada II: The Yigael Yadin Excavations, 1963-65. Final Reports. The Latin and Greek Documents, Hannah M. Cotton and Joseph Geiger* (Jerusalem: Israel Exploration Society, 1989). Fitzmyer does not discuss the use of Nabatean by Jews, but the documents of the Babatha archive show that Jews moved back and forth from Judaea and Peraea to Nabatean regions. Among the Masada finds are several jars indicating the presence of refugees in the fortress who were most comfortable writing in Nabatean script. Jar 468 bears a proper name which is apparently Nabatean, and jars 514 and 515 are inscribed with Nabatean cursive script. See Aviram, *et al.*, *Masada I*, 40 and 44, and plates 32 and 39, respectively. In addition, note 4Q343, a letter in Nabatean, on which see P. Benoit, et al., 'Editing the Manuscript Fragments from Qumran', *BA* 19 (1956), p. 96.

22   On *linguae francae* see W.J. Samarin, 'Lingua Francas of the World', in *Readings in the Sociology of Language*, ed. J. Fishman (The Hague: Mouton, 1968), pp. 660-72.

23   For the Assyrian period see e.g., H. Tadmor, 'The Aramaization of Assyria: Aspects of Western Impact', in *Mesopotamien und seine Nachbarn*, eds. H.-J. Nissen and J. Renger (Berlin: Dietrich Reimer Verlag, 1982), pp. 49-70. For the

to the breakdown of the Persian empire, Fitzmyer sees a number of distinct 'local dialects' emerging from the *lingua franca*.[24] Although in the case of Palestinian Aramaic he would acknowledge some differences between the spoken and written forms, he sees them as slight.[25] For him, the *lingua franca* became the vernacular, and as time passed, it changed somewhat as spoken languages are wont to do. At the time of its emergence Qumran Aramaic is essentially the spoken language of Judaea. Therefore, for Fitzmyer linguistic differences from text to text constitute a valid measure of language change. It follows that they are also precious indicators of a text's date of composition.

This view portrays Aramaic influence on the people of Judah—and later, the Jews—as coming almost entirely through a single channel: the language spoken by the élite. Presumably the prestige of its speakers made this *lingua franca* so attractive to lower sectors of society that they, too, strove to acquire it. Thus this form of Aramaic eventually filtered down and even villagers in outlying hamlets came under its sway. Yet the historical and sociological obstacles standing in the way of this explanation are formidable.

It must be recalled that Judaean interaction with Aramaic speakers did not begin with the rise of the Persians or even the Assyrians. David fought against the Aramaic kingdoms of Aram-Zobah and Aram-Beth-Rehob. Later, the kingdom of Aram-Damascus became the foremost Syrian Aramaean state, and during the ninth and eighth centuries BCE this kingdom was embroiled in the disputes between Judah and Israel.[26]

In that period the region of the upper Transjordan, reaching to Ramoth-Gilead in the south, came to comprise a mixed Israelite-

later periods see e.g., J. Greenfield, 'Aramaic in the Achaemenian Empire', in *The Cambridge History of Iran. Vol. 2: The Median and Achaemenian Periods*, ed. I. Gershevitch (Cambridge: University Press, 1985), pp. 698-713 and 918-22.

24   J.A. Fitzmyer, 'The Phases of the Aramaic Language', in *Wandering Aramaean*, pp. 61-2 and 71-4.

25   Note Fitzmyer's declaration in 'Methodology in the Study of the Aramaic Substratum of Jesus' Sayings in the New Testament', in *Jésus aux origines de la christologie*, ed. J. Dupont (Louvain: Leuven University, 1975), p. 86: 'I remain very skeptical about the alleged differences between the literary and spoken forms of Aramaic of this period.' Cf. his statements in 'Languages of Palestine', p. 39, and his review of M. Black, *An Aramaic Approach to the Gospels and Acts* (Oxford: Clarendon Press, [3]1967), in *CBQ* 30 (1968), pp. 417-28.

26   E.g. 1 Kgs 15.18-19.

Aramaean population.[27] The region was alternately a part of Aram-Damascus and then of Israel. This situation must have resulted in some measure of cultural and linguistic assimilation.[28] In battles against Shalmaneser III of Assyria between 853–845 BCE, Israelite soldiers fought shoulder-to-shoulder with Aramaeans. During this same period, of course, Israel had a multifaceted relationship with Judah, and so presumably served as a kind of conduit for a certain degree of Aramaic influence. Under king Hazael Aram-Damascus conquered regions as far south as the Arnon in the west and Gath in the east, and forced Judah to pay tribute.[29] At the time of the Syro-Ephraimite war Rezin of Damascus annexed territory down to Ramoth-Gilead, and waged war against Jotham and Ahaz of Judah. The latter king went so far as to introduce the Damascus cult at Jerusalem. He 'passed his son through fire,' evidently in the manner of the Aramaean rites for Hadad-melek.[30] In the postexilic period the Judaeans worshipped Hadad-Rimmon of Damascus in the plain of Megiddo.[31] And, of course, the 'Jews' of Elephantine, whether they hailed from Israel or—as I suspect—Judah, worshipped the Aramaean god Bethel.[32] Thus the Judaean interaction with the Aramaean tribes of Syria, whether through war or trade, whether direct or through Israelite channels, was considerable.

After the Neo-Assyrian empire rose to power, it was their policy to punish vanquished enemies with mass deportation and population exchange. Bustenay Oded estimates that over the several centuries in which this deportation was practiced, some 4.5 million people were involved.[33] Such huge population shifts had the potential to alter the linguistic map of the region profoundly, and Judaea was in the thick of much of the movement.

One mechanism by which this linguistic effect might have been

---

27   1 Chr. 2.23 and 7.14.
28   The linguistic effect is perhaps seen in the Aramaic or Aramaizing inscription from Deir 'Alla. For the most recent studies on this text see J. Hoftijzer and G. van der Kooij, *The Balaam Text from Deir Alla Re-evaluated* (Leiden: Brill, 1991).
29   2 Kgs 12.17-18.
30   2 Kgs 16.3.
31   Zech. 12.11.
32   See the discussion in B. Porten, *Archives From Elephantine* (Berkeley: University of California Press, 1968), pp. 164-89. Porten seeks to minimize the evidence for syncretism, but in my view the sources point to a different conclusion.
33   B. Oded, *Mass Deportations and Deportees in the Neo-Assyrian Empire* (Wiesbaden: Dr. Ludwig Reichert Verlag, 1979), p. 20.

realized was trade. Peoples from the east, largely if not entirely Aramaic or Chaldean tribesmen, replaced or were added to the native populations in important stations on the Mediterranean coastal trade route, such as the cities of Phoenicia and Gaza.[34] This trade route passed not far west of Judah, and a branch turned east through Gezer to Jerusalem. Even where the native population remained, the Assyrians placed themselves and Aramaic-speaking elements of their population along the major trade routes throughout the empire, in order to guarantee that they stayed open. Mercantile activity in the west would thus involve speakers of more or less diverse Aramaic dialects.[35]

Of perhaps the greatest significance for Judah were two particular relocations, placing Chaldeans and other eastern Aramaean tribes in Ashdod and Samaria. Tiglath-Pileser III installed Chaldeans and others in Ashdod, some as charioteers and cavalry; Sargon II resettled Ashdod and its daughter villages with more deportees from the east.[36] As the native and deported elements blended, the linguistic character of Ashdod presumably changed, with the spoken Aramaic dialects of the deportees an important ingredient in the recipe. This fact is meaningful for Judah because, according to Neh. 13.23-4, certain members of the Jerusalem temple community intermarried with people from Ashdod. A significant proportion of the children of these marriages were unable to speak Hebrew, knowing only אשדודית. Scholars are divided on the question of what language this designation represents,[37] but in light of the ethnic makeup of Ashdod it is plausible that it refers to an eastern or spoken dialect of Aramaic.[38] It is unlikely to refer to the *lingua*

---

34 For Phoenicia, Tiglath-Pileser III settled tribes from Babylonia in Simirra, and Esarhaddon built Kar-Esarhaddon near Sidon and populated it with Aramaeans. Sargon II settled deportees (of uncertain origin) in Nahal-Musur near Gaza. See Oded, Mass Deportations , pp. 27-8 and 65-7.

35 Oded, *Mass Deportations*, p. 44, n.20 and 49.

36 Oded, *Mass Deportations*, pp. 27, 51-2 and 63.

37 For the discussion see e.g., H.G.M. Williamson, *Ezra, Nehemiah* (Waco, Texas: Word, 1985), p. 398.

38 For the use of Aramaic in Ashdod one may note the ostracon found there, thought to date to the mid-fifth century, only a generation or so before Nehemiah's confrontation with those who had intermarried. Unfortunately the inscription is so short that dialect characteristics are not apparent; indeed, even the language is not absolutely certain. See J. Naveh, 'An Aramaic Ostracon from Ashdod', *Atiqot* 9-10 (1971), pp. 200-1.

franca form of the language, since that was known as אֲרָמִית.[39] Incidentally, if even the members of the exclusivist *golah* group were intermarrying in numbers sufficient to endanger the continued role of Hebrew, it seems fair to assume that among the 'peoples of the land' (Judaeans not belonging to the *golah*) the rate of intermarriage with surrounding peoples—some Aramaic speaking—was even greater.[40]

The settlements of deportees from the east by Sargon II, Esarhaddon and Assurbanipal in the city and province of Samaria (including Gezer) was again portentous for Judah.[41] All of these settlers came from the regions near Babylon and presumably, therefore, spoke various dialects of Aramaic.[42] Since these settlers essentially replaced the élite of Israel in Samaria, which became the capital of the Assyrian province of the same name and then, later, of the Persian province, their language habits would have been influential. Further, during the Achaemenid years Samaria may have ruled Judaea at times, and certainly had considerable influence through intermarriage and cultic connections.[43] Intermarriage between the ruling circles of Jerusalem and Samaria continued into the Hellenistic period at least.[44] Perhaps marriages linking north and south were not uncommon at the lower levels of society either. And of course, at the beginning of the Persian period there was the influence of the repatriated Jews coming from Babylon. While these people may well have retained Hebrew as a home language during the period of the exile, they presumably had also acquired one or more spoken varieties of Aramaic and, in certain cases, command of the written *lingua franca* form as well.

In the early centuries of its advance into Judah, then, Aramaic came

39   2 Kgs 18.26.
40   It is generally agreed that the *golah* group opposed the assimilationist tendencies which characterized the 'peoples of the land.' I assume that such assimilation would manifest itself not only in a greater openness to the religious practices of the surrounding peoples, but also in less clearly defined group boundaries.
41   Oded, *Mass Deportations*, pp. 28-9 and 96. The biblical texts are 2 Kgs 17.24-41, Ezra 4.1-2 and 9-10.
42   For their provenance as near Babylon and not northern Syria see R. Zadok, 'Geographical and Onomastic Notes', *JANESCU* 8 (1976), pp. 113-26.
43   For intermarriage, note Neh. 13.28. For cultic connections, many proofs could be adduced, but the implications of Cowley 30 and the reply (Cowley 27) will suffice to make the point. See Cowley, *Papyri*.
44   Thus Josephus *Ant*. 11.306-12.

by various avenues and, doubtless, in various forms. East met west within its borders. One influence, and a weighty one, was that of the *lingua franca*. But spoken dialects more or less divergent from the standard must have been an important influence as well. Adjusting the focus to a later period—the centuries during which the Aramaic DSS may have been composed (c. 200 BCE to c. 70 CE)—speakers of different forms of Aramaic continued to flow into Judah. For example, when the Parthians conquered Babylonia in the second century BCE, Jewish refugees would have flooded Jerusalem and vicinity. Peaceful intrusion in the form of pilgrimage from Babylonia and elsewhere would again have brought Eastern Aramaic speakers to Jerusalem, some deciding to settle permanently. Such movements would have added to the linguistic complexity in Judaea.

By now the point is clear, and further historical elaboration is unnecessary. What this broader view of Aramaic influences supports is the second model explaining the role of Aramaic at the time of the scrolls: the model of diglossia. At the time of the Hasmonean rise to power, different forms of Aramaic, when and where it was used, served for the written as opposed to the spoken language.[45] The written language was a standard form based on the old *lingua franca* of Achaemenian days. The people of Judaea were familiar with a reasonably extensive literature in this written standard, including Tobit, portions of Enoch, the Book of Noah, and a number of court tales centered on the person of Daniel.[46] The spoken dialects were more or less distinct from that standard,[47] and seldom achieved permanence in writing except by inadvertence. Thus, with regard to Aramaic, the

45 Beginning with the time of the Hasmonean revolt, the situation may have changed, as Hebrew came to the fore in an expression akin to modern nationalism. A form of classical Hebrew was now a more significant written language than Aramaic within Judaea. Nevertheless, Aramaic texts composed earlier continued to be copied, and some Aramaic works were written. I hope to address this point in more detail elsewhere.

46 For a stimulating analysis of the Aramaic literature circulating in Judaea in pre-Hasmonean times, see E.J. Bickerman, *The Jews in the Greek Age* (Cambridge: Harvard University Press, 1988), pp. 51-65.

47 The degree of difference between the written standard and any given vernacular dialect would be in part a function of the amount of exposure the vernacular's speakers had to the prestigious written form. This exposure could come either through a person's own reading (on literacy see the comments below) or through aural exposure to the reading of another.

situation was what one linguist has called 'classic diglossia.'[48] Divergent dialects stood in complementary distribution according to function. The high language (H) was the written standard, spoken but seldom; it required education to handle it correctly, and since most of the population consisted of peasants with little or no education, the number of people who could do so was relatively small. Their knowledge of the vernacular dialects of daily life (the low [L] dialects), however, probably rendered the H broadly intelligible. Situations of diglossia are extemely common throughout world history; they may even be the norm. Certainly they were such in the ancient Near East, where spoken languages were never used for formal writing except at the foundation of political entities, or when political upheaval and reform would briefly realign the spoken and written forms.[49] Subsequent to such 'paradigm shifts,' the two forms would once more diverge as the L continued to evolve while the H remained essentially frozen. Thus not only historical considerations, but also sociological norms, argue against Fitzmyer's model in favor of diglossia. Fitzmyer's is intrinsically much less satisfactory an explanation of the facts,

---

48   R. Fashold, *The Sociolinguistics of Society* (Oxford: Basil Blackwell, 1984), p. 55 (in response to the seminal article by C. Ferguson, 'Diglossia', Word 15 [1959] pp. 325-40). For a full discussion of the present state of diglossia studies, including J. Fishman's modification of Ferguson's concept, see F. Britto, *Diglossia: A Study of the Theory with Application to Tamil* (Washington, D.C.: Georgetown University Press, 1986), pp. 5-53. Important applications of the concept to Semitic languages (including Palestine, but not reaching the same conclusions as the present study) are J. Blau, 'The Beginning of the Arabic Diglossia: A Study of the Origins of Neoarabic', *Afroasiatic Linguistics* 4/3 (1977), 175-202; T. Harvainen, 'Diglossia in Jewish Eastern Aramaic', *StudOr* 55 (1984), pp. 95-113; M.H. Goshen-Gottstein, 'The Language of Targum Onkelos and the Model of Literary Diglossia in Aramaic', *JNES* 37 (1978), pp. 169-80; P. Lapide, 'Insights from Qumran into the Languages of Jesus', *RevQ* 8 (1972-76), pp. 483-501, esp. 485-9; C. Rabin, 'Hebrew and Aramaic in the First Century', in *Compendia Rerum Iudaicarum ad Novum Testamentum. Section 1. The Jewish People in the First Century: Historical Geography, Political History, Social, Cultural and Religious Life and Institutions*, eds. S. Safrai and M. Stern (Philadelphia: Fortress Press, 1976), 2, pp. 1007-39, and B. Spolsky, 'Jewish Multilingualism in the First Century: An Essay in Historical Sociolinguistics', in *Readings in the Sociology of Jewish Languages*, ed. J. Fishman (Leiden: Brill, 1985), pp. 35-50.
49   An interesting discussion of this point with regard to Egypt is found in J. Baines, 'Literacy and Ancient Egyptian Society', *Man* N.S. 18 (1983), pp. 572-99.

requiring as it does a sociolinguistic anomaly for this region. Diglossia is, of course, essentially the situation envisaged by Jonas Greenfield's 'Standard Literary Aramaic,' although he does not use the term.[50]

The meaning of this model for the linguistic analysis of the Aramaic DSS is simply that the authors and copyists of these texts were working in a different dialect (and, perhaps, in some cases in a different language) than they spoke. On occasion they would inadvertently introduce a nonstandard Aramaic word or form into the text.[51] These forms are particularly what the advocates of linguistic dating isolate. Do such accidents make it possible to date a manuscript? The answer is no, for reasons that may already be clear but will become more so after a consideration of the book culture and the place of the Aramaic DSS in it.

The DSS and the Book Culture in Late Second Temple Palestine

In order to consider the Aramaic DSS in the context of the book culture one must first be convinced that the DSS were not—or at least not entirely—the product of a small group living on the shores of the Dead Sea *sine ulla femina, omni venere abdicata, sine pecunia, socia palmarum.*[52] The question is related to—but distinct from—the long dormant but now recently revived debate about Qumran origins.[53] I am

---

50   J. Greenfield, 'Standard Literary Aramaic', in *Actes du Premier Congrès International de Linguistique Sémitique et Chamito-Sémitique. Paris 16-19 juillet 1969*, eds. A. Caquot and D. Cohen (The Hague: Mouton, 1974), pp. 280-9. See also his 'Aramaic and Its Dialects', in *Jewish Languages: Themes and Variations*, ed. H. Paper (New York: n.p., 1978), pp. 29-43.

51   I would also certainly not rule out the possibility of occasional insertion of nonstandard forms for flavor, nuance, precision or style.

52   Pliny, *HN* 5.73, describing the Essenes.

53   For long the overwhelmingly majority opinion has held that the Qumran scrolls, apart from the biblical texts, were the products of an Essene or other sectarian community living at the site. In this view even the copies of biblical books were almost entirely products of their scribes. N. Golb has raised objections to this interpretation in a series of articles, among them 'The Problem of Origin and Identification of the Dead Sea Scrolls', *Proceedings of the American Philosophical Society* 124 (1980), pp. 1-24; 'Who Hid the Dead Sea Scrolls?' *BA* 48 (1985), pp. 68-82; 'Les manuscrits de la Mer Morte: une nouvelle approche du problème de leur origine', *Annales Économies Sociétés Civilisations* 40, 5 (1985), pp. 1133-49, and 'Khirbet Qumran and the Manuscripts of the Judaean Wilderness: Observations on the Logic of Their Investigation', *JNES* 49 (1990), pp. 103-14. With the

more narrowly concerned with the scrolls as scribal objects. From the beginning of scrolls research it has been acknowledged that such a group could not have copied all of the scrolls, for some are thought to antedate the occupation of Qumran. And certainly any community living at Qumran did not actually author all the literary works found nearby, most obviously the biblical texts, but also such works as Enoch and Jubilees. These works existed, in some form at least, prior to the establishment of the site of Qumran. Thus on any analysis at least some of the scrolls are the products of the broader book culture, and I would argue that the great majority of the scrolls constitute a cross section of that trade (although it is still unclear how representative a cross section).[54]

Underscoring this recognition is the fact that even granting the dubious reconstruction of a scriptorium on the site,[55] the remains scarcely support the assumption of full-scale scribal book production there.[56] Indeed, the scribal evidence of the scrolls themselves belies that picture. This evidence is manifold, including: (1) the fact that of the biblical scrolls, no two texts demonstrably share an immediate

anticipated 'official' publication of 4QMMT, advocates of a Sadducean connection are now being heard. See e.g., L. Schiffman, 'The New Halakhic Letter (4QMMT) and the Origins of the Dead Sea Sect', *BA* 53 (1990), pp. 64-73.

54   Texts such as *1 Maccabees* are conspicuous by their absence. Further, there is a corpus of nonbiblical literature that appears to be more or less closely related, sharing significant terms and concepts, and a much larger body that lacks a definable inner relationship as well as an obvious connection with the smaller 'central' corpus.

55   The remains consist of two or three inkwells and two tables, upon which, in the usual reconstruction, the scribes are imagined to have written. The difficulties with this picture are twofold: first, the tables are too low (only about 17 inches high) to function as writing tables; and second, all the evidence for the ancient period pictures scribes writing either while standing, or, if sitting, with the writing materials on their knees. At best, these tables could have been 'couches' upon which the scribes sat while writing. See de Vaux's description in R. de Vaux, *Archaeology and the Dead Sea Scrolls* (Oxford: Clarendon Press, 1973), pp. 29-32, and the analysis of B. Metzger, 'When Did Scribes Begin to Use Writing Desks?' in *Historical and Literary Studies: Pagan, Jewish, and Christian* (Grand Rapids: Eerdmans, 1968), pp. 123-137, and 'The Furniture of the Scriptorium at Qumran', *RevQ* 1 (1958-59), pp. 509-15.

56   Note Golb's point (note 53) that no remains of leather, papyrus sheets, etc.— such as were found buried in the ruins at Masada and should presumably, therefore, have survived at Qumran as well—have in fact turned up.

prototype; neither did any MS give rise to identifiable daughter copies;[57] (2) the lack of autographic texts;[58] (3) the apparent lack of any

57   One of the original editors, P. Skehan, speaks to the point in 'The Qumran Manuscripts and Textual Criticism', *VTSup* 4 (1957), p. 149, concerning approximately 100 Biblical maniuscripts from Cave 4: 'At the end of two years' acquaintance, in varying degrees, with these materials, the writer is still not aware of internal evidence which would urge that any one of these manuscripts was copied from another identifiable manuscript among the finds, or that any two had a common immediate prototype. Put in another way, this is to say ... that their origins are to some extent necessarily diverse ...' In a letter dated 8 October 1990, Eugene Ulrich informed me that to the best of his knowledge, Skehan's judgment still holds true. As the 4Q biblical texts are about to go to press, he cites one possible exception. In his 'Orthography and Text in 4QDan[a] and 4QDan[b] and in the Received Masoretic Text', in *Of Scribes and Scrolls*, eds. H. W. Attridge, J.J. Collins and T.H. Tobin (New York: University Press, 1990), pp. 29-42, Ulrich tentatively suggests that 4QDan[b] may have been copied from 4QDan[a]. Another possible exception to Skehan's generalization is the relationship between 11Ps[a] and 11QPs[b]: according to J.A. Sanders, the two mss agree not only in order and content, but also agree at various points against the MT version of some Psalms. Sanders stops short, however, of concluding that the two texts share the same *Vorlage*, and from claiming that one was copied from the other. See his 'Cave 11 Surprises and the Question of Canon', *McCQ* 21 (1968), p. 287. But even if both these instances of possible interrelationship prove out, my point remains essentially unchanged: one would expect *significant* evidence of internal copying and recopying in a small scribal community, if indeed such had produced all or most of the mss. E. Tov, who has published several studies attempting to identify scribal characteristics peculiar to 'Qumran scribes', concedes in 'Hebrew Biblical Manuscripts from the Judaean Desert: Their Contribution to Textual Criticism', *JJS* 39 (1988), p. 5, 'It now seems likely that many, if not most, of the [biblical] texts found in this region [the Judaean Desert] were copied in other parts of Palestine, so that most of them can be taken as Palestinian texts.'

58   As a matter of principle in working with literary texts the presumption should always be against identifying a given ms as an autograph; the odds against it being such are overwhelming. In an early article E. Hammershaimb studied the pattern of scribal errors in the then-published DSS and concluded: (1) there were apparently no autographs; and (2) the scrolls could not have been produced or copied at Qumran. See his 'On the Method Applied in the Copying of Manuscripts in Qumran', *VT* 9 (1959), pp. 415-18. Autograph literary texts may be identified on the basis of a number of phenomena, if parallels from the Cairo Genizah (where autographs of known works by Maimonides, for example, have been identified) are allowed to bear any weight. Such works were not ordinarily written on scrolls, but rather on single sheets or other expensive media. If necessary, the author wrote in the margins and on both sides. Economy was the motive here, and there was no

'signature' of a scribal school (e.g., peculiar techniques or linguistic habits), odd for an ingrown separatist group;[59] (4) the very large number of individual hands among the scrolls;[60] and (5) the existence of personal copies among the scrolls. As the first items in this list have been discussed at some length elsewhere, I want to focus only on the last two: multiplicity of hands and personal copies.

need for a handsome appearance such as might be desirable in a scribal copy. The handwriting in autographs is rough; most authors did not possess calligraphic hands. The lines are often more widely spaced than in a professional scribal text, and other matters of presentation, such as marking of guidelines, are partially or wholly absent. Because the author was thinking while writing, not infrequently the language was inept. While reworking the writer would strive to improve on it. This fact, along with his ordering of his thoughts, would often result in much crossing out and adding in above or below the lines. In light of such criteria, the oft-echoed suggestion of Fitzmyer and Kaufman that 1QapGen may be the autograph cannot be accepted (Fitzmyer, *Genesis Apocryphon*, 19; Kaufman, 'Job Targum', p. 327 n. 62). None of the Aramaic DSS are autographs.

59   In an early but massive study of the scribal phenomena of the six major scrolls from Cave 1, M. Martin concluded that they showed no evidence either of sectarian origin or of origin in a single scribal school. See M. Martin, *The Scribal Character of the Dead Sea Scrolls*, 2 vols. (Louvain: University of Louvain, 1958) passim. More recently E. Tov challenged this conclusion in 'The Orthography and Language of the Hebrew Scrolls Found at Qumran and the Origin of These Scrolls', *Textus* 13 (1986), pp. 31-57. Even Tov, however, admitted that at least some of the nonbiblical scrolls could not be the products of a community at Qumran. In identifying those which were, in his view, products of the group, he isolated those characterized by plene orthography and the use of peculiar grammatical forms, such as the masculine singular and plural independent pronouns הואה and המה. But he prudently conceded (p. 39) that the linguistic uniqueness of these features might be merely apparent, and could disappear in the light of further discoveries. In fact just such discoveries are now known. In several literary texts from Masada Tov's diagnostic forms appear. Ironically, however, their editor suggests that they were brought to Masada by members of the Qumran sect. See S. Talmon, 'Fragments of Scrolls from Masada', *ErIsr* 20 (1989), pp. 279-80 (Heb.), and idem, 'A Joshua Apocryphon from Masada', in M. Goshen-Gottstein, S. Morag and S. Kogut (eds.), Studies in *Hebrew and Other Semitic Languages Presented to Professor Chaim Rabin on the Occasion of His Seventy-Fifth Birthday* (Jerusalem: Academon, 1990), pp. 147-53 (Heb.). For a critique of Tov's method and conclusions see J. Lübbe, 'Certain Implications of the Scribal Process of 4QSam^c', *RevQ* 14 (1989), pp. 255-65.

60   Golb has noted this point very briefly in 'Observations', p. 103.

Scribal Hands

According to R. de Vaux, the site's excavator, Qumran was occupied for approximately 200 years, i.e., some eight generations.[61] Its suggested population at any one time never exceeded 200 persons, and even that figure was attained only in the latter years of the site's lifespan.[62] With such a modest number of inhabitants—most of whom were presumably occupied with matters of day-to-day sustenance—it is remarkable that among the scrolls scholars have identified hundreds of individual hands. The words of John Allegro, one of the original group involved in reconstructing the materials from the Caves during the late 1950's, speak clearly to this point. Describing the difficulties of making joins among the often exceedingly meager manuscript materials, he says:[63]

> One of the saving factors has been that of the four hundred or so manuscripts we have had to deal with, surprisingly few were written by the same scribe, so that by recognizing the idiosyncracies of one's own scribes one could be fairly sure that the piece belonged to his document.

Since Allegro penned those words, the number of manuscripts

---

61   The position defended by E.-M. Laperrousaz would reduce the number of generations to no more than seven. See his *Qoumrân: L'établisssement essénien des bords de la Mer Morte. Histoire et archéologie du site* (Paris: Picard, 1976), pp. 28-33, and 'Bréves remarques archéologiques concernant la chronologie des occupations esséniennes de Qoumrân', *RevQ* 12 (1985-7), pp. 199-212.

62   De Vaux, *Archaeology and the Dead Sea Scrolls*, 86. H. Stegemann (oral communication) has observed that no more than fifty people could have squeezed into the site's 'communal meeting hall', which for him would imply a much lower population than de Vaux's estimate. I am not sure that this is a legitimate argument, since e.g., the synagogue at Masada could have held only a fraction of those we know lived there from 66-74 CE.

63   J. Allegro, *The Dead Sea Scrolls: A Reappraisal* (New York: Penguin Books, (1964), pp. 55-56. Allegro's subsequent activities had the effect of destroying his scholarly credibility, but here he is describing not just his own methodology, but that of the editorial group as a whole. Obviously all agreed that the diversity of hands was an essential control for reconstructing the texts. That the hands do indeed number in the hundreds can be seen merely by glancing through Eisenman and Robinson.

identified has doubled,[64] and the number of hands identified has increased proportionately. How is it possible to reconcile the multiplicity of scribal hands with the small number of Qumran's inhabitants—or even with the number of the Essenes generally? According to ancient testimony the entire group of adherents numbered no more than some 4,000.[65] Nor is it apparent why, on the conventional view that the texts originated at the site of Qumran, virtually no scribe copied more than a single text.[66]

If a community at Qumran had produced the texts in question, one would have expected a scribal profile more nearly like that of the well known 'Jewish' military colony at Elephantine and Syene. True, the two communities are certainly not comparable in every respect; but both are commonly imagined as self sufficient. With a population of 1800–3000 men (and thus a total population of four to five times that number), the Elephantine community was more than fifty times larger than estimates for Qumran. Yet it relied upon only a dozen or so

---

64   In the estimate of H. Stegemann, 'Some Aspects of Eschatology in Texts from the Qumran Community and in the Teachings of Jesus', in *Biblical Archaeology Today*, ed. R. Amitai (Jerusalem: Israel Exploration Society, 1985), p. 421, n. 4, the mss total about 823. This figure is somewhat uncertain because of the fragmentary condition of many of the manuscripts, but the actual total will not have been greatly different. For the fullest available description, comprising 668 of the texts, see F. García Martínez, 'Lista de MSS procedentes de Qumrán', *Henoch* 11 (1989), pp. 149-232.

65   Philo, *Quod Omnis Probus*, 75; Josephus, *Ant.* 18.20.

66   In a few cases only does it seem scribes may have copied more than one ms, a fact that proves nothing in particular. J.M. Allegro, DJD 5, p. 58, suggests that the scribe of 4Q175 is identical with that of 1QS. E. Ulrich, '4QSam^c: A Fragmentary Manuscript of 2 Samuel 14-15 from the Scribe of the Serek Hayyahad (1QS)', *BASOR* 235 (1979), p. 20, argues that this same scribe was responsible for 4QSam^c, 1QSa, 1QSb, and certain supralinear corrections in 1QIs^a. J.P.M. van der Ploeg, 'Les manuscrits de la Grotte XI de Qumrân', RevQ 12 (1985-87), p. 9, and 'Une halakha inédite de Qumrân', in *Qumrân: sa piété, sa théologie et son milieu*, ed. J. Carmignac (Paris: Duculot, 1978), p. 107, maintains that the scribe who copied the second exemplar of the Temple Scroll from Cave 11 was identical with one of the three scribes of the Habbakuk *pesher*. A problem with arguments of this sort is that thus far no adequate paleographic study of the DSS mss exists, in which each letter of each ms is gathered into one source and placed side-by-side for scholars to study. In view of this lack, it is easy to fall into mistaken identifications and false distinctions.

scribes.[67] And this total served over a period of three or four generations. Consequently only three or four were active in a given generation—and even then, not all were full-time scribes.

The only way to reconcile the extraordinary number of hands with scribal production at Qumran is to argue that the community consisted almost exclusively of scribes. Then, somehow, one must explain why the vast majority of these scribes limited themselves to a single (often *parvum*) opus. The resulting picture is so absurd that it simply cannot be right. The multiplicity of hands among the scrolls argues overwhelmingly that they must represent, to a greater or lesser extent, a cross section of the book culture.

Personal Copies

Reinforcing this conclusion is the identification among the DSS of personal copies—i.e., copies that did not ordinarily circulate publicly and that were not produced by scribes. The papyri of Egypt provide a helpful context for analyzing such texts. They have preserved various types of ancient books, among which are (1) the school text; (2) the amateur copy; (3) the scholar's private copy; (4) the ordinary trade book; and (5) the *edition de luxe*. Little work has been done in looking among the DSS for books produced by others than scribes—categories (1) through (3)—but the identification of such materials among the DSS has important ramifications for any attempt at linguistic dating of the Aramaic works. This point is especially important in reference to amateur and scholarly copies, because the authors of such texts may not follow scribal conventions and may not write the standard language very well. Also, as we shall see, sometimes such texts did enter the stream of scribal transmission. Their identification points to the presence among the scrolls of private collections.

In seeking to identify personal copies, one can begin with a process of elimination. Extremely rough, untutored hands may be those of schoolboys just learning how to write—category (1) above (not to be confused with 'slow writers'—Greek βραδέως γράφοντες).[68] Such

---

67   See B. Porten, *Archives*, pp. 32-33 for the population, and 192-194 for the number and identity of the scribes. For more details on the activities of the major scribes, see B. Porten and A. Yardeni, *Textbook of Aramaic Documents from Ancient Egypt* (2 vols.; Winona Lake: Eisenbrauns, 1989), 2, pp. 188-189.

68   E.G. Turner, *Greek Papyri: An Introduction* (Princeton: University Press,

hands occur among the Egyptian Greek papyri even in long passages of literature. It is very unlikely that such copies circulated even privately; they would therefore have no potential impact on scribal copies.

On the other extreme, it is possible to identify the work of professional scribes in several ways. The most obvious approach is to isolate calligraphic book hands. This approach is promising but not foolproof, since there are instances where this type of hand is known to be the work of educated officials or intellectuals rather than of professional scribes.[69] (In some cases, therefore, book hands will appear in private copies, but there is no way to distinguish these instances from the work of scribes.) Another clue to the work of professionals is evidence of stichometric calculation. Scribes would receive payment according to the number of lines they copied. But the most certain way to recognize professional work is to identify the handwriting of scribes who have copied more than one work.[70] After eliminating the MSS that are clearly the work of either untutored or professional hands, then, some of those that remain will fall in the realm of personal copies.

Further progress in identifying personal copies is possible by typological script analysis. In the ancient world generally, including Judah, scribes used book hands for literary works, but ordinarily copied documents in a fluent cursive writing. The intelligentsia also wrote in a cursive or semi-cursive script when writing personal letters and the like.[71] Encountering a literary text in a cursive type script, therefore,

---

1968), pp. 88-9 groups the two types of writers together. Such a grouping may be adequate for certain purposes, but for the present inquiry the two must be kept separate. The 'slow writer' was a person who was so marginally literate that he or she ordinarily could not read and was able only to sign a legal text and, perhaps, laboriously scrawl one or two additional words. Therefore, unlike a schoolboy who might copy out a literary text in the course of his lessons, the slow writer would never be responsible for a continuous text. From the perspective of the book trade such hands do not exist. See H. Youtie, 'βραδέως γράφων: Between Literacy and Illiteracy', *Greek, Roman and Byzantine Studies* 12 (1971), pp. 239-61.

69   Lewis notes the example of a village clerk—not a position held by scribes, as in Ptolemaic Egypt scribes were usually slaves—who apparently wrote a beautiful book hand in copying some anthologies of Greek verse. These are preserved among the Tetubnis papyri. See N. Lewis, *Greeks in Ptolemaic Egypt: Case Studies in the Social History of the Hellenistic World* (Oxford: Clarendon Press, 1980), pp. 122-23.

70   Cf. Turner, *Greek Papyri*, pp. 92-93, and see note 66 above.

71   There are thus three basic gradations of writing: the formal professional

one may infer that it did not circulate in the regular book trade. A famous example is the papyrus containing Aristotle's *Politics of Athens*. Four distinct cursive hands copied out this work—which was known only by title prior to the nineteenth century—apparently as a student's copy.[72]

A final potential indicator of personal copies is the quality of materials invested in the scroll's production. In the Palestine of the DSS, leather was, on the evidence, the preferred material for literary texts. While in earlier centuries papyrus had apparently played this role in the Near East, by the first century it had fallen in esteem throughout the ancient world (Egypt excepted).[73] The reasons for this decline are not entirely clear, but it seems that the contributing factors were in part aesthetic and—at least in Palestine—in part religious.[74]

script, the cursive used by the scribes for documents and by the intelligentsia generally, and the 'vulgar' script which common folk used for signatures and simple notations. It should be noted that not all documents preserved from this period are in cursive script; for example, some of the Bar Kochba contracts are written in square script. Such cases are exceptional, however, and are I think largely attributable to two factors: (1) some of the texts were not written by scribes at all, but by ordinary people, either because no scribe was available or simply because they were able to do it and saw no need to purchase a scribe's services; and (2) the decision on the part of certain scribes to write in the square script so that the client could read the contents, as for example on the *scriptura exterior* of double documents. In general see J. Naveh, 'A Paleographic Note on the Distribution of the Hebrew Script', *HTR* 61 (1968), pp. 68-74; F.M. Cross, 'Epigraphic Notes on Hebrew Documents of the Eighth-Sixth Centuries B.C.: II. The Murabbaᶜat Papyrus and the Letter Found Near Yabneh-Yam', *BASOR* 165 (1962), pp. 34-46, and 'Epigraphic Notes on Hebrew Documents of the Eighth-Sixth Centuries B.C.: III. The Inscribed Jar Handles from Gibeon', *BASOR* 168 (1962), pp. 18-23.

72   See F.G. Kenyon's somewhat imaginative description of the process of producing the copy in *Books and Readers in Ancient Greece and Rome* (Oxford: Clarendon Press, 1951), p. 71.

73   P.E. Easterling, 'Books and Readers in the Greek World: 2. The Hellenistic and Imperial Periods', in *The Cambridge History of Classical Literature I: Greek Literature*, eds. P.E. Easterling and B.M.W. Knox (New York: Cambridge University Press, 1985), pp. 18-19.

74   M. Haran ignores these factors in 'Book-Scrolls at the Beginning of the Second Temple Period: The Transition from Papyrus to Skins', *HUCA* 54 (1983), pp. 111-22. Instead he sees three reasons for the switch in Palestine: (1) the desire to use skin rather than papyrus for canonical materials because skin is more durable; (2) the need to accommodate the D source of the Pentateuch on a single scroll, only possible with skin; and (3) Jewish mimicry of the Persian use of skins

It is likely that in many cases papyrus was less costly.[75] Unfortunately, with the data at our disposal it is impossible to be certain about the relative expense of leather and papyrus at any given time and place.[76] And it is necessary to distinguish here between different grades of leather; the amount of labor invested differed markedly between the lower grades and those ordinarily use for book scrolls.[77] Evidently the lower grades were not so expensive as to rule out their use for ephemera.[78] Though it is not certain that economic concerns were a factor in dictating the preference for leather, it does seem that papyrus was substantially cheaper than good quality leather. Thus papyrus, being relatively inexpensive, lacked that aura of quality desired by most owners of fine books. More important, from the perspectives of calligraphy and general appearance good quality vellum was immensely preferable.

As for religious factors, the use of leather for prestigious literary works was later canonized by the Tannaitic dicta on particular biblical scrolls. These scrolls had to be written on parchment or they were of no use for the task at hand.[79] A man could not fulfill his obligation to read

for writing material. All three of these reasons are open to question. We have archaeological evidence of papyri lasting hundreds of years, and, according to ancient sources, books on papyrus could last centuries. The original length of the D source is impossible to know; but some papyrus rolls from Egypt exceed 100 feet, capacious enough for D on any view. As for the third point, although the Persians used skin for writing, they also used papyrus, at least in Egypt. Palestine is close enough to Egypt that it was probably not too expensive to import papyrus, as it may have been in other Persian regions.

75   Turner, *Greek Papyri*, p. 5. On p. 12 Turner suggests that another factor favoring the use of leather was the increasing use of iron compounds in inks. These compounds acted as a mordant on papyrus but not on leather.

76   We have figures for the cost of papyrus and leather, but no comparative figures for the cost of papyrus and parchment during the same period of time. See C.H. Roberts and T.C. Skeat, *The Birth of the Codex* (London: Oxford University Press, 1987), pp. 7-8.

77   The discussion of this point in M.T. Clanchy, *From Memory to Written Record: England, 1066-1307* (Cambridge: Harvard University Press, 1979), pp. 93-5, although dealing with another scribal context, is helpful.

78   Note the use of leather to record a debt of a single sela[c] (i.e., just four zuz) in M. Broshi and E. Qimron, 'I.O.U. Note from the Time of the Bar Kokhba Revolt', *ErIsr* 20 (1989), pp. 256-61 (Heb.).

79   The text reads הספר על—according to the traditional understanding, here the equivalent of קלף. For a discussion of rabbinic evidence on matters related to

the scroll of Esther at Purim if the scroll from which he read were made from papyrus.[80] Given that the vast majority of the DSS are on leather,[81] as are the Masada and Murabbaᶜat literary texts, it is possible that a religious connection between books and leather was substantially older than the compilation of the Mishnah.[82]

In any event, despite uncertainty about the reasons, it is indisputable that in the time and region under discussion leather was the principal medium for literary works. Thus, on encountering such a work copied on papyrus, it is necessary to ask why the scribe chose such a medium. Certainly such scrolls would not fetch a first-class price on the market; they might even have been religiously objectionable. Several possible explanations for such manuscripts come to mind. In certain cases, perhaps, papyrus may have been chosen because the literary work was rather short.[83] Papyrus would also be the usual choice of anyone who was copying a scroll from a friend's copy or a library copy. It would, in other words, often be the preferred material for personal copies. This choice reflected the desire to save money. If one were to go to the trouble of having a scribal copy made, it might as well be done on leather, since labor costs often exceeded the cost of materials.[84]

books, mostly relying on post-Tannaitic sources, see M. Bar-Ilan, 'Scribes and Books in the Late Second Commonwealth and Rabbinic Period', in *Mikra: Text, Translation, Reading and Interpretation of the Hebrew Bible in Ancient Judaism and Early Christianity*, ed. M.J. Mulder (Philadelphia: Fortress Press, 1988), pp. 21-38.

80   *m.Meg.* 2.2.

81   Strictly speaking, the skins from Qumran, and those used by Jews in Talmudic times, were neither leather nor parchment. They underwent some chemical treatment to facilitate writing, but not a full tanning. For a detailed discussion see M. Haran, 'Bible Scrolls in Eastern and Western Jewish Communities from Qumran to the High Middle Ages', *HUCA* 56 (1985), pp. 37-38.

82   One notes that of the 127 biblical scrolls from Cave Four, only three are written on papyrus. For these texts see E. Ulrich, 'The Biblical Scrolls from Qumran Cave Four: A Progress Report of their Publication', *RevQ* 14 (1989), pp. 207-228.

83   H. Stegemann makes the point that when rolled up, papyrus rolls are substantially bulkier than are leather ones. Thus if storage space and ease of use were a concern, papyrus might be the choice for shorter literary works. See his 'Methods for the Reconstruction of Scrolls from Scattered Fragments', in *Archaeology and History in the Dead Sea Scrolls,* ed. L. Schiffman (Sheffield: JSOT Press, 1990), pp. 195-6.

84   See note 77 above.

Yet some people might be in a situation where even papyrus was unavailable. In these cases it was common to copy out a work on the back of a scroll already inscribed on the *recto*. Since such opisthographs never circulated by purchase, they are virtually certain indicators of private copies.

In summation, after eliminating texts that exhibit the markers of schoolboys and professional scribes, a literary work on papyrus, especially if written in a cursive or semi-cursive script, is likely to be a personal copy. An even clearer indication of such origin is opisthographic inscription.

The DSS include about one hundred texts written on papyrus. They break down according to their place of discovery as follows:[85] Cave 1

85   1Q70 consists of 32 fragments in at least 5 hands. The editors assign them to at least 5 different texts, broken down as follows: 1-6, 7-10, 11-12, 13-19 (more exactly, 13, 15, 18 and 19), and 20-. See D. Barthélemy and J.T. Milik, DJD 1: pp. 148-149 and plate 37. 1Q70*bis* apparently belongs with the fifth group; see p. 155. The texts from Cave 4 are 4Q163 (see Allegro, DJD 5, pp. 17-27 and plates 7-8), 196, 222-23, 249, 255, 257, 273, 302, 310-11, 324b, 331, 347, 353, 358-9, 361, m130 (unidentified papyrus fragments not yet assigned an official number), 382, 384, 391, 398, 432, 465, 478, 482-490, 496-500, 502-503, 505-506, 509, 512, 515-520, 558 and 559. 4Q516-520 are unclassified fragments, so it is uncertain how many texts they represent. 4Q520 fr. 38 is perhaps a contract, for it is in Aramaic and in a cursive script. Otherwise the texts are all copies of literary texts. For the 4Q texts other than 4Q163, see M. Baillet, DJD 7 and Reed, *List*. The Cave 6 texts are 6Q3, 6Q4, 6Q5, 6Q7-10, 6Q16, 6Q18, 6Q22-24, 6Q26, 6Q30-31. The last number designates two or more texts. Of these 6Q scrolls, apparently not all are literary texts. 6Q26, written in a cursive script, may be a bill of sale, a contract, or a list of apportionments. The text makes use of scribal abbreviations, such as ס (= סאה?), and numeration. It may be in Mishnaic Hebrew (cf. הן in line 1, and הלי [*si vera lectio*] in line 3), although its condition is so fragmentary that it is impossible to be certain. 6Q29, also in cursive script, is perhaps a contract or bill of sale. Fr. 1 includes the cipher for '60', and fr. 2 apparently reads בכסף. For all the texts, see M. Baillet, J.T. Milik and R. de Vaux, DJD 3. The texts from Cave 7 are 7Q1-19. 7Q1 is on carefully prepared papyrus, in Greek uncials of the type known as 'Zierstil', and apparently contains a portion of Exodus. 7Q2 is likewise a well-prepared papyrus in Greek uncials, and is thought to preserve a portion of the apocryphal Letter of Jeremiah. The remaining mss are so fragmentary that it is impossible to characterize their contents. See DJD 3. The single fragment from Cave 9 is on well-prepared papyrus. The hand may be semi-cursive, insofar as such conclusions are warranted on the basis of only 6 surviving letters; it has a fine calligraphic *lamedh*, but a cursive *qoph*. It is impossible to determine whether the text is in Hebrew or Aramaic, or its genre. See DJD 3.

has 5; Cave 4, 57; Cave 6, 19; Cave 7 between 5 and 23; and Cave 9, 1. Many of these papyrus texts are written in book hands. Accordingly, although some are likely to be private copies, they could also possibly be professional copies for the cheap book trade. Since our interest centers only on the most certain evidence for private copies, they need not be considered further here. But those papyrus texts that are inscribed in semi-cursive or cursive hands, and especially the few opisthographs (whether on papyrus or leather), warrant further comment.

6Q7 is a copy of the book of Daniel, on poorly prepared (thus cheap) papyrus, and in a semi-cursive script. The manuscript shows no signs of correction (correction may hint at professional work). At Dan 10.15 it preserves an apparent Aramaism of the sort that could creep in if the copyist, particularly if he were most at home in Aramaic, were not careful—as many non-professionals were not.[86] 6Q8 is perhaps a portion of the lost 'Book of Noah,' or of the Enochic 'Book of Giants,'[87] like 6Q7 written on inferior papyrus and including some cursive letter forms. 6Q9, titled by its editors an 'Apocryphon of Samuel-Kings,' is carefully written, but has some cursive ligation.[88] 6Q22 is too fragmentary to characterize as to genre, but it is in semi-cursive script. 6Q23, an Aramaic apocalyptic text, is also written in a semi-cursive hand.[89] 6Q30 is a literary text in cursive script.[90] Among

---

86   For MT נתחי פני ארצה the text reads נתחי אפי ארצה. Trade copies of texts, which were often the product of second-grade scribes and even private individuals, were notorious in antiquity for their inaccuracies. Copies of copies of copies, with each generation introducing new errors, could result in texts that were almost unintelligible. Yet, inexplicably perhaps for modern scholars, people continued to copy such texts, and, presumably, to make some sense out of the garbled mess. See the comments by Kenyon in *Books and Readers*, p. 74.

87   The original editors identified it as an 'Apocryphon to Genesis.' For its assignment to the Book of Giants, see Milik, *Books of Enoch,* pp. 300-301 and 309. F. García Martínez rejects this idea in favor of seeing the fragment as part of the 'Book of Noah', of which he believes portions are preserved in Enoch, Jubilees and certain DSS fragments. For his reasoning see '4Q Mes. Aram. y el libro de Noé', *Salmanticensis* 28 (1981), pp. 230-1.

88   Cf. fr. 21, line 1 בקולו.

89   Milik suggests (*Books of Enoch*, p. 91) that this MS represents a copy of the 'Words of Michael', a text known from two other yet unpublished copies from Cave 4. The remains here are so fragmentary, however, that it is unclear how such a certain identification is warranted.

90   That it is a literary text seems certain from line 3, עד[ת בוגד]ים.

the Cave 6 materials, at least these scrolls are almost certainly personal copies.

Texts on papyrus and in cursive scripts from Cave 4 include 4Q163, a pesher on Isaiah. Some of the fragments of this text are much more cursive than others; either the text is in a so-called 'mixed script,' or two people have worked on it, one writing a cursive hand.[91] 4Q488 is an apocryphon in Aramaic, whose remains are too exiguous to characterize any further. It is inscribed in a semi-cursive script and shows no signs of correction. Similar is 4Q489, perhaps an apocalyptic text in Aramaic, lacking correction and in a semi-cursive hand.[92] 4Q490 may belong to the same text as 4Q489; the hand seems to be the same, again lacking correction. Perhaps the same man made two personal copies that happened to survive in the Qumran collections. 4Q516 the editor calls 'fragments divers;' they are in a semi-cursive script, and derive from several different literary texts.[93] 4Q517 is a similar situation. The number designates 87 fragments inscribed on the *recto*; it is impossible to be sure how many different texts they originally comprised. At least one hand of the fragments appears to be cursive.[94] Thus, estimating very conservatively, from Caves 4 and 6 come approximately a dozen mss inscribed only on the *recto* that are most likely personal copies. To these one must add the opisthographs, which are summarized in Table 1.[95] Most of these manuscripts are very fragmentary, but two warrant further comment. The eleventh item in this chart is particularly intriguing. It appears that a scribe or scholar 'made selections' (a common procedure in the ancient world) on the *recto*, producing an ἐκλογή.[96] He began with 4Q509, a festal prayer

---

91 The latter interpretation is that of J. Strugnell, 'Notes en marge du Volume V des Discoveries in the Judaean Desert of Jordan', *RevQ* 7 (1970), p. 189. The cursive fragments include frgs. 2, 3, 46, 47 and 49.

92 The text is so fragmentary that one cannot be certain of its language, much less its genre. The basis for my very tentative characterization is the reading of רוח, a common term in apocalyptic visions. It should be noted that although the term was more common in Aramaic than in Hebrew, it does occur a few times in Hebrew texts among the DSS, in connection with visionaries.

93 Baillet tentatively suggests that they may be related to 4Q484 and 4Q488–4Q489.

94 Fragment 25.

95 An additional opisthograph appears among the Masada texts. See Talmon, 'Fragments', 283-4 (Heb.).

96 See note 117 below.

	Recto	*Verso*
1.	1Q70 1-6 Unknown work in calligraphic hand	Unknown work in cursive script
2.	1Q70 7-10 Unknown work in book hand	Unknown work in cursive script
3.	4Q249 Midrash Sepher Moshe (Cryptic A)	4Q250 Unknown work in Cryptic A (*second hand*)
4.	4Qpap Hodayot-like (no number)	4Q255 papS^a (*second hand*)
5.	4Q257 papS^c	Illegible inscription (*second hand*)
6.	4Q259 S^e	4Q319 Otot
7.	4Q460 Pseudepigraphic Text	4Q350 Account of Cereal (Greek)
8.	4Q324 Mishmarot C^c	4Q355 Account of Money (Aramaic)
9.	4Q377 Torah-like Text	4Q377 (*second hand*) Probably a different literary work from recto
10.	4Q417 Sapiental Text I^c	4Q417 Sapiental Text I^c (may be a different work) (*second hand*? mostly illegible)
11.	4Q509 Festal Prayers (3rd exemplar) 4Q505 Words of the Luminaries (2nd exemplar) 4Q509 resumes (*All in one hand*)	4Q496 (*second hand*) War Rule (6th examplar) 4Q506 (*third hand*) Words of the Luminaries (3rd exemplar)
12.	4Q499 Liturgical text	4Q497 (*different hand*) Text related to War Rule
13.	4Q503 Daily prayers	4Q512 (*different hand*) Purification ritual
14.	4Q518 Uncertain genre (*Several hands*)	4Q519 (illegible) Uncertain genre
15.	Effaced (Probably more than one ms)	4Q520 Uncertain genre (*At least four hands*)
16.	4QEn^a Enochic Book of Watchers (1 Enoch 1–36)	4Q338 Patriarchal genealogy (*different hand*)

Table 1. Opisthographs Among the Dss

text, added some lines from 4Q505 (another liturgical text known as the 'Words of the Luminaries'), and then returned to the first text for another selection. Some time later another writer reused the scroll and wrote a few lines of the War Rule on its *verso*. These first two hands are standard book hands. Later still, a writer with a much cruder and more cursive hand reused the scroll yet again for a portion of the

'Words of the Luminaries'. The last person was certainly not a professional scribe; probably even with the second hand the text had ceased to circulate in the market for books.

The other ms requiring comment is that of 4QEn[a].[97] This opisthograph is inscribed on very thick, very stiff leather—not, it would seem, a good grade. The lines of writing descend at an angle to the southwest at some points, rather than being straight across as is usual with a scribal hand. Guidelines are missing, and a peculiar symbol (otherwise unknown) marks a supralinear insertion. The script does not fit the typology for Jewish scripts developed by Frank Moore Cross, a problem that leaves its editor, J.T. Milik, at a loss.[98] Further, the language of the text is markedly different from that of the other Aramaic DSS. Along with a spelling that is stingy with matres lectionis—usually, by the canons of typological dating, a sign of an early text—some linguistically 'advanced' forms occur. Noteworthy are: the use of לת for לא אית,[99] frequent use of the particle ד rather

---

97   Published in Milik, *Books of Enoch*, pp. 139-63 and plates 1-5.

98   Milik first says the script ' . . . does not fit very well into the scribal traditions of the Jewish copyists of Judaea or even Egypt; the scribe would perhaps be dependent upon the Aramaic scripts and the scribal customs of Northern Syria or Mesopotamia.' He does not specify which characteristics of the script he finds anomalous, nor precisely which scripts it reminds him of; comparing the script with what Naveh calls 'cursive Seleucid Aramaic', and with approximately coeval northern Mesopotamian scripts, I find nothing to support Milik's tentative suggestion. Later he has another try at it: '4QEn[a] is perhaps a school-exercise, copied by a young scribe from the master's dictation' (quotations from Milik, *Books of Enoch*, pp. 140 and 141 respectively). In spite of his admission that he really cannot locate the script of this text within Cross's typology, Milik dates the text by paleography anyway. Both Sokoloff and Beyer have relied upon this dating without hesitating at Milik's admission of difficulty (see below). And his very early dating of the ms—amounting really to a guess—has found its way into the secondary literature. There various broad syntheses rely upon it to guide their characterization of Second Temple literature and ideas. See e.g., F. García Martínez, 'Estudios Qumranicos 1975-1985: Panorama critico (I)', *EstBib* 45 (1987), pp. 125-206. On the scripts see J. Naveh, 'An Aramaic Inscription from El-Mal—A Survival of 'Seleucid Aramaic' Script', *IEJ* 25 (1975), pp. 117-23, and idem, 'The North-Mesopotamian Aramaic Script-type in the Late Parthian Period', *IOS* 2 (1972), pp. 293-304.

99   2.14.

than די,[100] use of ית,[101] the spelling of *shewa mobile* with *yod*,[102] the use of דוק in the *Aphel* to mean 'look at',[103] the appearance of the fronted demonstrative הדן,[104] and the use of the 'short' form of the suffixed possessive pronoun.[105] This complex of characteristics has frustrated Sokoloff in his attempt at dating the text by linguistic typology,[106] and has defied Klaus Beyer's attempts at explanation as well.[107] Once it is

100 E.g., 2.4, 2.6, etc.

101 5.4.

102 See מיבישין. This phenomenon is common in medieval mss, but rare at this early date.

103 This lexical variant was previously unknown prior to Middle Aramaic. See Sokoloff, *Dictionary*, s.v., and chapter six below.

104 Milik convincingly reconstructs this word, partially broken, on the basis of the Greek. See 1.4.

105 Thus בסרכן in place of the expected בסרכהן at 2.1.

106 In his 'Notes on the Aramaic Fragments', pp. 202-3, Sokoloff struggles to date the text based on its linguistic phenomena. On the basis of the same list of morphological features he used to date 11QtgJob, the text should be late; but on the basis of its orthography, it ought to be early. Further compounding his difficulties is Sokoloff's adherence to Milik's very early paleographic dating of the text, even though Milik himself was diffident on this point. Finally, pulled in opposite directions by conflicting indicators, Sokoloff offers an explanation of the text for which there is otherwise absolutely no evidence: 'We may have in 4QEn^a a local Palestinian orthography which was employed in the earlier copies of Enoch, but which was displaced in the later ones by that of Standard Literary Aramaic' (p. 203).

107 Beyer, *Texte*, p. 227, dates 4QEn^a to c. 170 BCE, and classifies it as belonging to a dialect he calls 'Jewish Old Palestinian.' He further says that because of its age and dialect, it cannot come from Judaea, but must instead derive from northeastern regions of the Transjordan. In order to evaluate these conclusions, it is necessary briefly to consider Beyer's dialect classifications more generally—no easy task, since where they are not confused they are confusing. On pp. 28-44 and 49-58, Beyer discusses first Achaemenid Imperial Aramaic and subsequent written dialects derived from it, and then contemporary spoken dialects which arose from 'Old Western Aramaic.' Eventually these spoken dialects took written form, for the most part (the existence of some Beyer merely infers from later evidence). In Palestine Imperial Aramaic gave way in 142 BCE to Hasmonean Aramaic. For Beyer, virtually all of the Aramaic DSS are inscribed in this dialect. In 37 BCE, with Herod's rise to power, Hasmonean Aramaic ceased to be used, except for some legal formulae. Instead Greek served as the language of government, and private documents began to be written in 'Judaean.' Unlike Hasmonean, which evolved from the Achaemenid *lingua franca*, Judaean represented the written use of a vernacular. But its Herodian use in Jerusalem and Judaea was not the first time a

recognized that 4QEn[a] is a personal copy, however, the intractable difficulties with its script and language evaporate. It need not be squeezed into the mold of what is expected from scribal copies. The ms is one of some forty among the DSS that exhibit the signs of personal copies.[108]

form of Judaean had been turned to a literary task. In an earlier incarnation, which Beyer labels 'Jewish Old Palestinian', (yes, the dialect of 4QEn[a]) it had been used in the area of Caesarea Philippi. It was thus a Transjordanian spoken dialect which, in written form, came to displace Hasmonean in Judaea. Now the confusion begins; for 'Jewish Old Palestinian' is further a subdivision of 'Old East Jordanian.' Old East Jordanian (otherwise referred to simply as 'East Jordanian') embraces the following: Jewish Old East Jordanian (apparently another name for Jewish Old Palestinian), Pagan Old East Jordanian, Christian Old East Jordanian, Jewish Middle-East Jordanian, and above all Christian Palestinian Aramaic. Thus Beyer specifically distinguishes between East Jordanian and Judaean, while, as noted above, he sees Judaean as derived from, or the same as, East Jordanian. Puzzled, the reader supposes this situation might be explained by a bifurcation of the earlier Old East Jordanian into two or more later dialects, but this apparently is not the explanation, for Beyer lists no East Jordanian dialect contemporary with Judaean. In fact, as one searches his book it develops that the one and only example of Jewish Old Palestinian is 4QEn[a]. Beyer never explains fundamental questions involved with that dialect, such as 'Why was it ever written down at all, and by what group or governmental authority was it employed as a conscious alternative to the earlier Imperial Aramaic?', and 'How could a written language from a politically insignificant region of Palestine ever come to dominance in Jerusalem, eventually to displace Hasmonean as a written language?' To my mind Beyer was forced to his wildly improbable divisions here in part by his acceptance of a date of 170 BCE for 4QEn[a]. It is clear that this date represents his interpretation of Milik's discussion of the text's paleography. Beyer lets that date checkmate him when he seeks to explain the text's language. In fact his 'Jewish Old Palestinian' is a chimera. It never existed. But Beyer is nevertheless right to see a connection with many of the Jerusalem sepulchral inscriptions—his 'Judaean' dialect (*Texte*, pp. 335-62)—since (as indicated by their cursive script, the sort used by someone used to writing on leather, papyrus, or ostracon, but not well suited to lapidary use) many of these were inscribed by family members rather than masons working from copy provided by a scribe. Accordingly they manifest exactly the sort of language one might expect: that of an educated person who is not a scribe—the equivalent of a personal copy. For a further discussion of some of the problems raised by Beyer's rabbit-like multiplication of dialects, see the review of his work by S.F. Bennett in *Maarav* 4 (1987), pp. 243-60, esp. 245-9.

108   This number is undoubtedly lower than the real number of personal copies among the DSS, for I have purposely excluded semicursive and cursive texts written on leather, along with the scribal hands written on papyrus already noted.

Thus the most satisfactory explanation for the scribal phenomena of the DSS is to regard them as the product of the wider Hebrew and Aramaic book culture. A very brief consideration of this culture will bring to the fore the significance of placing the Aramaic scrolls in that context. Its vicissitudes will be most evident in considering three major elements: (1) publication; (2) reproduction; and (3) circulation.

The Dynamics of the Book Culture

By the first century, Judaea—and Palestine as a whole—was in many respects an integral part of the broader culture of the Greco-Roman world.[109] With due caution, it is often possible to analyze Judaean cultural phenomena using models constructed on analogy with that broader culture. This approach is helpful for the question of the book culture in Palestine.[110] Very little information on the trade and use of books has come down in Hebrew and Aramaic sources of the first century and earlier. A fair amount of data, however, survives in approximately contemporary Greek and Latin literary sources. In addition the arid regions of Egypt have preserved large numbers of literary and non-literary papyri, the study of which contributes substantially to information about the book culture drawn from the literary sources.[111]

An author in first-century Palestine might publish his work by any of

109 See M. Hengel, *Judentum und Hellenismus, Studien zu ihrer Begegnung unter besonderer Berücksichtigung Palästinas bis zur Mitte des 2 Jh.s v.Chr.*, 2 vols. (Tübingen: J.C.B. Mohr, ²1973). For scholarly reaction to some of Hengel's broad claims, see the reviews by J.C.H. Lebram, *VT* 20 (1970), pp. 503-24 and A. Momigliano, *JTS* 21 (1970), pp. 149-53, and the review articles by L.H. Feldman, 'Hengel's *Judaism and Hellenism* in Retrospect', *JBL* 96 (1977), pp. 371-81 and F. Millar, 'The Background to the Maccabean Revolution: Reflections on Martin Hengel's 'Judaism and Hellenism'', *JJS* 29 (1978), pp. 1-21.

110 For a brief application of Greco-Roman models to the book culture of Palestine (dealing only with Greek books) see M. Hengel, *The 'Hellenization' of Judaea in the First Century after Christ*, trans. J. Bowden (Philadelphia: Trinity Press International, 1989), pp. 19-29 and 75-81.

111 In addition to the works on aspects of the book trade which are specifically cited below, the following discussion relies at various points on W. Schubart, *Das Buch bei den Griechen und Römern* (Berlin and Leipzig: De Gruyter, 1921); Kenyon, *Books and Readers*; and E.G. Turner, *Athenian Books in the Fifth and Fourth Centuries B.C.* (London: H.K. Lewis & Co., 1952).

three methods. First—and probably most frequently—he could deposit the work in the temple at Jerusalem.[112] Often this would entail a public reading, and in any case other intellectuals would encounter it there, for considerable learned discussion and ferment took place in and around the temple courtyards. This method was the most ancient, and the procedure by which some of the biblical prophets, for example, had published their words.[113] But it was not appropriate for every sort of writing. For this reason an author might decide to deposit the principal copy, if not with a group, then with a wealthy and influential friend. This 'Maecenas' would see to it that copies of the work were made and distributed.[114] It appears that Josephus published the Semitic version of his *Jewish War* in like manner (under Flavian patronage?). It was evidently addressed to the elders and leaders of local Eastern communities, and one may imagine that other Semitic books could be published in the same way, both within and without Palestine.[115] Finally, like Martial, an author might provide an authorial copy to one or more *librarii* (later *bibliopolae*) to copy and sell.[116] Of course, an author might employ more than one of these methods.

112 S. Lieberman, 'The Publication of the Mishnah', in *Hellenism in Jewish Palestine* (New York: Jewish Theological Seminary of America, 1950), 83-99. For a discussion of the passages in Josephus and Tannaitic literature which connect holy books with the temple at Jerusalem, see R. Beckwith, *The Old Testament Canon of the New Testament Church* (Grand Rapids: Eerdmans, 1985), pp. 80-86.

113 A number of passages in the Hebrew Bible connect books and writings with holy places and temples. Cf. Exod. 25.16, 21; 40.21 on the tables of the Ten Commandments; Deut. 10.1-5, 31.24-26 on the 'Book of Deuteronomy;' Josh. 24.26 on the written covenant between Joshua and the people; 1 Sam 10.25 on Samuel's 'Law of the King;' and 2 Kgs 22.8, etc. on the finding of the Book of the Law in the temple during the reign of Josiah. For Jer. 36 see J. Philip Hyatt, 'The Writing of an Old Testament Book', *BA* 6 (1943), pp. 71-80.

114 H.I. Marrou, 'La technique de l'édition à l'époque patristique', *VC* 3 (1949), pp. 222-24.

115 The wording of Josephus' description (ἅ τοῖς ἄνω βαρβάροις τῇ πατρίῳ συντάξας ἀνέπεμψα; and cf. *War* 1.6) makes it clear that copies were sent to Eastern diasporate communities, and, given our knowledge of diasporate Jewish organization, it is probable that he addressed his work to community leaders who were in a position to see to it that the work was distributed and read. On this Semitic (Aramaic? Hebrew?) version of *War* see e.g., T. Rajak, *Josephus: The Historian and His Society* (Philadelpha: Fortress Press, 1983), pp. 174-84.

116 H.L.M. van der Valk, 'On the Edition of Books in Antiquity', *VC* 11 (1957), pp. 1-10.

The Greek terms ἐκδιδόναι and ἔκδοσις, used regularly of publication, refer literally to an author's 'abandonment' of his work to the public.[117] Once he had released his book, the public could easily copy it before passing it on. And it was not at all unusual for readers to introduce 'improvements' in the course of a book's circulation. In fact, once a work was published, the author had no control over its circulation. Common trade copies were notoriously prone to error and distortion, a fact that led to the prestige of so-called 'autograph copies'—certifiably made from the author's original.[118] Some 'authors' would pirate the work of others, a process known as 'making extracts' (ἐκλέγειν).[119] By this method many anthologies arose. An author's work might appear in truncated or extended form, combined with extracts from other authors, while ironically no one read his original book.[120]

In the first century book production was largely a private matter. After an author had published a work, it was usual to produce scribal copies one at a time. In certain circumstances multiple copies could perhaps be produced simultaneously by means of dictation, but there is no convincing evidence that *scriptoria* as such existed prior to the Middle Ages.[121] Even the solitary scribe, however, would read his exemplar aloud, one line at a time, and sometimes repeat each word aloud again as his hand formed the letters.[122]

Upon deposit with a bookseller, all profits from a book would accrue

---

117 B.A. van Groningen, 'EKDOSIS', *Mnemosyne* 16,4 (1963), pp. 1-17.

118 Cf. Lucian, *Ind.* 4.

119 See the discussion of opisthographs above. I discuss another text among the DSS which may well be a collection of extracts in my *A Critical Study of the Temple Scroll from Qumran Cave 11* (Chicago: Oriental Institute, 1990), pp. 152-3, on which see now Reed, *List*, 4Q265.

120 Apparently this was what happened to Menander, for example.

121 See the discussion by T.C. Skeat, 'The Use of Dictation in Ancient Book-Production', *Proceedings of the British Academy* 42 (1956), pp. 179-208.

122 In general, the ancients always read aloud, even when alone. They also commonly pronounced the words aloud as they were writing. See J. Balogh, who has collected all the evidence for the ancient and medieval periods in 'Voces Paginarum', *Philologus* 82 (1927), pp. 84-109 and 202-240. For additional discussion see e.g., G.L. Hendrickson, 'Ancient Reading', *Classical Journal* 25 (1929-30), pp. 182-96; W.B. Sedgwick, 'Reading and Writing in Classical Antiquity', *Contemporary Review* 135 (Jan-June 1929), pp. 90-94; and E.S. McCartney, 'Notes on Reading and Praying Audibly', *CP* 43 (1948), pp. 184-87.

to that individual, not to the author. Booksellers charged different rates according to a book's calligraphic quality. They would employ one or more copyists, professional scribes who earned their livelihood in this manner. In the Greco-Roman world generally, most such copyists were slaves, but those connected with the temple at Jerusalem often were lower-class freemen, and even occasionally belonged to the upper classes.[123] Indeed, one of the major differences between Judaea and the empire generally was the exalted position held by certain scribes among the Jews. Alongside such Jewish intellectuals, however, were the lowly village scribes and simple copyists.

If a work generated a large demand, copies could perhaps be produced in multiples by dictation, as noted. But for most works the bookseller would stock only one copy; indeed, sometimes he would stock none at all, keeping only the exemplar. Its presence with him would be known to prospective customers, and if the need should arise, a scribe could copy out a short work from the authorial copy while the customer waited.

A number of factors must be borne in mind when considering the circulation of books in Palestine. These factors include the extent of literacy (by which I mean here the ability to read, as opposed to the much more restricted ability to write)[124] and the cost of books—factors affecting demand—as well as the breadth of circulation and the availability of libraries. With regard to the first, it is probable that

123 For the most recent and sociologically informed study of the scribe, see A. Saldarini, *Pharisees, Scribes and Sadducees in Palestinian Society* (Wilmington: Michael Glazier, 1988), esp. pp. 241-76.

124 How widespread 'literacy' was depends, of course, on how it is defined and measured. For example, in certain circumstances individuals would learn how to read, but not how to write. Is that literacy? If a person can write, how facile must he be before he is considered literate? Certainly many more people could sign their name than could write a letter; the ability to compose original literary works will have been still rarer. For discussions of the significance of literacy in the development of ancient society, and of the difficulties of defining and measuring ancient literacy, see e.g. J. Goody and I. Watt, 'The Consequences of Literacy', in *Literacy in Traditional Society*, ed. J. Goody (Cambridge: Cambridge University Press, 1986), pp. 27-68; R.S. Schofield, 'The Measurement of Literacy in Pre-Industrial England', in idem, pp. 311-25; W.V. Harris, 'Literacy and Epigraphy I', *Zeitschrift für Papyrologie und Epigraphik* 52 (1983), pp. 97-111; and F.D. Harvey, 'Literacy in Athenian Democracy', *Revue des Études Grecques* 79 (1966), pp. 585-635.

Palestine enjoyed what has been called 'craftsman's literacy.'[125] The term stands in contrast to the 'scribal literacy' (wherein only those with scribal training, much less than one percent of the population, can read and write) that had characterized earlier Ancient Near Eastern societies, and to the 'mass literacy' of today. It refers to a society in which most craftsmen can at least read, while women, unskilled laborers, and peasants generally cannot. In the Greco-Roman world males of the upper classes—among the Jews the Jerusalem aristocracy and their retainers, and local aristocracies such as village elders and property owners—could read.[126] Merchants stood somewhere between the upper classes and the peasants, and in the Greco-Roman world were perhaps fifty percent literate. On the whole perhaps ten to fifteen percent of the population of Judaea was literate.[127] Given that the Jewish population of first century Palestine, while impossible to calculate precisely with the data at our disposal, nevertheless certainly totaled well over a million, the number of potential readers was, conservatively, over 100,000.

The expense of producing an ancient book is difficult to assess. Naphtali Lewis has amassed data which suggest that for most of classical antiquity, the cost of materials plus copying for a work of moderate size would equal approximately five days' pay on the wage scale of a day-laborer.[128] Accordingly the total price of such a work

125 For the term see W.V. Harris, *Ancient Literacy* (Cambridge: Harvard University Press, 1989), pp. 7-8.

126 In Judaea there is evidence for upper class literacy already in the First Temple period. See Naveh, 'Distribution of the Hebrew Script', pp. 68-74; A.R. Millard, 'An Assessment of the Evidence for Writing in Ancient Israel', in *Biblical Archaeology Today*, pp. 301-12, and the 'Responses' to Millard by A. Demsky and J. Naveh, pp. 349-54.

127 This figure is based on Harris' conclusions for literacy in Greek and Latin in the first century Roman Empire—see *Literacy*, pp. 328-30. The figure may seem very low, and indeed it is a conservative estimate, but it must be borne in mind that the percentage is greatly reduced when one adds in the uneducated peasant masses, and the fifty percent of the population which was female. It does not take into account, however, the Jewish obligation to study the scriptures, which may have raised the figure somewhat. (Of course, even that obligation need not involve reading for every individual, since study could be done in groups, only one member of which need be literate.) Also, it does not take into account the matter of which language an educated Jew would first learn to read. The entire question of literacy among Second Temple Jews is in need of study.

128 N. Lewis, *Papyrus in Classical Antiquity* (Oxford: Clarendon Press, 1974),

averaged about 5-6 *drachmae*. For social milieux more elevated than the day-laborer's, these costs would not be prohibitive. In Jerusalem, for example, books would be well within the means of people such as merchants. Consequently anyone of sufficiently elevated social standing to be literate would be likely to have enough money to satisfy the desire for reading material.

How broadly did literary works circulate? No single answer can be given to this question, as many variables would be involved. But in Egypt the works of all the major (and many of the minor) Greek writers were copied and recopied in small towns in whose dumps the papyri chanced to survive until their discovery in the nineteenth century.[129] Analogy suggests that many Jewish works circulated widely, throughout Palestine and even, perhaps, the diaspora. For Palestine some direct evidence, although difficult to evaluate, comes from the manuscript finds associated with Masada, Naḥal Ḥever and Murabbaᶜat. Seventeen literary works survived the centuries at Masada, including nine or ten nonbiblical texts.[130] It is hard to say who owned them, as the group present when Masada fell was not identical to that which first took the fortress, and included in its ranks some refugees.[131] But of the three find-spots, Masada has the best claim to represent a cross-section of society. The excavations in the four Caves at Murabbaᶜat revealed at least eight literary texts (two or more nonbiblical) that may reasonably be assigned to the refugees who fled there in the waning period of the Bar Kochba revolt.[132] These people were probably village aristocracy and gentry, to judge from the quality of their material possessions, and the amounts of money changing

pp. 129-34. The evidence for subsistence income in Palestine at this period is sparse and difficult to interpret with any confidence. For contemporary Egypt the situation is somewhat more certain, thanks to the plentiful finds of papyri. It appears that in both regions the average annual income generated by subsistence farming was between 150-200 *drachmae*. See S. Applebaum, 'Judaea as a Roman Province; the Countryside as a Political and Economic Factor', in *ANRW* 2.8, pp. 374-77.

129 N. Lewis, *Life in Egypt under Roman Rule* (Oxford: Clarendon Press, 1983), pp. 59-64.

130 See the summary offered by Talmon, 'Fragments', p. 278 (Heb.); it differs somewhat from Yadin's preliminary report. It is uncertain whether one text is Genesis or Jubilees.

131 See Chapter Two above.

132 I.e., Mur 1-6 and 108-9. Mur 110-12 may fit in here.

hands in their contracts. The refugees of Naḥal Ḥever belonged to the same segment of society and hailed from En Gedi. Along with the extraordinary documentary finds from these Caves, a number of literary texts were unearthed: two biblical scrolls from the Cave of Letters, a Hebrew prayer, a literary text from the Cave of Horror, and, of course, the famous Greek parchment scroll of the Twelve.[133]

It is impossible to know what proportion of the books these groups of refugees and revolutionaries brought with them survived to be discovered by modern archaeologists. And it is impossible to know what proportion of the books they owned these groups managed to salvage. But the picture they suggest is consonant with the much better attested situation in Egypt of the time: fair numbers of Semitic and Greek literary works circulated in the outlying villages of Judaea. Circulation will have been aided by the steady flow of literate people to and from Jerusalem. The priests participating in their courses would come to Jerusalem for periodic service in the temple and then return to their widely-scattered homes. Peasants and freemen would also frequent Jerusalem for religious or economic reasons. Among diasporate Jewry, there is evidence for an early circulation of Semitic works among the Jews of Egypt;[134] in the east, the Jews of Babylon

---

133 See Reed, *List*, and for the Minor Prophets scroll see E. Tov, DJD 8.

134 In the *Letter of Aristeas* 30, describing what is missing from the royal library, one reads τοῦ νόμου τῶν Ἰουδαίων βιβλία σὺν ἑτέροις ὀλίγοις τισὶν ἀπολείπει· τυγχάνει γάρ Ἑβραϊκοῖς γράμμασι καὶ φωνῇ λεγόμενα, ἀμελέστερον δέ, καὶ οὐχ ὡς ὑπάρχει, σεσήμανται ... 'scrolls of the Law of the Jews, together with a few others, are missing; they are composed in the Hebrew language and script, but rather carelessly copied, not as they should be.' One may deduce from the mention of 'a few others' that, in addition to the Bible, books in Hebrew or Aramaic circulated among the Jews of Alexandria in the second century BCE. That they were carelessly copied implies that they were not official productions. It would seem, therefore, that a Hebrew and Aramaic book culture existed. If its dating is correct, the Nash papyrus may be further evidence of such. For a critical text of Aristeas see H. Swete, *An Introduction to the Old Testament in Greek* (New York: Ktav, 1968), pp. 531-606. For literature about, and options for understanding, the problematic seshvmantai, see V. Tcherikover, 'The Ideology of the Letter of Aristeas', *HTR* 51 (1958), p. 75 and n. 33. For the Nash papyrus see the anonymous 'Un papyrus hébreu pré-massorétique', *RB* 1 (1904), 242-50, and for its (paleographic!) dating see W.F. Albright, 'A Biblical Fragment from the Maccabaean Age: The Nash Papyrus', *JBL* 56 (1937), pp. 145-76. It should be considered that the Jews of Egypt during Roman-Byzantine times still wrote letters in Hebrew, some of which—probably only the tip of the iceberg—have been

may reasonably be assumed to have been familiar with at least some Palestinian works.[135]

For the Hellenistic and Roman period we know of Greek public libraries at Alexandria, Pergamum and Macedon. Given the likelihood that every major Hellenistic town had one,[136] it follows that in Judaea, at least Jerusalem had a public library. Such a library is mentioned already in 2 Macc. 2.13-15.[137] The larger Greek cities of Palestine probably had libraries as well. Herod evidently possessed a fine royal library.[138] In addition to these large institutions—some of which held thousands of rolls—smaller institutions such as gymnasia, houses of study and synagogues housed more modest collections. Medical schools, such as the Asclepion at Pergamum, gathered specialist collections. An inscription from Cos, dating to the second century BCE, records the endowment of a local library with hundreds of books.[139]

The literary sources say little about private libraries, but the extensive finds of literary papyri in Egypt mentioned above prove that some individuals even in provincial towns had collections. In Rome, private libraries among the wealthy became so common that Seneca

preserved in the Cairo Genizah and elsewhere. Thus, whatever the significance and provenance of the LXX translation of the Pentateuch into Greek, some Egyptian Jews retained a knowledge of Semitic and an interest in Semitic books.

135 In this connection it is worth noting that the mss of CD found in the Cairo Genizah are in Babylonian hands. It is, of course, impossible to know how long the work had existed among the Jews of Mesopotamia, or how it got to them in the first place. It need not be assumed, however, as it often is, that it began to circulate there only with the rise of the Karaites.

136 F.G. Kenyon and C.H. Roberts, 'Libraries', in *The Oxford Classical Dictionary* (Oxford: Clarendon Press, ²1970).

137 See the discussion in J. Goldstein, *II Maccabees* (Garden City: Doubleday, 1983), pp. 186-7. As public libraries were often attached to gymnasia, it is noteworthy that, according to 2 Macc. 4.12, a gymnasium was founded in Jerusalem in about 170 BCE. Its subsequent fate in the revolt against Antiochus IV and hellenizing members of the priestly and upper classes is unknown.

138 B.Z. Wacholder, *Nicolaus of Damascus* (Berkeley: University of California, 1962), pp. 81-6, estimates on the basis of Nicolaus' references to various Greek works in his writings that Herod's library contained over forty Greek authors. His methodology is questionable; the mere fact that Nicolaus had read an author does not prove that he had found him among Herod's scrolls. Nicolaus was, after all, a widely traveled man. Nevertheless this Caveat does not empty Wacholder's analysis of value; many of the works surely were among Herod's volumes.

139 Easterling, 'Books and Readers in the Greek World', p. 24.

thought them as essential for a well-equipped house as a bath.[140] One Roman private library is known to have numbered 30,000 scrolls.[141] Compared to earlier times, intellectual circles of the Greco-Roman world were awash in books.

A person who wanted to obtain a certain book had a number of options. He (it would almost always be a male) could, of course, simply buy it from a bookseller. He might also go to a library to examine the work. Ordinarily he could not check it out, as users of modern libraries do, although instances of borrowing are recorded. Because many books were not available by either of these procedures, however, or because he could not afford to buy the book new, a reader would sometimes resort to other means of acquisition. He might make his own copy from a friend's. A postscript to a letter found in Egypt, dating to 173 CE, is very suggestive along these lines. It reads:[142]

> Make and send me copies of Books 6 and 7 of Hypsicrates'
> Komodoumenoi . . . For Hypocration says that they are among
> Polion's books. But it is likely that others, too, have got them. He
> also has his prose epitomes of Thersagoras' works On the Myths
> of Tragedy.

Below this postscript another person has written:

> According to Harpocration, Demetrius the bookseller has got
> them [the books being sought]. I have instructed Apollonides to
> send me certain of my own books which you will hear of in good
> time from Seleucus himself. Should you find any, apart from
> those which I possess, make copies and send them to me.
> Diodorus and his friends also have some which I haven't got.

This is a clear statement of how books could be copied and passed around among educated readers. Copying from another person's book, or from a library copy,[143] must have been a common way to obtain

---

140 Seneca, *Tranq.* 9.
141 Mentioned in the Suda, s.v. 'Epaphroditus.' See Kenyon and Roberts, 'Libraries', p. 608.
142 The translation is a slightly modified form of Turner's, *Introduction*, p. 87. Lewis, *Life in Egypt*, p. 60, refers to the same papyrus.
143 Turner mentions a text in the British Museum which reads: ἐκ βιβλιοθη(κας) Πραξί(ου) Ἡρακλειδης ἀπέγραψεν. See Turner, *Introduction*, p. 181 n. 37.

books unavailable locally, or to expand a private library at minimal cost. Thus arose the personal copies so clearly evident among the DSS. Later, of course, such copies could serve as scribal Vorlagen, when one or more of the circle of scholars and friends decided he wanted a fine copy of the work in question and hired a scribe to do the work. Unfortunately, we have no way of knowing how common such twists of a book's fate might have been. Presumably it will have been connected directly or indirectly with a particular book's popularity and (not exactly synonymous) the esteem in which it was held, among other variables.

Conclusion

The authors and copyists of the Aramaic DSS wrote in a dialect that they did not ordinarily speak. In such a diglossic situation spoken forms will enter a written text from time to time, but with unpredictable frequency.[144] It could happen at the time of original composition, or at any point in the continuous process of making copies.

Ancient writers read aloud as they copied, whether working alone or by dictation. In fact four separate acts were involved in copying: (1) reading aloud to oneself (usually one line at a time); (2) holding the line briefly in one's memory; (3) dictating this material aloud to oneself; (4) moving the hand to write the words.[145] The type of scribal error most relevant to the question of linguistic dating is the 'error of the mind.' Here an error occurs at step (2) of the copying process. Errors of the mind, in contrast to other types of scribal errors, are linguistic rather than graphic.[146] The scribe processes his line mentally and in the process may adjust the language in various ways. In the transmission of

144 For a good discussion of a diglossic situation much like Palestine, and with comparable evidence of such in the textual tradition, see R. Browning, 'Greek Diglossia Yesterday and Today', in *International Journal of the Sociology of Language* 35 (1982) pp. 49-68. A very interesting example of the variations among scribal contemporaries in their ability to handle an H language related to, but different from, their vernacular appears in Skeat's discussion of the three scribes of Codex Sinaiticus. See his 'Use of Dictation', p. 192.
145 See B.M. Metzger, *The Text of the New Testament: Its Transmission, Corruption and Restoration* (New York: Oxford University Press, 1968), pp. 16-17.
146 For an illuminating discussion of this type of error see J. Andrieu, 'Pour l'explication psychologique des fautes de copiste', *Revues des études latines* 28 (1950), 279-92.

the Greek New Testament, for example, the most frequent results of this type of error are the substitution of synonyms and variation in the order of words.[147] In ancient Palestine it is easy to imagine that at step (2) spoken language forms might contaminate a text intended as what we call Standard Literary Aramaic. For an original בדי, the conjunction בדיל might be inserted;[148] for an original derived stem infinitive of the form קטלה(ה), a מקטלה could appear;[149] קטלון might be used for the perfect 3 c. pl.;[150] where the original had used the demonstrative דנה, the copyist might insert הדן.[151] All of these forms were evidently used

---

147 Metzger, *Text*, pp. 192-93. Note in this regard the words of two classical scholars well aware of the problems posed by the transmission of a language in manuscript form: 'In all kinds of text word order is subject to fluctuation. The number of variants of this kind is large enough to suggest that inferences about the word order of Latin and Greek prose should be made with great care.' Thus L.D. Reynolds and N.G. Wilson, *Scribes and Scholars: A Guide to the Transmission of Greek and Latin Literature* (Oxford: Clarendon Press, ²1974) p. 207.

148 בדיל appears at 11QtgJob 29.7, while otherwise Qumran Aramaic witnesses the 'earlier' בדי (e.g., 1QapGen 2.20). Yet the form בדיל must have been known among the Jews of Palestine by c. 250 BCE at the latest, since Eccl 8.17 contains a Hebrew calque on the Aramaic conjunction בדיל די: בשל אשר (note the 'next step' in the evolution of the Hebrew, בשל ש, in 4QMMT and Mur 46.7—and not otherwise in 'Mishnaic' Hebrew). It is therefore probable that בדיל was used in spoken dialects of Aramaic in Palestine well before the composition of any of the Aramaic DSS. On בדיל in general see J. Ribera, 'La partícula bedyl: su origen y evolución en arameo', *Aula Orientalis* 5 (1987), pp. 306-9.

149 Possibly here 1QapGen 10.15 ושרית למשחיה ביום; cf. למקימה and למעמקה in a somewhat later deed: M. Broshi and E. Qimron, 'A House Sale Deed from Kefar Baru from the Time of Bar Kochba', *IEJ* 36 (1986), pp. 201-14. Both forms occur in line 6 of the deed. Even 'Syriac' infinitival forms appear in the Babatha Archive materials; see J. Greenfield, 'The Infinitive in the Aramaic Documents from the Judaean Desert', in M. Goshen-Gottstein, S. Morag and S. Kogut (eds.), *Studies in Hebrew and Other Semitic Languages Presented to Professor Chaim Rabin on the Occasion of His Seventy-Fifth Birthday* (Jerusalem: Academon, 1990), pp. 77-81.

150 This form is known from the later written dialects, and evidently arose by analogy with the indicative *nun* of the imperfect. Note אקטרון in a fragment of 4Q547 Testament of Amram[e], PAM 43.567.

151 In addition to the form mentioned above in 4QEn[a], note 4QAmram[b] 2.2, reading הדן ע[י]רא, 'this watcher' (restoration virtually certain in the context), and cf. the uncertain 1QapGen 2.6 הדא ב]ן. A calque on this demonstrative occurs in one of the 4Q copies of CD, 4QD[a] (= 4Q266). In a portion preserving the end of the Admonition, one reads והזה פרוש המשפטים אשר יעשו בכול קץ הרשע, 'and this is the exact statement of the ordinances which they shall observe during the entire

in the spoken dialects of the time when the Aramaic DSS were composed and copied.[152] Further, since L dialects different from the H had a long history in Palestine, these phenomena and others like them are not necessarily 'late'; theoretically they could date to the Persian period, or even earlier.[153] They simply appear late because our knowledge is based on texts whose dialect excluded them.

The number of spoken forms intruding in any given text will depend upon many variables, including the ability of the original author to write the standard, the number of times the text has been copied, and the ability and intentions of its copyists. In the case of the Qumran Aramaic scrolls, apart from the fact that none of them is an autograph, we know absolutely nothing about any of these variables. Scribes copied, and sometimes very faithfully. But they also sometimes modernized or leveled irregularities they found in their *Vorlagen*.[154]

---

wicked era.' The context clearly rules out understanding the initial *heh* as interrogative. Note that in biblical Hebrew, predicative זה is always anarthrous. For this portion see J.T. Milik, 'Milki-ṣedeq et Milki-reša' dans les anciens écrits juifs et chrétiens', *JJS* 23 (1972), p. 135 and now PAM 43.277. It may be of relevance for L dialects of the DSS period that the deictic ܟܢ is attested in the contemporary Syriac Birecik inscription. This inscription is especially important in the present context because it contains a date, the equivalent of 6 CE. For the most recent edition, with photographs, see A. Maricq, 'La plus ancienne inscription syriaque: celle de Birecik. Notes posthumes mises en œuvre par Jacqueline Pirenne et Paul Devos', *Syria* 39 (1962),pp. 88-100.

152 When the linguistic paradigm shifted, probably as a result of the disastrous wars with Rome—especially that of Bar Kochba—these spoken forms came to full expression in a new written standard. All are common in later forms of Jewish Palestinian Aramaic. Again, sociolinguistic analogy suggests this interpretation of the evidence. Note the words of S.A. Kaufman, 'On Methodology in the Study of the Targums and their Chronology', JSNT 23 (1985), p. 123: ' ... literary language almost always reflects the colloquial speech of an earlier period.'

153 It will be recalled that the *mem* preformative for infinitives of derived stem verbs is the norm in the Hermopolis papyri, usually dated (paleographically) to a period prior to the Persian conquest. Further, there is general agreement that the Aramaic dialect represented in these papyri stems from Syria—i.e., the west, not too distant from Palestine. Might it not be that such forms were also a part of some contemporary Palestinian spoken dialects of Aramaic?

154 An interesting example of modernizing is attested at 4QEn⁸ 3.25, where the scribe first faithfully copied די from his *Vorlage*, then partially erased it and modernized to דֹ. A much more uncertain example of the same conversion may appear at 5.17 of the same MS.

And at other times the opposite occurred, and they inserted archaic forms.[155] Of course, a work copied by a modernizing scribe at one stage in its transmission might fall to an archaizing scribe the next time.

If the scrolls had been entirely the product of a small and insular group, and if they had circulated exclusively within the confines of that group, perhaps it would be possible somehow to allow for sociolinguistic variables. Perhaps then a better case could be made for linguistic dating as a reliable method when applied to the Aramaic DSS. But, as we have seen, the scribal phenomena of the DSS as a whole speak eloquently to the fact that they had a far wider circulation. Some of these manuscripts were probably authored or copied in rural villages. Geography thus enters the picture, and somewhat different scribal practices—some, such as orthography, of relevance to linguistic dating—will naturally be evident (although perhaps to some extent 'diluted' or disguised by subsequent copying).

155 Indeed, some authors of the period of the Aramaic DSS still used for their compositions archaic forms which had long since fallen out of general use. Thus two ossuary inscriptions dating from the Herodian period, or perhaps slightly later, still use the relative זי. See J. Naveh, 'Varia Epigraphica Judaica', *IOS* 9 (1979), 17-23. Mur 72, an ostracon containing a portion of a literary text (an autograph?) is another possible example of this phenomenon. Although J.T. Milik, the editor of the relevant portion of DJD 2, dated the text to the period 125-75 BCE by paleographic analysis, his conclusion has been questioned. S. Segert in his 'Zur Orthographie und Sprache der aramäischen Texte von Wadi Murabbaat', *ArOr* 31 (1963), pp. 129-30 connected the writing of 72 with that of Mur 30, which bears the date 134. Y. Yadin also hesitated at the early date, and stated 'one should connect it [the ostracon] with the habitation of Masada during the period of the [First] Revolt' (translation mine). He did not give the reasons for his suggestion. See his 'The Excavation of Masada—1963/4: Preliminary Report', *BIES* 29 (1965), p. 132 n. 108 (Heb.). The fact is that Milik's early date is difficult archaeologically; perhaps this was the problem which struck the Israeli archaeologist. Virtually none of the evidence obtained in the excavations of the Caves of the Wadi Murabbaᶜat can be interpreted as favoring their habitation at the time of Milik's date, whereas all of that evidence can happily be reconciled with the proposition that they were uninhabited between the Iron Age and the time of the First Revolt. In the light of its possible late date, then, it is interesting to observe that Mur 72 writes זי and זנה. Of course, if either the sepulchral inscriptions or Mur 72 were subjected to linguistic dating, they would falsely be considered earlier than any of the Aramaic DSS. For Mur 72 see DJD 2: 172-4 and plate 52. For the archaeology of the Murabbaᶜat Caves see R. de Vaux, 'Archéologie', in DJD 2, pp. 3-49, esp. 10-12 (on Cave 2, where Mur 72 was discovered).

Not the least of the ramifications of seeing the scrolls in the context of the book culture is that it emphasizes our ignorance of the pedigree of any given ms among the scrolls. Although the major Aramaic DSS as we have them are apparently scribal—not amateur or scholarly— copies, we cannot be at all certain the same was true of their *Vorlagen*. One or more of these works may derive, proximately or distantly, from a personal copy such as 4QEn^a. We have noted the manner in which scholars copied books for themselves and each other, sometimes employing a scribe, sometimes not. Such private copies are the sort most likely to depart from whatever norms of spelling and usage existed, and, of course, to contain spoken language forms. If, as is not unlikely, a text with a private copy in its background came to us in a scribal hand, we would have no way of recognizing its bastardized genealogy; submitted to linguistic dating, it would often appear late. Yet it might be only two copies removed from a Ptolemaic period autograph. And it is not inconceivable that an older work copied once by a less faithful or able scribe might contain more 'late' linguistic phenomena than a younger one four or five manscript generations old, each of whose copyists had been careful and well-educated. *We simply do not know how much change has taken place in any given text since it left the author's hand.* An unknown number of generational copies and scribal hands will have obscured the language of the autograph to an unknown extent.

In a diglossic scribal context, then, *the presence of 'late' linguistic phenomena in a given text is meaningless for dating.* It says nothing of when a given form first appeared or first became commonly used. A form's absence in texts does not prove it had not yet arisen in speech. Consequently the relative frequency of diagnostic forms in any two scrolls does not necessarily indicate priority at the level of the autographs.[156] And not only has linguistic dating overlooked the implications of diglossia for its approach—it has simply paid no serious attention to the phenomena of the book culture in the Greco-Roman period. In such neglect of the vicissitudes of scribal and non-scribal transmission lies the method's fatal flaw. Of course, it may be that linguistic dating as practiced has here or there yielded approximately correct results; but can we recognize their probity?

---

156 If such forms were extremely common, perhaps more could be made of them; but it must be remembered that in most instances we are talking about two or three forms in one text versus none in another.

In short, linguistic dating of the Aramaic DSS is an exercise in futility. The method has not come to terms with fundamental theoretical difficulties, the heart of which is an irremediable ignorance. In this instance linguistic dating cannot work. Indeed, its application to these books strikes one as a final ironic twist in their fate, a pellucid illustration of Terence's ancient dictum.

Chapter Four

THAT WHICH HAS BEEN IS THAT WHICH SHALL BE:
4QFLORILEGIUM AND THE מקדש אדם

Introduction

Ever since its preliminary publication by Allegro in the late 1950s,[1] the Qumran work known as 4QFlorilegium (=4Q174; henceforth 4QFlor) has been controversial. Scholarly attention has focused particularly on the first thirteen lines of column one. This portion, by no means transparent even where fully preserved, is further beclouded by lacunae at crucial junctures. Among the questions that it has raised are: how many temples are in view? Historically and metaphysically speaking, which temples are these? What is the meaning of the enigmatic phrase מקדש אדם and, concomitantly, of the elements that characterize it in 1.6-7?

With the publication of the Temple Scroll (henceforth TS) in 1977, a new light was cast on these questions, and the study of 4QFlor received fresh impetus. The two texts seem to be mutually illuminating. Of course, there is little hope for a well-grounded reappraisal of 4QFlor apart from an accurate understanding of the TS, and it is particularly when dealing with the TS that recent studies of 4QFlor have been unconvincing. Consequently, before turning the discussion to 4QFlor itself, it is necessary to consider the relevant phenomena of the TS. Building in part on an understanding of that text, in what follows I will

---

1   'Further Messianic Reference in Qumran Literature', *JBL* 75 (1956), pp. 174-87; 'Fragments of a Qumran Scroll of Eschatological Midrashim', *JBL* 77 (1958), pp. 350-54. The *editio princeps* is J.M. Allegro, DJD 5, 53-57 and plates XIX-XX. The extensive restudy of the texts of DJD 5 by J. Strugnell should be consulted for improved readings and the alignment of fragments. See 'Notes en Marge du Volume V des Discoveries in the Judaean Desert of Jordan', *RevQ* 7 (1970), pp. 220-25. Also, many of the studies of 4QFlor that are cited below suggest improved readings and restorations.

4QFlorilegium and the מקדש אדם 153

propose new answers to the central questions of 4QFlor 1.1-13.[2] I will
argue that the author of this Hebrew text would have understood the
view of history held by Qoheleth and quoted in the title of this essay.
He, also, believed that the end would be like the beginning, although
unlike the third century sage his view of history was not so much
cyclical as circular. His use of the term מקדש אדם, thus far elusive, is
in fact allusive. Before essaying that argument, however, I turn to the
text,[3] its translation and a general overview of the portion in question.

Text and Translation of 4QFlorilegium 1.1-13

Text

1 [ולוא ירגז עו]ד אויב [ולוא יוסי]ף בן עולה ⁴[לנלות]ו כאשר
בראישונה ולמן היום אשר

---

2   The reasons for believing that it is legitimate methodology to approach
4QFlor via the TS will become apparent in the ensuing discussion.
3   For the text I largely follow D. Dimant. See her '4QFlorilegium and the Idea
of the Community as Temple', in *Hellenica et Judaica: Hommage à Valentin
Nikiprowetzky,* ed. A. Caquot, M. Hadas-Lebel and J. Riaud (Paris: Éditions
Peeters, 1986), pp. 165-89, esp. 166-7 for the text. For the options that scholars
have suggested for the lacunae, her notes on pages 167-70 represent the most recent
discussion and evaluation.
4   Dimant adopts the restoration of לענות, in accordance with the text of 2 Sam.
7.10, and perhaps this suggestion is indeed correct. It was the original restoration of
Allegro and most scholars have since acquiesced to it. But in view of the textual
corruption of Nathan's oracle in the MT, both here and in the parallel text of 1
Chronicles 17, it might be worth considering a restoration based on the text of 1
Chron. 17.9. There the MT reading is the very difficult לבלותו. The corresponding
reading of the Peshitta is perhaps preferable: ܠܡܒܠܝܘܬܗ i.e., a *Pael* or *Aphel*
infinitive of *gl'* plus 3ms suffix. The reading suggests that the translator had before
him a Hebrew *Vorlage* that read לנלותו. If the author of 4QFlor also knew such a
text, it seems likely that he would cite it here. That citation would suit his
interpretation of the biblical text, that foreign elements had polluted the First and
Second temples (cf. the use of the root שמם below, and the meaning 'defile' for that
root as suggested by D. Flusser, 'Two Notes on the Midrash on 2 Sam. vii', *IEJ* 9
[1959], p. 91 n. 9). The root גלה would conveniently allow him punning
interpretations on the basis of the similar roots גלה and גלא, both of which can
mean 'defile' in DSS Hebrew. See the notes on both roots in E. Qimron, *The
Hebrew of the Dead Sea Scrolls* (Atlanta: Scholars Press, 1986), p. 89.

2 ‏[צויתי שפטים] על עמי ישראל הואה הבית אשר ⁵[יכוננו ל]וא[
‏באחרית הימים כאשר כתוב בספר

3 ‏[מושה מקדש אדוני כ]וננו ידיכה יהוה ימלוך עולם ועד הואה
‏הבית אשר לוא יבוא שמה

4 ‏[   ]עד עולם ועמוני ומואבי וממזר ובן נכר וגר עד
‏עולם כיא קדושי שם

5 ‏יגנל]ה [כבוד] עולם תמיד עליו יראה ולוא ישמוהו עוד זרים
‏כאשר השמו בראישונה

6 ‏מקדנש י]שראל בחטאתמה ויואמר לבנות לוא מקדש אדם
‏להיות את מקטירים בוא לוא

7 ‏מעשי תורה ואשר אמר לדויד ונ[הניחו]תי לכה מכול אויביכה
‏לפניו אשר יניח להמה מכ]ול

8 ‏בני בליעל המכשילים אותמה לכלותמ[ה באונ]מה כאשר באו
‏במחשבת בליעל להכשיל בנ[י

9 ‏אונ]ר ולחשוב עליהמה מחשבות און ל[נמען ית]פשו לבליעל
‏במשגת אשמה vacat

10 ‏[והג]יד לכה יהוה כיא בית יבנה לכה והקימותי את זרעכה
‏אחריכה והכינותי את כסא ממלכתו

11 ‏[לעול]ם אני אהיה לוא לאב והוא יהיה לי לבן הואה צמח דויד
‏העומד עם דורש התורה אשר

12 ‏[יקום] בצי[ון ב]א[]חרית הימים כאשר כתוב והקימותי את סוכת
‏דויד הנופלת הואה סוכת סוכת

13 ‏דויד הנופל[ת א]שר יעמוד להושיע את ישראל   vacat

Translation

1 [...*and no*]*enemy* [*shall disturb aga*]*in*, [*nor*]*wicked man*
[*'defile'*] *it as happened at the first, even from the day on which*
2 [*I appointed judges*] *over my people Israel.'* (2 Sam. 7.10-11a)[6]

5 Here Dimant suggests restoring ‏יכין. Her suggestion apparently derives from
her understanding of the Temple Scroll, particularly of TS 29.10, and from her
ideas about the relationship of the ‏מקדש אדם to the temple of Exod. 15.17. Y.
Yadin had originally advocated ‏יעשה, based on the biblical text of 2 Sam. 7.10—
see 'A Midrash on 2 Sam. 7 and Pss.1-2(4Q Florilegium)', *IEJ* 9 (1959), p. 95. In
his publication of the Temple Scroll, however, Yadin changed his mind—because
of his interpretation of that scroll—and suggested restoring ‏יברא. See Y. Yadin,
The Temple Scroll, 3 vols. plus supplement (Jerusalem: Israel Exploration Society,
1983), 1, p. 185. My understanding of the TS and its relation to this text has
likewise colored my suggestion for the lacuna.
6 As a number of scholars have pointed out, the lemma almost certainly began

This refers to the house that [they will prepare] for [him] in the
End of Days, as it is written in the book

3   of [Moses, *'A Temple of the Lord]you are to prepare (with)
your hands; Yahweh will reign forever and ever.'* (Exod.
15.17)[7] This refers to the house that no [...] will enter

4   forever, nor Ammonite nor Moabite nor bastard nor foreigner
nor alien forever. For his holiness will be rev[eale]d there;

5   eternal [glory] will always be seen resting upon it. Strangers
shall not defile it again, as they defiled at the first

6   the Temp[le of I]srael, because of their sins. To that end he
ordered that they build him a Temple of Adam, and that in it
they sacrifice to him {before him}[8]

7   proper sacrifices. And as for what he said to David, *'I [will
give] you [rest] from all your enemies'* (2 Sam 7.11b); this
means that he will give them rest from [al]l

8   the Sons of Belial, who cause them to stumble so as to destroy
the[m through] their [wickedness], just as they entered in with
the plan of Belial, which was to cause the S[ons] of

9   Li[ght] to stumble; and they plotted against them wicked
schemes, [in order that they might be sei]zed by Belial through
guilty error.

10   *'And Yahweh ann[ounces] to you that he will build you a house,
and that "I will raise up your seed after you, and I will
establish the throne of his kingdom*

11   *[forev]er. I will be a father to him, and he will be my son."'* (2
Sam. 7.11c, 12b, 13b-14a) This refers to the Shoot of David,
who is to arise with

12   the Searcher of the Torah, and who will [arise] in Zi[on at the

---

in the column preceding the text as preserved, i.e., with the beginnning of verse 10
of the biblical text. Thus it would include the Hebrew word מקום. In its meaning
'temple' that term evidently underlies the midrashic interpretation that follows.

7   My translation attempts to render the text as the author of 4Q Flor construed
it. The result is not a modern scientific translation, nor are the textual readings it
presupposes necessarily those that modern textual criticism would consider
original. For example, I do not suppose that the reading of אדוני here is likely to be
original rather than יהוה, nor that my translation is likely to be what the author of
Exod 15.17 really meant. For a justification of the translation of line 3 in particular,
see note 63 below.

8   It would appear that the text as it stands is disturbed, for either לוא or לפניו is
otiose.

E]nd of Days, as it is written, '*And I shall raise up the Booth* [9] *of David that is fallen.*' (Amos 9.11) This refers to the Branch of
13   David that is fall[en, w]ho shall arise to save Israel.

Purpose and Method

4QFlor 1.1-13 is an exegesis of Nathan's dynastic oracle to David. Implicitly it argues that the proper application of the biblical text is to the eschatological period, the End of Days. The Qumran text reinterprets the two themes that are the central concerns of the biblical text: the temple and the Davidic dynasty. The temple of the biblical text becomes the eschatological temple; the dynasty finds fulfillment in a messianic Davidide.

The reader encounters various methods of interpretation in 4QFlor. Its author used certain exegetical devices known from Qumran *pesharim,*[10] but the text is not—or at least not exactly—a *pesher.*[11] The author apparently knew his method as מדרש[12] and, indeed, the exegesis proceeds largely through devices common to rabbinic midrash. One notes especially the combination of biblical verses by *gezerah shavah.* Thus the word מקום of 2 Sam. 7.10 leads to the term מקדש of Exod. 15.17. The word והקימותי of 2 Sam. 7.12b connects to the same word in Amos 9.11.[13] As I hope to show—and as it is important to emphasize—in such manner the author sometimes alludes to biblical

9   As first noted by L. Silberman, 'A Note on 4Q Florilegium', *JBL* 78 (1959), pp. 158-9, the author of the midrash evidently read the MT סוכה, 'booth', also as a word for 'branch.' Thus his comment in lines 12-13 is to suggest the alternate reading, and thereby support his exegesis of 2 Samuel.

10   For an analysis of these techniques, see M.P. Horgan, *Pesharim: Qumran Interpretations of Biblical Books* (Washington, DC: Catholic Biblical Association of America, 1979), pp. 237-47.

11   For a discussion of the genre of the text, see G. Brooke, *Exegesis at Qumran: 4Q Florilegium in its Jewish Context* (Sheffield: JSOT Press, 1985), pp. 139-46.

12   Column 1, line 14. Note that the term does not appear in lines 1-13, however, and therefore it is uncertain whether the author would have characterized those lines in the same way—cf. the comments of W.R. Lane, 'A New Commentary Structure in 4Q Florilegium', *JBL* 78 (1959), pp. 343-46. The lacunose condition of the portions of 4QFlor that follow on line 14 prevents a meaningful comparison of the techniques used.

13   The author evidently knew of a tradition that varied from the MT, which reading is אקים.

verses that he *never actually quotes*. Along with *gezerah shavah*, the
wordplay in lines 12-13 between terms meaning 'branch' and 'booth' is
reminiscent of the rabbinic *lo' tiqra*. Admixed with interpretations
secured by these techniques are the declarative 'this is that' statements
known from the *pesharim*. The modern reader of the Bible searches in
vain for the textual mandate behind such identifications. Where their
reasoning can be traced, they often involve subtle exegetical
triangulation and allusion; but ultimately their authority is that of the
author or his tradition. Perhaps some or all of these expositions depend
upon traditional written sources to which the author had recourse.

Previous Scholarship on 4QFlorilegium

Both before and since the publication of the TS in 1977,[14] scholars have
been divided on the question of how many distinct temples the terms
מקדש ישראל, מקדש אדוני and מקדש אדם represent. They have
further disagreed as to the nature and identity of those temples, as Table
1 indicates:

---

14   Y. Yadin, מגילת המקדש, 3 vols. and supplemental plates (Jerusalem: Israel
Exploration Society, 1977). Because Yadin substantially revised his work with the
issuance of the 1983 English edition *The Temple Scroll,* references here are to the
latter publication.

Scholar and Year of Writing[15]	#1 מקדש אדוני	#2 מקדש ישראל	#3 מקדש אדם
Flusser, 1959—2 Temples	Future, God-Built	Present	=#1; Physical
Gärtner, 1965—2 Temples	Future, God-Built	does not discuss	=#1; Qumran Community
Gaster, 1976—2 Temples	Future, metaphysical	Past (Undefined)	=#1; Qumran Community
McNicol, 1977—2 Temples	Future, God-Built (?)	2nd Temple	=#1; Physical (?)
Schwartz, 1979—3 Temples	Future, God-Built	Past and Present (2nd Temple)	Solomonic Temple
Ben-Yasher, 1981—2 Temples	Future, God-Built	Past and Present (1st and 2nd)	=#1; Physical
Yadin, 1983—2 Temples	Future, God-Built	Past (Undefined)	=#1; Physical
Wacholder, 1983—2 Temples	Future, God-Built	Past	=#1; Physical (Undefined)
Dimant, 1986—3 Temples	Future, God-Built	Past and Present	Present; Physical and Community
Knibb, 1987—2 Temples	Future, God-Built	Past (Undefined)	=#1; Qumran Community
Vermes, 1987—3 Temples	Future, God-Built	Past (Undefined)	Present; Qumran Community

Table 1. The Temples of 4QFlorilegium

15   D. Flusser, 'Two Notes;' cf. the revised form in his *Judaism and the Origins of Christianity* (Jerusalem: Magnes Press, 1988), pp. 88-98; B. Gärtner, *The Temple and the Community in Qumran and in the New Testament* (Cambridge: CUP, 1965), pp. 30-42; T. Gaster, *The Dead Sea Scriptures* (3rd ed., Garden City, N.Y.: Doubleday, 1976), pp. 446-47; A. McNicol, 'The Eschatological Temple in the Qumran Pesher 4QFlorilegium 1.1-7', *Ohio Journal of Religious Studies* 5 (1977), pp. 133-41; D.R. Schwartz, 'The Three Temples of 4Q Florilegium', *RevQ* 10 (1979-81), pp. 83-91; M. Ben Yasher, 'Noch zum Miqdaš 'Adam in 4Q Florilegium', *RevQ* 10 (1979-81), pp. 587-88; Y. Yadin, *Temple Scroll*, 1, pp. 182-87; 2, p. 129; B.Z. Wacholder, *The Dawn of Qumran: The Sectarian Torah and the Teacher of Righteousness* (Cincinnati: Hebrew Union College Press, 1983), pp. 93-94; D. Dimant, '4Q Florilegium;' M. Knibb, *The Qumran Community* (Cambridge: Cambridge University Press, 1987), pp. 258-62 and G. Vermes, *The Dead Sea Scrolls in English* (3rd ed., Sheffield: JSOT Press, 1987), pp. 293-94.

Scholars have construed either two or three temples in 4QFlor,
according as they have identified or distinguished between the מקדש
אדוני and the מקדש אדם. They have interpreted the latter either as a
physical temple or as a metaphysical entity equivalent to the Qumran
community. A consensus has formed on the identification of the first
temple, but the same cannot be said for the others. In fact, the
differences in scholarly opinion are even greater than the table
represents. For example, Yadin and Wacholder appear in the table to
hold the same views, but in reality their positions are radically
different—a function of their interpretations of the TS, as we shall see
below.

Also for the meaning of מקדש אדם—clearly the key to the entire
text—the table affords only an approximation of the different scholarly
conceptions. Four basic views of the phrase's precise denotation have
developed, scholars variously suggesting that the phrase signifies:

(1). 'A sanctuary made by men standing among men' (Lohse,
Schwartz, Dupont-Sommer, Allegro, Lane, Carmignac, McNicol,
Moraldi and Maier).[16]
(2). 'A sanctuary made by God standing among men' (Flusser, Yadin
and Ben-Yasher).
(3). 'A sanctuary made by men consisting of men' (Gaster, Knibb,
Gärtner and Dimant [with a twist]).
(4). 'A sanctuary made by God consisting of men' (Baumgarten,
Vermes and Brooke).[17]

---

16   In addition to the references already cited, see: E. Lohse, *Die Texte aus
Qumran* (3rd ed., Munich: Kösel Verlag, 1981), p. 257; A. Dupont-Sommer, *The
Essene Writings from Qumran,* trans. G. Vermes (Gloucester: Peter Smith, 1973),
p. 312; J. Carmignac, É. Cothenet and H. Lignée, *Les textes de Qumran* (2 vols.;
Paris: Letouzey et Ané, 1961-63), 2, p. 282; L. Moraldi, *I manoscritti di Qumran*
(Turin: Unione Tipografico-Editrice Torinese, 1971), p. 573, and J. Maier, *Die
Texte vom Toten Meer* (2 vols.; Munich: E. Reinhardt, 1960), 1, p. 185.
17   In addition to the authors already cited, see Brooke, *Exegesis at Qumran,* p.
92, and J. Baumgarten, 'The Exclusion of 'Netinim' and Proselytes in 4Q
Florilegium', *RevQ* 8 (1972), pp. 87-96, republished in *Studies in Qumran Law*
(Leiden: Brill, 1977). In the latter volume, to which I refer here, he gives his
translation of the phrase on p. 76. More recently, Baumgarten has nuanced the
positions he took in this article, but his revised views do not appear to have affected
his understanding of the phrase in question. See his 'Exclusions from the Temple:

The translations offered are variants of either 'a temple among men' or 'a temple of (i.e. consisting of) men.'

The other elements of lines 6-7, which one might hope would resolve the ambiguity of this phrase, unfortunately only heighten it, as they are themselves ambigious. Consequently they, also, have given rise to divergent interpretations, largely but not solely controlled by the individual scholar's understanding of מקדש אדם.

Interpreters have explained the words מעשי תורה as either 'works of Law' in a general sense, without particular reference to the sacrificial cultus,[18] or as referring specifically to sacrifices made in conformity with the Law.[19] Those who have taken the latter view have sometimes thought in terms of a broad equivalence to the entire cultus. Others construe the phrase more narrowly. Most who subscribe to this narrower interpretation see a reference to incense. And a few students of the text have advocated a different reading altogether, מעשי תודה, 'works of thanksgiving.'[20] Following this reading,[21] there may be no allusion to sacrifice at all, whether general or specific. Thus, not only do scholars see מקדש אדם in four fundamentally different ways, but the phrase מעשי תורה elicits at least as many different views.

Tied in with the ambiguity of that phrase is the next element of the line, מקטרים. The word is susceptible of two basic meanings. In the Hebrew Bible the root קטר refers either specifically to the burning of incense, or simply to the act of sacrifice in general. With this wide semantic domain the term can equally well support virtually any of the interpretations of מעשי תורה. Most students of 4QFlor explain the word in accordance with whether they believe מקדש אדם to mean a physical or a metaphysical temple. The 'burning of incense,' if given a metaphorical nuance, is compatible with the idea of a metaphysical temple.

Proselytes and Agrippa I', *JJS* 33 (1982), pp. 215-25.

18　Thus Baumgarten, Gaster, Lohse, Vermes, Knibb, Gärtner, Moraldi and Maier.

19　So Flusser, Dimant, Allegro, Lane, Dupont-Sommer, McNicol and Carmignac.

20　Strugnell first suggested this option in 'Notes en marge', p. 221, and Brooke, *Exegesis at Qumran,* p. 92, adopts it. The image that this reading conjures is congenial to some in view of Amos 4.5.

21　Dimant, '4Q Florilegium', p. 169, argues that the reading is materially impossible. I do not agree, but, as I hope to show below, the reading nevertheless cannot be correct on exegetical grounds.

Finally, even ויואמר has divided interpreters. Scholars align on its meaning as a function of their concept of מקדש אדם, and of who they understand to be that temple's builder. In fact, however, ויואמר has received insufficient attention. As I hope to show, a determination of its meaning and structural function is crucial to the interpretation of 4QFlor 1.1-13. I shall return to it below, after considering the matter of the temples of the TS, and how they may elucidate the מקדש אדם.

The Temples of the Temple Scroll

The TS is a long text, one of the longest found in the Caves near Qumran. It begins with a general exhortation based on Exodus 34 , Deuteronomy 7 and perhaps Deuteronomy 12.[22] Although the early columns of the text are badly broken, enough remains to show that this exhortation did not exceed one or one and a half columns in length.[23] Thereupon begins a lengthy program for the construction of a temple complex surrounded by three concentric square courtyards. This description occupies virtually all of columns 3-46 of the TS, apart from a break in columns 13-29 for the insertion of a festival calendar. Beginning in column 45 (and thus overlapping in part the building instructions), appear a series of purity laws, derived by midrashic techniques from portions of Numbers and Leviticus.[24] From column 51 to 66, the redactor of the scroll presents a form of the laws of Deuteronomy 12-26,[25] arranged topically and with some very interesting omissions that will be noted shortly. Therewith the scroll ends abruptly.

Of great import for the understanding of the scroll is the fact that the redactor has eliminated the name of Moses where it should appear in his biblical excerpts. This omission has the effect of rendering the biblical portions direct communication between the scroll's author and God. Although scholars have generally overlooked the second option, this phenomenon can be taken in either of two ways.

22 For the significance of Deuteronomy 12 for the Temple Scroll, see M.O. Wise, *A Critical Study of the Temple Scroll from Qumran Cave 11* (Chicago: Oriental Institute, 1990), pp. 155-6 and 161-7.
23 This point assumes, of course, that no sheets are missing from the beginning of the scroll. Each sheet of the extant TS contains three or four columns.
24 Wise, *Critical Study,* pp. 315-18.
25 Idem, pp. 240-60.

First, the author of the scroll could be perpetrating a pseudepigraphon. He could be claiming to have discovered a long-lost writing from the hand of Moses. Such literary works were common in late Second Temple Judaism, of course, and this is the interpretation that Yadin preferred.[26] Wacholder and other writers on the TS have followed him.[27]

But it is also possible that the author was more audacious. Rather than claiming merely to have found a book written by the archetypal prophet, the redactor could be insisting that Moses' mantel has fallen to him. In other words, perhaps he is claiming to be that 'prophet like Moses' (Deut 18.15) whom certain elements of society in the late Second Temple period expected as a herald of the eschaton. In that case the TS is intended as a new Deuteronomy, a new Law for the land governing the eschatological period. The redactional phenomena of the scroll favor this option, and I have argued for it elsewhere.[28] The difference between the two options of interpretation is, of course, profound, and of pivotal significance for the understanding of 4QFlor. This significance becomes manifest through a consideration of TS 29.7b-10.[29]

7 [ו]שכנתי
8 אתמה לעולם ועד ואקדשה [את מ]קדשי בכבודי אשר אשכין
9 עליו את כבודי עד יום הבריה אשר אברא אני את מקדשי
10 להכינו לי כול הימים כברית אשר כרתי עם יעקוב בבית אל

---

26   Yadin's view was present already in his preliminary reports in 1967, made within months of acquiring the scroll. See 'מגילח המקדש', in *Jerusalem Through the Ages: The Twenty-Fifth Archaelogical Convention October 1967* (Jerusalem: Israel Exploration Society, 1968), pp. 72-84; 'The Temple Scroll', *BA* 30 (1967), pp. 135-39, and 'Un nouveau manuscrit de la Mer Morte: 'Le Rouleau du Temple',' *CRAIBL* (1967), pp. 607-16. He continued to hold this view until the end; for its clearest expression see *The Temple Scroll: The Hidden Law of the Dead Sea Sect* (London: Weidenfeld and Nicolson, 1985), pp. 226-28.

27   For Wacholder, see *The Dawn of Qumran,* 112-19; for other scholars holding this view see Wise, *Critical Study,* esp. 31-33.

28   Wise, *Critical Study, passim.*

29   For a justification of the translation and general consideration of certain ramifications of this text, see my 'The Covenant of Temple Scroll XXIX, 3-10', in *RevQ* 14 (1989), pp. 49-60. For the text, I have followed Yadin (*The Temple Scroll,* 2: 128-29) except for line 9, where I prefer Qimron's reading of הבריה. See E. Qimron, 'מן העבודה במלון ההסטורי', *Leshonenu* 42 (1978), p. 142.

(7b)...[and] I shall dwell (8) with them forever and ever, and sanctify my [te]mple with my glory, for I shall cause (9) my glory to dwell upon it until the Day of Creation, when I myself shall create my temple, (10) to establish it for me forever—according to the covenant that I made with Jacob at Bethel...

In the TS, this portion constitutes a redactional seam, bridging between two of the scroll's major sources. It apparently differentiates between two temples, the one for which the scroll provides a verbal blueprint and the one which, in the Day of Creation, God himself will create. Once again, as in 4QFlor, the question is the identity of the temples.

For Yadin and virtually all who see in the TS a pseudepigraphic writing *stricto sensu,* the future temple that God will create is a single eschatological temple. Accordingly the previous temple whose construction the TS details is an idealized First Temple, the one that Solomon should have built. And since the Second Temple was intended to be a rebuilding of the Solomonic one, it is simultaneously an idealized Second Temple. Thereby it represents an implicit criticism of the temple standing in Jerusalem in the author's day.

Among those who have reexamined 4QFlor in the light of the TS, all but Wacholder have adopted Yadin's view of the TS temples. As a result they have identified the מקדש אדם of 4QFlor with the temple of the Day of Creation.[30] In contrast, for Wacholder the temple whose construction the TS orders is not distinct from that which God will create; in other words, he sees only one, not two temples in TS 29. Yet he believes that one temple is nevertheless the same as the מקדש אדם of 4QFlor. Consequently (despite certain problems with his view in the context of the TS), for the interpretation of the first temple of 4QFlor he falls together with Yadin.[31]

But if the TS is a new Deuteronomy intended to serve for the eschaton, and simultaneously one recognizes in TS 29.7b-10 reference to two temples, that interpretation is problematic. If the TS is an eschatological Deuteronomy, then, of course, *both* temples of TS 29 are eschatological temples. Such a possibility is not at all unlikely. Other literary works of the Second Temple period also conceived of a two-

---

30   Thus Schwartz, 'Three Temples', p. 86 n. 11, and Dimant, '4Q Florilegium', pp. 187-88.

31   Wacholder, *Dawn of Qumran,* p. 27.

stage eschaton.[32] If the views of the author of the TS approximated to the schema of those other books, the first stage would constitute a messianic millennium, and the second would be nothing less than a New Creation.

In such an eschatological scheme, the מקדש אדם of 4QFlor is best considered as identical with the temple that the TS orders 'Israel' to build. It is a temple for the End of Days, but it would function only in the first stage of the eschaton. It would later be supplanted by the temple created by God. The terminology of 4QFlor happily supports this interpretation provided that the first and third temples, the מקדש אדוני and the מקדש אדם, can be shown to be identical.

As a first step in considering this equation it is instructive to dwell for a moment upon the the term אחרית הימים. 4QFlor 1.2 specifies that the מקדש אדוני will function during this period.[33] But what precisely did the author have in mind by his use of אחרית הימים? If such a question can be answered at all, the answer appears to lie in another of the DSS texts, the Damascus Covenant (CD). The substantial number of *termini technici* that appear in both CD and 4QFlor seems to require that the two texts have a definable relationship.[34] If so, then it is legitimate to use CD to loose the knots of 4QFlor, and in particular to clarify the purport of אחרית הימים. Unlike 4QFlor, CD rather clearly defines the term.

32　This idea is clearly present in 2 (Syriac) Baruch and 2 Esdras, but there are hints of it also in much earlier works. It appears in the Apocalypse of Weeks in 1 Enoch (91.12-17, 93.1-10) and less clearly in Jubilees. See e.g., D.S. Russell, *The Method and Message of Jewish Apocalyptic* (Philadelphia: Fortress, 1964), pp. 291-297.

33　In fact all the events, persons and institutions with which the midrash is concerned are said to exist or take place in the אחרית הימים.

34　Brooke finds eleven significant verbal connections between the two texts. Not all of his suggestions are equally convincing, but the four instances of technical terms or phrases occurring in both texts are hard to explain unless some relationship exists between them. The technical terms are: יתפשו לבליעל (1.9 *[si vera lectio]* and CD 4.16-18); דורש התורה (1.11 and CD 6.7, 7.18 ['A' text]—note, however, that although this term appears nowhere else in DSS literature as a formal title, its use does not seem to be quite identical in the two texts); אחרית הימים itself (only in 4QFlor, 1.2, 12, 15, 19 and CD 4.4 and 6.11, the *pesharim* and 1QSa as a term for the eschaton); and the unqualified use of בני צדוק (1.17 and CD 4.3). See Brooke, *4Q Florilegium*, 206-209. Since Brooke wrote, the term אחרית ימים has come to light in additional texts, and not all of them are 'sectarian' (i.e., apparently connected to CD or 1QS); cf. 4Q509 7 5 and 4Q504 iii 13-14.

In the ideology of the Damascus Covenant, God has a legal case (ריב) against Israel, because they have forsaken his commandments.[35] Only a remnant has remained faithful to him, holding to the covenant that he made with the patriarchs. According to CD 1.8, this righteous remnant, now in 'exile,' will inherit the land, displacing the present wicked inhabitants.[36] During the present exile, the CD community adheres to laws that their founder laid down sometime in the past. According to CD 6.11,[37] however, the community did not regard these laws as eternally valid. They were valid only until the eschaton began, only for the present period, known as the Wicked Era—the קץ הרשע.[38] In the community's perspective, the satisfaction of God's lawsuit, inheriting the land, and the end of the Wicked Era would all be simultaneous with the beginning of the eschaton or End of Days. In the context of CD it is thus possible to show that the terms 'Wicked Era' and 'End of Days' are precise technical terms.

At this point column 29 of the TS re-enters the discussion. Although lack of space precludes a full discussion of the point here, I have previously argued that the redactor of the the TS was a member of the CD community.[39] Furthermore, he explicitly connects his first temple, and presumably also his entire new Law, to the preliminary stage of the eschaton.[40] And presumably, as a member of the CD community, he would know that period by its technical name of אחרית הימים. If so, given its technical sense he would further distinguish between that era and the subsequent one to be inaugurated by God's creation of a temple. Apparently he and his community would know the last period—or, minimally, its inception—as יום הבריה;[41] this is the term

---

35   On the ideology of the text I follow the interpretation of P.R. Davies, *The Damascus Covenant: An Interpretation of the 'Damascus Document'* (Sheffield: JSOT Press, 1983), pp. 66-67 and 128. For the lawsuit, cf. CD 1.2-4.

36   See H.W. Huppenbauer, 'Zur Eschatologie der Damaskusschrift', *RevQ* 4 (1963-64), p. 573. The 'exile' need not be literal, on which note especially M. Knibb, 'Exile in the Damascus Document', *JSOT* 25 (1983), pp. 99-117.

37   The text states that the group will live by the laws בכל קץ הרשע ... עד עמד יורה הצדק באחרית הימים. Note the force of עד, which implies a change at the inception of the eschaton.

38   CD 6.10, 6.14, 12.23-13.1, 15.6-7, and probably the broken 15.10.

39   I follow Davies in the view that the CD community was not the same as the community of the *pesharim* and 1QS.

40   See Wise, *Critical Study,* esp. pp. 133-89.

41   Perhaps the full technical name of the period would be קץ הבריה החדשה.

by which it is identified in TS 29.9.[42] Thus one can distinguish three distinct periods, all known by technical names, as follows:

1. קץ הרשע: the present and the past, or at least some of the past.
2. אחרית הימים: the near future.[43]
3. יום הבריה: the remote future.

Since 4QFlor specifically states that the מקדש אדוני will exist in the אחרית הימים, it follows that—despite what may seem to be the straightforward meaning of the quotation from Exod 15.17—the phrase מקדש אדוני does *not* designate the temple that God will create. (The quotation must have meant something different to the author of 4QFlor than it did to the Massoretes. I will attempt to explicate this understanding below.) That temple will not exist until the Day of Creation. And—a most important point—since the text specifies that it will come into existence in the End of Days, the מקדש אדוני does *not* refer to a temple that exists in the present, the Wicked Era. Therefore the author cannot have in mind a 'community as temple,' as so many scholars have thought, if by that concept one means a community with which he is contemporary.[44] The reference must be to a physical temple that does not yet exist, but which will come to function in the first period of the eschaton.

---

42   That this term, also, was a technical term in certain circles is suggested by the use of 'New Creation' for a similar or identical concept in Jubilees 4.26.

43   Some scholars have suggested that this term encodes a concept of inaugurated eschatology, and thus means not only the near future, but also in some sense the present—cf. e.g., Brooke, *4Q Florilegium*, pp. 177-78. In my view, there is no unambiguous use of the term that supports such an idea, while there are many texts that indicate that the term applies to the future. They do so by their use of imperfect verb forms and inceptive infinitives. See CD 6.10-11, 1QpHab 2.5-6 and 9.6, 1QSa 1.1, 4QpIsᵃ 8-10 17, 4QpNah 3-4 ii 2, 4Q Catena 1-4 5, and 4QpIsᵇ II 1. Admittedly the question is a complex one, made more difficult by the composite character of certain of these texts, their generally uncertain interrelationship, and the use of tenses in the *pesharim*. Until these difficulties are solved, however, the provisional indications are that אחרית הימים does not embrace an inaugurated eschatology.

44   Ever since Gärtner's discussion, this idea has become a commonplace in New Testament scholarship. Yet not all New Testament scholars have accepted it uncritically; cf. e.g. E. Fiorenza, 'Cultic Language in Qumran and in the NT', *CBQ* 38 (1976), pp. 159-68.

A striking confirmation of this understanding of 4QFlor appears in
the way in which the TS has redacted the portions that it excerpted
from a Deuteronomy source.[45] Turning to a consideration of those
portions, let the fact be underscored: according to TS 29 the period
during which the TS (or at least its temple) will function is terminated
by the Day of Creation. At that point a new order will begin, and it is
problematic to what extent the laws of the TS were then intended to
continue. As it stands, however, the laws and temple are for the period
the CD community called אחרית הימים.

According to 4QFlor 1.4, the enforcement of certain biblical (and
nonbiblical) prohibitions against foreign entry was to constitute a
crucial difference between the מקדש אדוני and the מקדש ישראל. In
contrast to the מקדש ישראל, no Ammonite or Moabite or bastard or
גר or בן נכר was to enter the temple of the End of Days. The latter
two categories are especially interesting. In every case when sifting the
laws of the Deuteronomy source, the TS has eliminated those that
applied to them. By omitting all references to these two foreign
elements in its new Law for the land, the scroll is, of course, tacitly
denying them residence in eschatological Israel.

In conformity with this principle, the TS omits those passages that
concern—or even mention—the גר (in this period the term can be
taken either as 'proselyte' or 'resident alien').[46] It deletes Deut 14.28-
29, 15.8-18,[47] 23.25-26, 24.14-15, 24.17-23, 26.1-11 and 26.12-15.
Likewise, the redactor of the scroll removed 15.1-7 and 23.20-21
because they legislated for foreigners, none of whom would be around;
no legislation for them was necessary. Both the TS and 4QFlor deny
the גר and the foreigner participation in the eschatological cultus. The
extraordinary preoccupation with these two groups confirms that their
authors had the same—or at a least very similar—view of the eschaton.

We have thus far considered the temples of the TS and the
appellations that the CD community applied to various periods in
history. Those considerations have developed evidence that favors

---

45   On the character and extent of this source in the Temple Scroll, and for
reasons supporting the view that the redactor used such a source and not the biblical
Deuteronomy, see Wise, *Critical Study,* pp. 35-60.

46   Idem, 169-70, n. 29, and in more detail in my 'The Eschatological Vision of
the Temple Scroll', *JNES* 49 (1990), pp. 155-72.

47   This portion is omitted because of the parallel passage Lev. 25.47-54, which,
while 'interpreting' it, mentions the גר.

associating the מקדש אדוני with the first stage of the eschaton, as opposed to the stage of God's personal intervention. We must now ask what light these observations may shed on the מקדש אדם.

The Meaning of מקדש אדם

The Meaning and Function of ויאמר

In order to understand the meaning of מקדש אדם it is necessary to understand how it relates to the מקדש אדוני. If they are identical, then 4QFlor speaks of two temples; if they are distinct, the text describes three. I have suggested above that the two terms are simply different expressions for the same temple. The proof of this view hinges largely on the meaning and function of ויאמר.

Scholars construe ויאמר in one of two ways. Many have followed Allegro's original interpretation, 'and he purposed'.[48] This is a well-attested meaning of אמר in certain contexts; evidently a deep-structure phrase such as בלבו remains unexpressed.[49] In choosing this interpretation of the phrase for 4QFlor 1.6, however, interpreters are clearly guided by their belief that the Temple of the Lord is the same as the מקדש אדם. Since the Temple of the Lord is described by the quotation from Exod 15.17—the common interpretation of which is that it refers to a temple that God will build—it follows that ויאמר cannot be directed outward. It must be something that God 'says to himself.' If this is the proper interpretation of ויאמר, then it virtually requires that the unexpressed subject of the infinitive לבנות is God, i.e., 'and he purposed that he should build.'

Yet this understanding is difficult in view of the subsequent להיות. Again, the subject of the infinitive is unexpressed. The most natural interpretation is that ויאמר governs both infinitives; certainly one would expect the author to avoid intolerable ambiguity and make the subject of the two infinitives the same. But on Allegro's understanding of ויאמר they cannot be the same, since להיות is further explicated by מקטרים. Thus Allegro's understanding results in very awkward

---

48　Allegro, 'Fragments', p. 352. Thus Lane, Flusser, Brooke, Baumgarten, and Yadin.

49　E.g., Deut. 8.17 for the full phrase, and Gen. 20.11, 26.9, 1 Sam. 20.26, etc. for the apocopated form.

grammar. This fact alone does not disqualify it, of course, but it does encourage the search for a better interpretation.

Thus many scholars prefer to understand ויאמר straightforwardly as 'he said' or 'he commanded.'[50] With this interpretation the infinitives make good sense, for it is then obvious that the unexpressed subject of both is the people, i.e., 'and he commanded that they should build.' But then another problem arises: 'Where does he say it?' A virtue of Allegro's position is that with his view 4QFlor is 'self-contained;' ויאמר simply refers back to the quotation from Exodus 15. Virtually none of the scholars who have adopted the second understanding of ויאמר seem to have appreciated the difficulty with their view.[51] Considering the centrality of the expression to the author's exposition, one would certainly expect him to indicate where in the Hebrew Bible God commanded Israel to build the מקדש אדם. He does, after all, provide explicit scriptural warrant for each of his other major claims. Thus there are grave difficulties with either approach to ויאמר.

Yet a solution does exist that avoids all these problems. It begins with the concept of narrative function. The meaning of ויאמר is inextricably bound up with the word's function in the midrash. How does it advance the argument? Does it refer forward, to an undiscussed portion of the lemma? Or does it perhaps refer backward?

The proper context in which to set this question is that of the formal structural elements that recur in many of the Qumran biblical commentaries. Several studies have shown that the structure of the Qumran *pesharim* was highly stylized, characterized by the repetition of key interpretive words.[52] For example, three of these elements appear in 4QFlor 1.1-13 (a fact that has resulted in the work's frequent classification as a *pesher*). These elements are הואה after a lemma, the

---

50   So Gaster, Lohse, Vermes, Dupont-Sommer, Knibb, Dimant, Schwartz, Carmignac, Moraldi, and Maier.

51   Wacholder, however, does, and in *The Dawn of Qumran*, 254 n. 376 suggests the phrase may refer to the TS. If in fact the phrase does refer to a source other than the Hebrew Bible (which we suggest below is probably not the case) it seems more likely that the author of 4QFlor was referring to a source such as 43.366 fragment one. This fragment, part of a 'proto-TS', specifically commands the building of a temple in the name of Moses. It further stipulates the offering of specified sacrifices that are not detailed in the Hebrew Bible. See Wise, *Critical Study*, pp. 46-50.

52   See Horgan, note 10 above, and J. Fitzmyer, 'The Use of Explicit Old Testament Quotations in Qumran Literature and in the New Testament', *NTS* 7 (1960-61), pp. 297-333.

secondary use of כאשר כתוב, and the use of ואשר אמר preceding a
lemma. Thus, although 4QFlor is not strictly a *pesher*, it does often use
pesher techniques. Might it then be that ויואמר is an element such as
these, specifically a variant of one that uses the verb אמר?

On closer examination, the answer appears to be no. In every case of
an interpretive element involving אמר in the *pesharim,* the verb is
unconverted, and introduced either by כאשר or אשר הואה. Further, the
biblical lemma always follows immediately. In 4QFlor 1.6, no lemma
either precedes or follows ויואמר. In fact, in the published nonbiblical
works from Qumran this narrative use of ויואמר has no parallel. If it is
not a structural element with analogs in other texts, how then does the
term relate to the biblical text that 4QFlor is explaining?

Schwartz argues that it and the words that follow in 1.6-7 are a
paraphrase of 2 Sam 7.13a, הוא יבנה בית לשמי.[53] These words are, of
course, left out of 4QFlor; in Schwartz's opinion, the author
paraphrases them here while referring to the temple that Solomon built.
Schwartz is thereby able to explain what is for him otherwise a
difficulty—the omission of the first portion of verse 13 from the
midrash. His idea also explains why the next citation is specifically said
to refer to David: the preceding one had referred to Solomon.

But in spite of these apparent virtues, Schwartz's explanation of the
function of ויואמר falls well short of conviction. Apart from the
improbability of the basic thesis that undergirds his suggestion,[54] he has
apparently overlooked the fact that 13a is not the only omission from 2
Sam. 7.10-14. The author of 4QFlor also omitted a phrase from 7.12,
אשר יצא ממעיך. The common thrust of the omitted portions makes
the author's intention plain. He purposely deleted them both in order to
clarify that the son of David in view was not Solomon. Since the author
sought to establish the messianic intention of the text, to retain these
phrases—most naturally applying to an immediate son of David—
would needlessly have complicated things.[55]

---

53 Schwartz, 'Three Temples', p. 88.
54 Schwartz never explains why it was important for 4QFlor to discuss the
temple of Solomon as distinct from the defiled Second Temple. His distinction
between those two temples strikes me as arbitrary, since from the perspective of the
author of 4QFlor they were both defiled.
55 Many scholars have argued that the additions to the text of this portion in 1
Chron. 17.11 are also for the purpose of clarifying the messianic import of the
oracle, but this interpretation is not without its difficulties. See e.g. H.G.M.

The only other writer on 4QFlor who has specifically addressed the function of ויואמר is Dimant.[56] It is her position that the term introduces a new topic in the midrash, deriving from the last phrase of the biblical lemma, ולמן היום אשר צויתי שפטים על עמי ישראל. She sees a connection by *gezerah shavah* between the terms ויואמר and צויתי. Such a connection certainly could make sense, but Dimant then strains to connect the terms צויתי and מקדש אדם by the same process.[57] She is forced to this unlikely effort by her view that a one-to-one correspondence exists between the midrash and the text of 2 Samuel. For her, every phrase of the biblical text, and often even the word order, must find a reflex in the interpretation.

But the relationship does not appear to be nearly that tight. Instead, 4QFlor often loosely strings its phrases around key words chosen from the biblical text. In the case of the last phrase of the lemma, for example, it is the word immediately preceding ולמן, בראשונה, which the author developed. He worked it into his exegesis at 1.4, in the course of describing the defilement of the previous temples. Therefore it is unnecessary to detach the words following בראשונה as Dimant has done. The author of 4QFlor implicitly incorporated them by incorporating בראשונה.

It thus seems that neither Schwartz's nor Dimant's analysis satisfactorily explains the interpretive function of ויואמר. A different approach is needed. I suggest beginning with the structure of lines 10-13 of the midrash. This portion interprets 2 Sam 7.11c-14a, and its rhetorical structure can serve as an analytical control for that of the earlier lines. That structure is as follows. First appears a lengthy quotation from the biblical text, sometimes skipping words or phrases. Then the author explicates the quotation, introducing his identification of the biblical בית with the צמח דוד by means of the structural word הואה. He next offers further support for his identification by quoting the text from Amos, introducing that quotation with the element כאשר

Williamson, *1 and 2 Chronicles* (New Century Bible; Grand Rapids: Eerdmans, 1982), p. 135.

56   Dimant, '4QFlorilegium', pp. 176-77.

57   She further connects שפטים with מעשי תורה by suggesting that the midrashist read משפטים or שיפוטים. The latter term, however, does not occur in the Hebrew Bible, and while it is attested in Tannaitic Hebrew, its meaning there is 'vanity.' The dropping of initial *mem* in the case of the first word is unconvincing; she can show no parallels for such an interpretive procedure in other Qumran literature.

כתוב. Finally he explicates the original identification even more fully, once again introducing his explanations by the word הואה. That this last portion is indeed further explication (and not the introduction of some new topic) is clear by virtue of the repetition of סוכת דויד. The structure and movement of lines 10-13 can therefore be schematized as follows:

A. Biblical Quotation
B. Identification/Explication—introduced by הואה
C. Further Support—introduced by כאשר כתוב
D. Additional Explication—introduced by הואה

Turning now to the disputed earlier portion of the midrash, the underlying structure is immediately recognizable as identical:

A. Biblical Quotation—2 Sam 7.10-11a
B. Identification/Explication—line 2, introduced by הואה
C. Further Support—a quotation of Exod 15:17, introduced by
כאשר כתוב
D. Additional Explication—lines 3b-7, introduced by הואה

If the author's method is consistent—and his repeated formal structuring suggests that it is—then ויואמר neither introduces a new topic nor functions as a formal structural element. The term is merely part of the 'additional explication' that begins at line 3. True, the *waw* turns the reader's attention away from the immediate topic of lines 4-6a—the polluted First and Second Temples—but not in order to introduce a new temple.[58] Rather, the narrative resumes discussion of that temple that had already appeared in the earlier lines.

If this structural analysis is correct, then the מקדש אדם and the מקדש אדוני must be identical. The term מקדש אדם is in some way a further explication of the term מקדש אדוני. How did the author of 4QFlor arrive at the equation? The same way as he arrived at many other equations and explanations in his midrash: by the process of *gezerah shavah*.

---

58   It is one of the merits of Dimant's discussion that she recognizes that the *waw* cannot simply mean 'and.' She has correctly seen that it is explicative, establishing a causal connection between the lines immediately preceding and lines 6-7. See Dimant, '4QFlorilegium', p. 177.

Many writers have commented on the complexity of the midrash in 4QFlor.[59] As noted above, its author relies not only upon portions of the Bible that he explicitly quotes, but also upon portions to which he alludes. And his reference to those portions presupposes a certain interpretation of them. For example, when he states that no Ammonite, Moabite, bastard, etc., shall enter the eschatological temple, he is presupposing an interpretation of Deut 23.3-4, supplemented apparently by Ezek. 44.9.[60] The triangulation equates קהל (Deut 23.3) with מקדש (Exod 15.17). So also the author connects the מקדש אדם with the מקדש אדוני of Exod 15.17 by *gezerah shavah*.[61]

The verse to which 4QFlor alludes by its use of מקדש אדם is 2 Sam 7.19. This portion is in the context with which the midrash is explicitly concerned; it is only natural that it impinge upon the author's mind. Two separate terms within the last half of the verse would have drawn his attention. The last half of the verse reads:

אל בית עבדך למרחוק וזאת תורת האדם אדוני יהוה

In the terms בית and למרחוק the author perceived a reference to the temple of the End of Days.[62] He equated the term אדוני with the same term in Exod 15.17. By a midrashic understanding of the difficult וזאת תורת האדם אדוני—a phrase that has always perplexed commentators and exegetes—he further equated האדם and אדוני. That it was indeed to 2 Sam 7.19 that the author turned for his appellation מקדש אדם is further clear from the appearance of another key term of that verse, תורה, in 4QFlor 1.7, מעשי תורה. The collocation of these crucial ideas and terms from 2 Sam 7.19 within just two lines of 4QFlor where it is manifestly concerned with the context of that biblical portion cannot be mere coincidence.

To summarize to this point: ויאמר does not introduce a new topic. It refers back to what is already under discussion, the temple of the End

---

59   For a representative and enlightening discussion of how the midrash used the Hebrew Bible, see Gärtner, pp. 30-32. While I cannot agree with all that Gärtner says, his discussion gives some idea of the complexity involved in several derivations.

60   As recognized by Baumgarten and Dimant, among others.

61   Flusser, 'Note', 102, n. 11; Ben-Yasher, 'Noch zum Florilegium', p. 588.

62   Some rabbinic interpretation also considered this verse a reference to the eschatological temple, as is clear for example in Targum Jonathan, which renders the MT בית עבדך למרחוק as בית עבדך דאתי לעלמא.

of Days. If this conclusion is correct, then both 4QFlor 1.6-7 and the quoted Exod 15.17 must refer to the same temple. It also seems good to equate that temple with the temple that the TS orders Israel to build. Consequently the unexpressed subject of לבנות, the infinitive that ויאמר governs, is 'they.' One should interpret ויאמר as a command, and translate 1.6 as, 'To that end, he ordered that they build...'.[63] These conclusions furnish the interpretive parameters within which to construe the phrase מקדש אדם.

We can now turn our attention to its meaning. I would argue that the author of 4QFlor derived this term through a series of applications of *gezerah shavah* and that from the האדם of 2 Sam 7.19 he arrived at the equation אדם=האדם.[64] Furthermore, he understood both terms as referring not to mankind, but to Adam, the primal man.[65] In order to defend this assertion, we must now investigate the use of Adam in the eschatology of those Qumran texts that are related to 4QFlor and CD.

The מקדש אדם *as the Temple of Adam*

The name אדם appears in Qumran literature as an element in two construct phrases, כבוד אדם and נחלת אדם. The first phrase occurs three times, but only one of the occurrences, CD 3.20, provides

---

63 If the temple of line 6 is one Israel must build, and it is the same as the temple of Exod. 15.17, then clearly the author of 4QFlor understood the Exodus passage likewise as a command. He cannot have understood it in the way that all writers on 4QFlor have suggested (see Table 1, column #1 above). Rather than referring to a temple that God will build, the temple of the Day of Creation, he believed the reference to be to the first temple of the End of Days, which Israel would construct. Accordingly, he construed כוננו not as a *Polel* perfect 3cpl, agreeing with 'hands', but as a masculine plural imperative, governing an unexpressed 'you (all)', i.e., Israel.

64 Some rabbinic texts also connect 2 Sam. 7.19 to the first man Adam—cf. *Yalqut Shimoni* האזינו, *remez* תתקמם. The Vulgate takes the same tack: *ista est enim lex Adam Domine Deus.*

65 Although the definite article might seem to preclude this equation, and certainly would by the canons of modern grammar, it did not deter ancient interpreters. For example, Targum Onkelos consistently renders האדם in the MT of Gen 3 and 4 as the proper name Adam. So also Targum Neofiti, which even occasionally subsitutes האדם for the anarthrous form without intending a different meaning. Cf. Gen. 3.12 in comparison with the marginal reading, and especially 3.20. Incidentally, this equation explains the Masoretic pointing of אדם without the definite article at Gen. 2.20b, 3.17 and 3.20.

sufficient context to determine what the writer meant by it.[66] That context is CD 3.12-4:4 in the narrow sense, and 2.13-4:12 in the broader sense. נחלת אדם is found at 4QpPs37 iii 1-2, with parallel portions in the same composition affording insight into its meaning.[67] I shall examine the two phrases in turn.

כבוד אדם in CD 3:12-4:4

Text [68]

ובמחזיקים במצות אל	3.12
אשר נותרו מהם הקים אל את בריתו לישראל עד עולם לגלות	3.13
להם נסתרות אשר תעו בם כל ישראל שבתות קדשו ומועדי	3.14
כבודו עידות צדקו ודרכי אמתו וחפצי רצונו אשר יעשה	3.15
האדם וחיה בהם פתח לפניהם ויחפרו באר למים רבים	3.16
ומואסיהם לא יחיה והם התגוללו בפשע אנוש ובדרכי נדה	3.17
ויאמרו כי לנו היא ואל ברזי פלאו כפר בעד עונם וישא לפשעם	3.18
ויבן להם בית נאמן בישראל אשר לא עמד כמהו למלפנים ועד	3.19
הנה המחזיקים בו לחיי נצח וכל כבוד אדם להם הוא כאשר	3.20
הקים אל להם ביד יחזקאל הנביא לאמר הכהנים הלוים ובני	3.21
צדוק אשר שמרו את משמרת מקדשי בתעות בני ישראל	4.1
מעלי הם יגשו [אלי לשרתני ועמדו לפני להקריב]לי חלב ודם	4.2
הכהנים הם שבי ישראל	

---

66   It appears at 1QS 4.23 as a part of a general litany of blessings for the upright, and in the *Hodayot* at 17.15 in a broken context. Only a very general semantic overlap ties this phrase to the תפארת אדם of Ben Sira 49.16. According to J. Marböck, 'Henoch-Adam-der Thronwagen', *BZ* N.F. 25 (1981), p. 108, the phrase 'meint bei Ben Sira von Gott verliehenen Ruhm und Glanz . . .' Understanding חיי נצח as an appositional equivalent, he suggests on the same page that the CD phrase means cither 'immortality' or 'long life.' As I hope to demonstrate below, however, כבוד אדם goes beyond mere synonymity.

67   Other than these phrases, there are no other certain uses of אדם as a proper noun (and, indeed, scholars have sometimes failed to recognize even these uses). It seems relatively certain that the use at 4QpIsac 4-7 ii 8 is that of a proper noun, but the context is broken. Other possible uses—even perhaps eschatological uses to judge by the preserved vocabulary—occur at 4QpIsac fr.31 line 2, and 4Q178 fr. 4 line 2. Both contexts are broken.

68   Portions in brackets may have fallen out during textual transmission, and are here restored.

4.3 היוצאים מארץ יהודה והנלוים הם הנ[ל]וים עמהם ובני צדוק
הם בחירי

4.4a ישראל קריאי השם העמדים באחרית הימים

Translation

3.12b ...But among those who held to God's commandments

13 —those who remained of them—God established his eternal covenant for Israel, by revealing

14 to them those hidden things in which all Israel had erred: his holy sabbaths and glorious

15 feasts and righteous testimonies and truthful ways and pleasing sacrifices,[69] *'which man*

16 *shall do and thereby live.'* (Lev. 18.5) He opened before them, and they dug, a well of many waters

17 —those who refuse it shall not live—but they defiled themselves in human sin and impure ways,

18 and they said, 'It belongs only to us.' But God in his wondrous mysteries atoned for their evil and forgave their sin.

19 He built for them *'a sure house in Israel,'* (2 Sam. 7.16) whose like has never existed from ancient times until

20 now. Those who hold to it will possess long life and all the glory of Adam. It is just as

21 God promised them through the prophet Ezekiel, saying *'The priests and the Levites and the sons*

4.1 *of Zadok who preserved the proper service of my temple when the sons of Israel apostatized*

4.2 *from me—it is they who shall approach [me for my service and stand before me to sacrifice] to me.'* (Ezek. 44.15) 'The priests' refers to those of Israel who have returned,

4.3 who went out from the land of Judah. 'The [Levites' refers to th]ose who joined them (shall join them?). And 'the sons of Zadok' refers to the chosen of

---

69 Cf. CD 6.20 להרים את הקדשים כפירושיהם, 'to offer the sacrifices according to their exact specifications.' This was a basic point in which all who joined the community had to be educated. Cf. also 6.18-19.

4.4 Israel, those foreknown by name who shall arise at the End of Days.[70]

Discussion

This is a difficult text, pregnant with different possibilities of interpretation. A full discussion of all the problems must await another occasion; a few comments will suffice here.[71] The portion is part of a historical discussion that begins at 2.14, whose basic intent is to show that the community of CD is the true heir to God's promises to Israel.[72] The author sees the community as a faithful remnant which, according to 3.12-16, has received new revelation concerning the festival calendar and proper sacrifices. As all Israel had previously gone astray in these areas, in the author's view the proper cultus has been neglected since the time of the patriarchs. To his day the proper sacrificial procedures have never been followed. Without that proper service, as the quotation from Leviticus proves, there is hope neither of life nor of forgiveness.

The passage goes on to state that, although God had showed them the true interpretation of the Scriptures[73] (= the 'Well'; cf. 6.4), for a period of time the group continued in error.[74] Still, God forgave them and made them understand their place in his eternal plan. They were to give

---

70 This last definition establishes that the community expected the fulfillment of the verse from Ezekiel only in the End of Days, for according to 2.11, קריאי השם were to be found in every generation, not just the last.

71 For a full discussion of different views concerning some of the textual *cruces,* see Davies, *Damascus Covenant,* pp. 76-95.

72 The two major source-critical studies of CD are those of Davies and J. Murphy-O'Connor. Davies divides the Admonition of CD into four sections: (1) the History (in three parts, comprising all told 1.1-4.12a), (2) the Laws, (3) the Warnings and (4) the New Covenant. See Davies, *Damascus Covenant, passim.* Murphy-O'Connor includes our portion within his 'Missionary Document' of 2.14-6.1. See his 'An Essene Missionary Document? CD II,14-VI,1', *RB* 77 (1970), pp. 201-29. For a preliminary discussion of the merits of both positions, see P. Callaway, *The History of the Qumran Community: An Investigation.* Journal for the Study of the Pseudepigrapha Supplement Series 3 (Sheffield: JSOT Press, 1988), pp. 91-99.

73 Perhaps this is what is meant by the statement that he had given them revelation.

74 Cf. 1.8-10.

rise to a messianic son of David (hence the reference to 2 Samuel), and also to serve in the eschatological temple that would someday be built. They, and those who came to belong to them, would enjoy long life and 'all the glory of Adam.'[75] This phrase seems to imply a reversal of the Adamic curse (Gen. 3.16-19) during the eschaton. The author proves this last assertion by an appeal to Ezek. 44.15.

Ezekiel 44 occurs, of course, in the context of Ezekiel 40–48, a portion that many late Second Temple Jews understood as describing an eschatological temple. It is therefore very significant that the CD community interpreted 44.15 as a reference to themselves and those who would join them up to the very beginning of the End of Days (note the appearance of that term in 4.4). By citing this passage, the author of CD stakes his claim: because the community had preserved and (to the degree possible) practiced the proper cultus during the Wicked Age, it was they who would serve as God's priests and ministers in a physical eschatological temple. It is unnecessary to underscore the obvious parallels between this concept and the phenomena of the TS, with its extensive provisions for a future sacrificial cultus and architectural plans for that temple.[76]

Thus this passage of CD explicitly connects the temple of the End of Days with the name Adam. It says that the 'glory of Adam' consists in part of the practice of the true cultus—never before administered—in that temple.[77] It would only be natural for the community of CD to refer

75 In connection with my comments on הֲאָדָם in 2 Sam. 7.19 and its equation with Adam, notice the word-play between הֲאָדָם of the Leviticus quotation and אָדָם in line 20. The author is apparently arguing for a connection between proper worship and the glory of Adam.

76 In terms of the claims of this passage of CD, it is interesting to note that the sacrificial calendar of the TS includes festivals known from no other source, and sacrificial stipulations likewise unattested elsewhere. These matters were, of course, not found in the Hebrew Bible precisely because they were נסתרות (3.14).

77 The idea of Adam as a keeper of the Law is central to his depiction in Jubilees. That work characterizes him as the first of the virtuous patriarchs of Israel, obedient to the Mosaic law even though, from a straightforward reading of the Pentateuch, it did not yet exist. The disobedience to God's command not to eat from the tree is played down. Unlike Eve, Adam does not hide from God afterwards, and rather than being expelled from the garden, he and Eve simply leave. See Jubilees 3, and the discussion in J.R. Levison, *Portraits of Adam in Early Judaism.* Journal for the Study of the Pseudepigrapha Supplement Series 1 (Sheffield: JSOT Press, 1988), pp. 89-97. Note also that CD 3.14 disregards

to that eschatological period in Edenic terms,[78] and to that temple as the Temple of Adam.

4QpPs 37 and the נחלת אדם

At 4QpPs^a 1-10 iii 1-2, a portion that is interpreting Psalm 37:18-19a, the following text occurs:

Adam's rebellion and begins its account of past disobedience with Genesis 6. The notion of Adam as knowing and obeying the Law also appears in rabbinic literature. One example concerns Gen. 2.15. This verse says that God 'took the man (Adam) and placed him in the garden of Eden' לעבדה ולשמרה. Although the MT infinitives have 3fs suffixes agreeing with 'garden', some rabbinic commentators interpreted the final *heh* of לעבדה as the rare variant spelling of the 3ms suffix. That option allowed them to interpret לעבוד as 'to serve, to worship.' Once that interpretive move was made, the connection of the second verb with the garden was likewise severed, and it required a new feminine antecedent. Of course, there could be only one choice. The resultant understanding of the phrase was 'to serve him (God) and to observe it (the Torah).' It would seem that this interpretation arose because a comparison of biblical portions disallowed the straightforward understanding of the words: before Adam sinned, working and protecting the garden were unnecessary (cf. Gen. 2.6 and 3.24). Similarly, Targum Neofiti rendered the last two words of Gen. 2.15 as למהוי פלח באוריתא ולמטור פקודיה , 'to be serving the Torah and to observe its commandments.' See the comments in B. Levy, *Targum Neofiti 1: A Textual Study* (2 vols.; New York: University Press of America, 1986), 1, p. 92.

78   It is interesting that Jubilees, which in one form or another was known to the CD community (CD 16.3-4), portrays Eden in exalted terms. Eden is said to be 'holier than any place on earth', and is equated with the holy of holies in the sanctuary (3.9-12). It is where Enoch took up residence after being taken up; there he sits recording mankind's judgment and condemnation. Because of his presence there, the waters of the flood did not reach to Eden (4.18-19). In the new creation, Eden will be one of four places set apart for the hallowing of the earth, along with Mount Sinai, Mount Zion, and the 'mountain of the east' (presumably Mount Lubar, where the ark came to rest—4.26). This last point means that the author of Jubilees envisioned an eschaton in which Eden figured prominently, but held a somewhat different idea of the relationship between Eden and Zion than did Ezekiel (see below). It would appear that the ideas underlying CD at this point are closer to Ezekiel's perspective. For the equation of the Garden of Eden with the temple in Qumran literature, note also 4Q251 Halakha A, where the typology underlies the purification periods after their creation before Adam and Eve could enter Eden.

‎1 שבי המדבר אשר יחיו אלף דור בישועה ולהם כול
‎2 נחלת אדם ולזרעם עד עולם

1 [Its meaning concerns...][79] those who have returned to the
  wilderness, who will live for a thousand generations in
  prosperity. To them belongs all
2 the inheritance of Adam, and to their progeny, forever.

In these lines the members of the text's community, who call
themselves the יחד,[80] are said to be sole heirs to the 'inheritance of
Adam.' The text affirms that when the inheritance is realized, the
beneficiaries will enjoy extended life spans, as will their children. The
period described by the text will evidently be one in which, while
people live a long time, they will die and bear children. The faithful
will live in 'prosperity' or 'security' or even 'victory,' depending on the
nuance intended by the term ישועה. An earthly eschatological period is
in view here, characterized in part by a reversal of the Adamic curse.
Insofar as it goes, this description jibes completely with the concept of
כבוד אדם in CD.

A comparison with a second passage from the same literary work
provides further details and justifies the translation 'inheritance of
Adam.'[81] Explicating Psalm 37.22, 1-10 iii 10-11 read as follows:[82]

‎10 פשרו על עדת האביונים אשר לה]ם נחלת כול הגדול[ים אשר]

79   The preceding portion has been lost, but the restoration פשרו על is certain.
See Horgan, *Pesharim*, 213-14.
80   For the יחד as the community, see 1-2 ii 14 and 3-10 iv 19. Davies has
suggested that members of this group exercised the final (?) redaction of CD and
that they were thus, in some way, the descendants of that earlier community. See
Davies, *Damascus Covenant*, 175-79. Even if the relationship between these texts
is less clearly defined, all that is necessary for our purposes is that they share the
same world of discourse. Such is manifestly the case.
81   The term can be taken as either an objective genitive, 'the inheritance that
Adam bequeathed', or as a subjective genitive, 'the inheritance that Adam
inherited.' The first option is clearly preferable.
82   For the text and restorations, see Horgan, *Pesharim*, pp. 217-218. For the best
discussion of options for reading and restoring the text of line 10 after כול, see D.
Pardee, 'A Restudy of the Commentary on Psalm 37 from Qumran Cave 4
(Discoveries in the Judaean Desert of Jordan, vol. v, no 171)', *RevQ* 8 (1973), pp.
165, 168 and 185.

‫11 ירשו את הר מרום ישרן‪[‬אל ובה‪[‬ר קודשו יתענגו...‬

10 Its meaning concerns the Congregation of the Poor, [to
wh]om belongs all the inheritance of the Great [Ones; for]
11 they shall inherit the high mountain of Isra[el, and] shall
delight [in] his holy [moun]tain...

The notion of inheritance connects this text to the previous passage.
Again, in context the period of inheritance appears to be the eschaton.
This text helps explicate the other in that it apparently equates נחלת
אדם with נחלת כל הגדולים and the 'high mountain of Israel.' All
three phrases are descriptive of the community's eschatological
inheritance. Although the exact meaning of the 'inheritance of the
Great Ones' (*si vera lectio*) is unclear, the juxtaposition of the
'inheritance of Adam' with the 'high mountain of Israel' is very
helpful. Also helpful is the appearance in this text of the term יתענגו.
Since neither הר מרום ישראל nor ענג is common in the Hebrew Bible,
their presence affords the possibility of uncovering the textual basis and
backtracking along the paths of exegetical reasoning behind the text's
claims.

הר מרום ישראל occurs only three times in the Hebrew Bible, all in
Ezekiel: 17.23, 20.40 and 34.14. The term is associated with Eden, and
represents God's paradisal abode.[83] Contextually, Ezek. 17.23 is part of
an oracle of salvation that counters the oracle of judgement of 17.1-21.
The text associates the Davidic line, which it refers to as a 'tender
shoot' with this mountain.[84] Further, it is intriguing to note the
appearance in verse 23 of the verb שתל, a word meaning 'to plant.' Its
association with the mountain might naturally lead a practicioner of
gezerah shavah to think of Exod. 15.17. There, too, appears a verb for
planting in נטע, and there, too, appears a reference to God's mountain.
Significantly, that verse describes the mountain as God's 'inheritance'
(נחלה). It would certainly be no great leap for the author of 4QFlor—

83   The direct connection between the mountain and Eden appears in Ezek 28.11-
19, the famous parable of the king of Tyre. See especially 28.14 and 28.16. The
casting of this parable in terms of the primeval Adam is well known. See e.g., W.
Zimmerli, *Ezekiel*, 2 vols., trans. R. Clements (Philadelphia: Fortress, 1979; 1983),
2, pp. 81-95.
84   The possibilities for exegetical association of this idea with the messianic
branch imagery of 4QFlor and the צמח דוד require no emphasis.

the complexity of whose exegesis we have already noted—to connect
these two verses.

If he made such a connection—and given his terminology, there is
reason to suspect that he did—and if he were aware of the ideas
encountered in the *pesher* on Psalm 37, the resultant equations would
be very interesting. The term נחלה refers to the mountain, but in
Exodus the mountain is said to be God's, while the *pesher* texts taken
together say that it is Adam's (and, of course, the community's).
Therefore, by the canons of *gezerah shavah*, נחלת אדם=נחלת אדוני.
Recalling that Exod. 15.17 further speaks of the מקדש אדוני, the next
step in association is, of course, מקדש אדם=מקדש אדוני! These
equations are not incongruous by the exegetical lights of the author of
4QFlor. They would serve to reinforce the juxtaposition between the
two temples that he had derived from 2 Sam 7.19. In terms of the
meaning of מקדש אדם, the equations associate Eden with the
mountain; and once we have Eden, we also have Adam.

Ezek 20.40 belongs in the larger context of Ezek. 20.27-44. These
portions associate the mountain of God with the exiles who return from
all the nations to inherit the land. They will receive the land just as God
swore to give it to their forefathers; however, those who are rebellious
will not share that gift. These ideas are clearly congruent with the
ideology of the CD community, who saw themselves in exile while
those who rebelled against God ruled. This text would surely have
attracted their attention and invited their ponderings. Ezek. 20.40 reads:

כי בהר קדשי בהר מרום ישראל נאם אדוני יהוה שם יעבדני כל
בית ישראל כלה בארץ שם ארצם ושם אדרוש את תרומתיכם ואת
ראשית משאותיכם בכל קדשיכם

For on my holy mountain, the high mountain of Israel, says the
Lord Yahweh, there will the whole house of Israel serve me, in the
land; there I will receive them with favor, and there I will demand
your gifts and offerings of firstlings, all your holy gifts.

Several interesting things happen in this passage. First, the high
mountain that elsewhere in Ezekiel is associated with Eden is here
identified also with Jerusalem, 'my holy mountain.' Second, the text
says that it will be here that those who inherit the land will practice the
cultus. Given that at the time Ezekiel wrote, as it was thought, no
temple stood on the site of Jerusalem, the passage implicitly requires

the building of a new temple. It therefore establishes a connection with
the eschatological temple of Ezekiel 40–48, which in 40.2 is said to
stand on 'a very high mountain.'

Ezek. 20.40 furnishes a basis, then, for understanding the idea of
נחלת אדם as partially cultic. (It will be recalled that כבוד אדם also
had cultic overtones.) The text also provides warrant for connecting
these phrases with the time of inheritance, i.e. the End of Days. It
indicates that at that time, a new temple must be built in Jerusalem.
And it equates Jerusalem with the 'high mountain' which, as we have
already seen, is also associated with Eden. In 'Eden,' then, will stand
an eschatological temple—none other than the first temple of the TS,
which is a development of that found in Ezekiel 40–48.[85] One of its
names will be that by which 4QFlor 1.6 knows it, the Temple of Adam.

Parallel portions of Ezekiel strengthen the connection between the
'high mountain,' the inheritance and Eden. Ezek. 34.14, the third
occurrence of הר מרום ישראל, is part of such a passage. It promises
the enfranchising of the scattered and powerless and the expulsion of
the wicked leaders of Israel. It is once again reminiscent of the ideology
of CD, and echoes the ideas of the *pesher* on Psalm 37. Ezekiel 36 does
not mention the 'high mountain,' but it does parallel the
Heilsgeschichte of chapters 20 and 34. What is particularly interesting
is the appearance in 36.35 of the phrase 'garden of Eden.' The language
of all these chapters describes the future inheritance in terms
deliberately reminiscent of the luxuriant fertility of that paradise.
Ezekiel employs an *Urzeit/Endzeit* typology, which is adopted by the
Qumran texts under discussion.

This typology is inherent in a number of the uses of ענג in the
Hebrew Bible. Perhaps the most interesting of these passages is Isa.
55.2,[86] which says in part ותתענג בדשן נפשכם, 'you shall delight
yourself in abundance.' The portion informs not only 4QpPs[a] 1-10 iii
11, but also apparently CD 1.7-8. Those lines declare, 'And he caused
to grow forth a root from Israel and Aaron, to inherit the land and to
grow fat (ולדשן)[87] in the goodness of his soil.' This represents a
summary of several of the ideas found in our portions of 4QpPs[a], CD
and 4QFlor. Like Ezekiel, all these texts employ to some extent an

85   All commentators on the TS have agreed on this relationship. See Wise,
Critical Study, pp. 64-86.
86   Note also Isa. 55.3-5 and 12-13.
87   Read as *Niphal* infinitive construct with apocopated intervocalic *heh.*

Urzeit/Endzeit typology. And it is in the context of that typology that one can best understand the three terms כבוד אדם, נחלת אדם and מקדש אדם.

Summary and Conclusions

This discussion of 4QFlor 1.1-13 began with the hope of offering a new understanding of three crucial questions involved with the portion. Those questions were: how many temples are in view in 4QFlor? Which temples are they? And, what is the meaning of 1.6-7, and particularly of מקדש אדם? Having summarized the answers of previous scholarship, I have proposed my own suggestions, which it is now appropriate to summarize in turn.

4QFlor speaks of only two temples. One is the temple that it calls the 'Temple of Israel.' This temple was (is) defiled, and represents typologically both the First and Second Temples of Israel's history. The other temple has two designations, each arising from one of the biblical texts that the author of 4QFlor wove into his interpretive construct. One name for this second temple is מקדש אדוני, the 'Temple of the Lord.' This name primarily derives from Exod. 15.17. The other designation for this temple is the one that has presented so many difficulties, מקדש אדם. It comes primarily from 2 Sam. 7.19; I shall return to its meaning in a moment. This binomial temple is the temple that Israel is to build for the first stage of the eschaton, the End of Days. It is the same as the temple described with so much detail in the TS. According to TS 29.8-10, it is distinct from yet another temple, that of the latter portion of the eschaton. That period begins with the Day of Creation, and features a temple that God himself will create.

I have argued that the phrase מקדש אדם ought to be translated 'Temple of Adam.' The basis for this view is twofold: the eschatological character of this temple, and the meaning of parallel epithets in two other texts, CD and 4QpPs[a]. There occur respectively the phrases כבוד אדם and נחלת אדם. Through analysis of these phrases in context, and in light of their exegetical basis in the Hebrew Bible (particularly in Ezekiel), it became clear that they represented an *Urzeit/Endzeit* typology.

Since מקדש אדם refers to an actual physical temple, and not to the idea of 'community as temple,' it follows that מעשי תורה and מקטרים should be taken literally rather than allegorically. Furthermore, the phrase מעשי תורה probably refers not merely to lawful deeds, but to sacrifices. This understanding is requisite because of the association of the phrase with the temple; it reflects a nuance that the verb עשה already possesses in the Hebrew Bible.[88] Since מעשי תורה is a general expression for sacrifices, מקטרים must mean 'to offer' and not 'to offer as incense.' With the solution to מקדש אדם these other parts of the puzzle fall readily into place.

The CD community and its heirs believed that, though now disenfranchised, they would inherit the land in the End of Days. Then they would worship God in a new temple on the holy mountain. The land would regain its Edenic luxuriance, and they would offer to God, for the first time since the beginning, a proper worship. As advocates of this typology, it was entirely natural that they should call the future temple by a name that reflected their view. The term carries no overtones of an ἔσχατος 'Αδάμ.[89] Rather, the use of מקדש אדם captured the author's hope and conviction that he and others of like mind could someday return to Eden whence Adam was banished. The cycle of God's relation with man would be complete and at the same time, just beginning.

---

88   Cf. 1 Chron. 23.28 for מעשה with a meaning of 'offering', and note the frequent use of the verb עשה in the Hebrew Bible for 'perform a sacrifice' (also in Qumran literature—TS 24.10, etc.). When applied to the temple cultus, 'to do the Law' means 'to perform the proper sacrifices at the proper time.' Cf. e.g., Deut. 31.12 for the biblical usage in a general sense; this phrase and the related 'to do the command(s)' are typically Deuteronomic. The opposite of מעשי תורה in Qumran sectarian literature is apparently מעשי תועבות. In 1QpHab 12.8-9, the Wicked Priest is charged with performing these and thereby defiling the temple. Thus, it is possible to preserve the sanctity of the temple only by offering מעשי תורה.
89   For the typology First Adam/Last Adam in Jewish and early Christian literature, see G. Kittel, ed., trans. and ed. G. Bromiley, *Theological Dictionary of the New Testament* (Grand Rapids: Eerdmans, 1964), s.v. "'Αδάμ', by J. Jeremias.

Chapter Five

PRIMO ANNALES FUERE: AN ANNALISTIC
CALENDAR FROM QUMRAN

Introduction

It has been said that although the Greeks liked history, they never made it the foundation of their lives.[1] Second Temple Jews, on the contrary, did. Because they saw themselves in continuity with Abraham, Isaac and Jacob, and because for them history and religion were indistinguishable, they returned again and again to the biblical narratives. There they found not only the story of earlier generations, a record of the past as seen from a given perspective—what we today would call historical writings—but also, in a very real sense, a record of the future. For no matter what else they may have thought of the prophets of Israel, no one doubted that the essence of prophecy was prediction.[2] The Bible therefore needed very little in the way of supplementation. Wrapped together in its scrolls were history told and history foretold. Perhaps that is why the literature of the Second Temple period is so destitute of historical writings. Only 1 Maccabees and, some might argue, 1 Esdras continue the biblical tradition of historiography during these years.

The discovery of nearly a thousand literary works near the site of Qumran has done nothing but reinforce this impression, to the chagrin, naturally, of the historian hungry for new facts (or, at least, new perspectives on old facts). Most of these literary texts allude to current events, if at all, with the ambiguous generalities usual to their genres. Those Qumran texts that apparently do concern historical events and real persons, the *pesharim,* are almost equally ambiguous. Anyone who

1   A. Momigliano, *The Classical Foundations of Modern Historiography* (Berkeley: University of California Press, 1990), p. 20.
2   See J. Barton, *Oracles of God: Perceptions of Ancient Prophecy in Israel after the Exile* (Oxford: Oxford University Press, 1986), *passim.*

has spent time trying to decipher the coded signficance of 'Ephraim' and 'Manasseh', of 'the seekers after smooth interpretations' and 'the Man of the Lie'—not to mention 'the Teacher of Righteousness'—is well acquainted with the frustrations inherent to the interpretation of this body of literature. With so few unambiguous statements in the sources, it is hardly surprising that historical reconstructions based on the scrolls are often convincing to none but their authors.

Apparently the authors of Qumran's quasi-historical works felt no need to break away from encoded references or to use the proper names of their *dramatis personae*. Perhaps they preferred to conceal these identities. The 'wise' would recognize them anyway, and it might be dangerous for their accusations to be too transparent. To this general pattern there are apparently only two exceptions. One is the well known portion of the *pesher* to Nahum that refers to an Antiochus and a Demetrius—probably, if scholarly consensus is right, Antiochus IV Epiphanes and Demetrius III Eucaerus.

The second exception was communicated by J.T. Milik early on in research on the Qumran finds. In 1957 he described a group of texts he called *mishmarot;* as their name suggests, these texts concern the priestly rotation in and out of service in the temple at Jerusalem. One of them seemed to be of outstanding importance. As Milik described it,[3]

> Un ouvrage, représenté par deux mss. différents, mais malheureusement réduits à quelques petites parcelles, s'apparente au même group de Mishmarot, mais avec des additions d'un intérêt exceptionnel . . . occasionnellement se retrouvent la mention des . . . événements historiques. Ainsi 'Salamsiyon a tué' . . .

Unfortunately Milik never published the fragments. Interested scholars had to wait until the recent publication of a fascimile edition to get more information.[4] Now that the *mishmarot* text containing proper

---

3   J.T. Milik, 'Le travail d'édition des manuscrits du désert du Juda', *SVT* 4 (1957) pp. 25-6. Milik also referred to this text in *Ten Years of Discovery in the Wilderness of Judaea,* trans. J. Strugnell (London: SCM, 1959), p. 73. Here he said, 'there is an Essene calendar giving the dates of certain historical events which were celebrated annually.' He seems to be thinking of *Megillat Taanit* in making this judgment about the text's function. While there are obvious analogies between the two texts, there is no evidence that the dates in the Qumran text were celebrated.
4   Eisenman and Robinson, *A Facsimile Edition of the Dead Sea Scrolls,* Washington: BAS, 1991.

names has seen the light of day, I propose here to discuss aspects of its reading and interpretation. Rather than two manuscripts, it seems that six copies of this work have survived. Each copy is extremely fragmentary, but it may still be possible to recognize certain historical events to which reference is made, and perhaps even to show that the work contains hitherto unknown information about these events.

Reading and Translation of the Texts

The official designations of the six copies of this calendar are 4Q322-4Q324c, otherwise 4QMishmarot C^a, C^b, C^c, C^d, C^e and C^f.[5] 4QMishmarot C^f is inscribed in a cryptic script known as cryptic script A, and is extremely fragmentary, such that I will not consider it here. The other copies also include some fragments too small to yield information for the purposes at hand. The following is, then, my reading of the larger portions of the five texts 4Q322 (MS A), 323 (MS B), 324 (MS C), 324a (MS D) and 324b (MS E).[6]

Manuscript A (4Q322)

Fragment 1

[	]א בעשר [בחודש הששי	] .1
בעשרים ואחד]	[בארבעה עשר בו ביא]ת ידעיה בששה עש]ר בו	] .2
[	[בו באיח חרים בעשרים ו]שבעה בחודש [הששי	] .3
[	הושיב ג.]	] .4
[	גו]אים וגם .]	] .5
[	מ]רורי הנפש .]	] .6
[	אסורים]	] .7

Fragment 2

[	ל]חת לו יקר בערב]ים	] .1
[	ביום אר]בעה לשבט זה]	] .2

5　I follow the index given in Reed, *List*.

6　Since the surviving fragments lack the formulae associated with the calendar, it is not certain that 4QMishC^e is a copy of the work. For my reading of the texts, I have also consulted B.Z. Wacholder and M. Abegg, *A Preliminary Edition of the Unpublished Dead Sea Scrolls, Fascicle One* (Washington, D.C.: Biblical Archaeology Society, 1991), pp. 77-85, and have on occasion preferred their restorations (e.g. B3:6)

]ה שהוא עשרים בחודש [‏]. 3
].יסוד באה שלמציון] ‏]. 4
] להקביל את [פני ‏]. 5
]ב הרקנוס מרד [על ארסטבולוס ‏]. 6
] להקביל] ‏]. 7

Fragment 3

] [...] ‏]. 1
] ראש הג]אים הרג ש[‏]. 2
] ביום ח]מישי בידעיה ז[. ‏]. 3

Fragment 4

]].ם כרצו]ן ‏]. 1

Manuscript B (4Q323)

Fragment 1

]ה בתשע]ה בחודש השמיני ביאת שכניה [‏]. 1
] ביום [ ] בשכניה א] בששה עשר בה ביאת אלישיב[‏]. 2
].[בעשרים ושלו]שה בה ביאת יקים <בשנים ביקים .[◁ ויום ר]ביעי ביקים [‏]. 3
]].בס..[יו]ם שני בחודש הת]שיעי ‏]. 4

Fragment 2

] יום רב]יעי בחזו[י]ר [זה א]חד בע[שירי] ‏]. 1
].בארבעה בה ביאת הפ]צץ באחד [ע]שר בה [ביאת פתחיה] ‏]. 2
].בשמונה עשר בה ביא]ת יחזקאל בעשר]ים וחמשה בה ביאת[‏]. 3
] יכי]ן הע[ב]ודה .[‏]יכין ‏]. 4
] בשנים בה] ביאת [גמול ‏]. 5

Fragment 3

]] שהוא [‏]. 1
]].[‏]. 2
]]ש[‏]. 3
]].ות[... ‏]. 4
]].. אשנ]ים ‏]. 5
]]. ונגד אר]סטבולוס ‏]. 6
] א]מרו בע[‏]. 7
] שבעים .[‏]. 8
]] שהוא [‏]. 9

Manuscript C (4Q324)

Fragment 1

1. [בעשרים ושלושה בה] ביאת [אלישיב בשלושים בה ביאת יקים]
2. [אחר שבת ביקים זה אח]ר בש[שי בשבעה בה ביאת חופה]
3. [בארבעה] עשר בה [ביאת ישבאב] ..פות בע[שרים ואחד]
4. [בה ביאת בלג]ה בעשרים [ושמונה ב]ה ביאת אמ[ר יום]
5. [רביעי באמר זה א]חד בשביעי באר[ב]עה בה ביאת ח[זיר]
6. [יום ששי ב]חזיר שהוא עשרה בשביעי שיום [הכפורים בה]
7. [   ]   לברית באחד עשר בשביעי ביאת [הפצץ   ]

Manscript D (4Q324a)

Fragment 1 Column 2

5. יום [   ]. [   ].[בל]. [   ]   בעשרים ואחד]
6. [בו]א ביאת ש[עור]ים בעשרים ושמונה בוא ביאת מלכ[י]ה]
7. יום רביעי [ב]מלכיה זה אחד בחודש העשירי   *vacat*
8. בא[רבע]ה בע[ש]ירי ביאת מי[מ]ין באחד עשר בוא ביא[ת הקוץ]

Fragment 2

1. [   ]   ב[עשרים
2. [ואחד בוא ביאת פתחיה בעשרים ושמו[נה
3. [בוא ביאת יחזקאל ביום 3/2/1 בי]חזקאל שהוא
4. [29/30/31 בחודש הששי יום] הרג אמליוס
5. [יום רביעי ביחזקאל זה אחד בחוד]ש השביעי
6. [בארבעה בוא ביאת יכין באחד עשר בוא ב]י[את] גמול
7. [   ] יום רביעי בגמול ש[הוא
8. [חמשה עשר בחודש השביעי חג הסכות בוא] הרג אמליוס

Fragment 3

1. [   ]ש[ ]. אצל .[   ]
2. [בעשרים ושמונה בוא ביאת י]שוע יום רביע[י בישוע זה אחד בחודש]
3. [העשירי   שה]וא עש[רה   ]

Fragment 4

1. [איש יהודי א] [

Manuscript E (4Q324b)

Fragment 1 Column 1

1.] כוהן ג[ד]ול כ.רי
2.] יוחנן להבי את

Fragment 1 Column 2

1. ..[
2. מן]
3. [
4. [
5. אנוש]
6. ת הזוי[.
7. שלמצ<י><ן]

Translation

Manuscript A Fragment 1
(1) on the tenth [of the sixth month (i.e., of the second year of the priestly rotation) . . .] (2) [on the fourteenth of it, the arriva]l of (the priestly course of) Jedaiah; on the sixtee[nth of it . . . on the twenty-first] (3) [of it the arrival of (the priestly course of) Harim; on the twenty]-seventh of the [sixth] month [   ] (4) he returned . . . (5) [gen]tiles and also . . . (6) [b]itter of spirit . . . (7) prisoners . . .
Fragment 2 (1) [to] give him honor among the Nabat[eans . . .] (2) [on the fou]rth [day] of this course's service . . . (3) which is the twentieth of the [   ] month . . . (4) foundation, Shelamzion came . . . (5) to visit . . . (6) Hyrcanos rebelled [against Aristobulus . . .] (7) to visit . . . **Fragment 3** (2) [the leader of the ge]ntiles murdered . . . (3) [on the fi]fth [day] of (the service of the priestly course of) Jedaiah . . .
Fragment 4 (1) according to the wi[ll of . . .]
Manuscript B Fragment 1 (1) on the nin[th of the eighth month (i.e., of the second year of the priestly rotation), the arrival of (the priestly course of) Shecaniah . . .] (2) On day [ ] of (the service of the priestly course of Shecaniah, [On the sixteenth of it (i.e., the eighth month), the arrival of (the priestly course of) Eliashib]; (3) [on the twenty-thi]rd of it, the arrival of (the priestly course of) Jakim; on the second (day of the service of the priestly course of) Jakim, [   ]; and on the fo[urth] day of (the service of the priestly course of) [Jakim,   ] (4) . . . the second day of the ni[nth] month . . . **Fragment 2** (1) [the four]th [day]

of (the service of the priestly course of) Hez[i]r, [this day is the fi]rst (day) of the te[nth month (i.e., of the second year of the priestly rotation);] (2) [on the fourth day of it (i.e., the tenth month), the arrival of (the priestly course of) Happi]zzez; on the eleve[nth] of it, [the arrival of (the priestly course of) Pethahiah;] (3) [on the eighteenth of it, the arriv]al of (the priestly course of) Jehezkel; on the twen[ty-fifth of it, the arrival] (4) [of (the priestly course of) Jachin;   Jach]in, the se[r]vice . . . (5) [. . . on the second of it (i.e., the eleventh month)], the arrival of [(the priestly course of) Gamul . . .] **Fragment 3** (1) which is . . . (5) me[n . . .] (6) and against Ar[istobulus . . .] (7) [and] they [sa]id . . . (8) seventy . . . (9) which is . . .

Manuscript C Fragment 1 (1) [on the twenty-third of it (i.e., the fifth month of the fifth year of the priestly rotation)], the arrival of [(the priestly course of) Eliashib; on the thirtieth of it, the arrival of (the priestly course of) Jakim;] (2) after the sabbath, while Jakim is serving, this is the fir]st of the six[th month; on the seventh of it, the arrival of (the priestly course of) Huppah;] (3) [on the four]teenth of it, [the arrival of (the priestly course of) Jeshebeab;] . . . on the twen[ty-first] (4) [of it, the arrival of (the priestly course of) Bilg]ah; on the twenty-[eighth of i]t, the arrival of (the priestly course of) Imm[er; day] (5) [four (of the service of the priestly course of) Immer is the fi]rst day of the seventh month; on the four[t]h of it, the arrival of (the priestly course of) He[zir;] (6) [the sixth day of] (the service of the priestly course of) Hezir, which is the tenth day of the seventh month, this is [the Day of Atonement;] (7) [ ] for the covenant; on the eleventh day of the seventh month, the arrival of (the priestly course of) [Happizzez. . .]

Manuscript D Fragment 1 Column 2 (5) day [on the twenty-first] (6) [of i]t (i.e., of the ninth month of the fifth year of the priestly rotation), the arrival of (the priestly course of) S[eor]im; on the twenty-eighth of it, the arrival of (the priestly course of) Malchi[jah;] (7) the fourth day of (the service of the priestly course of) Malkijah is the first day of the tenth month. (8) On the f[ourt]h day of the te[n]th month, the arrival of (the priestly course of) Mija[m]in; on the eleventh of it, the arriv[al of (the priestly course of) Hakkoz;] **Fragment 2** (1) [. . . on the] twenty-(2) [first of it (i.e., of the sixth month of the sixth year of the priestly rotation), the arrival of (the priestly course of) Pethahiah; on the twenty-eig]th (3) [of it, the arrival of (the priestly course of) Jehezkel; on the first (or, the second; or, the third) day of (the service of the priestly course of) J]ehezkel, which is (4) [the twenty-ninth (or, the thirtieth; or, the thirty-first) day of the sixth month, the Day] of the Massacre of Aemelius; (5) [the fourth day of (the service of the priestly course of) Jehezkel is the first day of] the seventh [mon]th; (6) [on the fourth of it (i.e., of the seventh month), the arrival of (the priestly course of) Jachin; on the eleventh of it, the arr]iv[al of] (the priestly course of) Gamul; (7) [the fourth day of (the service of the priestly course of) Gamul, whi]ch is (8) [the fifteenth day of the seventh month, is the Festival of Booths; on that day,] Aemelius murdered . . . **Fragment 3** (2) [on the twenty-eighth of it (i.e., of the ninth month of the sixth year of the priestly rotation), the arrival of (the priestly course of) Je]shua; the four[th] day of [(the service of the priestly course of) Jeshua is the first day of the] (3) [tenth month . . . wh]ich is the ten[th . . .] **Fragment 4** (1) a Jewish man . . . **Manuscript E Fragment 1 Column 1** (1) the hi[g]h priest (2) Yohanan to bring the . . . **Fragment 1 Column 2** (2) from . . . (5) a man (7) Shelamzion . . .

Discussion

The regular patterning of this work, together with a knowledge of the underlying system of priestly rotation, make many of the suggested restorations certain. In common with a significant number of works from Qumran, the author reckoned by a solar calendar of 364 days. With this calendar structuring his calculations, he distributed the twenty-four priestly courses over a six-year period. This is the length of time required for any given course to return to serve at the same week it had first served. Thus, for example, the course Delaiah served in the first month of the first year of the cycle, beginning with day four of that month (1/4 Year One). Although Delaiah served twice a year, it would require six years before the course returned in month one day four. This sexennial cycle structured the recording of holy times in all the Qumran *mishmarot*. The cycle was eternal, deriving from the Creation narrative of Genesis 1. Every sabbath, month, year and festival was denominated by the name of the relevant priestly family. As the calendar under discussion shows, the system also structured chronography and, in a certain sense, historiography.

1 Chr 24.1-18 describes how the order of the priestly courses was once determined by the fall of the lot. As it is laid out in Chronicles, the order was as follows: (1) Jehoiarib (spelled Joiarib in the Qumran texts) (2) Jedaiah (3) Harim (4) Seorim (5) Malchijah (spelled Malachijah in the Qumran texts) (6) Mijamin (7) Hakkoz (8) Abijah (9) Jeshua (10)

Shecaniah (11) Eliashib (12) Jakim (13) Huppah (14) Jeshebeab (15)
Bilgah (16) Immer (17) Hezir (18) Happizzez (19) Pethahiah (20)
Jehezkel (21) Jachin (22) Gamul (23) Delaiah and (24) Maaziah (often
spelled Moaziah in the Qumran texts). The Qumran *mishmarot* use the
same names for the courses—apparently indicating that their system
postdates 1 Chronicles 24—but in a different order. Rather than
beginning with Jehoiarib, the Qumran texts begin with Gamul.[7] Thus
the cycle begins not with (1) above, but with (22). Probably the reason
for this change is that the list given in 1 Chronicles began the rotation
in the autumn. Jehoiarib rotated into service at the beginning of the
seventh month, Tishri. In contrast, the Qumran calendar texts assume a
vernal New Year, beginning in Nisan. The different beginning derives
once again from an understanding of the Creation narrative. The
creation happened in the spring, and so an eternal order based on the
creation must therefore also begin at that time. The vernal New Year
meant that the priestly rotation would begin with Gamul.

Indications are that the Qumran calendar originally comprised one
full six year cycle. The time of each course's arrival was noted, as were
'New Moons'[8] and the major festivals of the religious calendar.
Interwoven with these data were entries dating significant events
(significant to whom is a question to which we will return). The major
festivals were often double-dated using formulae introduced either by
שהוא or זה. Often, but not always, the author applied the same double-
dating technique to significant events. Like the New Moons and
festivals, the events included in the work may have been celebrated—
or, as appropriate, mourned. At the least they were memorialized. The
most obvious analogy is *Megillat Taanit,* but the Qumran work was
much more extensive: in addition to the 312 entries describing the
rotation of the courses (52 x 6), there were entries for six years' worth
of festivals and an unknown number of historical events. Assuming that
the entry for each course required about half a line (the space occupied
by entries in the extant portions), it is hard to believe that the complete

7   One could determine that Gamul is first simply by a complete study of the
relevant texts, but one text, 4Q320 Mishmarot A, makes that inference explicit. The
text reads 'on the fourth, on the sabbath, the sons of Gamul (shall serve) in the first
month, in the first year.' See PAM 43.330, fragment 1, lines 3-5.
8   The text speaks of אחד בחורש because in the Qumran system the
astronomical New Moon only occasionally fell at the beginning of the month. See
Chapter 6 below.

work numbered fewer than 200 lines; it may have been much longer. Only a small percentage of the presumed original dated entries survive, as Table 1 illustrates (references are to manuscript, fragment and line):

MONTH	1	2	3	4	5	6
YEAR 1	-	-	-	-	-	-
2	-	-	-	-	-	-
3	-	-	-	-	-	-
4	-	-	-	-	-	-
5	-	-	-	-	C1:1	-
6	-	A1:1-7	-	-	C1:2	D2:1-4
7	-	-	-	-	C1:5	D2:5-8
8	-	B1:1-3	-	-	-	-
9	-	B1:4	-	-	D1:5-6	D3:2
10	-	B2:1-4	-	-	D1:7-8	D3:3
11	-	B2:5	-	-	-	-
12	-	-	-	-	-	-

Table 1. Dated Entries in the Qumran Chronicle

As is clear in the table, no two copies of the calendar overlap.[9] The preserved portions of the texts refer to about twenty events, some of which are dated according to the system described. The dates of others have not survived. The events are as follows:[10]

(1) A1:1 6/10 Year Two—an event.

(2) A1:2 6/16 Year Two—an event.

(3) A1:3-7 6/27 Year Two—one or more events involving 'gentiles', the 'bitter of spirit' and 'prisoners.'

(4) A2:1 Undated—an event involving 'honor among the Nabateans.'

(5) A2:4 Undated—an event involving שלמציון.

(6) A2:6 Undated—a rebellion involving הרקנוס.

(7) A3:2 Undated—a murder by a gentile leader.

(8) B1:1-2 Between 8/9 and 8/16 Year Two—an event.

(9) B1:3 8/25 Year Two—an event.

---

9   It is possible that D2 immediately precedes A2. The two mentions of Shelamzion do not seem to refer to the same event, judging by line lengths and lacunae.

10   I omit events that are implied by the spacing of lacunae between course arrivals, e.g. C1:3-4.

(10) B1:3 8/27 Year Two—an event.

(11) B1:4 9/2 Year Two—an event.

(12) B2:3-4 Between 10/25 and 11/2 Year Two—an event involving, perhaps, the temple service (עבודה).[11]

(13) B3:6 Undated—one or more events involving, perhaps, opposition to an Aristobulus.

(14) C1:6-7 7/10 Year Five—an event involving the 'covenant.'

(15) D2:4 Between 6/28 and 6/31 Year Six—a murder or massacre involving אמליוס.

(16) D2:8 7/15 Year Six—a murder or massacre involving אמליוס.

(17) D4:1 Undated—an event involving 'a Jewish man.'

(18) E1:2 Undated—one or more events involving יוחנן.

(19) E2:7 Undated—one or more events involving שלמציון.

What was the nature of this calendar? It is notable that all the proper names preserved belong to the Hasmonean period. יוחנן is perhaps John Hyrcanus I (135/4-104 BCE);[12] הרקנוס is then John Hyrcanus II (63-40 BCE), שלמציון is Salome Alexandra (76-63 BCE),[13] and אמליוס is the

---

11   It is intriguing to note that 164 BCE, when Judas Maccabaeus restored the temple service, was a Year Two according to the Qumran system (see below). The reference here seems to be about a month too late to refer to Judas' actions, but depending on whether the intercalations of the Seleucid and Jewish calendars were out of synch with each other in 164, the equation is not impossible. Both J. Goldstein and B. Bar-Kochva, for example, argue that the two calendars intercalated differently at this time, but come to very different conclusions. Goldstein thinks that the dedication took place on 16 October, 164, while Bar-Kochva argues for 14 January 163. Bar-Kochva's date is close to the Qumran text's dated event. See J. Goldstein, *1 Maccabees* (Garden City, N.Y.: Doubleday, 1976), pp. 165 and 283, and B. Bar-Kochva, *Judas Maccabaeus: The Jewish Struggle Against the Seleucids* (Cambridge: Cambridge University Press, 1989), pp. 278-9, 564-5, and Table 3 on p. 282 (the dedication took place on '14 January 164', an apparent misprint for '14 January 163').

12   For the chronology of this reign and of the later Hasmoneans, see Schürer 1, pp. 200-202 n. 1. It is certainly possible that this 'John' is someone other than Hyrcanus I, but this seems the best suggestion given the calendar as a whole.

13   In the face of potential objections, one must consider whether the person here mentioned is certainly the queen of that name. First there is the problem of the names's spelling. Alexandra's Semitic name is spelled variously in rabbinic sources: שלמצה, שלמתו, שלמצו and שלציון (Jastrow, *s.v.*). Still, there can be little doubt that these are all corruptions of the form found here, a conclusion on which all modern researchers into the onomastics of the period seem to agree. See particularly T. Ilan, 'The Greek Names of the Hasmoneans', *JQR* 78 (1987), p. 7 n.

Roman general M. Aemilius Scaurus. Of course, it may be fortuitous that no names from the Herodian period and later have been preserved. Any characterization of the work must be appropriately tentative, but I would hypothesize that this Qumran work was a 'Hasmonean Chronicle.' I base this suggestion not only on the names, but also on the fact that the few events that can be analyzed point to the Hasmonean period. It is on several of these events that I want to focus in the following discussion, in particular considering fragment 2 of manuscript A and fragment 2 of manuscript D. In order to set this discussion in the proper context, an overview of the relevant historical period may be helpful.

Historical Overview

Sources for the period from Alexandra's reign to the Roman conquest (76-63 BCE) are not rich. Essentially all that we have are Josephus'

---

28. But there remains the problem of the name's apparent frequency. It has been argued that fully fifty percent of women in the Second Temple period bore the names Mariamme and Salome, with the latter understood as a shortened form of שלמציון (thus T. Ilan, 'Notes on the Distribution of Jewish Women's Names in Palestine in the Second Temple and Mishnaic Periods', *JJS* 40 (1989), pp. 186-200, esp. p. 192). If this assertion is correct, it might be thought to imperil the present identification. But a number of considerations must be borne in mind here. Ilan's identification of Salome as a short form of Shelamzion is problematic. No text or ossuary actually bears both names for the same woman and, perhaps significantly, when the name שלמציון appears in Greek, it is always vocalized with the Aramaic form of the first element, 'peace' (thus Σελαμψιών and variants; Ilan's numbers 162, 195, 202, 207, 217 and 218 in 'Notes'). Salome, on the other hand, is always vocalized as Hebrew when it appears in transliterated form. It seems curious that the Aramaic element should be Hebraized when the hypocoristic is used and yet never appears in Hebrew form in the full name. To my mind this fact makes the identification of the two names questionable. Of course, strange things sometimes happen with hypocoristics, and if the identification is correct, then one may note that the name שלמציון is never attested prior to Alexandra and that, in all probability, its popularity derived precisely from its association with the Hasmoneans (thus R. Hachlili, 'Names and Nicknames of Jews in the Second Temple Period', *ErIsr* 17 (1984), p. 191 [Heb.]). Finally, there simply is no other שלמציון of sufficient political significance to be associated with the nationally important events of our text, unless one wants to argue that the reference is to some otherwise unknown individual. Therefore, it is probable that this text refers to the Hasmonean queen.

parallel narratives,*War* 1.107-58 and *Antiquities* 13.405-14.79.[14] While there are some differences of emphasis and characterization,[15] the two accounts are especially close for these years. In both cases the Jewish historian's major resource was the history of Nicolaus of Damascus.[16] For *Antiquities* he had done additional research and also used Strabo, Livy and other classical and, perhaps, native authors.[17]

Apart from Josephus a few late rabbinic legends and several of the *Psalms of Solomon* are relevant. That is all—the full extent of our source material for a pivotal point in Second Temple Jewish history. Thus impoverished, we lack a stereoscopic perspective, even if it is perhaps possible to recount the main events. As Efron has noted, Josephus describes the period entirely from the Roman point of view:[18]

> No flaw is found in Roman intervention and the suppression of Jewish independence. In the battles for Jerusalem the memory of the Jewish warriors is not perpetuated nor their names mentioned, while outstanding Roman officers are listed . . . An aura of nobility surrounds Pompey, Antipater is characterized as wise and resourceful, while Hyrcanus is weak and despicable and Aristobulus arrogant and rash. Inner divisions, folk institutions, or national and religious aspirations within the Jewish people are almost entirely disregarded.

Presumably a partisan Jewish concept of the people and events involved would differ markedly. Although not much is preserved, precisely that, I will argue, is what A2 and D2 represent. If that assertion is correct, it is hardly necessary to emphasize their potential value to the historian.

---

14   Allowing that the reference to Hyrcanus in A2:6 concerns the period subsequent to Rome's conquest would include in this discussion *War* to 1.273 and *Antiquities* to 14.369. As noted, however, nothing in the preserved portions can be dated later than about 62 BCE, so for the present I leave these portions of Josephus aside.

15   For some of the differences in Josephus' characterizations of the Hasmoneans—unfortunately, excluding Aristobulus II and Hyrcanus II—see G. Fuks, 'Josephus and the Hasmoneans', *JJS* 41 (1990), pp. 166-77.

16   For an interesting example of Josephus' treatment of Nicolaus' work in the context of *Ant.* 13, see B.Z. Wacholder, *Nicolaus of Damascus* (Berkeley: University of California Press, 1962), pp. 59-60.

17   S.J.D. Cohen, *Josephus in Galilee and Rome* (Leiden: Brill, 1979), pp. 50-51.

18   J. Efron, *Studies on the Hasmonean Period* (Leiden: Brill, 1987), p. 229.

At the death of Alexander Jannaeus (103-76 BCE) power passed into the hands of his wife, Alexandra (76-67 BCE).[19] With her reign began a signal change in policy, intended to heal the nation of those disputes that had ravaged it in the latter years of Jannaeus. Josephus informs us that Alexandra assuaged the antagonisms of the Pharisees, who had opposed her husband, by ceding to them virtual control of the government. They responded by reinstituting some of their ordinances abolished years earlier after a falling out with Hyrcanus I, and by exer- cising such sovereign powers as the sending and recalling of exiles and the freeing of prisoners. Indeed, Josephus characterizes her reign as one in which 'she held nominal rule, but the Pharisees held the power.'[20]

Alexandra appointed her elder son Hyrcanus II high priest, not only because of his age, but also—at least as Josephus, depending on the anti-Hasmonean Nicolaus, describes it—because of his lethargic character. She did not want his much more energetic brother, Aristobulus, in that position; she feared that he would use it as a springboard for his very considerable ambitions. And in fact, as things developed, this fear was well placed.

Shortly after Alexandra had anointed the Pharisees, they began to agitate for revenge against those councilors of Jannaeus who had urged him to put eight hundred insurgents to death.[21] Among those victims of Jannaeus' anger had been a substantial number of Pharisees. Josephus does not say much about the progress of this pogrom, other than to indicate that it made a beginning with a certain Diogenes and was followed by additional executions carried out in the victims' own homes. The focus of this attack was the highest levels of society, but it also extended to lower echelons.[22] The leaders of the group under attack turned to Aristobulus for help, and he did intercede on their

19   For the purposes of this discussion I have not felt it necessary to provide a reference for each and every statement, since the relevant portions of Josephus' works have already been indicated. In what follows I will provide specific references only when Josephus' writings disagree (and the disagreement is pertinent to this analysis), when I have quoted a text or its precise wording is otherwise significant, or when it is necessary to consider the meaning of the Greek.

20   *Ant.* 13.409, τὸ μὲν οὖν ὄνομα τῆς βασιλείας εἶχεν αὐτή, τὴν δὲ δύναμιν οἱ Φαρισαῖοι.

21   *Ant.* 13.410; cf. 13.380.

22   Note *War* 1.114, which states that 'the most eminent' of the imperiled sought refuge with Aristobulus, implying that there were others who, lacking such social eminence, could not hope to approach the queen's son.

behalf. As a result, instead of being executed, Alexandra allowed them to go into voluntary exile, stationed in various fortresses around the country. The apparent continuity between Aristobulus' faction and the powerful aristocrats that had earlier advised Jannaeus is notable.

Later the queen fell ill, and Aristobulus took this occasion to make a bid for the throne. He went to the fortresses where his allies had been stationed and, within a short time, twenty-two of them were under his control. He also sought and obtained alliances with various local princes; soon he possessed a large army. Alexandra and her Pharisee advisors were so alarmed that they took Aristobulus' wife and children hostage but, before any further action could be taken, Alexandra died.

Hyrcanus now assumed the royal mantle, adding that to his role as high priest. Aristobulus immediately declared war. In the first battle, fought near Jericho, Aristobulus won a resounding victory, sending Hyrcanus fleeing back to the citadel in Jerusalem. Here he took some prisoners from those of Aristobulus' faction who had sought refuge in the temple—and, of course, he still had Aristobulus' wife and children. But Hyrcanus had no stomach for more war, and now proposed to his brother that they reach terms. He agreed to abdicate the throne and, apparently, his office of high priest, on condition that he be allowed to live peacefully off the income of his considerable properties.[23] This proposal was fully acceptable to Aristobulus. In the sight of all the people and with the appropriate weighty oaths the agreement was sealed in the temple.

There things might have remained but for the interference of Herod's father, the Idumean Antipater. This man was unhappy with the arrangements because of his own ambitions for power. Antipater realized that these ambitions stood a much greater chance of fulfillment if the weak Hyrcanus were in power than if the dynamic Aristobulus ruled. Thus he began to foment discontent, addressing himself to members of the Jewish aristocracy as well as to Hyrcanus. Antipater argued that Aristobulus had seized power illegally since Hyrcanus was in fact the elder brother. Hyrcanus had sold his birthright for a mess of pottage. Furthermore, he urged, Hyrcanus could never be safe as long as Aristobulus ruled. His brother would perceive him as a threat and do away with him at the first opportunity. Antipater continued these

23   For Aristobulus as high priest as well as king—denied by some scholars—cf. *Ant.* 14.41, 97 and 20.243-44. Note also Aristobulus' coins (if such they are; the point is moot) which declare him high priest.

slanders and false charges—false, at least, according to Josephus—for some time. He even suggested a safe haven for the deposed Jewish monarch: the kingdom of the Nabateans, ruled then by Aretas III (87-61 BCE?),[24] with whom Antipater enjoyed good relations. The Arab king, said Antipater, might prove a powerful ally for Hyrcanus.

Finally Antipater's importunities bore fruit. Hyrcanus fled to Petra with him. Once there Antipater relied upon judicious bribery to convince Aretas to help Hyrcanus. Hyrcanus himself, now having come around fully to Antipater's perspective, offered to restore land and cities that the Nabateans had lost to the Jews under Alexander Jannaeus. Persuaded, Aretas led a substantial force against Aristobulus and defeated him in battle. Aristobulus retreated to the temple, where the Arab forces besieged him. Most of Jerusalem now went over to Hyrcanus; only the priests, says Josephus, remained loyal to Aristobulus. The siege continued into the Passover celebration of 65 BCE.

At about that time Pompey, who was campaigning in the east, sent two envoys to Syria, one of whom was M. Aemilius Scaurus.[25] Their assignment: to exploit the power vacuum then existing in that region. Scaurus heard of the struggle going on in Judaea and left Damascus to investigate for himself. He received envoys from both brothers, and, although they offered equal bribes, Aemilius decided in favor of Aristobulus. Given the poor equipment of the Nabatean forces and Hyrcanus' natural passivity, he judged the siege could not succeed. He commanded Aretas to raise it or suffer the consequences at the hands of Rome. Aretas scurried to obey, and Scaurus returned to Damascus. Meanwhile, as Aretas and Hyrcanus marched home to Petra, Aristobulus launched an attack, inflicting a devastating defeat on his unsuspecting foes.

Until the autumn of 64 BCE, Aristobulus stood tenuously supreme, attempting all the while to win Pompey himself over with gifts. At that time Pompey decided to reconsider the Judaean question. Representatives came to him from Aristobulus, Hyrcanus, and a third

---

24   On the problem of the dates of Aretas' rule, see G.W. Bowersock, *Roman Arabia* (Cambridge: Harvard University Press, 1983) pp. 24-25 and 34.

25   The other was Gabinius. For 65 BCE as the date of Scaurus' coming to Syria, see T.R.S. Broughton, *The Magistrates of the Roman Republic* (2 vols.; New York: American Philosophical Association, 1952) 2, p. 164. M. Sartre, 'Rome et les Nabatéens à la fin de la République', *REA* 81 (1979), p. 42, allows for the possibility of 66.

group comprising members of the priestly aristocracy who had soured
on the Hasmoneans and wanted to return to their ancestral hierocracy.
Aristobulus did not perform well at this audience; he also managed to
alienate Scaurus by revealing to Pompey the earlier bribe. The
arguments of the two brothers were those that had characterized their
respective cases all along. Hyrcanus argued for his right of
primogeniture. Aristobulus charged his elder brother with
incompetence too great to be countenanced in the ruler of a nation.
According to Josephus (following Nicolaus, presumably), Hyrcanus at
this point pressed a telling accusation.[26] He said that the nation would
not have rebelled (ἀποστῆναι) against Aristobulus had he been less
violent. Here is a clear statement that some Jews of that period viewed
Hyrcanus' actions (for he, after all, was the leader) as nothing less than
rebellion. This is a point to which I shall return, but let it be noted:
Josephus nowhere uses a term for 'rebel' with regard to Aristobulus.

Pompey did not wish to make an immediate decision as to which
brother should rule. That very indecision amounted, of course, to
something of a reversal of Scaurus' earlier position favoring
Aristobulus. Pompey preferred first to investigate the situation among
the Nabateans. Aristobulus did not think that his case would be
improved by waiting, and apparently decided to defy the Romans and
raise arms to keep himself in office. He left Pompey immediately and
set out for Judaea. It seems that Aristobulus believed that while
Pompey was in Nabatea he could solidify his own military position
enough to give the Romans a fight or, better yet, pause; they might then
decide simply to ratify the *status quo ante* rather than suffer the
difficulties of a military campaign. But Pompey was not so easily
outwitted. He recognized Aristobulus' intentions. Rather than marching
to the Arab regions, he followed the Judaean king immediately.
Hyrcanus accompanied the Roman general with sycophantic
compliance.

Aristobulus took refuge in the mountain fortress Alexandrium.
Pompey came to the site and ordered the Judaean to abandon his plans
and descend. Now Aristobulus tried to play both sides, obeying
Pompey in the hope that he might grant him the kingdom after all, but
returning to the fortress after each session of palaver. Thus he could
make at least a pretense of independence and prepare in case war were

26   *Ant.* 14.43, οὐκ ἂν οὐδ' ἀποστῆναι λέγων τὸ ἔθνος αὐτοῦ.

necessary. Pompey once again ordered him to give up the fortress and to inform his fortress commanders throughout the land to give up their strongholds as well. Aristobulus was forced to obey, but then went on to Jerusalem to prepare for war.

Consequently Pompey led his army against Aristobulus, camping first at Jericho. There, apparently having recognized the hopelessness of his cause, the Jewish king met him and sued for peace. He promised Pompey money and agreed to admit the Romans into Jerusalem. Pompey acceded to these arrangements. Gabinius was dispatched with some troops to get the money and take control of the city. When they arrived at Jerusalem, however, Aristobulus' partisans[27] refused to keep their leader's bargain. Gabinius returned empty-handed. Pompey, enraged, arrested Aristobulus, whom he doubtless suspected of complicity in the double-cross, and marched against Jerusalem.

The city was divided between the radical adherents of Aristobulus and the rest of the population, which evidently included, but was not identical with, Hyrcanus' supporters. The party of Aristobulus, unable to enforce their will, occupied the temple and cut the bridge connecting it to the upper city. The partisans of Hyrcanus then admitted Pompey's forces to Jerusalem; the Romans took control of the city and began the siege, Hyrcanus helping in any way possible. The siege dragged on for several months. Pompey sent for siege engines and catapults from Tyre, taking advantage of the weekly sabbaths to raise the earthworks on which to anchor the battering rams. The Jews could only watch helplessly. Their law forbade any but a defensive war on the holy days, and the Romans—doubtless aided by Hyrcanus' tutoring—refused to attack while working on the sabbaths. All during the period of the siege, even when missiles rained into the courtyards, the priests within the temple carried on with the required sacrifices and other ceremonies.

Finally the temple fell, perhaps in July 63 BCE, or perhaps in late September or early October of that same year. The precise date is debated and, as our text may shed some light on this problem, we shall have to take it up in more detail below. The Roman forces now rushed

---

27   Reading στασιωτῶν at *Ant.* 14.56 rather than στρατιωτῶν, in accordance with Niese's suggested emendation. The difference is only two letters, a common sort of textual corruption, and with the emendation the text of *Ant.* accords with *War* 1.140, οἱ τὰ ᾽Αριστοβούλου φρονοῦντες. The point is that Aristobulus' adherents were not primarily soldiers, but priests, as noted earlier and as the sequel would show.

into the holy places and began a general slaughter. Even more of Aristobulus' supporters died at the hands of those Jews who belonged to Hyrcanus' faction. While the slaughter raged the priests continued their duties, some dying as they approached the altar to offer sacrifice. Some 12,000 Jews died, according to Josephus.[28] Others were taken to Rome as prisoners, eventually lending a great impetus to the Jewish community there.

Now Pompey did that for which—at least according to traditional Jewish piety—he would lie some years hence without a grave, 'pierced on the mountains of Egypt.'[29] Along with his staff, he entered the sanctuary and penetrated to the Holy of Holies where, of course, none but the high priest was ever permitted to go. Presumably his staff included his principal generals, among them Aemilius and Gabinius. Their curiosity was natural enough in view of the wildly distorted stories about the forbidden contents that circulated among the gentiles. Pompey may therefore have hoped to glimpse a golden ass head,[30] but of course all he found was an empty room. Subsequently he acted swiftly to restore the temple cultus and granted the high priesthood to Hyrcanus. But he denied him the other office he had sought, that of king, and drastically reduced the territories of Judaea. These he gave to the new governor of Syria and Coele-Syria, Aemilius. Aristobulus and his family were among those led off in chains to Rome (although Aristobulus and two of his sons did escape and lead brief rebellions against Rome at different times during the next two decades). It was the end of Jewish independence a scant eighty years after it had been born under the early Hasmoneans.

The significance of the quarrels between Aristobulus and Hyrcanus was well recognized among the Jews of the first century. As Josephus wrote,[31]

---

28 A variant found in Niese's mss. LAMW and in the Latin tradition of Josephus reads 22,000.

29 *Pss. Sol.* 2.26, almost universally regarded as a reference to Pompey's death in 48 BCE.

30 That the Jews worshipped such a head was propagated in antiquity by at least three writers: Mnaseas, Apion, and Damocritus. For the texts, see M. Stern, *Greek and Latin Authors on Jews and Judaism,* 3 vols. (Jerusalem: Israel Academy of Sciences and Humanities, 1976-84) 1, pp. 97-8, 409-10 and 531.

31 *Ant.* 14.77-78.

> For this misfortune which befell Jerusalem Hyrcanus and
> Aristobulus were responsible, because of their dissension. For we
> lost our freedom and became subject to the Romans . . . and the
> royal power which had formerly been bestowed on those who were
> high priests by birth became the privilege of commoners.
> (Translation by Marcus)

Josephus refers to the overwhelming shame and sorrow the Jews still
felt, some century and a half later. These feelings focused on foreign
control of the high priesthood, a recurrent theme in the Qumran texts.
Clearly Josephus—and presumably most of his contemporaries—did
not share the perspective of modern historians, who are apt to argue
that even without the division of the Hasmonean house the nation could
not have stood before the Romans. The Jewish understanding of divine
sovereignty precluded such conclusions. That is precisely why the
events we have briefly considered were so important to them. Things
could have been different.

Historical Analysis

It is now possible to reach some tentative conclusions about certain
events that may be chronicled in fragments A2 and D2. Further, while
many of its entries must remain tantalizingly opaque, it may be possible
now to advance somewhat further in our understanding of the work as a
whole. The reference in fragment A2:1, לתת לו יקר בערבים, may
refer to the relations between Hyrcanus and Aretas. The phrase may
easily be taken as connoting an alliance between the two in which the
Jewish would-be king attained to a new status in Nabatea. The earlier
relations between the Nabateans and the Hasmoneans had been
uniformly inimical, so far as we are informed. Alexander Jannaeus, in
particular, waged war with his Arab neighbors on more than one
occasion. Thus, apart from Hyrcanus, this expression could apply to no
Hasmonean. It is perhaps impossible entirely to rule out that the
reference is to some later Jewish ruler such as Herod. But given the
almost universal hatred with which that tyrant was regarded by his
Jewish subjects, it is hard to believe there would have been much
interest in recording the fact that the Idumean had good relations with
the Nabateans. Further, as noted several times, no later names occur;
we lack a textual mandate to search the Herodian and post-Herodian
periods for possible references. It therefore seems methodologically

preferable to explain uncertainties in the text using Hasmonean history if at all possible. In that vein the phrase could conceivably describe the relations between Rome and Nabatea at this period, but that seems improbable for the same reason that a reference to Herod does: why would a Jewish author, writing for other Jews (as the use of Hebrew makes clear), care to record the fact that Rome at this time moved on the Arabs? The Roman designs on Arabia had no necessary implications for the fate of the Jews. What we know of Second Temple historiography therefore makes a reference to Roman-Arab relations a very poor second choice.[32]

If one wished to move from the general to the specific and speculate further as to the agent implied by the infinitive לתת, and as to the reference of לו, it would seem that the first is either Antipater or Aretas; in either case it follows that the second is Hyrcanus. Antipater was the force behind Hyrcanus' decision to flee to Nabatea. Once there, he bribed Aretas with gifts and incessantly urged the king to help Hyrcanus.[33] Aretas was eventually receptive and did indeed give Hyrcanus honor among the Arabs, allowing him to stay in Petra as a suppliant. He gave Hyrcanus even more honor by agreeing to march on Aristobulus with him.[34] Further, if, as I will suggest below, fragment A2 is to be dated as a fragment belonging to Year Three of the calendar's cycle, the timing implied is appropriate. The calendar would then indicate that Hyrcanus spent about two weeks in Nabatea before marching on Aristobulus. According to *Ant.* 14.19, Aretas and Hyrcanus marched on Aristobulus with a force of fifty thousand, meeting in battle in some unspecified place. After the defeat, Aristobulus fled to Jerusalem. We may imagine, therefore, that the initial battle took place in regions of Judaea bordering on Nabatean territory. If so, no great time would have been spent in marching from

---

32 Note the classic discussion of Jewish historiography in E.J. Bickerman, *The God of the Maccabees,* trans. H.R. Moehring (Berlin: Schocken Verlag, 1937; English trans. Leiden: Brill, 1979), pp. 9-23.

33 See especially *Ant.* 14.14-15. It is not clear how much time passed at Petra.

34 The use of ערבים for the Nabateans, in place of their self-designation נבטו, is unsurprising. It was common Greco-Roman usage. Josephus, for example, uses both names, but much more frequently prefers 'Arabs.' When he wishes to refer to Arab nations or groups other than the Nabateans, he uses a fuller expression such as Ἀράβων τε τοὺς πορρωτάτω. Cf. e.g.,*War* 1.6, referring, as I suppose, to Jewish communities in areas such as the Arabian Penninsula. For what little we know of these communities see Schürer 3:15-17.

Petra to the battle, and the events Josephus narrates may reasonably fit within a period of two weeks.

I doubt that it is possible to discern what event underlies A2:3-5—if, indeed, the lines all refer to a single event.[35] It would seem that Salome Alexandra came to some place, and it is likely, as the sequel will show, that it was for no friendly purpose. Whatever the calendar is describing here, it seems that it occurred in 72 BCE. The reasoning behind this suggested date is based on a tentative but reasonable concatenation of evidence, as follows:

(1) First, 63 BCE was almost certainly a Year Six in terms of the cycle of priestly rotations (see below on Aemilius).

(2) Given that 'peg', the years of Alexandra's reign would be, in terms of the calendar's system, approximately as follows:

76 = Year Five
75 = Year Six
74 = Year One
73 = Year Two
72 = Year Three
71 = Year Four
70 = Year Five
69 = Year Six
68 = Year One
67 = Year Two

(3) The event appears to be double-dated in line A2:3, wherein it is described according to the regular pattern in terms of some course's service. The course name ends in *heh,* and the date is the twentieth of some month. The month cannot be months eleven or twelve because the phrase begins בחודש, requiring, according to the formula, a subsequent ordinal number between 'first' and 'tenth.' (The ordinals for months eleven and twelve would be stated as בעשתי עשר החודש or בשנים עשר החודש.) Any month when the twentieth was a sabbath should be omitted; it is unlikely that Shelamzion would 'come' (באה

---

35   Note that Milik's original interpretation of this event as having to do with a murder was based on his reconstruction of the relevant words as [הר]גה שלמצי[ון (see PAM 42.334). Subsequent to that reconstruction, another fragment was joined to the MS (as shown in the latest photograph, PAM 43.336), resulting in the new reading given here and, of course, entirely changing the nature of the entry.

i.e., journey) on the sabbath. Table 2 lays out the possibilities (dates indicate beginning of service by month, day, and year of the cycle):

NAME	DATE	DATE
Delaiah	8/16/5	7/18/6
Maaziah	10/18/3	
Jedaiah	5/16/3	4/18/4
Malchijah	2/16/1	1/18/2
Abijah	10/18/5	
Shecaniah	5/16/5	4/16/6
Bilgah	8/16/3	7/18/4
Pethahiah	8/16/4	7/18/5
Huppah[36]	2/16/3	1/18/4

Table 2. Service of Courses Ending in *Heh*

(4) According to A2:6, Hyrcanus was involved in an event that was dated, so it appears, by the name of a course ending in *beth*. The courses whose names end in that letter are Jehoiarib, Eliashib and Jeshebeab, but only the first two serve after another course whose name ends in *heh*. Jehoiarib follows Maaziah, and Eliashib follows Shecaniah. Therefore, referring to Table 2, the event involving Alexandra should date to the service of Maaziah or Shecaniah, and thus date either 10/18/3, 5/16/5 or 4/16/6.

(5) Whatever year of the cycle Alexandra's event occurred in is also the year in which Hyrcanus' revolt took place (see below). But we know from Josephus that the revolt took place in late 67 BCE or early 66 BCE. That rules out years Five and Six of the cycle, since 67 was a Year Two and 66 a Year Three.

(6) The result: Alexandra's event occurred in a Year Three. As it happens, the only Year Three in her reign was 72 BCE. We can tentatively conclude, then, that Alexandra 'came' somewhere, probably for inimical purpose, late in the year 72 BCE.

If these deductions are correct, further reconstructions for A2 are possible. Lines 2-3 could be read:

36 Although spelled with an *aleph* in the Bible, the Qumran texts sometimes spell this name with a *heh*.

2. [יום אר]בעה לשבט זה [בשמונה עשר בו ביאת]
3. [מעזיה בשנים במעזי]ה שהוא עשרים בחודש [העשירי]

Lines 5-6 could be read:

5. [ ] להקביל את [פני . . . בעשרים וחמשה בו ביאת]
6. [ויריב בX ביוירי]ב הרקנוס מרד [על ³⁷ארסטבולוס]

The reference to Hyrcanus in A2:6 is the first clue to the *Tendenz* of this Qumran calendar. Provided that the reading מרד is correct, it appears that the text identifies with the supporters of Aristobulus. The reading of מרד is uncertain because the final letter is damaged, but this uncertainty is not as great as it might seem. The remaining ink cannot simply be read as any letter at all; most possibilities are ruled out by the surviving traces. For example, the final letter cannot be a *waw*, thus ruling out a reading such as [מרו]רי הנפש—a reading that one might have favored since the phrase does occur in the calendar at A1:6.

Further, the formulaic character of the text favors the reading of a simple verb at this point. Other alternatives are conceivable, but the repeating formulae lead one to expect that the *beth* preceding Hyrcanus' name belongs to the name of a course. Given a course name in that position, either a verbless clause or a simple verb should follow almost immediately. Leaving aside the question of what letters the traces would allow for the third radical of the verb, what verbs begin with *mem* and *resh?* Considering both Biblical and Postbiblical Hebrew, the only options that come to mind are: מרד, 'to rebel' (but in the Bible, only rebellion against one's father or against God); מרח, 'to rob'; מרט, 'to polish' (of a sword); מרץ, 'to be sick' (only in derived stems); מרק, 'to scour or polish'; מרר, 'to be bitter;' and מרס, 'to crush; to rub' (of flour or sacrificial portions). Sifted by the dual criteria of semantics and material reading, none of these options survives. Further, if it is correct to read the *beth* preceding Hyrcanus as the name of a course, a prepositional phrase beginning with מן cannot make sense. We are calculating probabilities here, of course, not solving equations. Certainty remains elusive. Nevertheless, the best option by far seems to be מרד.

Now, מרד is not a neutral term. It implies that the person carrying

---

37   For the spelling of the name in rabbinic literature see Jastrow and Dalman, s.v. The two lexica do not agree on the rabbinic manuscript tradition. I have followed Dalman, who is usually more accurate in such matters, and, as it happens, the form he cites accords well with the use of *matres lectionis* in Qumran literature.

out the action, the 'rebel', is out of power and seeking to get it. In the Hebrew Bible the term always carries that implication in the realm of human events; otherwise it describes sinful relations with God.[38] Here another question arises. Did the text link the name of Hyrcanus to מרד, or was there a syntactic break between the two words? If the author meant that Hyrcanus was rebelling, then, as noted, the text may originally have read something like ביוירי]ב הרקנוס מרד על אריסטבולוס, 'in Jehoiarib Hyrcanus rebelled against Aristobulus.' The general reference would be to the time when the older brother had abdicated his rights as high priest.[39] Aristobulus then became the legal resident of that office and, probably, king as well.[40] Hyrcanus agreed to that arrangement at first. For a period of time, then, it was the uncontested truth that Aristobulus was ruler. When, at the instigation of Antipater, Hyrcanus later sought to annul this agreement, the situation would be described differently according to whom one supported. For those favoring Aristobulus, Hrycanus was illegally seeking that which was no longer rightfully his; he was a rebel. For those favoring Hyrcanus, the earlier agreement ceding Aristobulus the throne had never been valid. It contradicted the absolute right of primogeniture to which Hyrcanus was heir. Aristobulus was a rebel.

Accordingly one might argue that the Qumran text be restored differently, e.g., ווכשיש]ב הרקנוס מרד [בו אריסטבולוס[41], 'and when Hyrcanus began to reign as king, Aristobulus rebelled against him.' A restoration with a syntactic break between הרקנוס and מרד probably would require that the text favored Hyrcanus. But we have already seen that the formulaic movement of the work does not point to such a restoration. Perhaps equally important, if one adopts that reading or something similar, the result is a literary work lacking a consistent perspective (see below on Aemilius). That is highly unlikely. All Jewish historical literature—Kings, Chronicles, Ezra–Nehemiah, 1 and

---

38   For the first meaning, see Neh. 6.6, Isa. 25.5, Gen. 14.4, 2 Kgs 24.20, etc. For the second meaning, among many possible examples note for clarity Josh. 22.29 and Dan. 9.5.

39   *Ant.* 14.4-7.

40   For Aristobulus as high priest, denied by some scholars who hold that Hyrcanus continued in that office while giving up only the throne, see *Ant.* 14.41, 97, and 20.243-44.

41   For unqualified ישב as meaning 'sit as king or ruler', see Exod. 18.14, Ps. 61.8, Mal. 3.3, Isa. 10.13, etc.

2 Maccabees, Josephus himself—seeks to fix blame and give praise, according to its author's view of which actors were faithful to God. With due regard for the hermeneutical circle, therefore, I suggest that the first restoration is more likely to represent the thrust of the missing words. In the mind of this text's author, Hyrcanus' claims were illegitimate. The author sided with Aristobulus.

Fragment D 2 is potentially the most informative portion of our text, since it may refer to details of the history of this period which, unlike those discussed above, were not previously known. But for precisely that reason we are on even less certain footing in attempting to interpret these lines. Both D 2:4 and D 2:8 refer to Aemilius Scaurus, and both appear to link the Roman general with the killing of some person or persons. The references raise a number of questions. Do both lines refer to the same occasion, or are two separate events in mind? In either case, is it possible to suggest what those events may be?

To consider the first question first: in accordance with the structure of the calendar, the words בחודש השביעי in line 5 logically require that the concern of lines 3 and 4 is with the sixth month. Since several lines then intervene between the mention of the seventh month and the second occurrence of הרג אמליוס, as does the name of a course, גמול, which rotated in after יחזקאל of line 3, it is almost certain that two separate occasions are meant. The two occasions are presumably separated by no more than a week or two, however, because only one priestly course, Jakin, stood in the rotation between Gemul and Jehezkel. The proposed restoration accords with structural considerations and the lengths of the lines.[42] (The surviving words

---

42   The proposed reconstruction does not allow for the mention of the Day of Atonement. Apparently this festival was omitted by scribal error, and either was left out altogether, or was written in above the line in the missing portions. No reconstruction that mentions it can be made to fit the surviving words. That fact might seem to weaken my argument here rather badly, but such is really not the case. It must be appreciated that the Qumran *mishmarot* texts are extremely regular and formulaic in their structure. Precisely that regularity is what makes possible virtually complete restorations of many of these texts. Thus, when it is said that this fragment can only fit the sixth year of the rotation of the courses, the statement must be taken seriously: the fragment simply cannot fit anywhere else. From a scribal perspective, the regular formulae of these texts could easily result in the sort of error I am proposing. In fact, 4Q321 Mishmarot B[a] contains a scribal error that illustrates this difficulty very well. In column 3, the scribe forgot the words הואה יום הזכרון ('is the Day of Atonement') and had to write them in above the line

require that this portion fit in the sixth year of the priestly cycle; see below.)

The second question is much more difficult. We have noted above what Josephus has to say of the part that Scaurus played in the drama of the last years of Hasmonean rule. Nowhere is there any mention of executions or murders at the hand of the Roman general. Scaurus comes on stage at the time that Hyrcanus and Aretas had Aristobulus caged up in the temple at Jerusalem.[43] Sent to Syria as Pompey's legate, the Roman general heard both Hyrcanus and Aristobulus out, then, accepting bribes from each, ordered Aretas to raise the siege. At this time Scaurus favored Aristobulus. When Pompey himself came to Syria and decided to rehear the Judaean case, Scaurus is again mentioned as present.[44] Because Aristobulus revealed to Pompey that he had earlier bribed Scaurus, he and Scaurus became enemies. Josephus does not mention Scaurus at all in his description of the siege in Jerusalem. Nor does his name appear in the context of the slaughter in the temple when it fell to Pompey.

Where Scaurus was during this time is not entirely clear. Presumably he was with Pompey. In *Ant.* 14.79, after narrating the fall of the Jewish nation, Josephus mentions that Pompey appointed him governor (i.e., *proquaestore propraetore*) of Syria. Shortly thereafter, Scaurus marched against Petra. That would be in 62 BCE, as the parallel passage in *War* 1.159 makes clear. Petra proved a very difficult city to take, and this fact, together with a bribe from Aretas, convinced Scaurus to end the brief war. Josephus knows of no major battles. That is the last the Jewish historian has to say about his term as governor. One has the impression that he knew nothing else about that period, which was at any rate very brief—about one year. That Josephus had no sources for the period just after the fall of Aristobulus is obvious from the fact that immediately after describing the episode in Nabatea, he begins to narrate events that took place when Gabinius was governor. He places these things 'sometime later' (χρόνῳ δὲ ὕστερον).[45] Evidently then Josephus was unaware of the two governors of Syria who intervened between Scaurus and Gabinius, L. Marcius Philippus (61-60 BCE) and

(see PAM 43.328). I think the very same thing happened here.

43　*Ant.* 14.29-33.
44　*Ant.* 14.37.
45　*Ant.* 14.82. His passage in *War* 1.160 is of course no better informed.

Cornelius Lentulus Marcellinus (59-58 BCE).[46]

To what killings by Aemilius could the Qumran calendar then be referring? Any answer will be largely unsupported by evidence from Josephus. Among the conceivable anwers to this question, two suggest themselves as most plausible: (1) the text refers to the siege and fall of the temple in 63 BCE, which culminated in the massacre of thousands of Jews; or (2) the text refers to events that took place in the year after the fall of the temple, when Scaurus was governor of Syria and may have been called upon to quell disturbances in Judaea. To my mind the first alternative is clearly preferable, since Josephus—who is at any rate well informed about catastrophic events during this period of Jewish history—knows of none during Aemilius' tenure as governor. Further, that the Qumran fragment would have referred to the fall of the temple somewhere may be taken as axiomatic given what is preserved of the text. The end of Jewish independence and of rule by the Hasmonean dynasty was a tremendous shock to Jewish life. Pompey's entrance into the Holy of Holies was a similarly powerful blow to Jewish sensibilities. Both of these disasters were remembered and echo in contemporary literature such as the *Psalms of Solomon*. It is probably best, therefore, to see fragment D2 as referring to that time. If the second alternative (or some other) is nevertheless correct, there is no way to confirm it and little more to say. The first alternative, however, merits more discussion.

If the 'killing' in line 4 refers to the actual fall of the temple and Scaurus' involvement in the subsequent slaughter—an involvement likely in spite of Josephus' silence on the matter[47]—then הרג אמליוס in line 8 may be tied to something that Josephus mentions in passing. He reports that a short time after the temple fell, Pompey determined who had been the leaders of the revolt and had them beheaded.[48] Josephus does not say who was the actual agent of the executions, nor which officer had charge of carrying out Pompey's orders. Scaurus, as one of his principal generals, might well have been the man.

---

46 Cf. Appian, *Syr.* 51.

47 According to *Ant.* 14.72 and *War* 1.152, members of Pompey's staff entered the temple with him. Scaurus would certainly figure as part of that group if he were at Jerusalem at all. If so, then he also would have taken part in the fighting, and with major responsibilities.

48 *Ant.* 14.73. Cf. *Pss. Sol.* 8:20, ἀπώλεσεν ἄρχοντας αὐτῶν καὶ πᾶν σοφὸν ἐν βουλῇ.

Certain Jews would have taken notice of Scaurus' actions and recorded them as found in the Qumran text. Those Jews, however, would require a particular reason to focus on Scaurus as the evildoer rather than Pompey. Josephus, relying on Strabo and Nicolaus—and in addition taking a Roman rather than Jewish perspective on these events—focuses on Pompey as the Roman leader. Which Jews might have focused on Scaurus? Those of Aristobulus' party, naturally, those who were the victims of the Roman general. The reason for such a focus is not hard to seek: having been bribed, Scaurus had originally sided with Aristobulus. Later, when Aristobulus and Hyrcanus were pleading their case with Pompey, it is obvious that Scaurus did not speak up for Aristobulus; if he had, Aristobulus would have had no evident reason to besmirch him by revealing his graft to Pompey. From Aristobulus' perspective, then, Scaurus had committed treachery of the most contemptible sort. If it is a bad thing to be bought, it is twice as bad not to stay bought. It would be understandable if Aristobulus and his supporters considered Scaurus the principal cause of their subsequent disasters. If he had kept faith, Pompey might well have decided in favor of Aristobulus and the sequel avoided.

Perspective is everything in historiography, of course, guiding the selection of names and events that should be mentioned. In the case of the fall of the temple in 63 BCE, there is quite possibly an example that parallels the highlighting of Aemilius Scaurus' role by one source in the face of complete silence about it in another. In 54 BCE Aulus Plautius, *curule aedile* in that year, minted a coin on which an otherwise unknown Bacchius Judaeus strikes a suppliant pose.[49] The coin is most easily explained as commemorative of Pompey's Judaean campaign; the time lag of nine years is not problematic for Roman

49	The reverse side of the coin shows a bearded figure in eastern dress, kneeling with a camel at his side. He extends his right hand offering an olive branch. The inscription on the exergue reads BACCHIVS, while the right side reads IVDAEVS. See H.A. Grueber, *The Coins of the Roman Republic in the British Museum* (3 vols.; London: British Museum, 1910) 1, p. 490, nos. 3916-19, and A.E. Sydenham, *The Coinage of the Roman Republic* (London: Spink & Son, 1952), p. 156 no. 932. A. Schalit, *König Herodes, der Mann und sein Werk* (Berlin: Walter de Gruyter, 1969), p. 9 n. 29, suggests that Bacchius was a troublemaker in the Lebanon who was put down by Pompey along with other local chieftains. E. Mary Smallwood, *The Jews Under Roman Rule* (Leiden: Brill, 1981), p. 26 n. 16, argues the position adopted here.

numismatics.⁵⁰ Bacchius was an otherwise unrecorded leader in the Jewish revolt, more prominent in the actual warfare than was the imprisoned Aristobulus. He probably led the forces within the temple. Here then is a man who was perhaps the most important Jewish leader of the war from the perspective of the Roman leadership, yet he did not merit even a mention in Josephus' accounts. That fact is a salutary reminder that we really know very little about the detailed course of these events.

If it is correct to see fragment D2 in connection with the fall of the temple, then a most significant corollary follows: we can now be quite certain of the season when the fall occurred. As alluded to above, the date of the fall of the temple to Pompey has long been problematic. When Josephus penned *War,* he knew no exact date for the fall. He noted merely that it was in the third month of the siege.⁵¹ Writing *Antiquities* years later, he had done additional research on the question, having read Strabo and other historians. He was now able to specify that the temple fell 'in the third month [of the seige], on the Fast Day (τῆς νηστείας ἡμέρᾳ), in the hundred and seventy-ninth Olympiad, in the consulship of Gaius Antonius and Marcus Tullius Cicero.'⁵² The 179th Olympiad stretched from 64-60 BCE; the consulship of Antonius and Cicero was in 63 BCE. Therefore the temple fell sometime in 63 BCE, but there scholarly agreement ceases.

The first problem is Josephus' mention of 'the Fast Day.' In Jewish usage of the time, that expression (Hebrew צוֹם יוֹם) can only refer to Yom Kippur, i.e., the tenth day of the seventh month, Tishri.⁵³ This date would approximate to the last few days of September or the beginning of October. But modern scholarship does not take seriously Josephus' assignment of the fall to the Day of Atonement. It is considered an error, for which two explanations have been offered. Possibly he may have assimilated the date of the fall in 63 BCE to that of the fall of Jerusalem to Herod in 37 BCE; for the latter there exists a good explanation of an autumn dating.⁵⁴ The Jewish tendency to

---

50　It may be significant that the reverse of the Plautius coin is adapted from that of Aemilius Scaurus.

51　*War* 1.149.

52　*Ant.* 14.66.

53　Note especially 1QpHab 11.6-8 and m.Men 11.9.

54　J. Kromayer, 'Forschungen zur Geschichte des II. Triumvirats', *Hermes* 29 (1894), pp. 569-70 n. 3.

assimilate traditions in this way is well illustrated by the designation of
9 Ab as a day of mourning. Fully five disasters were said to have
occurred on this one day. Perhaps then this is the explanation of
Josephus' date. More frequently, however, scholars embrace a
suggestion first made by Herzfeld.[55] Herzfeld proposed that Josephus'
blunder arose because he found recorded in his pagan sources that the
conquest took place on a fast-day. As was natural for a Jew, Josephus
supposed the phrase to refer to the Day of Atonement. In fact, however,
the phrase designated a sabbath. Gentile authors often mistakenly
believed the sabbath was a day of fasting.[56] Most particularly Strabo—
whose narrative of the events Josephus refers to here explicitly[57]—says
the final assault occurred 'on the day of fasting, when the Jews abstain
from all labor' (τὴν τῆς νηστείας ἡμέραν, ἡνίκα ἀπείχοντο οἱ
Ἰουδαῖοι παντὸς ἔργου).[58]

Once Josephus' reference to the Day of Atonement is dismissed, the
fall of the temple is no longer tied to the seventh month. It could have
happened on any sabbath in any month for which there is otherwise
some evidence. Modern scholarship divides at this point, some saying
Pompey took the temple in the early summer, others preferring the fall.
The basis for the division is how one assesses the time frame of the
events between Pompey's start for Judaea and the conquest of the city.
Schürer, for example, regards this sequence of events as 'long', and
says that it 'cannot have happened within the space of a few months.'[59]
He therefore dates Pompey's triumph to the late autumn. Other scholars
argue that the siege began shortly after Pompey received news of
Mithridates' death, which occurred early in 63 BCE.[60] Since the siege
lasted into the third month but was over before the fourth month began,

55   L. Herzfeld, 'Wissenschaftliche Aufsätze', *MGWJ* 4 (1855), pp. 109-15.
56   E.g., Justinus, *Epit.* 36.2.14; Suet., *Aug.* 76.2; Mart. 4.4. 7.
57   *Ant.* 14.68.
58   Strabo 16.2.40. It is possible, by analogy with the verb νηστεύω, that the
noun νηστεία may here not mean 'fasting' in the strict sense of abstaining from
food, but rather 'abstinence' in general, in this case from work. Here Strabo's use
of the verb ἀπείχοντο is significant. Thus Strabo may have correctly understood
the meaning of *shabbat,* and not considered it a fast-day.
59   Schürer I: 239-40, n. 23. Agreeing with a date in the late fall is P. Schäfer,
'The Hellenistic and Maccabean Periods', in *Israelite and Judaean History,* eds.
J.H. Hayes and J.M. Miller (London: SCM Press, 1977), p. 604.
60   *Ant.* 14.53.

according to this view the date of the fall was late June or early July.[61]

The Qumran text would appear to vindicate the position that argues for an autumnal dating. D2:5 specifically refers to the seventh month, and line 6 to the course גמול. It is therefore likely that the events of lines 5-6 took place during the week when גמול was in service, and that in this particular year, that week occurred in the seventh month. According to the six-year system represented by some of the Qumran mishmarot texts, גמול would serve in the seventh month only once in any six year span. That would occur in the sixth year of the cycle, when the course would rotate into service on 7/11 and rotate out of service on 7/18, the 'eighth day.'[62] It is equally important to notice that Jehezkel, mentioned in line 3, would serve from 6/28 to 7/3 in the sixth year. Thus, if it is right to see the two instances of הרג אמליוס as involved with the fall of the temple, the following scenario results: some time in the week during which Jehezkel served, Aemilius was guilty of the first instance of killing. Perhaps that was the actual fall of the temple. Between eight and fourteen days later he was guilty of the second instance. This would be a reasonable time to allow for the identification, trial and execution of Jewish leaders such as Bacchius. In the sixth year, the sabbaths of the two priestly rotations here relevant would have occurred on 7/3 and 7/17. Each is only a week from the Day of Atonement, 7/10. Nevertheless, neither גמול nor יחזקאל ever served on a Day of Atonement at any time in the six-year cycle. Thus the text implies a date very near the Day of Atonement, but rules out the possibility that Josephus could be correct in assigning the fall to that day.[63]

A date within a week of the Day of Atonement only results, of course, if one follows the solar calendar of 364 days that structures the

---

61   Thus Smallwood, *Jews Under Roman Rule,* pp. 565-6; R. Marcus, note *ad loc. Ant.* 14.66.

62   Cf. 11QTemple 45.5. The 'eighth day' was counted in terms of the old course. Thus the first day on which any course served was a Sunday and the last day was the following Sabbath. It rotated out on the second Sunday. Probably the day began in the evening according to this system.

63   If the fall happened only a week in either direction from that day, of course, the tendency to assimilation referred to above might well have resulted in a Jewish tradition, which became known to Josephus between *War* and *Antiquities,* in which Pompey did profane not merely the temple, but the holiest day of the year. After all, it is only a conjecture (even if a very persuasive one) that Josephus attached the fall to the Day of Atonement because of Strabo's phrase τὴν τῆς νηστείας ἡμέραν.

mishmarot texts. The lunisolar calendar of 354 days with periodic intercalation of a month would lose ten days a year to the solar calendar until it drew even by intercalation. Every three years a month would be intercalated to synchronize the lunisolar calendar with the progression of the seasons. That, at any rate, is the way the author of 1 Enoch 74.10-16 schematized the relations between the two systems.[64] Leaving aside the vexed problem of intercalation of the solar calendar, when the seventh month of that calendar began, the lunisolar calendar would have advanced over it by twenty-five days. A week into Tishri by the solar calendar would mean the lunisolar calendar had already entered the eighth month, Marheshvan. In terms of the solar calendar, Pompey took the temple in late September or early October 63 BCE; in terms of the lunisolar calendar, the fall would equate to late October or early November of that year.[65] Regardless of which system of dating is employed, if the Qumran text does describe the involvment of Aemilius with Pompey's conquest of the temple, then that event must now be dated to the autumn.

Conclusions

I have suggested in the foregoing analysis that the Qumran calendar refers to events involving Alexandra in 72 BCE, the rebellion of

64   The description is confused, however, and fails to deal with certain problems that would arise over the course of many years. The question that must be asked, however, is whether the description nevertheless represents the actual state of Jewish knowledge in the first century BCE or so. The tannaitic system, for example, lags well behind the predictive schemes of some pagan contemporaries. On the Enoch passage see O. Neugebauer, 'The 'Astronomical' Chapters of the Ethiopic Book of Enoch (72 to 82)', Appendix A in M. Black, *The Book of Enoch or 1 Enoch* (Leiden: Brill, 1985), pp. 398-401.

65   It would probably be mistaken to say that either the lunar or solar system was always operative in the temple in the period of the Second Temple. Presumably it varied according to who was in power, or to which advisors the high priest listened. For example, Aristobulus may have regulated the temple by a solar calendar, since the authors of our text, who favor him over Hyrcanus II, advocated that calendar. It is unlikely that they would have approved of Aristobulus if he were deviant on such an important matter as the proper season for the festivals of God. At the time when 4QMMT was composed, the temple was evidently regulated by a lunar calendar, but the letter seems to presuppose that change was possible. One must remember that control of the temple and its cultus was equivalent in Judaea to political control. As different parties came to power, such halakhic matters as the proper calendar might change accordingly.

Hyrcanus against Aristobulus in late 66 BCE,[66] and the fall of the temple to Pompey and his leading generals, especially M. Aemilius Scaurus, in the fall of 63 BCE. The Qumran text apparently provides new details about the last item in this list, and perhaps about the second as well.

What about the general character and *Tendenz* of the work? I noted above that the text was possibly a catalogue of events of the Hasmonean period. Notable is the apparent focus on national figures, not sectarian ones. Still, the work seems to represent the interests of a particular party within the political spectrum of that period. This party favored Aristobulus against Hyrcanus II in the civil war of the 60's BCE. They suffered, so it seems, at the hands of M. Aemilius Scaurus, and therefore focused on him rather than on Pompey when recalling the fall of the temple and the defeat of Aristobulus' faction. Who was this faction?

Josephus locates Aristobulus' power base in two sectors of society: among powerful aristocrats, and among the priesthood. Presumably, then, the authors of our text arose from one of those groups or an amalgamation of them. These groups were essentially the same ones that had supported Alexander Jannaeus in the civil war of his reign.[67] While Alexandra ruled they were out of power (hence my suggestion above that she 'came' somewhere for inimical purposes). With Aristobulus at their head, they made a renewed bid for power when the queen died. Their opponents included the Pharisees. In Josephus the politics of this period focus on the Pharisees and are unusually clear: the Pharisees were out of power under Jannaeus; they came to full power under Alexandra; they were the basis of support for Hyrcanus II.[68] During all this period they were opposed by certain of the

66   According to Josephus, *Ant.* 15.180, Hyrcanus ruled only three months after the death of his mother. Thereupon Aristobulus took power and ruled for three and one-half years. If the restorations of fragment A 2 above are correct, the Qumran chronicle may provide new details on the events of the year when power changed hands. It suggests that Hyrcanus rebelled sometime between 10/25-11/1 of Year Three, i.e., of 66 BCE. That date approximates to 11/22-11/28 in the lunisolar calendar. Thus Aristobulus ruled at least ten or eleven months before Hyrcanus rebelled.

67   Cf. *War* 1.114, *Ant.* 13.411 and *Ant.* 13.417.

68   For a perceptive analysis of the question, 'When were the Pharisees *really* in power?', note E.P. Sanders, *Judaism: Practice and Belief, 63 BCE-66 CE* (London: SCM, 1992), pp. 380-412.

Jerusalem élite and elements of the priesthood. I suggest, then, that it was from the ranks of these Pharisaic opponents that this Qumran calendar emerged.

Such would not be surprising in view of two considerations. First, a prayer on behalf of Alexander Jannaeus has now been identified among the Cave 4 materials.[69] Clearly, its author and those who preserved the prayer favored Alexander. And second, the Qumran pesharim are uniformly critical of the Pharisees.[70] These authors opposed the Pharisees and, it now seems evident, supported those whom the Pharisees opposed.

These points belie what has become a commonplace in Qumran studies, namely the assertion that those who cached the scrolls opposed the Hasmonean dynasty. Matters are more complicated. In fact, the readers of these texts did not oppose all the Hasmoneans. They apparently opposed only those who countenanced Pharisaic domination of the Jerusalem power structures. Less certainly, one might argue that they opposed Hasmoneans who allied themselves with Rome or were insufficiently 'nationalist.'[71] Further, this Qumran calendar suggests that its authors were very much involved with national politics down to the time of Pompey's victory, if not later. It may be, therefore, that scholars ought once again to consider Dupont-Sommer's proposal identifying the 'Wicked Priest' with Hyrcanus II.[72]

Of course, these are narrower questions. Both here and in the broader framework of Second Temple Jewish history the Qumran calendar has a contribution to make. True, this text is not straightforward historiography; it is not, for example, a chronicle. A chronicle is interested in chronology: in sequence, in years, in eras. This text does not view time that way. It is a calendar, interested in the eternal cycles of time. Nevertheless, many of its entries presuppose one or more

---

69   4Q448. For a preliminary edition, with a few misreadings, see E. and H. Eshel and A. Yardeni, 'A Scroll from Qumran Which Includes Part of Psalm 154 and a Prayer for King Jonathan and His Kingdom', *Tarbiz* 60 (1992), pp. 296-324 (Heb.).

70   Presuming, of course, that the 'seekers after smooth things' of those texts are correctly identified as the Pharisees.

71   One notes in this regard the absence of 1 Maccabees from the Qumran writings. Perhaps this absence is purely fortuitous, but recall that the hero of that book, Judas Maccabaeus, made a treaty with Rome (chapter 13).

72   A. Dupont-Sommer, *The Essene Writings from Qumran,* trans. G. Vermes (Gloucester, Mass.: Peter Smith, 1973), pp. 351-7.

chronicles or the equivalent. The situation is illustrated by some modern calendars. These calendars note that February 2 is Lincoln's birthday and June 6 is D-Day. Such modern calendars presuppose a knowledge of historical personages and events. This Qumran work is analogous. Thus, while it is no annal, the designation 'annalistic calendar' seems appropriate.

The work cites actual names and refers to the actions of people well known to us from other sources. Because it is so fragmentary, its contributions to historical understanding will necessarily be limited. Nevertheless, one recalls Cicero: *primo annales fuere, post historiae factae sunt.*[73] Chronicles must precede history. Not all historians will agree with Cicero's order, or even his distinctions, but none would dispute the connection of chronicle and history. To the bare bones of a chronicle's year-by-year recounting of events, a writer of history may add explanation—a particular perspective on the events. The Qumran text does not write history, but it does go beyond mere chronicling; it does add perspective. For that reason, and because—unlike the *pesharim*—it avoids encrypted references, this annalistic calendar is the nearest thing to historiography yet to emerge from the DSS. Its tantalizing remains render all the more tragic the loss of the whole work. One is reminded that, like the apostle Paul, the ancient historian must learn to be content, whether with much or, as here, with little.

73   *De or.* 2.12.

Chapter Six

OBSERVATIONS ON NEW CALENDRICAL TEXTS FROM QUMRAN

Introduction

Among the *mishmarot* texts from Qumran Cave Four are several that include a form of synchronistic tables. A portion of these texts concerns equivalences between solar and lunar calendars. Calculating in terms of rotating priestly courses and the solar calendar so ubiquitous in the Qumran writings, these texts chart the day on which a given lunar month ends. They further record for each lunar month the date on which a mysterious thing called *dwqh* falls. These texts are denominated Mishmarot B[a] and B[b], otherwise 4Q321 and 4Q321[a].[1] They originally belonged to the lot of J.T. Milik, and have now fallen to Shemaryahu Talmon and Israel Knohl for their 'official' edition.[2] The structure of a typical portion, selected from 4Q321, is as follows:[3]

6 [ה]שנ[ית] הראשון בש[נ]ים במלאכיה בעשר[ים בראשון ו]דוקה
7 [בשלושה בחרים בשבעה] בוא

'[The] seco[nd] (year): The first (lunisolar month ends on) the se[co]nd day (of the service of the priestly course of) Malachiah, which is the twentie[th of the first month (by the reckoning of the solar calendar). And] *dwqh* (7) [is on the third day of the service of the priestly course of Harim, on the seventh] of it (i.e., of the month, as reckoned by the solar calendar).'

These texts raise questions important not only for their own understanding, but for the understanding of the Qumran caches as a

---

1   I follow the index given by Reed, *List*.
2   For the complete list of editors see most conveniently E. Tov, 'The Unpublished Qumran Texts from Caves 4 and 11', *JJS* 43 (1992), pp. 101-36.
3   Readings and restorations are my own.

phenomenon. The answers to these questions feed directly into how one construes the relationship between the advocates of the 'Qumran calendar' and the rest of their society. The most obvious question is, of course, 'What was the purpose of these texts?' But that question probably cannot be answered before solving a second puzzle: 'What is the meaning of the term *dwqh*'? Judging from the context, this word helps define the underlying system of these *mishmarot*. It attaches to the sixteenth day of twenty-nine day lunar months, and to the seventeenth day of thirty day months. Thus if one is to apprehend the purpose of these timetables, it is necessary to determine the underlying system, an important element of which apparently resides in a word of unknown meaning.

Although Milik never published these texts, he did signal his understanding of them in his book *Ten Years of Discovery in the Wilderness of Judaea*. There, in an obscure note buried at the rear of the volume, he wrote:[4]

> Further study of the Mismarot from Cave IV, not yet finished, seems to favour the assumption that the Essenes computed the beginning of *their* lunar month from the full moon, not the new moon. Nevertheless, in one of their synchronistic tables, in addition to the correspondence between the day of their solar calendar and the first day of their lunar month they also note the day of the solar month on which the *new* moon falls; this correspondence is called *dauqah* . . . which in Rabbinic literature means 'precision (obtained by an observation),' the root *dwq* meaning 'to examine, observe.' (Italics are Milik's)

The guarded wording of this statement is notable. Milik says that his study is 'not yet finished,' but that it 'seems to favour' a certain 'assumption.' Clearly Milik was uncomfortable with his tentative conclusions. Perhaps this discomfort arose from an inability to explain why a group that adhered to a solar calendar and polemicized so strongly against its lunar rival should turn around and embrace that rival's uglier sister. And, of course, it must have seemed strange to find in his text a peculiar lunar system for which there is otherwise no evidence in biblical or Second Temple texts, whereas these same texts are so full of evidence for the more familiar version that began the month with the new moon. Milik's conclusions reflect his connection

4   Milik, *Ten Years*, p. 152 n. 5.

of *dwqh* with the new moon, but he does not explain why he makes that connection.

Milik explicitly states that his study was not yet complete, thus leaving room for a possible change in his tentative conclusions. But Talmon and Knohl, having taken the baton from Milik, apparently intend to run straight ahead in the direction signalled by their predecessor. In a preliminary report given in Mogilany, Poland, on 24 July 1991, they embraced Milik's explanation of the underlying system of 4Q321 and 4Q321a. The only point with which they disagreed was the understanding of *dwqh*. They connected this substantive not with Milik's root דוק but with דקק. In their view the mysterious word means 'denigration' (in the old meaning 'total blackness'). Accordingly, the calendars record the days of the moon's invisibility. The reason for this concern: moonless days were regarded as unlucky; therefore it was best to know when they fell. Activities could then be timed to avoid those days.[5]

In a paper entitled 'The Qumran Calendar,' given at the meetings of the *Society of Biblical Literature* on 24 November 1991, Ben Zion Wacholder completely agreed with Milik's explanation of the sytem used in these calendars. Thus, they reflect a lunar calendar that began each month with the full moon, and the word *dwqh* refers to the 'new crescent.' Wacholder did not offer an etymology for the word, nor, when questioned, explain why it should mean what he thinks it means.[6]

Is the emerging consensus on these texts correct? I think not; I will presently investigate the possible meanings for the term *dwqh*. On the basis of this investigation and some other considerations, I will suggest a different understanding of the system being used in the Qumran synchronistic calendars. Turning next to another Qumran literary work, I want to examine the calendrical portions of 4Q252, a 'Genesis Florilegium.' The remarkably adroit exegesis of this commentary on Genesis is interesting in its own right, and sheds new light on certain polemics of the Second Temple period.

---

5   This summary of Talmon's and Knohl's position is based on my own notes of their report, and the 7-page handout they gave their auditors, entitled 'A Calendrical Scroll from Qumran Cave IV—Mish Bᵃ (4Q83).' I cannot account for the discrepancy between the number they give this text and the official numeration.

6   This statement of Wacholder's postion is based on my own notes taken during his presentation and the subsequent questioning, and his four-page handout entitled 'The Qumran Calendar.'

דוקה *and the Qumran Synchronistic Calendars*

It is a truism that a word's meaning and its etymology are not the same thing. The way a word is used in daily speech may have little obvious connection with its etymology, and most native speakers of a language would not know the etymology of a given word if asked. Consequently, when one encounters a new word in an ancient text or inscription, one does not turn first to a study of its etymology. The best way to determine its meaning is to study the context in which it is used. Not infrequently, however, the context is sufficiently 'pliable' that a fairly large range of meanings seem possible. Such is especially the case when the new word appears either very rarely or, as in the present situation, only in one context (though the context occurs repeatedly). When context is an inadequate guide to a word's semantic range, one must then consider possible etymologies. In this way it may be possible to eliminate meanings that the context of the new word might have allowed, but that seem so far from the word's etymology that they would be unlikely to develop. The context in which דוקה appears in the calendrical texts allows all the meanings for the term that have been suggested, and indeed, additional meanings as well. In order to decide between these possibilities, we must consider the question of etymology, focusing on the two likely Semitic roots that have been suggested: דקק and דוק.

The basic meaning of דקק in the Northwest Semitic dialects is 'to crush, pulverize; to be small or fine.' Biblical Hebrew generally uses the verb with reference to things that require grinding or crushing: corn (to be made into bread), gold, and foreign or illicit gods. The Hebrew adjective דק means 'thin, small, fine.' The texts apply it to 'thin' cattle, 'withered' men and corn, and 'small' manna. The basic sense of 'crushed' appears when the adjective modifies incense and dust. Once דק modifies hair (i.e., 'fine' hair) and once it refers to a low whisper (1 Kgs 19.12, קול דממה דקה).[7] Postbiblical Hebrew usage essentially follows the lines of Biblical Hebrew, but the adjective דק much more often means 'small' in the postbiblical period.[8] In Ugaritic the substantive *dqt* refers to a female 'small cattle' used for sacrifice.[9] The

7   For the Biblical Hebrew evidence, see BDB and KB s.v. דקק and derivatives.
8   For postbiblical Hebrew usage see Jastrow and Dalman, s.v. דקק and derivatives.
9   For Ugaritic see C. Gordon, *Ugaritic Textbook, Glossary, Indices* (3 vols.;

Punic phrase לבנת דקת denotes 'fine' incense.[10]

Imperial Aramaic uses דקק of seed (presumably vocalized as *dqyq*),[11] while Biblical Aramaic employs the verb in both the *Peil* ('to be shattered') and in the *Haphel* ('break something into pieces').[12] Illustrating early Palestinian Aramaic, 4QEn^e uses the *Pael* passive participle מדקק to mean 'ground,' referring to bark.[13] Later Palestinian Aramaic introduces one interesting permutation; while the verb דקק means 'to crush, break to pieces' and the adjective דקיק commonly indicates something is 'small or young,' when used of fever דקיק apparently means 'hectic' (i.e., virulent?).[14] Other Aramaic dialects demonstrate the same basic usage: the root refers to the act of breaking things into pieces, or to the result of that act—small or broken things.[15]

The evidence from other branches of the Semitic languages is consonant. In Akkadian, the verb *daqāqu* means 'be small,' while the common adjective *daqqu* means 'small.' Other forms from the same root express permutations of the basic idea of being small.[16] Classical Arabic and Geez also know the root and use it in the familiar way: the verb means 'crush, pulverize' and adjectival and nominal forms mean 'be small, be thin'.[17]

In contrast to דקק, the root דוק is uncommon, both in Northwest Semitic and in Semitic more generally. Attestations are largely confined to Aramaic, where it is widespread. There the basic meaning is 'to look at something carefully.'

Rome: Pontifical Biblical Institute, 1965) s.v. *dqq*.

10 See *DISO* and R.S. Tomback, *A Comparitive Semitic Lexicon of the Phoenician and Punic Languages* (Missoula, Montana: Scholars Press, 1978), s.v. *dq*.

11 *DISO* s.v. *dqq*.

12 See BDB Aramaic section s.v. דקק.

13 Milik, *Books of Enoch,* 232 (= Enoch 31:3).

14 Sokoloff, *Dictionary,* s.v.v. דקק and דקיק. Sokoloff has only one usage that he glosses 'hectic', which seems a strange way to describe a fever. As indicated, I suppose that this entry means something like 'virulent.'

15 See e.g., R. Payne Smith, s.v. ד ק and related forms.

16 See CAD s.v. *daqāqu* and derivatives.

17 For Arabic see E.W. Lane, *Arabic-English Lexicon* (8 vols; Librairie du Beirut, 1968), s.v. *daqqa* and derivatives; for Geez see W. Leslau, *Comparitive Dictionary of Geez* (Wiesbaden: Otto Harrassowitz, 1987) s.v. *daqaqa* and related forms.

Biblical Hebrew may perhaps contain the verb at Gen 14.14. Though the MT reads וירק, the LXX ἠρίθμησεν has suggested to some an emendation to וידק, understood as derived from דוק.[18] The meaning then would be something like 'muster.' Otherwise, the substantive דיק, used six times in 2 Kings, Jeremiah and Ezekiel and apparently meaning 'bulwark, siege-wall,' probably derives from this root. Apart from these possible Hebrew examples and the Aramaic evidence to be considered shortly, the only other major Semitic language where the root דוק occurs is Arabic. There *dāqa* means 'taste.'[19]

The earliest Aramaic attestation of דוק is 4QEnᵃ, where the *Aphel* verb means 'look at;' otherwise the root does not appear until the later dialects.[20] The Babylonian Talmud uses the verb in the *Peal* to mean 'examine carefully;' in the *Pael* to mean 'to analyze, prove; calculate exactly;' and in the *Aphel* to mean 'to examine, wait attentively.' דוקא can be used as an abstract substantive meaning, as Milik notes, 'precision,' but the much more common usage is as an adverb, 'exactly.' The substantive דוקיא refers to 'exact meaning.'[21]

The verbal usage of the root is attested in Christian Palestinian Aramaic and in Mandaic,[22] but it is in Syriac that דוק is most productive. This richness is to a certain extent, of course, nothing more than a reflection of the fact that, in contrast to sister dialects, so much literature has survived in Syriac. As a verb, Syriac evidences the *Peal*, 'to gaze, especially from afar; to take astronomical observations; to observe, regard;' the *Pael*, 'to regard, gaze upon;' and the *Aphel*, 'to look forth or look out.' The noun ܕܘܩܐ means variously 'the sense of sight; one who observes; a watch tower; an astronomical observation.' ܕܘܩܣܐ is employed for 'instruments for making (astronomical) observations.' ܕܘܩܐ is an observer or spectator. ܕܒܩܘܬܐ refers to the act of looking at something. Leaving aside the very rare Syriac usages, these are the most significant and should suffice for our purposes.

---

18 See KB s.v. דוק.
19 See Lane s.v. *dāqa*.
20 For the Qumran evidence see Milik, *Books of Enoch*, 157 (= Enoch 9.1).
21 For the Talmudic evidence see Jastrow and Dalman, s.v. דוק and derivatives. Note that many of Jastrow's suggested derivatives should instead be attached to דקק.
22 For CPA see Schulthess s.v. דוק, and for Mandaic see Drower and Macuch, s.v. DWQ.

What, then, of the suggestions scholars have made for the meaning of
דוקה? Milik and Wacholder have suggested that the term refers to the
day of the moon's new crescent. Whether the term derives from דוק or
דקק, that suggestion seems possible. If the term derives from דקק,
then דוקה is a specialized word for the moon's 'smallness.' As we
have noted, the semantics of דקק include the concept of size, and
forms of the root frequently refer to something being small. Thus the
day of the moon's first appearance, its new crescent, was the day of its
'smallness.'

If the word derives from the root דוק, then presumably דוקה means
something like '(astronomical) observation,' i.e., of the new moon.
Here the connection of the root with astronomical observations in
Syriac is particulary noteworthy, although, of course, there is no direct
evidence that other Aramaic dialects knew this nuance, particularly
those of Palestine. And, even if the nuance was a part of Palestinian
Aramaic, one must presumably postulate that דוקה was then borrowed
into Hebrew and so appears in our calendrical texts. Perhaps those
assumptions have deterred Talmon and Knohl, who prefer the root
דקק. But can their suggested meaning of 'denigration' square with the
etymological evidence?

Based on our survey of the forms and meanings connected in the
Semitic languages to דקק, the answer to this question can only be
negative. While forms of the root can refer to something small, i.e.,
(perhaps) difficult to see, no useage connects it to an invisible object.
Nor does it seem possible that the meaning 'denigration' would arise
from the root that Talmon and Knohl implicitly reject, דוק. The
semantics of that root have to do with sight—either the act of seeing
itself, or the object of seeing, the thing observed. Thus I think it
possible that דוקה may refer to the moon's first crescent, but not to the
time of its astronomical conjunction, its invisibility.

Of course, our survey would also allow דוקה other meanings,
meanings that have nothing to do with the moon's first appearance. For
example, a connection with the root דוק could suggest '(astronomical)
observation' of the *full moon*. Precisely that is my own conclusion,
based on the following considerations.

To this point scholarly discussions of the synchronistic calendars
have paid no meaningful attention to other Qumran works that concern
the movements of the moon. These works include portions of four

copies of Aramaic Enoch (4QEnastr[a,b,c,d]),[23] 4Q503 'Prières quoti-diennes,'[24] and 4Q317 'Phases of the Moon, Cryptic.'[25] Very signi-ficantly, these works all begin the month at the time of the new moon, not the full moon. Thus anyone suggesting that the synchronistic calendars begin the month at the full moon is really saying that the Qumran texts evidence two fundamentally different lunar systems. That position seems unlikely *prima facie.* Is it not possible to reconcile all the evidence without thus adding new epicycles?

In these other Qumran 'lunar texts,' each day of the month is characterized by the proportion of light and darkness in the moon's surface. The system divides the moon into fourteen parts, with the first day having no parts of light, the second day one part light and thirteen parts darkness, and so on. The fifteenth day has fourteen parts of light—this is the full moon. Then the waning half of the month begins, and the proportion of light decreases for each of the next thirteen days. By the fourteenth day after the full moon, the moon is once more dark, and the next month has begun.

This system is undeniably highly schematic and, from the perspective of modern astronomy (and even that of Babylonian and Greek astro-nomy contemporary with the Scrolls), very primitive.[26] It could never really 'work'—but then, neither could the Qumran solar calendar as presently understood. Both are schematized versions of reality that owe as much to theological principles as to heavenly observation. Two other points stand out. First, the month begins with the moon's astronomical conjunction. Rather than referring to the new crescent (as in the Bible), 'new moon' here would mean the first day of the moon's invisibility (as in modern astronomy). Second, the system accounts for only twenty-eight days, so that modifications would be needed to adapt it to a lunar calendar that alternated twenty-nine and thirty day months.

23   Milik, *Books of Enoch,* 273-97. The Aramaic texts of the Astronomical Book of Enoch show that the Ethiopic version of the book has greatly abbreviated what was originally a very substantial part of Enoch.
24   M. Baillet, DJD 7, 105-36 and, for important comments and corrections, J. Baumgarten, '4Q503 (Daily Prayers) and the Lunar Calendar', *RevQ* 12 (1985-7), pp. 399-408.
25   This work is inscribed in Cryptic Script A (hence the name). Milik published a portion in *Books of Enoch,* pp. 68-69. The complete work may be found in Eisenman and Robinson, and comprises PAM 43.375-43.380.
26   For a full discussion of the system see O. Neugebauer, 'Notes on Ethiopic Astronomy', *Or* 33 (1964), pp. 49-71.

The only logical way to adapt the lunar system here described, while still holding to its basic arithmetic principles, would be to add one or two days of darkness as the given month required. That would not be entirely unrealistic, since the moon is invisible for periods of one to three days depending on variables such as the observer's location and the time of the year.[27] The days would necessarily be added at the beginning of the month, so that in a twenty-nine day month, days one and two would be 'dark,' while in a thirty day month the third would be another dark day. The moon would therefore always be invisible for at least two days. In the observer's reality, of course, that would not be the case, but this element is no more problematic than are other aspects of the schematization.

What I would suggest, therefore, is that the Qumran synchronistic calendars have adapted an older schema to lunar months alternating between twenty-nine and thirty days. This suggestion accounts for all the phenomena of the texts: months begin with two or three days of darkness, then the proportion of light seen on the moon's surface begins to wax. It continues to wax for fourteen days. On the sixteenth day of twenty-nine day months, and on the seventeenth day of thirty day months, the moon is full. The texts mark that day with the term דוקה, meaning something like 'observation (of the full moon).' Then the moon's light begins to wane and so continues for thirteen days. The last day on which the moon is at all visible will be the twenty-ninth or thirtieth, depending on the month, and here it is tell-tale that the texts always calculate for this last day of a month (compare the section quoted above). The whole approach is reasonable for those who give priority to a solar calendar. The Egyptians, who also followed a solar calendar, reckoned lunar months in similar fashion. The system also bears a structural resemblance to lunar ephemerides known from the ancient world, which calculated the first visibility of the new moon (here, alternately day three and day four of the month), the last visibility of the old moon (day twenty-nine or thirty here), and

27   See the discussion in E.J. Bickerman, *Chronology of the Ancient World* (Ithaca, N.Y.: Cornell University Press, 1966), p. 18. He notes that in Babylon the time between conjunction and apparent new moon varies between 16 hours 30 minutes in March and 42 hours in September. In Athens, it oscillates between 23 and 69 hours. The Babylonian calendar calculated the period of the moon's invisibility as three days, the 27th through the 30th of the month. During this period, Sin was thought to visit the underworld.

opposition and conjunction of the sun and moon. All those central elements of the Mesopotamian works are present here also.

The proposed understanding is logically satisfying in terms of the polemics over solar supremacy. More important, it accounts for every feature of the synchronistic calendars, is compatible with possible meanings of דוקה, and explains all the Qumran lunar evidence with a single basic system. Last and least, the proposed understanding is just as compatible with astronomical reality as are the other options.

What emerges from this analysis is that the authors of the synchronistic calendars championed not only the supremacy of the solar calendar, but a lunar calendar that differs from those of the Bible and of rabbinic Judaism. Such is not to say that their lunar calendar was a mere local product; we simply do not know when the system of rabbinic Judaism began to be used. Perhaps the method of the Qumran texts was earlier and rather widely accepted. That does not seem likely, however, and not only because the late Second Temple period is bracketed by historical periods in which we know that the 'new moon' meant the first crescent. One reads in Jubilees 6—the famous portion advocating a 364-day solar calendar—that the people of Israel would 'forget the new moons' (Jub. 6.34). Apparently the author of Jubilees felt that the people of his time had gone astray regarding new moons, a deviance concomitant with their failure to acknowledge his solar calendar. Clearly his concept of new moons was only as acceptable as his calendar generally. Although the evidence falls well short of proof, I suspect that the author of Jubilees would have approved the new moons of the Qumran synchronistic calendars. Their system was his system.

In some measure the purpose of the synchronistic calendars was probably 'scientific.' That is to say, just as the Enochic literature reveals an interest in astronomical matters as an expression of human curiosity,[28] so too these works from Qumran. Further, given the texts' resemblance to the sort of ephemeris used in Mesopotamia as an adjunct to the interpretation of omina, it may be that the Qumran texts served a similar function. More broadly, proper calendric reckoning had an overriding religious dimension. This aspect is clearly evident from the simple fact of polemics about the calendar. Time was holy. Its proper measure was a religious act, guided by a right understanding of

---

28 See the interesting discussion of M. Stone, 'The Book of Enoch and Judaism in the Third Century BCE', *CBQ* 40 (1978), pp. 479-92.

the Bible. These calendars intend to express a proper appreciation of the lesser light that ruled the night, and to affirm its relation to the greater light that ruled the day.

4Q252: Chronology of the Flood and the 364-Day Calendar

4Q252 is a sort of florilegium, quoting various portions of Genesis and offering interpretive comments. In the 1950s John Allegro published a portion of the manuscript, which he called 'Patriarchal Blessings.'[29] Surprisingly, that portion and the remainder of the manuscript were subsequently omitted from Allegro's volume of *Discoveries in the Judaean Desert* (DJD 5). What apparently had happened was that other portions of Allegro's manuscript had been assigned to Milik, without it being realized that a manuscript was being divided between the two men. When it was discovered that all the portions represented a single work, Milik assumed responsibility for its final publication.[30] There matters stood until the recent release of the unpublished texts.

Remarkably, the author of this text realized, long before the rise of critical scholarship, that the Flood narratives of Genesis can be read as evidence for a solar calendar. Consequently he devoted his attention to drawing out these implications, and along the way, polemicized against other understandings of the passage current in his day. In particular, he seems to have reacted to the views found in the book of Jubilees. The relevant portions of 4Q252 read as follows:[31]

Column 1

1   [ובש]נֵת ארבע מאות ושמונים לחיי נוח בא קצם לנוח ואלוהים

2   [א]מר לא ידור רוחי באדם לעולם ויחתכו ימיהם מאה ועשרים

29   J.M. Allegro, 'Further Messianic References in Qumran Literature', *JBL* 75 (1956) 174-76; see also H. Stegemann, 'Weitere Stücke von 4 Q p Psalm 37, von 4 Q Patriarchal Blessings und Hinweis auf eine unedierte Handschrift aus Höhle 4 Q mit Exzerpten aus dem Deuteronomium', *RevQ* 6 (1967-69), pp. 211-17. The text is now being designated 'Pesher Genesis A, ' but it is not actually a pesher in its entirety. Only the portion interpreting the blessings of Jacob on his sons uses that term. For photographs see PAM 43.253 and 43.381.

30   So I infer from the comments of J.T. Milik, 'Milki-sedeq et Milki-rešac dans les anciens écrits juifs et chrétiens', *JJS* 23 (1972), p. 138.

31   Readings and restorations are my own.

3 [שנ]ה עד קץ מי מבול ומי מבול היו על הארץ בעת שש מאות שנה
4 לחיי נוח בחודש השני באחד בשבת בשבעה עשר בו ביום ההוא
5 נבקעו כול מעינות תהום רבה וארבות השמים נפתחו ויהי הגשם על
6 הארץ ארבעים יום וארבעים לילה עד יום עשרים וששה בחודש
7 השלישי יום חמשה בשבת ויגברו המ[י]ם על ה[א]רץ חמשים ומאת יום
8 עד יום ארבעה עשר בחודש השביעי [יום] שולשה בשבת ובסוף חמשים
9 ומאת יום חסרו המים שני ימים יום הרביעי ויום החמישי ויום
10 הששי נחה התבה על הרי הוררט ה[וא יום] שבעה עשר בחודש השביעי
11 והמים הי[ו ה]לוך וחסור עד החודש [העש]ירי באחד בו יום רביעי
12 לשבת נרא[ו] ראשי ההרים ויהי מקץ ארבעים יום להראות ראשי
13 הה[רים ויפ]תח נוח את חלון התבה יום אחד בשבת הוא יום עשרה
14 בע[שתי עשר] החודש וישלח [נוח] את היונה לראות הקלו המים ולוא
15 מצאה מנוח ותבוא אליו [אל ה]תבה ויחל עוד שבעת ימים א[חרים]
16 ויוסף לשלחה ותבוא אליו ועלי זית טרף בפיה הוא יום עשרים]
17 וארבעה לעשתי עשר החודש באחד בשב[ת וידע נוח כי קלו המים]
18 מעל הארץ ומקץ שבעת ימים אחר[ים וישל נוח את היונה ולוא]
19 יספה לשוב עוד הוא יום א[חד לשנים עשר] החודש [יום אחד]
20 בשבת ומקץ שלוש[י]ם [ואחד יום משלח]ה אשר לא י[ספה]
21 שוב עוד חרבו ה[מים מעל הארץ] ויסר נוח את מכסה התבה
22 וירא והנה [חרבו המים מעל פני האדמה] באחד בחודש הראיש[ון]

Column 2

1 באחת ושש מא[ות] שנה לחיי נוח ובשבעה עשר יום לחודש השני
2 יבשה הארץ באחד בשבת ביום ההוא יצא נוח מן התבה לקץ שנה
3 תמימה לימים שלוש מאות ששים וארבעה באחד בשבת בשבעה

4 vacat אחת ושש vacat   נוח מן התבה למועד שנה

5 תמימה vacat   ויקץ נוח מיינו וידע את אשר עשה

(1) in the 480th [year] of Noah's life their end came for Noah. And God (2) [sa]id, 'My spirit shall not dwell among men for ever.' So their days (i.e., those of antedeluvian humankind) were determined, one hundred and twenty (3) [yea]rs, until the time of the flood waters. Now the flood waters were on the earth beginning with the six hundredth year (4) of Noah's life. In the second month, on Sunday the 17th, on that very day (5) all the fountains of the great deep burst open, and the windows of heaven were opened. So the rain was on (6) the earth for forty days and forty nights, until the 26th of the third (7) month, Thursday. The wa[te]rs swelled upon the [ea]rth for one hundred and fifty days, (8)

until the 14th of the seventh month, Tuesday. And at the end of one hundred (9) and fifty days the waters abated, for two days, Wednesday and Thursday. On (10) Friday the ark rested upon the mountains of Ararat , the 17th of the seventh month. (11) Now the waters w[ere con]tinuing to abate until the [ten]th month. On the first of that month, Wednesday, (12) the peaks of the mountains bec[ame vis]ible. Forty days from the ti[me] when the mou[ntain] peaks became visible, (13) Noah [ope]ned the window of the ark, on Sunday, that is the 10th of (14) the [eleve]nth month, and [No]ah sent the dove to see whether the waters had lessened. But (15) it did not find any place to rest, and it returned to him [at t]he ark. He then waited seven [mor]e days (16) and sent it out again. It returned to him with a plucked olive leaf in its bill. [It was on the (17) 2]4th of the eleventh month that it came to him, on Sunda[y. So Noah knew that the waters had lessened] (18) on the earth. At the end of seven mo[re days Noah sent the dove out, but (19) it did not] return again. That was the fir[st day of the twelfth] month, [a (20) Sunday.] At the end of thirt[y -one days from the time he sent it], when it did not (21) return again, the wa[ters] had dried up [from the earth.] Then Noah removed the covering of the ark (22) and looked, and indeed [the waters had dried up from the surface of the ground], on the first day of the first month,
Column 2 (1) in the six hundred and first year of Noah's life. And on the 17th of the second month, (2) the earth was fully dry. On Sunday, on that day Noah left the ark, at the end of a full (3) year: three hundred and sixty four days. On Sunday, in the seventh (4)   one'and six. Noah from the ark at the appointed time, one full (5) year.

Column 1, lines 1-3 relate to Gen. 6.3. Two points are particularly noteworthy. (1) The author of the Qumran text arrived at his figure of 480 by subtracting the biblical figure of 120 from Noah's age at the time the Flood began. Thus he understood the limiting period of 120 years as referring to the number of years remaining to humankind before the Flood. Then the lives of virtually all people would end. He did not, then, understand the verse as a limitation of the individual human life span to 120 years, as do most modern commentators.[32] Presumably he would have realized the difficulty inherent in the 'modern' view, namely that all the postdiluvial patriarchs from Shem to

32   See the discussion in C. Westermann, *Genesis 1-11: A Commentary*, trans. J. Scullion (Minneapolis: Augsburg, 1984), p. 376.

Terah far surpassed that supposed limit. With his interpretation, the number 120 becomes a part of the chronology of the Flood. (2) Replacing the biblical text's ידון with ידור, our author in effect 'translated' that *hapax legomenon* in the same way as the LXX (οὐ μὴ καταμείνῃ) and the Vulgate (*permanebit*). Presumably he did not know the meaning of the biblical crux—for which no convincing etymology has ever been established—because of a putative use in the Hebrew of his own time; therefore, like modern scholars, he deduced its meaning from the context.

The author's understanding of the Flood's subsequent chronology breaks down as follows (dating in terms of the life of Noah):

(1) 17.2.600 The flood begins (line 4; Gen. 7.11).
(2) 26.3.600 The rain ceases to fall, forty days after it began (lines 6-7; Gen. 7.17). The author counted 17.2.600 as the first day in his calculations, thus counting days inclusively, as is usual in Qumran chronological reckonings.
(3) 14.7.600 The waters begin to recede, 150 days after the flood began (line 8; Gen. 7.24, 8.3). Thus the author counted the forty days of Gen. 7.17 as part of the 150 days. Counting in this way, the dates given in the biblical text can support a calendar of thirty days per month, with intercalation of two days between 17.2 and 14.7—precisely the 364-day calendar of many Qumran texts.

Note how the author recognized and answered a possible objection to his view that the Flood narratives supported this calendar. Modern scholars have actually raised this objection. For example, Baumgarten argues, in view of the 150 days mentioned in Gen. 7.24, that 'the . . . [figure] certainly does not fit the Jubilees calendar in which the interval between the 17th and [*sic;* read 'of'] the second month and the 17th of the seventh month is 152, not 150 days.'[33] On the contrary, our author found that the biblical text did allow—even favored—152 days for the period mentioned. His reasoning was based on a comparison of Gen. 7.24, 8.3 and 8.4, and was apparently as follows.

According to Gen. 7.24, the waters 'swelled' or 'increased' upon the earth for 150 days. Gen. 8.3 then says that the waters 'gradually

---

33 J. Baumgarten, 'The Calendar of the Book of Jubilees and the Bible', *Studies in Qumran Law* (Leiden: Brill, 1977), pp. 108-9 n. 15. Cf. R. Beckwith, 'The Earliest Enoch Literature and Its Calendar: Marks of their Origin, Date and Motivation', *RevQ* 10 (1979-81), pp. 379 and 387.

receded' (הלוך ושוב) from the earth, and 'lessened' or 'abated' (ויחסרו) מקצה one hundred and fifty days. The questions in this verse are the relationship of the verbs to one another—are they complementary, or does the second verb merely restate—and the meaning of *min* in מקצה. Our author understood the verbs as complementary, and the *min* as marking the beginning of the time period. Thus the waters swelled, then abated *beginning* with day 150. A comparison of this understanding of the crucial terms with a modern one may bring this point into sharper focus. The *New Revised Standard Version* translates 'and the waters gradually receded from the earth. At the end of one hundred fifty days the waters had abated.' The Qumran author would have translated the biblical text more like 'and the waters gradually receded from the earth, beginning to abate from the one-hundred fiftieth day.'

Since Gen. 8.4 specifies that the ark came to rest on the Ararat Range on the seventeenth of the seventh month (17.7.600), simple subtraction would show that, while the waters *began* to abate on the 150th day, two more days were required before they had fallen enough for the ark to rest. Thus the author found his two intercalated days. His reading of Genesis is completely legitimate. It has the advantage (for so ancient interpreters would certainly think) of finding new information in each element of the biblical text (i.e., Gen. 8.4 does not merely recapitulate Gen. 8.3).

It is possible that the Qumran text here refines Jub. 5.27, which reads 'And all of the water stayed on the earth five months, one hundred and fifty days'. The equation of five months to 150 days would have bothered our author, and some circles may have read Jubilees in that 'erroneous' way. Thus it was perhaps necessary either to refute or, more probably, to explain, this portion of the book. Our author would have said that Jubilees only refers to the time before the water began receding.

(4) 1.10.600 The tops of the mountains become visible (line 11; Gen. 8.5).

(5) 10.11.600 Noah opens a window of the ark and sends the raven (Gen. 8.6-7). The author of 4Q252 omitted this part of the biblical text, presumably because the raven was an unclean bird. Further, he did not need to record this date, because of his understanding of וישלח (see below).

(6) 17.11.600 Noah sends the dove out for the first time (lines 14-15).

Accordingly, the author understood the וישלח ('and he sent') of Gen.
8.8 as concealing an unstated lapse of seven days. This is a logical
assumption, since there would be no reason to send the dove and the
raven at the same time. Further, a seven-day lapse is suggested by what
follows.

(7) 24.11.600 The dove goes out a second time, and it returns with an
olive branch (lines 15-18a; Gen. 8.10-11).

(8) 1.12.600 Noah sends the dove out for a third time, and it does not
return (lines 18b-20a; Gen. 8.12).

(9) 1.1.601 Noah removes the covering of the ark (lines 20b-2.1; Gen.
8.13). The waters have completely receded.

(10) 17.2.601 The land is dry, and Noah exits the ark at the end of one
full year precisely (2.1-3; cf. Gen. 8.14). The statement here is
polemical—note the strength of the phrasing, which recapitulates the
date four different ways: (1) לקץ (3) ביום ההוא (2) באחד בשבת
לימים שלוש מאות ששים וארבעה (4) שנה תמימה. Rather than dating
the exit to the seventeenth of the month, the MT and all other witnesses
read 27.2.601. What is our author's exegetical reasoning?

First, his belief that the flood lasted exactly one year from the time
that the rain began to fall until the land was completely dry was not an
innovation; it was an ancient tradition.[34] It may be that this reading of
the text is actually the intention of the priestly redactor(s) who added
the dates to this portion of Genesis.[35] Whether that be so or not, based
on that antecedent tradition, the date of the MT—which the author of
the text certainly read in his scroll of Genesis—was regarded as a lunar
date, in contrast to all the other (solar) dates of the Flood narrative.

Next, he probably proceeded based on the chronology of Jubilees, as

---

34   Note 1 Enoch 106.15, 'There shall be a great destruction upon the earth, and
there shall be a flood and a great destruction for one year.' The LXX knew the same
tradition, which it made explicit in a way precisely the opposite of our text. Rather
than reformulating the date of the end of the flood, the LXX changed the date of the
beginning, reading in Gen. 7.14 'in the second month, on the twenty-seventh day of
the month . . .'

35   So e.g., E. Kutsch, 'Der Kalender des Jubiläenbuches und das Alte und das
Neue Testament', *VT* 11 (1961), p. 43: P calculated a year of twelve lunar months
(354 days) + 11 intercalated days to total 365 days, i.e., precisely one solar year.
The references to months in the Flood narrative are thus understood as lunar
months, with the date of Gen 8:14 as the only solar calendar date in the narrative. If
so, then P has read these references in a fashion diametrically opposed to that of our
author—and both ways 'work.'

opposed to that of the MT and other traditions.[36] In the Jubilees chronology, the flood began 'in the twenty-[seventh] jubilee of years ... in the sixth year [of the fifth week], in the second month.'[37] Dated *anno mundi,* then, the flood began in the year 1308 and ended in 1309. The Qumran writer then calculated the equivalence of this date in terms of the eternal sexennial system of the priestly *mishmarot.* This system was used to date all sabbaths and festivals, and could even be applied to chronography.[38] Almost certainly there existed works that rendered the chronology of the entire Bible in these terms.[39]

This calculation would have revealed to him that the flood began in year four of the 235th cycle of *mishmarot,* at which point both the solar and lunar calendars agree on the date 17.2. Accordingly, the flood ended in year five of the cycle. By then the two calendars will disagree on the date: solar 17.2 = lunar 27.2. This is the situation that the Qumran author recognized in Gen. 8.14. After yet another year, in year six of the cycle, the variance would have been ten days greater still: solar 17.2 = lunar 7.3. Thereafter, however, an intercalated month would harmonize the lunar with the solar date, equating the situation of the first year to that of the fourth.

The tradition that the flood lasted exactly one year was also known to the author of Jubilees (Jub. 5.31). That writer seems further to have known our author's method of calculation; he certainly knows his date of the seventeenth.[40] But Jubilees tried to have it both ways. The writer

---

36   The date of the Flood varies in the major textual traditions: it is *anno mundi* 1656 in the MT, 1307 in the Samaritan Pentateuch, and 2242 in the LXX. The Samaritan Pentateuch's date will not result in the requisite lunar dating ten days ahead of the solar one. The MT and the LXX will work: the MT dating would have the Flood beginning in year one of the cycle and ending in year 2, while the LXX date equates to the fourth year of the sexennial cycle, just as does Jubilees.

37   Jub. 5.22-23. In keeping with the logic of the Bible and Jubilees elsewhere, I have emended the text's 'twenty-second jubilee.' Cf. Jub. 6.18.

38   See Chapter Five above. It seems possible that the cycle of *mishmarot* and the need to have the dates work out right lies behind the slight difference in the dating of the Flood according to Jubilees vis à vis the Samaritan Pentateuch.

39   Cf. the Aramaic biblical chronology 4Q559, which tries to rationalize biblical chronology, but (at least in the surviving portions) does not refer to the *mishmarot.*

40   It is surely no coincidence that Jubilees identifies the date on which Eve was tempted by the serpent as the same one on which the Flood began, 17.2 (Jub. 3.17). There are many parallels in the stories of the (first) Creation and the (re)Creation that followed the Flood.

stipulated that the land was dry on 17.2, but that it was not until 27.2, the date given in all witnesses to the biblical text, that Noah sent the animals out of the ark. He further declared that Noah himself only exited the ark on 1.3 (Jubilees 5.32-6.1). The Qumran text seems to react to this understanding with its emphasis that Noah exited the ark 'on that very day' when the land was dry: none other than 17.2.

The text of column 2, lines 3-5 is clearly corrupt, having suffered from several scribal lapses. It appears that one point made in these lines was to emphasize yet again that the Flood lasted precisely a year. That is the apparent intent still recognizable in the phrase נוח מן התבה למועד שנה תמימה.

The modern student of 4Q252 can only respect the subtlety of its understanding. As noted, at several points the Qumran florilegium adumbrates modern critical understandings of the narrative of the Flood. Whether the 364-day calendar originally structured the Flood narrative,[41] or can only secondarily be imposed on it, is not yet certain. For our author, however, there was no question on this point. In terms of the thought world of Second Temple Judaism his argument would be very difficult to refute. Based upon the earliest biblical narrative containing evidence on the question, one imagines that it must have convinced many that the 'Qumran calendar' was indeed God's calendar.

---

41   As argued by A. Jaubert, 'Le Calendrier des Jubilés et de la Secte de Qumrân: Ses origines bibliques', *VT* 3 (1953), pp. 250-64.

BIBLIOGRAPHY

Aharoni, Y. *Excavations at Ramat Rahel: Seasons 1961 and 1962.* Rome: Centri di Studi Semitici, 1964.

Albright, W.F. 'A Biblical Fragment from the Maccabean Age: The Nash Papyrus', *JBL* 56 (1937), pp. 145-76.

Alexander, P.S. 1976 Review of *The Targum to Job from Qumran Cave XI*, by M. Sokoloff. *JTS* 27 (1976), pp. 166-8.

Allegro, J. 1956 'Further Messianic References in Qumran Literature', *JBL* 75 (1956), pp. 174-87.

—*The Dead Sea Scrolls: A Reapprasial.* 2nd ed. New York: Penguin Books, 1964.

—'An Astrological Cryptic Document from Qumran', *JSS* 9 (1964), pp. 291-4.

—*Discoveries in the Judaean Desert of Jordan V: Qumrân Cave 4, I (4Q158-4Q186).* Oxford: Clarendon Press, 1965.

Alon, G. 'The Levitical Uncleanness of Gentiles', in *Jews, Judaism and the Classical World,* 146-89. Translated by I. Abrahams. Jerusalem: Magnes Press, 1977.

Andrieu, J. 'Pour l'explication psychologique des fautes de copiste', *Revue des études latines* 28 (1950), pp. 279-92.

Anonymous. 'Un papyrus hébreu pré-massorétique', *RB* 1 (1904), pp. 242-50.

Applebaum, S. 'The Zealots: The Case for Revaluation', *JRS* 61 (1971), pp. 156-70.

—'Judaea as a Roman Province: the Countryside as a Political and Economic Factor', in *Aufstieg und Niedergang der römischen Welt: Geschichte und Kultur Roma in Spiegel der neueren Forschung* II.8, pp. 349-96. Edited by H. Temporini and W. Haase. Berlin: de Gruyter, 1972.

Archer, G.L. 'The Aramaic of the 'Genesis Apocryphon' Compared with the Aramaic of Daniel', in *New Perspectives on the Old Testament,* pp. 160-9. Edited by J. Barton Payne. Waco, Texas: Word, 1970.

Avi-Yonah, M.*The Holy Land from the Persian to the Arab Conquests (536 B.C. to A.D. 640): A Historical Geography.* Revised ed. Grand Rapids: Baker, 1966.

Avigad, N. *Hebrew Bullae from the Time of Jeremiah: Remnants of a Burnt Archive.* Jerusalem: Israel Exploration Society, 1986.

Aviram, J., G. Foerster and E. Netzer, (eds.). *Masada I: The Yigael Yadin Excavations, 1963-1965. Final Reports. The Aramaic and Hebrew Ostraca and Jar inscriptions, Yigael Yadin and Joseph Naveh. The Coins of Masada, Yaacov Meshorer.* Jerusalem: Israel Exploration Society, 1989.

—*Masada II: The Yigael Yadin Excavations, 1963-1965. Final Reports. The Latin and Greek Documents, Hannah M. Cotton and Joseph Geiger.* Jerusalem: Israel Exploration Society, 1989.

Bagatti, P.B. and J.T. Milik. *Gli scavi del 'Dominus Flevit' parte I: La necropoli del periodo romano.* Jerusalem: Topografia dei PP. Francesani, 1958.

Baillet, M. *Discoveries in the Judaean Desert 7: Qumrân Grotte 4 III (4Q482-520).* Oxford: Clarendon Press, 1982.

Baillet, M., J.T. Milik and R. de Vaux. *Discoveries in the Judaean Desert of Jordan III:*

Les 'petites grottes' de Qumrân. Oxford: Clarendon Press, 1962.

Baines, J. 'Literacy and Ancient Egyptian Society', *Man* N.S. 18 (1983), pp. 572-99.

Balogh, J. 'Voces Paginarum', *Philologus* 82 (1927), pp. 84-109 and 202-40.

Bar-Ilan, M. 'Scribes and Books in the Late Second Commonwealth and Rabbinic Period', in *Mikra: Text, Translation, Reading and interpretation of the Hebrew Bible in Ancient Judaism and Early Christianity,* 21-38. Edited by M.J. Mulder. Philadelphia: Fortress Press, 1988.

Bar-Kochva, B. *Judas Maccabaeus: The Jewish Struggle Against the Seleucids.* Cambridge: Cambridge University Press, 1989.

Barag, D. and D. Flusser. 'The Ossuary of Yehohanah Granddaughter of the High Priest Theophilus', *IEJ* 36 (1986), pp. 39-44.

Barkay, G. 1984 'Excavations on the Slope of the Hinnom Valley, Jerusalem', *Qadmoniot* 17 (1984), pp. 94-104. (Hebrew)

Barnett, P.W. 'Under Tiberius All was Quiet', *NTS* 21 (1975), pp. 564-71.

Barr, J. 'Hebrew, Aramaic and Greek in the Hellenistic Age', in *The Cambridge History of Judaism Volume Two: The Hellenistic Age,* pp. 79-114. Edited by W.D. Davies and L. Finkelstein. Cambridge: Cambridge University Press, 1989.

Barthélemy, D. and J.T. Milik. *Discoveries in the Judaean Desert I: Qumran Cave I.* Oxford: Clarendon Press, 1955.

Barton, J. *Oracles of God: Perceptions of Ancient Prophecy in Israel after the Exile.* Oxford: Oxford University Press, 1986.

Baumbach, G. *Jesus vom Nazareth im Lichte der jüdischen Gruppenbildung.* Berlin: Evangelische Verlag, 1971.

Baumgarten, J. 'The Beginning of the Day in the Calendar of Jubilees', *JBL* 77 (1958), pp. 355-60.

—'The Calendar of the Book of Jubilees and the Bible', in *Studies in Qumran Law,* 101-14. Leiden: Brill, 1977.

—'4Q503 (Daily Prayers) and the Lunar Calendar', *RQ* 12 (1985-87), pp. 399-408.

Beckwith, R. 'The Earliest Enoch Literature and Its Calendar: Marks of their Origin, Date and Motivation', *RQ* 10 (1979-81), pp. 167-202.

—*The Old Testament Canon of the New Testament Church.* Eerdmans: Grand Rapids, 1985.

Benoit, P., J.T. Milik and R. de Vaux. *Les grottes de Murabbaᶜat. Discoveries in the Judaean Desert II.* Oxford: Clarendon Press, 1961.

Benoit, P., M. Baillet, J.T. Milik, F.M. Cross, Jr., P.W. Skehan, J.M. Allegro, J. Strugnell, J. Starcky and C.-H. Hunzinger. 'Editing the Manuscript Fragments from Qumran', *BA* 19 (1956), pp. 75-96.

Berger, K. 'Hellenistisch-heidnische Prodigen und die Vorzeichen in der jüdischen und christlichen Apokalyptik', in *Aufstieg und Niedergang der Römischen Welt* II.23.2, pp. 1428-96. Edited by H. Temporini and W. Haase. Berlin: Walter de Gruyter, 1980.

Beyer, K. *Die aramäischen Texte vom Toten Meer.* Göttingen: Vandenhoeck & Ruprecht, 1984.

Bezold, C. and Boll, F. 'Reflexe astrologischer Keilinschriften bei griechischen Schriftstellern', *Sitzungsberichte der Heidelberger Academie der Wissenschaften* 7 (1911), pp. 3-54.

Bickerman, E.J. *Chronology of the Ancient World.* Ithaca, N.Y.: Cornell University Press, 1966.

—*The God of the Maccabees*. Translated by H.R. Moehring. Leiden: Brill, 1979.

—*The Jews in the Greek Age*. Cambridge, Mass: Harvard University Press, 1988.

Bidez, J. and F. Cumont. *Les mages hellenises*. 2 vols. Paris: Société D'Édition des Belles Lettres, 1973.

Bilde, P. *Flavius Josephus between Jerusalem and Rome*. Sheffield: JSOT Press, 1988.

Blau, J. 'The Beginnings of the Arabic Diglossia: A Study of the Origins of Neoarabic', *Afroasiatic Linguistics* 4/3 (1977), pp. 175-202.

Bordreuil, P. *Catalogue des sceaux ouest-sémitique inscrits*. Paris: Bibliothèque Nationale, 1986.

Bouché-Leclercq, A. *Histoire de la divination dans l'antiquité*. 2 vols. Reprint New York: Arno Press, 1879-92.

Bowersock, G.W. *Roman Arabia*. Cambridge: Harvard University Press, 1983.

Brandon, S.G.F. 'The Zealots: The Jewish Resistance Against Rome, A.D. 6-73', *History Today* 15 (1965), pp. 632-41.

Britto, F. *Diglossia: A Study of the Theory with Application to Tamil*. Washington, D.C.: Georgetown University Press, 1986.

Brockelmann, C. *Lexicon Syriacum*. 2nd ed. Reprint Hildesheim: Georg Olms Verlag, 1962.

Broshi, M. and E. Qimron. 'A House Sale Deed from Kefar Baru from the Time of Bar Kochba', *IEJ* 36 (1986), pp. 201-14.

Broshi, M. and E. Qimron. 'I.O.U. Note from the Time of the Bar Kokhba Revolt', *EI* 20 (1989), pp. 256-61. (Hebrew)

Broughton, T.R.S. *The Magistrates of the Roman Republic*. 2 vols. New York: American Philosophical Association, 1952.

Brown, F., S. Driver and C. Briggs. *A Hebrew and English Lexicon of the Old Testament*. Oxford: Clarendon Press, 1953.

Browning, R. 'Greek Diglossia Yesterday and Today', *international Journal of the Sociology of Language* 35 (1982), pp. 49-68.

Buth, R. 'Aramaic Word Order from the Perspectives of Functional Grammar and Discourse Analysis', Ph.D. Dissertation, UCLA, 1987.

Cameron, A. 'The Date and Identity of Macrobius', *JRS* 56 (1966), pp. 25-38.

Charlesworth, J. 'The Treatise of Shem', in *The Old Testament Pseudepigrapha*, 2 vols., ed. J. Charlesworth, 1: 472-86. Garden City, N.Y.: Doubleday, 1983-85.

—1987 'Jewish interest in Astrology During the Hellenistic and Roman Period', in *Aufstieg und Niedergang der Römischen Welt* 20.2, pp. 926-50. Edited by H. Temporini and W. Haase. Berlin: Walter de Gruyter, 1987.

Clanchy, M.T. *From Memory to Written Record: England, 1066-1307*. Cambridge, Mass.: Harvard University Press, 1979.

Cohen, S.J.D. *Josephus in Galilee and Rome: His Vita and Development as a Historian*. Leiden: Brill, 1979.

—'Masada: Literary Tradition, Archaeological Remains, and the Credibility of Josephus', in *Essays in Honour of Yigael Yadin*, pp. 385-405. Edited by G. Vermes and J. Neusner. Totowa, New Jersey: Allenheld, Osmun & Co, 1983.

Cowley, A. *Aramaic Papyri of the Fifth Century B.C.* Oxford: University Press, 1923.

—*Gesenius' Hebrew Grammar*. Edited and enlarged by E. Kautzsch. Revised by A. Cowley. Reprint Oxford: Clarendon Press, 1978.

Cross, F.M., Jr. 'Epigraphic Notes on Hebrew Documents of the Eighth-Sixth Centuries B.C.: II. the Murabbaᶜat Papyrus and the Letter Found Near Yabneh-Yam',

BASOR 165 (1962), pp. 34-46.

—'Epigraphic Notes on Hebrew Documents of the Eighth-Sixth Centuries B.C.: III. The inscribed Jar Handles from Gibeon', *BASOR* 168 (1962), pp. 18-23.

Cumont, F. *Astrology and Religion Among the Greeks and Romans*. Reprint New York: Dover, 1960.

Cumont, F., et alia, eds. *Catalogus Codicum Astrologorum Graecorum*. 12 vols. Brussels: in Aedibus Academiae, 1898-1953.

Dalman, G. *Grammatik des Jüdisch-Palästinischen Aramäisch*. Reprint Darmstadt: Wissenschaftliche Buchgesellschaft, 1981.

—*Aramäisch-Neuhebräisches Handwörterbuch zu Targum, Talmud und Midrasch*. Reprint Hildesheim: Georg Olms Verlag, 1987.

De Vaux, R. *Archaeology and the Dead Sea Scrolls*. Oxford: Clarendon Press, 1973.

Delcor, M. 'Le targum de Job et l'araméen du temps de Jésus', *Revue des sciences religieuses* 47 (1973), pp. 232-61.

—'Recherches sur un horoscope en langue hébraïque provenant de Qumran', in *Religion d'Israel et proche orient ancien*, 298-319. Leiden: Brill, 1976.

Dexinger, F. *Henoch: Zehnwochenapokalypse und offene Probleme der Apokalyptikforschung*. Leiden: Brill, 1970.

Dicks, D.R. *The Geographical Fragments of Hipparchus*. London: Athlone Press, 1960.

Drower, E.S. and R. Macuch. *A Mandaic Dictionary*. Oxford: University Press, 1966.

Dupont-Sommer, A. *The Essene Writings from Qumran*. Translated by G. Vermes. Gloucester, MA: Peter Smith, 1973.

Easterling, P.E. 'Books and Readers in the Greek World', in *The Cambridge History of Classical Literature I: Greek Literature*, pp. 1-41. Edited by P.E. Easterling and B.M.W. Knox. New York: Cambridge University Press, 1985.

Efron, J. *Studies on the Hasmonean Period*. Leiden: Brill, 1987.

Eisenman, R. *Maccabees, Zadokites, Christians and Qumran: A New Hypothesis of Qumran Origins*. Leiden: Brill, 1983.

Eisenman, R. and J. Robinson. *A Facsimile Edition of the Dead Sea Scrolls*. 2 vols. Washington, D.C.: Biblical Archaeology Society, 1991.

Eisler, R. *The Royal Art of Astrology*. London: Herbert Joseph, 1946.

Eriksson, S. *Wochentagsgötter, Mond, und Tierkreis: Laienastrologie in der römischen Kaiserzeit*. Stockholm: Almquist and Wiksell, 1956.

Eshel, E., H. Eshel and A. Yardeni. 'A Scroll from Qumran Which includes Part of Psalm 154 and a Prayer for King Jonathan and His Kingdom', *Tarbiz* 60 (1992), pp. 296-324. (Hebrew)

Fashold, R. *The Sociolinguistics of Society*. Oxford: Basil Blackwell, 1984.

Feldman, L.H. 'Hengel's *Judaism and Hellenism* in Retrospect', *JBL* 96 (1977), pp. 371-81.

—*Josephus and Modern Scholarship (1937-1980)*. New York: Garland Publishing, 1984.

Ferguson, C. 'Diglossia', *Word* 15 (1959), pp. 325-40.

Fitzmyer, J. Review of *An Aramaic Approach to the Gospels and Acts*, by M. Black. in *CBQ* 30 (1968), pp. 417-28.

—'The Aramaic 'Elect of God' Text from Qumran Cave IV', in *Essays in the Semitic Background of the New Testament*, 127-60. Missoula, MO: Scholars Press, 1974.

—'Methodology in the Study of the Aramaic Substratum of Jesus' Sayings in the New Testament', in *Jésus aux origines de la christologie*, pp. 79-102. Edited by J. Dupont. Louvain: Leuven University, 1975.

—'The First Century Targum of Job from Qumran Cave 11', in *A Wandering Aramean: Collected Aramaic Essays*, pp. 161-82. Missoula: Scholars Press, 1979.

—'The Languages of Palestine in the First Century A.D', in *A Wandering Aramean: Collected Aramaic Essays*, pp. 29-56. Missoula: Scholars Press, 1979.

—'The Phases of the Aramaic Language', in *A Wandering Aramean: Collected Aramaic Essays*, pp. 57-84. Missoula: Scholars Press, 1979.

Fitzmyer, J. and D. Harrington. *A Manual of Palestinian Aramaic Texts*. Rome: Pontifical institute Press, 1978.

Frank, E. *Talmudic and Rabbinical Chronology*. New York: Philipp Feldheim, 1956.

Frizzell, L. Review of *The Targum to Job from Qumran Cave XI*, by M. Sokoloff. *CBQ* 37 (1975), p. 427.

Fuks, G. 'Josephus and the Hasmoneans', *Journal of Jewish Studies* 41 (1990), pp. 166-77.

García Martínez, F. '4Q Mes. Aram. y el libro de Noé', *Salmanticensis* 28 (1981), pp. 195-232.

—'4Q 246: ¿Tipo del anticristo o libertador escatológico?' in *El misterio de la palabra*, pp. 229-44. Edited by V. Collado and E. Zurro. Madrid: Ediciones Cristiandad, 1983.

—'Estudios Qumranicos 1975-1985: Panorama critico (I)', *Estudios Biblicos* 45 (1987), pp. 125-206.

—'Lista de MSS procedentes de Qumrán', *Henoch* 11 (1989), pp. 149-232.

Gelb, I.J., et alia. *The Assyrian Dictionary of the Oriental institute of Chicago*. Chicago: Oriental institute, 1956-.

Golb, N. 'The Problem of the Origin and Identification of the Dead Sea Scrolls', *Proceedings of the American Philosophical Society* 124 (1980), pp. 1-24.

—'Who Hid the Dead Sea Scrolls?' *BA* 48 (1985), pp. 68-82.

—'Les manuscrits de la Mer Morte: un nouvelle approche du problème de leur origine', *Annales Économies Sociétés Civilisations* 40,5 (1985), pp. 1133-49.

—'Khirbet Qumran and the Manuscripts of the Judaean Wilderness: Observations on the Logic of Their investigation', *JNES* 49 (1990), pp. 103-14.

Goldstein, J. *I Maccabees*. Garden City, N.Y.: Doubleday, 1976.

—*II Maccabees*. Garden City, New Jersey: Doubleday, 1983.

Golomb, D. *A Grammar of Targum Neofiti*. Chico: Scholars Press, 1985.

Goodman, M. 'A Bad Joke in Josephus', *JJS* 36 (1985), pp. 195-99.

—*The Ruling Class of Judea*. Cambridge: Cambridge University Press, 1987.

Goody, J. and I. Watt. 'The Consequences of Literacy', in *Literacy in Traditional Society*, pp. 27-68. Edited by J. Goody. Cambridge: Cambridge University Press, 1986.

Gordon, C. *Ugaritic Textbook, Glossary, indices*. 3 vols. Rome: Pontifical Biblical institute, 1965.

Goshen-Gottstein, M.H. 'The Language of Targum Onkelos and the Model of Literary Diglossia in Aramaic', *JNES* 37 (1978), pp. 169-80.

Greenfield, J. 'Standard Literary Aramaic', in *Actes du Premier Congrès international de Linguistique Sémitique et Chamito-Sémitique*. Paris 16-19 juillet 1969, pp. 280-9. Edited by A. Caquot and D. Cohen. The Hague: Mouton, 1974.

—'Aramaic and Its Dialects', in *Jewish Languages: Themes and Variations*, pp. 29-43. Edited by H. Paper. New York: n.p, 1978.

—'Aramaic in the Achaemenian Empire', in *The Cambridge History of Iran. Vol. 2: The Median and Achaemenian Periods*, pp. 698-713 and 918-22. Edited by I. Gershevitch. Cambridge: Cambridge University Press, 1985.

—'The infinitive in the Aramaic Documents from the Judaean Desert', in *Studies in Hebrew and Other Semitic Languages Presented to Professor Chaim Rabin on the Occasion of His Seventy-Fifth Birthday*, pp. 77-81. Edited by M. Goshen-Gottstein, S. Morag and S. Kogut. Jerusalem: Academon, 1990. (Hebrew)

Greenfield, J.C. and Sokoloff, M. 'Astrological and Related Omen Texts in Jewish Palestinian Aramaic', *JNES* 48 (1989), pp. 201-14.

Grelot, P. Review of *The Targum to Job from Qumran Cave XI*, by M. Sokoloff. *RQ* 9 (1977), pp. 267-71.

Groningen, B.A. van. 'EKDOSIS', *Mnemosyne* 16, 4 (1963), pp. 1-17.

Grueber, H.A. *The Coins of the Roman Republic in the British Museum*. 3 vols. London: British Museum, 1910.

Hachlili, R. 'Names and Nicknames among the Jews in the Period of the Second Temple', *EI* 17 (1984), pp. 188-211. (Hebrew)

—*Ancient Jewish Art and Archaeology in the Land of Israel*. Leiden: Brill, 1988.

Hammershaimb, E. 'On the Method, Applied in the Copying of Manuscripts in Qumran', *VT* 9 (1959), pp. 415-8.

Haran, M. 'Book-Scrolls at the Beginning of the Second Temple Period: The Transition from Papyrus to Skins', *HUCA* 54 (1983), pp. 111-22.

—'Bible Scrolls in Eastern and Western Jewish Communities from Qumran to the High Middle Ages', *HUCA* 56 (1985), pp. 21-62.

Harrington, D.J. 'Palestinian Adaptations of Biblical Narratives and Prophecies I: The Bible Rewritten (Narratives)', in *Early Judaism and its Modern interpreters*, pp. 239-47. Edited by R.A. Kraft and G.W.E. Nickelsburg. Philadelphia: Fortress Press, 1986.

Harris, W.V. 'Literacy and Epigraphy I', *Zeitschrift für Papyrologie und Epigraphik* 52 (1983), pp. 97-111.

—*Ancient Literacy*. Cambridge, MA: Harvard University Press, 1989.

Harvainen, T. 'Diglossia in Jewish Eastern Aramaic', *Studia Orientalia* 55 (1984), pp. 95-113.

Harvey, F.D. 'Literacy in Athenian Democracy', *Revue des Études Greques* 79 (1966), pp. 585-635.

Hendrickson, G.L. 'Ancient Reading', *Classical Journal* 25 (1929-30), pp. 182-96.

Hengel, M. *Die Zeloten: Untersuchungen zur jüdischen Freiheitsbewegung in der Zeit von Herodes I. bis 70 n. Chr.* Leiden: Brill, 1961.

—*Judentum und Hellenismus, Studien zu ihrer Begegnung unter besonderer Berücksichtigung Palästinas bis zur Mitte des 2. Jh.s v. Chr.*, 2 vols. 2nd ed. Tübingen: J.C.B. Mohr, 1973.

—'Zeloten und Sikarier', in *Josephus-Studien: Untersuchungen zu Josephus dem antiken Judentum und dem Neuen Testament*, pp. 175-96. Edited by O. Betz, K. Haacker and M. Hengel. Göttingen: Vandenhoeck & Ruprecht, 1974.

—*Die Zeloten: Untersuchungen zur jüdischen Freiheitsbewegung in der Zeit von Herodes I. bis 70 n. Chr.* 2nd enlarged ed. Leiden: Brill, 1976.

—*The Zealots: investigations into the Jewish Freedom Movement in the Period from Herod I until 70 A.D.* Translated by D. Smith. Edinburgh: T & T Clark, 1989.

Herzfeld, L. 'Wissenschaftliche Aufsätze', *Monatsschrift für Geschichte und Wissenschaft des Judentums* 4 (1855), pp. 109-15.

Hestrin, R. et alia. *inscriptions Reveal*. Jerusalem: Israel Museum, 1972. (Hebrew)

Hoenig, S. 'Qumran Fantasies', *JQR* 63 (1972-73), pp. 247-67 and 292-316.

Hoftijzer, J. and van der Kooij, G. (eds.), *The Balaam Text from Deir Alla Re-evaluated.* Leiden: Brill, 1991.

Horsley, R.A. 'Josephus and the Bandits', *JSJ* 10 (1979), pp. 37-63.

—'The Sicarii: Ancient Jewish "Terrorists."' *JR* 52 (1979), pp. 435-58.

—'High Priests and the Politics of Roman Palestine: A Contextual Analysis of the Evidence in Josephus', *JSJ* 17 (1986), pp. 23-55.

—'The Zealots: Their Origin, Relationships and Importance in the Jewish Revolt', *NT* 28 (1986), pp. 159-92.

—*Sociology and the Jesus Movement.* New York: Crossroad, 1989.

Horsley, R.A. and J.S. Hanson. *Bandits, Prophets and Messiahs: Popular Movements at the Time of Jesus.* Minneapolis: Winston Press, 1985.

Hyatt, J. Philip. 'The Writing of an Old Testament Book', *BA* 6 (1943), pp. 71-80.

Ilan, T. 'The Greek Names of the Hasmoneans', *JQR* 78 (1988), pp. 1-20.

—'Notes on the Distribution of Jewish Women's Names in Palestine in the Second Temple and Mishnaic Periods', *JJS* 40 (1989), pp. 186-200.

Jastrow, M. *A Dictionary of the Targumim, the Talmud Babli and Yerushalmi, and the Midrashic Literature.* Reprint New York: P. Shalom Publishing, 1967.

Jaubert, A. 'Le Calendrier des Jubilés et de la Secte de Qumrân: Ses origines bibliques', *VT* 3 (1953), pp. 250-64.

Jean, C.-F. and J. Hoftijzer. *Dictionnaire des inscriptions sémitiques de l'ouest.* Leiden: Brill, 1965.

Jeremias, J. *Jerusalem in the Time of Jesus.* Philadelphia: Fortress, 1969.

Jones, C.W., ed. *Bedae opera, pars VI, 2.* Belgium: Typographi Brepols Editores Pontificii Turnholti, 1977.

Jongeling, B. Review of *The Targum to Job from Qumran Cave XI*, by M. Sokoloff. *JSJ* 6 (1975), pp. 117-20.

Kasher, A. *The Jews in Hellenistic and Roman Egypt.* Tübingen: J.C.B. Mohr, 1985.

Kaufman, S.A. 'The Job Targum from Qumran', *JAOS* 93 (1973), pp. 317-27.

—'The History of Aramaic Vowel Reduction', in *Arameans, Aramaic and the Aramaic Literary Tradition.* Edited by M. Sokoloff. Ramat-Gan: Bar-Ilan University, 1983.

—'On Methodology in the Study of the Targums and their Chronology', *JSNT* 23 (1985), pp. 117-24.

—'The Pitfalls of Typology: On the Early History of the Alphabet', *HUCA* 57 (1986), pp. 1-14.

Kenyon, F.G. *Books and Readers in Ancient Greece and Rome.* Oxford: Clarendon Press, 1951.

Kenyon, F.G. and C.H. Roberts, 'Libraries', in *The Oxford Classical Dictionary,* 2nd ed. 1970 .

Kingdon, H.P. 'Who Were the Zealots and Their Leaders in A.D. 66?' *NTS* 17 (1970), pp. 68-72.

Knibb, M.A. *The Qumran Community.* Cambridge: Cambridge University Press, 1987.

Kobelski, P. *Melchizedek and Melchireša^c.* Washington, D.C.: Catholic Biblical Associates of America, 1981.

Koffmahn, E. *Die Doppelurkunden aus der Wuste Juda.* Leiden: Brill, 1968.

Kromayer, J. 'Forschungen zur Geschichte des II. Triumvirats', *Hermes* 29 (1894), pp. 556-85.

Kutsch, E. 'Der Kalender des Jubiläenbuches und das Alte und Neue Testament', *VT* 11 (1961), pp. 39-47.

Kutscher, E.Y. 'Dating the Language of the Genesis Apocryphon', *JBL* 76 (1957), pp. 288-92.

—'The Language of the 'Genesis Apocryphon:' A Preliminary Study', *Scripta Hierosolymitana* 4 (1958), pp. 1-35.

—'Aramaic', in *Current Trends in Linguistics* 6, pp. 347-412. The Hague: Mouton, 1970.

—'The Genesis Apocryphon of Qumran Cave I', *Orientalia* 39 (1970), pp. 178-83.

—*A History of Aramaic Part I*. Jerusalem: Hebrew University, 1973. (Hebrew)

—*The Language and Linguistic Background of the Isaiah Scroll (1QIsa^a)*. Leiden: Brill, 1974.

Ladouceur, D. 'Josephus and Masada', in *Josephus, Judaism and Christianity*, pp. 95-113. Edited by L.H. Feldman and G. Hata. Detroit: Wayne State University Press, 1987.

Lane, E.W. *Arabic-English Lexicon*. 8 vols. Beirut: Librairie du Liban, 1968.

Laperrousaz, E.-M. *Qoumrân: L'établissement essénien des bords de la Mer Morte. Histoire et archéologie du site*. Paris: Picard, 1976.

—'Bréves remarques archéologiques concernant la chronologie des occupations esséniennes de Qoumrân', *RQ* 12 (1985-87), pp. 199-212.

Lapide, P. 'Insights from Qumran into the Languages of Jesus', *RQ* 8 (1972-76), pp. 483-501.

Lebram, J.C.H. Review of *Judentum und Hellenismus, Studien zu ihrer Begegnung unter besonderer Berücksichtigung Palästinas bis zur Mitte des 2. Jh.s v. Chr.*, by M. Hengel. *VT* 20 (1970), pp. 503-24.

Leslau, W. *Comparitive Dictionary of Geez*. Wiesbaden: Otto Harrassowitz, 1987.

Lewis, N. 1974 *Papyrus in Classical Antiquity*. Oxford: Clarendon Press, 1974.

—*Greeks in Ptolemaic Egypt: Case Studies in the Social History of the Hellenistic World*. Oxford: Clarendon Press, 1980.

—*Life in Egypt under Roman Rule*. Oxford: Clarendon Press, 1983.

Lewis, N., Y. Yadin and J. Greenfield. *The Documents from the Bar Kokhba Period in the Cave of Letters: Greek Papyri*. Jerusalem: Israel Exploration Society, 1989.

Licht, J. 'The Time Reckoning of the Judean Desert Sect and of Other Time Reckoners', *EI* 8 (1967), pp. 63-70. (Hebrew)

Liddell, H.G. and R. Scott. *A Greek English Lexicon*. 9th ed., with a supplement. Oxford: University Press, 1968.

Lieberman, S. 'The Publication of the Mishnah', in *Hellenism in Jewish Palestine*. New York: Jewish Theological Seminary of America, 1950.

Lignée, H. 'L'Apocryphe de la Genèse', in *Les Textes de Qumran 2*, 207-42. Edited by J. Carmignac, P. Guilbert, É, Cothenet and H. Lignée. Paris: Éditions Letouzey et Ané, 1961-63.

Lübbe, J. 'A Reinterpretation of 4QTestamonia', *RQ* 12 (1985-87), pp. 187-98.

—'Certain Implications of the Scribal Process of 4QSam^C', *RQ* 14 (1989-90), pp. 255-65.

Manitius, C. *In Arati et Eudoxi phaenomena commentariorum*. Lipsiae: Teubner, 1894.

Marc, P. 'Eine neue Handschrift des Donner- und Erdbebenbuchs', *Byzantinische Zeitschrift* 14 (1905), pp. 614-5.

Mariq, A. 'La plus ancienne inscription syriaque: celle de Birecik. Notes posthumes mises en œuvre par Jacqueline Pirenne et Paul Devos', *Syria* 39 (1962), pp. 88-100.

Marrou, H.I. 'La technique de l'édition à l'époque patristique', *Vigiliae Christianiae* 3 (1949), pp. 222-4.

Martin, M. *The Scribal Character of the Dead Sea Scrolls*. 2 vols. Louvain: University of Louvain, 1958.

Mayer, L.A. 'A Tomb in the Kedron Valley Containing Ossuaries with Hebrew Graffiti Names', *Bulletin of the British School of Archaeology in Jerusalem* 5 (1924), pp. 56-60.

McCartney, E.S. 'Notes on Reading and Praying Audibly', *Classical Philology* 43 (1948), pp. 184-7.

Meshorer, Y. *Ancient Jewish Coins, vol. 2: Herod the Great through Bar Cochba.* New York: Amphora, 1982.

Metzger, B. 'The Furniture of the Scriptorium at Qumran', *RQ* 1 (1958-59), pp. 509-15.

—'When Did Scribes Begin to Use Writing Desks?' in *Historical and Literary Studies: Pagan, Jewish, and Christian.* Grand Rapids: Eerdmans, 1968.

—*The Text of the New Testament: Its Transmission, Corruption and Restoration.* New York: Oxford University Press, 1968.

Milik, J.T. 'Prière de Nabonide et autres écrits d'un cycle de Daniel, fragments de Qumrân 4', *RB* 63 (1956), pp. 407-15.

—'Deux documents inédits du Désert de Juda', *Biblica* 38 (1957), pp. 245-68.

—'Le travail d'édition des manuscrits du désert du Juda', *Supplements to VT* 4 (1957), pp. 17-26.

—*Ten Years of Discovery in the Wilderness of Judaea.* Translated by J. Strugnell. London: SCM, 1959.

—'Milki-sedeq et Milki reša^c dans les anciens écrits juifs ets chrétiens', *JJS* 23 (1972), pp. 95-144.

—*The Books of Enoch: Aramaic Fragments of Qumrân Cave 4.* Oxford: Clarendon Press, 1976.

Millar, F. 'The Background to the Maccabean Revolution: Reflections on Martin Hengel's "Judaism and Hellenism."' *JJS* 29 (1978), pp. 1-21.

Millard, A.R. 'An Assessment of the Evidence for Writing in Ancient Israel', in *Biblical Archaeology Today*, pp. 301-12. Edited by R. Amitai. Jerusalem: Israel Exploration Society, 1985.

Momigliano, A. Review of *Judentum und Hellenismus, Studien zu ihrer Begegnung unter besonderer Berücksichtigung Palästinas bis zur Mitte des 2. Jh.s v. Chr.*, by Martin Hengel. *JTS* 21 (1970), pp. 149-53.

—*The Classical Foundations of Modern Historiography.* Berkeley: University of California Press, 1990.

Moraldi, L. 1971 *I manuscritti di Qumran.* Turin: Unione Tipografico, 1971.

Mueller, I. de. *Geoponica sive Cassiani Bassi scholastici de re rustica ecologae.* Lipsiae: Henrichus Beck, 1895.

Muraoka, T. 'The Aramaic of the Genesis Apocryphon', *RQ* 8 (1972-75), pp. 7-51.

—'The Aramaic of the Old Targum of Job from Qumran Cave XI', *JJS* 25 (1974), pp. 425-43.

—'On the Language of the Targum to the Book of Job from Qumran', *Proceedings of the Sixth World Congress on Jewish Studies* 1 (1977), pp. 159-65. (Hebrew)

—Review of *The Targum to Job from Qumran Cave XI*, by M. Sokoloff. *Bibliotheca orientalis* 35 (1978), pp. 318-22.

Naveh, J. 'A Paleographic Note on the Distribution of the Hebrew Script', *HTR* 61 (1968), pp. 68-74.

—'An Aramaic Ostracon from Ashdod', *Atiqot* 9-10 (1971), pp. 200-1.

—'The North-Mesopotamian Aramaic Script-type in the Late Parthian Period', *Israel Oriental Studies* 2 (1972), pp. 293-304.

—'An Aramaic inscription from El-Mal—A Survival of 'Seleucid Aramaic' Script', *IEJ* 25 (1975), pp. 117-23.

—'Varia Epigraphica Judaica', *Israel Oriental Studies* 9 (1979), pp. 17-23.

Ness, L.J. 'Astrology and Judaism in Late Antiquity', Ph.D. diss., Miami University, 1990.

Neugebauer, O. 'The Alleged Babylonian Discovery of the Precession of the Equinoxes', *JAOS* 70 (1950), pp. 1-8.

—'Notes on Ethiopic Astronomy', *Orientalia* 33 (1964), pp. 49-71.

—*The Exact Sciences in Antiquity.* 2nd ed. Reprint New York: Dover, 1969.

—'The 'Astronomical' Chapters of the Ethiopic Book of Enoch (72 to 82)', in M. Black, *The Book of Enoch or 1 Enoch.* Leiden: Brill, 1985.

Nickelsburg, G.W.E. *Jewish Literature Between the Bible and the Mishnah.* Philadelphia: Fortress Press, 1981.

—'The Bible Rewritten and Expanded', in *Jewish Writings of the Second Temple Period,* pp. 89-156. Edited by M. Stone. Philadelphia: Fortress Press, 1984.

Niese, B. *Flavii Josephi Opera.* 7 vols. Berlin: Weidmann, 1885-95.

Oded, B. *Mass Deportations and Deportees in the Neo-Assyrian Empire.* Wiesbaden: Dr. Ludwig Reichert Verlag, 1979.

Oppenheim, A.L. *Letters from Mesopotamia: Official, Business, and Private Letters on Clay from Two Millenia.* Chicago: University of Chicago Press, 1967.

Pardee, D. Review of *The Targum to Job from Qumran Cave XI,* by M. Sokoloff. *JNES* 36 (1977), pp. 216-7.

Pauly, A., Wissowa, G. and Kroll, W., eds. *Real-Encyclopädie der klassischen Altertumswissenschaft.* Stuttgart: J.B. Metzger, 1894-1919; S.v. 'Prodigium', by P. Händel.

Payne-Smith, R. *Thesaurus Syriacus.* 2 vols. Hildesheim: Georg Olms Verlag, 1981.

Pfeifer, G. Review of *The Targum to Job from Qumran Cave XI,* by M. Sokoloff. *Orientalische Literaturzeitung* 73 (1978), pp. 562-3.

Pingree, D. 'Mesopotamian Astronomy and Astral Omens in Other Civilizations', in *Mesopotamien und seine Nachbarn,* eds. H.-J. Nissen and J. Renger, 613-31. Berlin: Dietrich Reimer Verlag, 1982.

Ploeg, J.P.M. van der. 'Une halakha inédite de Qumran', in *Qumrân: sa piété, sa théologie et son milieu,* pp. 107-14. Edited by J. Carmignac. Paris: Duculot, 1978.

—'Les manuscrits de la Grotte XI de Qumrân', *RQ* 12 (1985-87), pp. 3-15.

Ploeg, J.P.M. van der, and A.S. van der Woude. *Le targum de Job de la grotte XI de Qumrân.* Leiden: Brill, 1971.

Porten, B. *Archives from Elephantine.* Berkeley: University of California Press, 1968.

Porten, B. and Ada Yardeni. *Textbook of Aramaic Documents from Ancient Egypt. Volume 2: Contracts.* Winona Lake, Indiana: Eisenbrauns, 1989.

Price, J. 1992 *Jerusalem Under Siege.* Leiden: Brill, 1992.

Puech, E. 'Notes sur le manuscrit de 11QMelkisédeq', *RQ* 12 (1985-87), pp. 483-513.

—'Un Hymne essénien en partie retrouvé et les Béattitudes', *RQ* 13 (1988), pp. 59-88.

Qimron, E. *The Hebrew of the Dead Sea Scrolls.* Atlanta: Scholars Press, 1986.

Qimron, E. and J. Strugnell. 'An Unpublished Halakhic Letter from Qumran', *Israel Museum Journal* 4 (1985), pp. 9-12.

Rabin, C. 'Hebrew and Aramaic in the First Century', in *Compendia Rerum Judaicarum ad NT. Section 1. The Jewish People in the First Century: Historical Geography, Political History, Social, Cultural and Religious Life and Institutions* 2: 1007-39. Edited by S. Safrai and M. Stern. Philadelphia: Fortress Press, 1976.

Rajak, T. *Josephus: The Historian and His Society*. Philadelphia: Fortress, 1984 .

Reallexikon der Assyriologie und Vorderasiatischen Archäologie, 1976-80. S.v. 'Kidinnu',

Reed, S. *Dead Sea Inventory Project: List of Documents, Photographs and Museum Plates*. Claremont: Ancient Biblical Manuscript Center, 1991-.

Reid, S.B. 'The Structure of the Ten Week Apocalypse and the Book of Dream Visions', *JSJ* 16 (1985), pp. 189-95.

Reynolds, L.D., and N.G. Wilson. *Scribes and Scholars: A Guide to the Transmission of Greek and Latin Literature*. 2nd ed. Oxford: Clarendon Press, 1974.

Richmond, I.A. 'The Roman Siege-Works of Masada, Israel', *JRS* 52 (1962), pp. 142-55.

Roberts, C.H. and T.C. Skeat. *The Birth of the Codex*. London: Oxford University Press, 1987.

Roth, C. 'The Zealots in the War of 66-73', *JSS* 4 (1954), pp. 332-55.

—*The Dead Sea Scrolls: A New Historical Approach*. New York: W.W. Norton & Company, 1965.

Rowland, C. *The Open Heaven*. New York: Crossroad, 1982.

Rowley, H.H. 'Notes on the Aramaic of the Genesis Apocryphon', in *Hebrew and Semitic Studies Presented to Godfrey Rolles Driver*, 116-29. Edited by D. Winton Thomas and W.D. McHardy. Oxford: Clarendon Press, 1963.

Russell, D.S. *The Method and Message of Jewish Apocalyptic*. Philadelphia: Westminster, 1964.

Sachs, A.J. and H. Hunger. *Astronomical Diaries and Related Texts from Babylonia*. 3 vols. Wien: Österreichischen Akademie der Wissenschaften, 1988-.

Saldarini, A. *Pharisees, Scribes and Sadducees in Palestinian Society*. Wilmington: Michael Glazier, 1988.

Samarin, W.J. 'Lingua Francas of the World', in *Readings in the Sociology of Language*, 660-72. Edited by J. Fishman. The Hague: Mouton, 1968.

Sanders, E.P. *Judaism: Practice and Belief, 63 BCE-66 CE*. London: SCM, 1992.

Sanders, J.A. 'Cave 11 Surprises and the Question of Canon', *McCormick Quarterly* 21 (1968), pp. 284-98.

Sarna, N. Review of *The Targum to Job from Qumran Cave XI*, by M. Sokoloff. *IEJ* 26 (1976), pp. 151-3.

Sartre, M. 'Rome et les Nabatéens à la fin de la République', *Revue des études anciennes* 81 (1979), pp. 37-53.

Schalit, A. *Namenwörterbuch zu Flavius Josephus*. Leiden, 1968.

—*König Herodes, der Mann und sein Werk*. Berlin: Walter de Gruyter, 1969.

Schäfer, P. 'The Hellenistic and Maccabean Periods', in *Israelite and Judaean History*, eds. J.H. Hayes and J.M. Miller, 539-604. London: SCM, 1977.

Scherrer, S.J. 'Signs and Wonders in the Imperial Cult', *JBL* 103 (1984), pp. 599-610.

Schiffman, L. Review of *The Targum to Job from Qumran Cave XI*, by M. Sokoloff. *JBL* 95 (1976), pp. 158-60.

—'The New Halakhic Letter (4QMMT) and the Origins of the Dead Sea Sect', *BA* 53 (1990), pp. 64-73.

Schofield, R.S. 'The Measurement of Literacy in Pre-industrial England', in *Literacy in Traditional Society*, 311-25. Edited by J. Goody. Cambridge: Cambridge University Press, 1986.

Schreckenberg, H. *Bibliographie zu Flavius Josephus*. Leiden: Brill, 1968.

—*Bibliographie zu Flavius Josephus: Supplementband mit Gesamtregister*. Leiden: Brill, 1979.

Schubart, W. *Das Buch bei den Greichen und Römern.* 2nd ed. Berlin and Leipzig: De Gruyter, 1921.

Schuller, E. *Non-Canonical Psalms from Qumran: A Pseudepigraphic Collection.* Atlanta: Scholars Press, 1986.

Schulthess, F. *Lexicon Syropalaestinum.* Amsterdam: APA Oriental Press, 1979.

Schürer, E. *The History of the Jewish People in the Age of Jesus Christ (175 BC-AD135).* 3 vols. New English Version. Revised and Edited by G. Vermes, F. Millar, M. Black and M. Goodman. Edinburgh: T. & T. Clark, 1973-87.

Schwartz, J. 'Ishmael ben Phiabi and the Chronology of Provincia Judaea', *Tarbiz* 52 (1983), pp. 177-200. (Hebrew)

Sedgwick, W.B. 'Reading and Writing in Classical Antiquity', *Contemporary Review* 135 (1929), pp. 90-94.

Segert, S. 'Zur Orthographie und Sprache der aramäischen Texte von Wadi Murabbaat', *Archiv Orientální* 31 (1963), pp. 122-37.

—'Sprachliche Bermerkungen zu einigen aramäischen Texten von Qumran', *Archiv Orientální* 33 (1965), pp. 190-206.

Skeat, T.C. 'The Use of Dictation in Ancient Book-Production', *Proceedings of the British Academy* 42 (1956), pp. 179-208.

Skehan, P. 'The Qumran Manuscripts and Textual Criticism', *VT Supplement Volume* 4 (1957), pp. 148-60.

Smallwood, E.M. 'High Priests and Politics in Roman Palestine', *JTS* N.S. 13 (1962), pp. 14-34.

—*The Jews Under Roman Rule.* 2nd ed. Leiden: Brill, 1981.

Smith, M. 'Zealots and Sicarii, Their Origins and Relation', *HTR* 64 (1971), pp. 1-19.

Smith, R. Payne. *Thesaurus Syriacus.* Oxford: University Press, 1879-1901.

Soggin, J.A. Review of *The Targum to Job from Qumran Cave XI,* by M. Sokoloff. *Rivista degli studi orientali* 50 (1976), pp. 404-6.

Sokoloff, M. *The Targum to Job from Qumran Cave XI.* Ramat-Gan: Bar-Ilan University, 1974.

—'Notes on the Aramaic Fragments of Enoch from Qumran Cave 4', *Maarav* 1 (1979), pp. 197-224.

—*A Dictionary of Jewish Palestinian Aramaic.* Ramat-Gan: Bar-Ilan University, 1990.

Sonne, I. 'The Zodiac Theme in Ancient Synagogues and in Hebrew Printed Books', *Studies in Bibliography and Booklore* 1 (1953), pp. 3-13.

Spolsky, B. 'Jewish Multilingualism in the First Century: An Essay in Historical Sociolinguistics', in *Readings in the Sociology of Jewish Languages,* pp. 35-50. Edited by J. Fishman. Leiden: Brill, 1985.

Starcky, J. 'Les quatre étapes du messianisme à Qumran', *RB* 70 (1963), pp. 481-505.

—'Un texte messianique araméen de la grotte 4 de Qumran', in *Ecole des langues orientales anciennes de l'institut Catholique de Paris: Mémorial de cinquantenaire 1914-1964,* 51-66. Paris: Bloud et Gay, 1964.

Stegemann, H. 'Weitere Stücke von 4QpPsalm 37, von 4Q Patriarchal Blessings, und Hinweis auf eine unedierte Handschrift aus Höhle 4Q mit Exzerpten aus dem Deuteronomium', *RQ* 6 (1967-69), pp. 193-227.

—'Some Aspects of Eschatology in Texts from the Qumran community and in the Teachings of Jesus', in *Biblical Archaeology Today,* pp. 408-26. Edited by R. Amitai. Jerusalem: Israel Exploration Society, 1985.

—'Methods for the Reconstruction of Scrolls from Scattered Fragments', in *Archaeology and History in the Dead Sea Scrolls*, pp. 189-220. Edited by L. Schiffman. Sheffield: JSOT Press, 1990.

Stern, M. 'Zealots', *Encyclopedia Judaica Yearbook* 1973.

—*Greek and Latin Authors on Jews and Judaism*. 3 vols. Jersualem: Israel Academy of Sciences and Humanities, 1976-84.

—'Sicarii and Zealots', in *Society and Religion in the Second Temple Period*, 263-301. Edited by M. Avi-Yonah and Z. Barras. New Brunswick: Rutgers, 1977.

Stone, M. 'The Book of Enoch and Judaism in the Third Century B.C.E', *CBQ* 40 (1978), pp. 479-92.

Strugnell, J. 'Notes en marge du Volume V des Discoveries in the Judaean Desert of Jordan', *RQ* 7 (1970), pp. 163-276.

Sukenik, E.L. 'Two Jewish Hypogea', *JPOS* 12 (1932), pp. 22-31.

Swete, H. *An introduction to the Old Testament in Greek.* New York: Ktav, 1968.

Sydenham, A.E. *The Coinage of the Roman Republic.* London: Spink & Son, 1952.

Tadmor, H. 'The Aramaization of Assyria: Aspects of Western Impact', in *Mesopotamien und seine Nachbarn*, pp. 449-70. Edited by H.-J. Nissen and J. Renger. Berlin: Dietrich Reimer Verlag, 1982.

Talmon, S. 'Waiting for the Messiah: The Spiritual Universe of the Qumran Covenanters', in *Judaisms and their Messiahs at the Turn of the Christian Era*, pp. 111-37. Edited by J. Neusner, W.S. Greeen and E. Frerichs. New York: CUP, 1987.

—'Fragments of Scrolls from Masada', *EI* 20 (1989), pp. 278-86. (Hebrew)

—*The World of Qumran from Within.* Leiden: Brill, 1989.

—'A Joshua Apocryphon From Masada', in *Studies in Hebrew and Other Semitic Languages Presented to Professor Chaim Rabin on the Occasion of His Seventy-Fifth Birthday*, pp. 147-57. Edited by M. Goshen-Gottstein, S. Morag and S. Kogut. Jerusalem: Academon, 1990. (Hebrew)

Tcherikover, V. 'The Ideology of the Letter of Aristeas', *HTR* 51 (1958), pp. 59-85.

—'Was Jerusalem a Polis?' *IEJ* 14 (1964), pp. 63-74.

—*Hellenistic Civilization and the Jews.* New York: Athenaeum, 1982.

Tester, S.J. *A History of Western Astrology.* Suffolk: Boydell Press, 1987.

Testuz, M. *Les idées religieuses du livre des Jubilés.* Paris: Librairie Minard, 1960.

Thackeray, H. St. John, R. Marcus, A. Wikgren and L.H. Feldman. *Josephus.* Loeb Classical Library, 9 vols. Cambridge: Harvard University Press, 1926-65.

Theissen, G. *Sociology of Early Palestinian Christianity.* Philadelphia: Fortress, 1978.

Thierens, A.E. *Astrology in Mesopotamian Culture.* Leiden: Brill, 1935.

Thompson, R. Campbell. *The Reports of the Magicians and Astrologers of Nineveh and Babylon.* 2 vols. London: Luzac, 1900.

Tomback, R.S. *A Comparative Semitic Lexicon of the Phoenician and Punic Languages.* Missoula, MO: Scholars Press, 1978.

Tov, E. 'The Orthography and Language of the Hebrew Scrolls Found at Qumran and the Origin of These Scrolls', *Textus* 13 (1986), pp. 31-57.

—'Hebrew Biblical Manuscripts from the Judaean Desert: Their Contribution to Textual Criticism', *JJS* 39 (1988), pp. 5-37.

—*Discoveries in the Judaean Desert VIII: The Greek Minor Prophets Scroll from Nahal Hever (8HevXIIgr).* Oxford: Clarendon Press, 1990.

—'The Unpublished Qumran Texts from Caves 4 and 11', *JJS* 43 (1992), pp. 101-36.

Turner, E.G. *Athenian Books in the Fifth and Fourth Centuries B.C.* London: H.K. Lewis & Co, 1952.

—*Greek Papyri: An introduction*. Princeton: University Press, 1968.

Ulrich, E. '4QSam^c: A Fragmentary Manuscript of 2 Samuel 14-15 from the Scribe of the Serek Hayyahad (1QS)', *BASOR* 235 (1979), pp. 1-25.

—'Daniel Manuscripts from Qumran. Part 1: A Preliminary Edition of 4QDan^a', *BASOR* 268 (1987), pp. 17-38.

—'Daniel Manuscripts from Qumran. Part 2: Preliminary Editions of 4QDan^b and 4QDan^c', *BASOR* 274 (1989), pp. 3-26.

—'The Biblical Scrolls from Qumran Cave Four: A Progress Report of their Publication', *RQ* 14 (1989-90), pp. 207-28.

—'Orthography and Text in 4QDan^a and 4QDan^b and in the Received Masoretic Text', in *Of Scribes and Scrolls*, pp. 29-42. Edited by H.W. Attridge, J.J. Collins and T.H. Tobin. New York: University Press of America, 1990.

Vadja, G. Review of *The Targum to Job from Qumran Cave XI*, by M. Sokoloff. *REJ* 14 (1975), pp. 169.

Valk, H.L.M. van der. 'On the Edition of Books in Antiquity', *Vigiliae Christianae* 11 (1957), pp. 1-10.

VanderKam, J. 'Studies in the Apocalypse of Weeks (1 Enoch 93:1-10; 91:11-17)', *CBQ* 46 (1984), pp. 511-23.

Vincent, L.-H. 'Chronique: Hypogée judéo-grec découvert au Scopus', *RB* 9 (1900), pp. 106-12.

Wacholder, B.Z. *Nicholaus of Damascus*. Berkeley: University of California, 1962.

Wacholder, B.Z. and M. Abegg, *A Preliminary Edition of the Unpublished Dead Sea Scolls, Fascicle One*. Washington, D.C.: Biblical Archaeology Society, 1991.

Weidner, E.F. 'Die astrologische Serie Enuma Anu Enlil', *AfO* 14 (1941-44), pp. 172-95.

—'Die astrologische Serie Enuma Anu Enlil', *AfO* 14 (1941-44), pp. 308-18.

—'Die astrologische Serie Enuma Anu Enlil', *AfO* 17 (1954-56), pp. 71-89.

—'Die astrologische Serie Enuma Anu Enlil', *AfO* 22 (1968-69), pp. 65-75.

Weinstock, S. 'A New Greek Calendar and Festivals of the Sun', *JRS* 38 (1940), pp. 37-42.

Wernberg-Møller, P. Review of *The Targum to Job from Qumran Cave XI*, by M. Sokoloff. *JSS* 24 (1979), pp. 119-20.

Westermann, C. *Genesis 1-11: A Commentary*. Translated by J. Scullion. Minneapolis: Augsburg, 1984.

Williamson, H.G.M. *Ezra, Nehemiah*. Waco, Texas: Word, 1985.

Wise, M. 'The Teacher of Righteousness and the High Priest of the Intersacerdotium: Two Approaches', *RevQ* 14 (1989–90), pp. 587-613.

—'The Eschatological Vision of the Temple Scroll', *JNES* 49 (1990), pp. 155-72.

—*A Critical Study of the Temple Scroll from Qumran Cave 11*. Chicago: Oriental Institute, 1990.

Yadin, Y. 'Expedition D—The Cave of the Letters', *IEJ* 12 (1962), pp. 227-57.

—'The Excavation of Masada—1963/64: Preliminary Report', *Bulletin of the Israel Exploration Society* 29 (1965), pp. 1-133. (Hebrew)

—'The Excavation of Masada—1963/64: Preliminary Report', *IEJ* 15 (1965), pp. 1-120.

—*Masada: Herod's Fortress and the Zealots' Last Stand*. New York: Random House, 1966.

—*Bar Kokhba*. London: Weidenfeld and Nicholson, 1971.

Yardeni, A. 'New Jewish Aramaic Ostraca from Israel', *Tarbiz* 58 (1988), pp. 119-35.(Hebrew)

Youtie, H. 'βραδέως γράφων: Between Literacy and Illiteracy', *Greek, Roman and*

Byzantine Studies 12 (1971), pp. 239-61.

Zadok, R. 'Geographical and Onomastic Notes', *Journal of the Ancient Near Eastern Society of Columbia University* 8 (1976), pp. 113-26.

Zeitlin, S. 'Dating the Genesis Apocryphon', *JBL* 77 (1958), pp. 75-6.

—'Josephus and the Zealots: A Rejoinder', *JSS* 5 (1960), pp. 388.

—'Recent Literature on the Dead Sea Scrolls: The Sicarii and the Zealots', *JQR* 51 (1960-61), pp. 156-69.

—'Zealots and Sicarii', *JBL* 81 (1962), pp. 395-98.

—'Masada and the Sicarii', *JQR* 55 (1964), pp. 299-317.

—'The Sicarii and Masada', *JQR* 57 (1966-67), pp. 251-70.

INDEXES

INDEX OF REFERENCES

BIBLE

APOCRYPHA AND PSEUDEPIGRAPHA

RABBINIC LITERATURE

INDEX OF AUTHORS

JOURNAL FOR THE STUDY OF THE PSEUDEPIGRAPHA

Supplement Series